THE THERAPIST WITHIN

The Therapist Within introduces an original, systematic approach for understanding and treating suffering clients through reflective processes, providing readers with the essential tools needed to alleviate their own personal suffering and live a fuller, more enjoyable life.

Developed from knowledge gleaned from his five decades of clinical work and his own journey with anxiety, isolation, and despair, Dr. Brenner's novel reflective psychotherapy is influenced by psychoanalytic psychotherapy, relational therapy, and psychodynamic psychotherapy. Advancing this innovative therapeutic method, the book provides a strong framework for guiding clients through the process of reflecting upon and re-encountering their life history, consciousness, inner and outer worldview, intrapersonal dynamics, and relationships, as well as for applying specific methods of intervention.

Rejecting conventional approaches to therapy, this book provides therapists with a holistic treatment plan to use with clients and will teach all readers to use self-reflection, meditation, and journal writing to achieve a greater sense of wellbeing and psychological strength.

Marlin Brenner, PhD, is a licensed clinical psychologist practicing in the Upper West Side of Manhattan. With over five decades of helping patients alleviate suffering, he arrived at a new approach, Reflective Psychotherapy, that reveals how one can find their own "therapist within".

"As a NY psychoanalytic psychotherapist and sex therapist, I often look for innovative, effective, and practical approaches to treatment. Dr. Brenner's new approach, Reflective Therapy, is not only relevant for clinicians, it is also essential for all those who seek self-empowerment and psychological freedom."

Valerie Pinhas, PhD, Licensed NY Psychoanalyst
and Certified Sex Therapist/Supervisor

"Dr. Brenner's book gracefully weaves experiences from a lifetime of clinical practice with tales from his own process of therapeutic self-analysis. The result is an invitation to self-exploration for anyone curious to find out more about their own 'personal truth'. Fortunately for the reader, this will not be a journey one has to embark on alone. Dr. Brenner provides several guiding concepts, examples, and techniques perfected over his 50 years of practice to help one remain honest, forgiving, and, at the same time, creative about the process of self-discovery."

Florian A. Cuc, PhD, Associate Professor in the Department of Clinical
Psychology and School Psychology at Nova Southeastern University.

"With over 50 years as a clinical psychologist, Marlin Brenner challenges us to enter uncharted psychological territory within our own minds. Offering a unique framework for understanding human development, he describes the 'heroic journey' first with a therapist, and then on our own, in which we cultivate the voice for more full, mature, and graceful lives. Through the use of self-reflective techniques from interpreting dreams to journal writing (with special emphasis on the written word) − he explains how social and pathological structures shape our lives and how nurturing creative connections with others and with ourselves reveals deeper truths and diminishes suffering. That effort is critical in these divided times and this deeply compassionate book could not be more welcome."

Deborah Chasman, Co-Editor-in-Chief: *Boston Review*

THE THERAPIST WITHIN

Applying Reflective Psychotherapy to
Help Alleviate Suffering

Marlin Brenner

NEW YORK AND LONDON

First published 2021
by Routledge
52 Vanderbilt Avenue, New York, NY 10017

and by Routledge
2 Park Square, Milton Park, Abingdon, Oxon, OX14 4RN

Routledge is an imprint of the Taylor & Francis Group, an informa business

© 2021 Taylor & Francis

The right of Marlin Brenner to be identified as author of this work has been asserted by him in accordance with sections 77 and 78 of the Copyright, Designs and Patents Act 1988.

All rights reserved. No part of this book may be reprinted or reproduced or utilised in any form or by any electronic, mechanical, or other means, now known or hereafter invented, including photocopying and recording, or in any information storage or retrieval system, without permission in writing from the publishers.

Trademark notice: Product or corporate names may be trademarks or registered trademarks, and are used only for identification and explanation without intent to infringe.

Library of Congress Cataloging-in-Publication Data
Names: Brenner, Marlin, author.
Title: The Therapist Within: Applying Reflective Psychotherapy to
Help Alleviate Suffering/Marlin Brenner.
Description: New York, NY: Routledge, 2021. |
Includes bibliographical references and index.
Identifiers: LCCN 2020038875 (print) | LCCN 2020038875 (ebook) |
ISBN 9780367174668 (paperback) | ISBN 9780367174606 (hardback) |
ISBN 9780429056970 (ebook)
Subjects: LCSH: Existential psychotherapy. | Psychotherapy.
Classification: LCC RC489.E93 B74 2021 (print) | LCC RC489.E93 (ebook) |
DDC 616.89/14–dc23
LC record available at https://lccn.loc.gov/2020038875
LC ebook record available at https://lccn.loc.gov/2020038876

ISBN: 978-0-367-17460-6 (hbk)
ISBN: 978-0-367-17466-8 (pbk)
ISBN: 978-0-429-05697-0 (ebk)

Typeset in Joanna
by KnowledgeWorks Global Ltd.

CONTENTS

Acknowledgments		vii
Part One **Theoretical Framework**		1
1	Empathic Envelope	3
2	Creative Connection	9
3	Symbiotic-Compensatory System	16
4	Pathological Structures	26
5	Encasing Worldview	39
6	Functional Structures	45
7	Self-Reflective System	53

vi   CONTENTS

Part Two
Psychotherapy   61

8   **Psychotherapeutic Process**   63

9   **Dreams and Visions**   69

10 **Journal Writing and Meditation**   80

11 **The Human Adventure/Heroic Journey**   86

Index   92

ACKNOWLEDGMENTS

To my family, my friend and collaborator, my patients, and Michael DiGennaro, thank you.

I couldn't have done it without you.

Part One

THEORETICAL FRAMEWORK

Part 1 of the book contains the essential building blocks of Reflective Psychotherapy. Through my own personal life experiences, and the lives of my patients, these concepts evolved and led to a deeper understanding of the psychotherapeutic healing process. None of these concepts emerged spontaneously, but over the course of 30 years, through the tools discussed in Part 2, each construct was imagined, cultivated, and eventually practiced in treatment, producing extraordinary results.

1

EMPATHIC ENVELOPE

One of my earliest memories of growing up in Harrisburg, Pennsylvania, takes place in a small backyard behind a rather modest two-story house. I was about 11 or 12 years old, and my father, a short, stout man – to be honest, he was obese – invited me to have a catch. He was wearing a baseball mitt and hurled a pitch my way that was executed with the elegance of a major leaguer. I was stunned. My father was not athletic nor, as far as I can remember, was he ever a baseball fan. No wonder our backyard catch stayed with me. It was so uncharacteristic of him and the kind of relationship we never had. Had this bonding experience occurred more often, I probably would not be writing about it right now almost 80 years later as a psychotherapist with a story to tell.

That experience, in fact, never happened again, and sometimes I wonder if it ever happened at all. You see, a much darker memory of my father – one that still evokes in me a sense of terror – is certainly more in keeping with the relationship we did have. I am perhaps 10 or 12, the age does not matter, and I am climbing the stairs to my bedroom, wracked with fear as

THEORETICAL FRAMEWORK

my father follows close behind carrying a leather strap. I know that I will be punished, that I will feel pain as the strap strikes my bottom, that I will cry, and that I will hear my mother's voice from the kitchen crying out, "Jake, don't hit the boy. Please leave him be". While I clearly remember the anxiety of anticipating the sting of that strap as well as the pain itself, what I can never recall is why I was being punished. What did I do? What could I have done to deserve such a beating? To this day, the answers remain a mystery. What is not so mysterious, however, is the reality that my father was an angry man and that his anger colored all aspects of my early years in a household that included my mother and a brother who was two years older than I.

My father died when I was 13. He suffered from a heart condition and I have sometimes wondered whether this is in part what drove his anger. After his funeral, a relative asked if I felt sad that he had died. I do not remember if I answered truthfully that I did not, but I do know with absolute certainty that I did not grieve his loss. Many years later, when I briefly saw a therapist, I broke down crying over my father's death. I have to wonder if those tears were for the man whose birthright I shared – or for the father I never had – a man who would have a catch with his son in a small backyard in Harrisburg, Pennsylvania.

When I delve deeply into the earliest days of my life, I encounter darkness accompanied by a profound fear. Even today, after five decades as a psychotherapist, I still feel it. Why? It is a question that has informed much of my life. I have often looked for answers in old photos that record the smiling face of a rather slightly built boy of perhaps seven or eight years old. I know that I am the subject of those photographs, but I fail to recognize the boy grinning into the camera. Those pictures, like many others of a supposedly happy childhood, do not capture the underlying sadness and sense of isolation I felt then and which still haunts me.

Where was my mother? Where was my father? My brother? I grew up in a family, but I cannot recall too many warm happy occasions usually associated with family gatherings. All I remember is the sensation of aloneness.

I shared a room with my older brother Lenard. We never became playmates or buddies or confidantes, as many brothers often do. After climbing into bed, I would break the silence and say, "Good night", waiting patiently for Lenard's reply – a somewhat muffled "Good night". It was an utterance that was momentarily reassuring, but it did not dispel my fear. So, I would say it again. "Good night". And he would echo back, "Good night".

EMPATHIC ENVELOPE

This exchange would go on for maybe ten minutes as Lenard drifted off into a hypnogogic state, mumbling automatically "Good night". I honestly believed he was able to bid me good night while sleeping soundly as I lay wide-awake trembling.

These bedtime "conversations" stay with me. What I cannot remember is if we ever engaged in real boy-talk. I never knew what he liked or disliked, what he did in school or outside the house. I never knew his friends and when I finally acquired a few of my own, I never introduced them to him. If I had asked him any questions – and I must certainly have – I never received any answers. Like my father, Lenard was emotionally absent from my life.

Years later, I attended his funeral in Harrisburg after he died of heart failure, a condition he fittingly shared with my father. Going to the service was like attending the burial of a complete stranger, though, for many years, we shared a mother, a father, and a bedroom. At the burial site, I said farewell to my brother under my breath, a barely whispered version of the "goodnight" I used to say as a boy. This time, however, the only response was a deafening silence that sealed forever the wall between us, a barrier that only intensified my isolation.

Although I earned a BS and MS in economics at Penn State, I was inevitably drawn to the study of psychology, driven by the emotional anxiety I had felt growing up. For a time, I went into therapy while I was in the Navy, but that experience did not give me the understanding or healing I needed. It was at that point that I started to explore on my own the nature of my psyche, relying on self-reflection, journal writing, meditation, and dream analysis.

In 1961, I received a Ph.D. in psychology from Columbia and, by 1966, began a private practice which is still thriving. However, I never again went into analysis with another therapist. What I share with you now is what I learned by initially confronting through self-analysis my troubled boyhood as well as every other phase of my life as a man. These findings became inextricably related to the kind of therapy I employ now, in which client and psychotherapist collaborate in understanding the repressed and incompletely understood content of the patient's mind. I firmly believe that we all possess the unique capacity for self-reflection, which can ultimately lead to a revelation of the most powerful and effective therapist - the therapist within.

Coming to terms with the past is at the heart of the therapeutic process. For both patient and therapist, the first goal is to uncover what caused the pain of depression, anxiety, or alienation. The second is for the patient to experience relief and healing. The more I engaged in self-reflection, the more I realized that just as my fears began in infancy, many of my patient's fears began then as well. As a result, I conceived of a concept I called the "Empathic Envelope".

Through my years of working as diligently as I could to deeply listen to each individual person's story, I began to see several broad, common aspects to their development and central ways in which any child's development can be derailed.

Let me explain. Children are born with an inherent expectation that there will be an abundant supply of all they will need to survive and grow. Such needs are met by significant others, usually a mother and father or anyone else who provides the physical and psychological support for a healthy development of both body and mind. The image of an envelope connotes an enclosed space of security with the capacity to expand as the child matures psychologically. The term "empathic" suggests reciprocity of feeling between the child and the other. This connection begins with nursing and feeding to be accompanied by tactile gestures of affection, such as touching, caressing, hugging, and kissing. The empathic envelope is a middle stage between the unconscious dependency that occurs in the womb and the ever-growing independence of a fully developed ego. What was once purely biological and unconscious gives way to the complexities of a burgeoning consciousness. As the envelope expands in time, social awareness increases. Sounds, words, and music invade the envelope and stimulate an even greater awareness of the external world.

An ideal empathic envelope requires loving parents or caregivers who behave similarly. The empathic envelope into which I was born was hardly perfect. From all I could remember and learn about my birth and boyhood, I concluded that my parents lacked the capacity to provide the kind of warmth and security children need. As I said, my father was distant. I never understood the source of his anger, though I often suspected, as any child might, that it had something to do with me. My mother, on the other hand, was a kind woman who performed her wifely and domestic duties adequately. She kept the house clean, cooked nutritious meals, and washed and ironed our clothes, all without ever complaining. She seemed to get special satisfaction out of getting my brother and me into bed at night with scrupulous regularity. I believe that doing so fed her sense of orderliness, a way to counter the moody hostility that my father brought into the house.

Nevertheless, I felt personally abandoned by her though she rarely ever left the house. She was never that far away from me even behind a closed door. She was there but to meet my emotional needs, she really was not "there" at all. I clearly wanted more from her than she was able to give. Realizing now that she was not so different from most women of her generation and class, I make no judgment. I strongly believe she did her best.

Through self-analysis and interactions with patients, I began to deepen and widen the concept of the empathic envelope. It became clear that an infant's physical and mental well-being depends on the positive behavior of mother, father, or caregiver. When that behavior is negative, the consequences can be dire and long term. What are negative behaviors? First and foremost is neglect. To leave a child unattended, unfed, unclean, untouched, for any length of time, will produce emotional scars. The physical consequences can be easily corrected. The psychological issues, however, can last a lifetime. Where there should have been some sense of fulfillment, there could be deprivation. Where there should be a sense of being loved, there may be a sense of being unwanted; instead of a sense of a positive growing connection with the significant others, there might be an overwhelming feeling of emptiness. Whatever happens within the original empathic envelope will have an enduring impact on the life of the individual. Reflecting on the persistent fear of isolation I experienced as a young boy, I must conclude that my mother, father, and brother were not mindful of the attention I surely craved. What child does not want undivided attention and unqualified love? We all desire empathic others to satisfy our needs. The healthy development of the psyche depends to varying degrees on how those needs are met. It is important to note that the empathic envelope that appears so secure for the child in early life may be easily disrupted. Significant others may face difficulties and change emotionally from being caring and attentive to be partially unavailable or dysfunctional. These changes – financial setbacks, illness, marital problems, divorce, addictions – will have profound effects on the dynamic relationship between child and caregiver, and will cause traumatic reactions.

To understand how vulnerable the empathic envelope can be, I offer this image. Picture a nomad child living with his parents within a tent in the desert. The space inside the flimsy walls of the tent, along with the presence of significant others, provides an illusion of an ideal form of security. As long as the nomad child exists within the confines of the tent with the support of the others, the child will continue to thrive and grow. The child, however, is unaware of the dangers and threatening forces lurking outside the tent. If he should accidentally leave the tent alone at night and enter the outside world, he will experience anxiety, terror, isolation, and the threat of death. These are automatic responses that occur in dangerous situations, and they act as a signal to the child to return to the security of the tent, using any means possible.

The experiences outside the tent without the significant others symbolize premature exposure to the potential dangers lurking within an unfamiliar environment. Without the support of the empathic envelope, the child is likely to experience the eruption of the terror associated with isolation. Such harsh reactions, which arise within the child's mind, can be devastating because the immature ego of the child is unable to handle the kind of vulnerability that leads to lasting psychological suffering.

When we consider the emotional states associated with being inside and outside the tent, we realize how dramatically different they really are. The state of mind within is secure. There will be ups and downs in this positive state due to the exigencies of interacting with significant others. If the child is outside the tent, or if the tent is invaded by outside dangers, there will be a generalized destabilization of the mind of the child.

While the empathic envelope is formed at birth, it is an ongoing ever-expanding entity. As we grow and mature, new others enter the envelope, at first relatives and close friends, but eventually, as our circle of others widens, so does the envelope. Each experience brings in others who become significant to the degree that they interact with us. Lovers and spouses are most important, and then children and grandchildren, but close friends and colleagues also have an empathic impact on our psychological wellbeing, providing us with the security we once experienced as infants. For religious people, communal empathic envelopes provide the strength to deal with the trials and adversities of everyday life. What greater significant other is there than God? Having faith and being part of a congregation of fellow worshippers allow for a powerful empathic envelope that can sustain one throughout life. But even nonbelievers are drawn to various kinds of communities that nourish and enrich the psyche. We are by nature tribal, and require a sense of belonging, an antidote to the debilitating effects of alienation and isolation.

2

CREATIVE CONNECTION

If there is one event that marks the first turning point in my life, it is the experience of entering third grade. I was nine years old and my family had moved from a small apartment building to a two-storeyed house on a treelined street in Harrisburg. In ways I could not have understood at the time, it was a small step up the social ladder for my family. For me, what mattered most was discovering a world that was both new and different, which is not to say that I did not bring along many of the old fears I had endured during the first eight years of my life. "Newness" has its own challenges, and I now realize that I must have felt anxious about being the new kid on the block. Making friends is hard enough for anyone, but my situation was unique, for I had never had friends before. Friendship was, indeed, something new and different. For other boys my age, making the transition from leaving old friends behind to starting new alliances was probably met with mixed emotions. I had no pals to feel sad about leaving, nor did I have any happy memories of what it was like to spend time with kids away from the presence of adults at home or in the classroom.

Being invited to join in the rough and tumble games of tag, street hockey, and cops and robbers introduced me to excitement I had never known before. The word "adventure" entered my vocabulary through games played outdoors rather than from tales found in books. There were no books in my house, and no one read to me stories of knights or soldiers battling enemies or fairy tales with heroes and monsters. So, you can imagine the thrill of overcoming danger vicariously and conquering made up fears on the streets and parks of the neighborhood, especially because those real fears of isolation that had been dominating my life still existed at home and in my bedroom at night.

Going to a new elementary school in the middle of the year was fraught with much trepidation. That was only natural, but thanks to the way memory can play tricks with our sense of reality, it has become easy for me to mythologize the experience as a rite of passage. Looking back from the perspective of eighty years, I rely on impressions that have stayed with me through deep reflection, meditation, and even dreams. I picture a young female teacher, younger than any I had seen before in my former school. She looked kind, not at all threatening. Her smile welcomed and reassured me, and by the way, she touched my shoulder, she clearly sensed how nervous I was. I wish I could remember her name, for many times, throughout the years, I felt compelled to write and tell her how important she was at this pivotal moment of my life.

She must have known that my family was Jewish because she introduced me to a group of boys who were also Jewish and who seemed to have formed a private clique of their own within the room. It was her intention to have them make me feel comfortable, to show me the ropes in a way that no adult ever could. Unless you are a third-grader, you probably cannot appreciate fully the social dynamics of nine-year-old boys. What makes the experience even more memorable is that I was introduced into a small circle of my peers with an identity that ensured my belonging. I had always known I was Jewish, but it meant no more to me than being aware of my gender, height, and weight, or being an American living in Pennsylvania. I eventually realized that being a Jew did not just connect me to others but that it also separated me from some, not only in that classroom but in all the classrooms throughout my education. I slowly learned and experienced over the years that anti-Semitism could be both subtle and overt. That was a small price to pay, however, for now, I finally had friends.

The only way to explain the impact of that experience on the rest of my years as a student from elementary school through college and graduate school is to jump ahead to another even more significant life-changing event. While I was in the Navy just after the Korean War ended in the early 1950s, I felt compelled to seek therapy for the very first time. The fears I had experienced from the very beginning of my life and had artfully concealed behind the false persona of a very smart, charming, articulate guy with a bright future in the financial field, began to resurface. There was an expectation among family and friends that I had a sure-fire career path leading to Wall Street or the business world. After all, I had a Master's degree in Economics from Penn State. What could go wrong? What happened, however, was a reckoning with the darkness that continued to haunt me. The therapist I had seen for a time failed to provide an insight into my suffering, nor did he offer any hope for relieving the psychological burden that was becoming more and more difficult to bear.

I was living alone in a small apartment in Manhattan, but the only thing I can remember about it is, oddly enough, an easy chair. I know that I must have had more furniture. Whatever that was is hardly discernable enough to describe. No. It was the chair that looms large in my memory and even that defies easy description. Was it leather or upholstered? Who knows? All that matters is the experience of settling into it one day after returning from a particularly futile session with my therapist. I felt helpless and then concluded that whatever therapy I was being sold was not working.

Sitting in that easy chair at that moment, feeling a sense of despair, I began the difficult journey into my own psyche, unaccompanied by any therapist or counselor. The sensation of entering into the deepest terrain of my mind all alone became the formative experience of my life and served as the very foundation of the kind of therapy I practiced with patients over the years. Ultimately, I gave a name to this sensation. I called it a Creative Connection.

What happened to me that day is comparable to what an artist experiences as a prelude to the act of creation, a process that initially requires getting in touch with feelings and profound truths embedded in the deepest recesses of the mind. It precedes the challenging effort of actually executing a work of art. The conception, the initial vision, is what I call the "creative connection". I do not believe that making or appreciating art is the only way to experience a creative connection. I feel, however, that art is a way to explain it.

12   THEORETICAL FRAMEWORK

The poem "Those Winter Sundays" by Robert Hayden (as cited in Glaysher, 2013, p. 41), an African–American poet of the twentieth century, touched me the first time I read it a few years ago. Whenever I read it to others, I detect a similar reaction. Eventually, I learned that the poem has been widely anthologized and is a favorite of high school teachers attempting to generate enthusiasm for poetry among students, especially those who have a natural aversion to the genre.

Those Winter Sundays

Sundays too my father got up early
and put his clothes on in the blueblack cold,
then with cracked hands that ached
from labor in the weekday weather made
banked fires blaze. No one ever thanked him.
I'd wake and hear the cold splintering, breaking.
When the rooms were warm, he'd call,
and slowly I would rise and dress,
fearing the chronic angers of that house,
Speaking indifferently to him,
who had driven out the cold
and polished my good shoes as well.
What did I know, what did I know
of love's austere and lonely offices?

The poem obviously describes a memory. The poet, or speaker, is looking back at a time when he was a boy and recalls something about the relationship he had with his father that he may never have consciously acknowledged before. Which raises the question, what triggered the memory in the first place? One can only speculate on what stirred this confession of ingratitude after many years. Perhaps, as an adult, he had learned of his father's death. Or, maybe, he is himself now a father and can appreciate the complexities of fatherhood in a more profound way.

The first stanza makes clear that the poet's father was a man who put the comforts of his family first, even on Sunday, a day of rest, when he "got up early" to warm the house. As the poet acknowledges, "no one ever thanked him". Is the poet feeling guilty? Probably. Is he experiencing regret? Of course. After all, he was able to get dressed in the warmth and put on shoes that his father had already shined, despite fearing the "chronic angers of that house". This is not merely a backward glance at a painful boyhood. It is rather a belated acknowledgment of his failure to understand "love's austere and lonely offices". What could he have known back then of such things? But now through self-reflection, he comes to terms with a serious flaw in his own humanity, something he had likely repressed.

I like to think that whatever specific event stimulated the writing of the poem, the experience of introspection was one of creative connection for Hayden. For some, to read this poem is to undergo a similar experience of creative connection. One man's painful but poignant memory of regret can ignite in others an empathic response. When we look back, we may all have to face the fact that there is unfinished business. Reflection, writing, and then reading can lead to awareness and even healing. Such is the power of art.

A creative connection is the necessary condition that allows for the development of insight, inspiration, and clarity of thought. This experience can be called a revelation of truth or a spiritual or meditative discovery/inspiration/exploration. It is akin to feeling the bliss of an uncomplicated, true connection to oneself or to another.

A creative connection is always a personal experience, but it is often experienced in the company of others. As I look back, my third-grade teacher was the liaison to my creative connection to the Jewish boys in the class with whom I now could identify and share a sense of belonging at the Jewish Community Center.

We can find examples of creative connections in the most truly caring interpersonal experiences, between caregiver and child, between teacher and student, and, of course, between therapist and patient. Even though creative connections are dependent upon an interpersonal or inter-relational situation, the experience is always a deeply personal one.

The very essential aspects of living, such as experiencing joy, contentment, pleasure and healthy attachments are all expressed through a strong, positive, creative connection. The foundation of all these experiences, I believe, is love. When I speak of love, I am speaking not only of romantic relationships and marriage, love of children, and love of loyal friends, but the more general experience of the love of life. Because of creative connections, the individual has access to an atmosphere within the mind where a source of appreciation, joyful wonder about life, and a sense of being loved are found. I do not mean to say that people who are capable of love are constantly in that positive state. Surely, not. There is usually access to both psychological states of love and suffering. But in truly loving people, the balance is more to the positive than to the negative.

I know that love is a product of positive early relationships with significant others. Yet it is also a result of the ability to experience strong, positive, creative connections, first between self and significant others within the empathic envelope, and with the passing of time, with an increasing number of others who value us.

We also have the capacity for a creative connection with our true self as we contemplate, meditate, and self-reflect. Returning to my apartment on that fateful day from a disappointing session with my therapist, I settled into my easy chair and engaged for the first time in self-reflection. It was then that I experienced a creative connection alone with myself. I received and encountered the truth and creativity released from my self-reflective system. By engaging myself in this very personal way, transformative changes ensued. The self-reflective system is a quiet presence within the mind that is gradually revealed to be one's strength of character, wisdom, one's capacity for generosity, compassion, and a deep and profound understanding of the nature of life.

Unfortunately, creative connections with others can fail due to the psychopathology within the mind of the significant other, such as narcissism, excessive rage or anger, insufficient attentiveness, and a profound failure to be empathic. For an infant, the failure to experience a creative connection will cause sizable psychological distress. Essentially, the infant will suffer emotional deprivation, psychological isolation, and a severe inability to handle unexpected and abnormal stress. All of these disturbances block the flow of positive energy that could have been received and encountered from the self-reflective system. Grievously, the maturing child is unable to utilize what should be a budding capacity for self-reflection and psychological growth. The disturbances within the child become the foundation of the psychological disturbances that cause suffering throughout life.

There are many people who suffer greatly in this world from failed creative connections. An early disturbance within efforts to produce creative connection interfere with clear thinking, true creativity, and the ability to use wisdom. Traumatic states of any kind can obstruct the open receptivity within the mind to receive the creative connection. If our early openness to creative connection is met with indifference, or worse, with rejection, we are less likely to remain open to such a connection in the future. These hindrances can make true creative connections difficult to obtain throughout the course of an entire lifetime. Disturbances can come from other sources in addition to an inadequate significant other. The child may produce the disturbances within themselves. Physical pain and bodily discomfort may interrupt creative connection as can psychophysical conditions like attention-deficit/hyperactivity disorders and other childhood behavioral disorders.

All disturbances within creative connection put some degree of unusual strain upon the immature ego of the child. Too much stress upon the ego, and too much failure in the effort to form a creative connection, can result in the withdrawal of part of the child's self away from the significant other, and into isolation. This does not mean that the entire self has withdrawn because part of the child's self continues to develop within the existing, imperfect connection with the caregiver. The withdrawn part of the child's self, however, may become the nucleus what I will call of a "pathological structure". The failure of creative connection leading to the creation of an early pathological structure will, in fact, divide the mind of the child.

The consequences of a divided mind are great. It is important to stress that not all disturbances within creative connections result in the formation of pathological structures. They may result, though, in some degree of obstruction in the typical development of the young child. Minor early traumas may delay development but severe trauma, resulting in the creation of pathological structures, will guarantee a split in the person's mind. That split makes life much more complicated for the individual, and will negatively affect childhood development. This will also, eventually, increase the possibility of lifelong suffering.

References

Glaysher, F. (ed.). (2013). *Collected Poems: Robert Hayden*. New York: Liveright Corporation, W.W. Norton Publisher.

3

SYMBIOTIC-COMPENSATORY SYSTEM

The decision to rely on self-reflection in dealing with my own therapy was at first a formidable challenge. It did, however, eventually lead to revelations that were effective in my own healing and played a significant role in the way I treated patients once I became a psychotherapist. Now, at the age of ninety, I have the luxury of looking back at experiences that seemed inexplicable at the time but can now be explained in light of the discoveries I have made.

From the time I entered the third grade as a nine-year-old until I tried and rejected therapy at the age of twenty-two while in the Navy, I was living what looked like a charmed life, at least to outsiders who didn't know anything about the fears I continued to have since my earliest days. For over a decade, I was able to conceal the darkness and keep it at bay.

Feeling connected to a tight-knit group of Jewish boys, playing basketball at the Center, going with them to movie matinees, and engaging in friendly competition for good grades, I got through my days in elementary and high school relatively happy. Not even the death of my father when I was thirteen could dispel this happiness or undermine confidence in the self I had projected to the world.

After my father died, the economic circumstances of our household did not change, thanks to the generosity of my father's sister. She had married Jacob Miller who owned several highly successful furniture stores for which my father worked as a salesman. The paycheck he earned every week to keep us alive and healthy continued after he died. My older brother, Lenard, started to work for the firm while still in high school and after college established himself as a highly capable businessman continuing to be part of the Miller establishment.

Although I worked for the company during the summers, I formed my own relationship with the family after my father died. My mother believed it would be "nice" to express our gratitude for the Millers' benevolence by my paying regular visits to them. They lived in a rather impressive house in one of the most fashionable neighborhoods of Harrisburg. Although the Millers were on one of the highest rungs of the social ladder, I was still able to walk to their house. In my adolescent way of starting to romanticize things, I saw in them a way of life to which I could aspire. Had I read the novels of F. Scott Fitzgerald or Horatio Alger, such aspirations might have made sense. But I did not learn through books about characters like Jay Gatsby and other believers in the American Dream who sought material and social success. There was just something special about the Millers that appealed to me. They were like us in that they too were Jewish, but they were not at all like the Brenners because of the way they dressed, the food they ate, the music they listened to, and the books they read. They may have lived within walking distance, but they might as well have lived on another planet. My mother not only encouraged my visits, but she also enjoyed hearing my accounts of what occurred while I was there, even if the time spent were only an hour. Mrs. Miller was her sister-in-law, but I cannot imagine a meaningful conversation taking place between them.

When it came time for my brother to attend college and then for me two years later, it was the Millers who paid for our education. What was remarkable was that there were no strings attached, no expectations for paying them back for what surely made a profound difference in our lives.

The Millers were real, but, at the same time, they represented a world of sophistication and culture which inspired me. As for Lenard, I doubt if he had similar notions. He viewed them as a way of furthering his career in business and, in that sense, he was correct. When Miller Furniture was eventually sold, Lenard, who had worked there for many years, assuming he was part of the family, did not receive any part of the sale. He was, like me, "family", but not quite among the immediate members. Lenard, nevertheless, started his own furniture company which was very successful. Apparently, he learned from the Millers the business strategies that led to the kind of material success he wanted for a happy life. What I learned, however, was quite different.

Leaving home and going to Penn State may not have had the same dramatic impact on my life as going into third grade, but it did allow me to grow and flourish intellectually and socially. The timid boy so afraid of isolation was fittingly concealed beneath the polished veneer of a confident undergraduate focusing on a bright future, not a dark past. This new self emerged quite boldly when I entered a public speaking contest. In high school, I was shy and reticent during class discussions; so, entering this contest in an unfamiliar setting was especially gutsy, if not downright perverse for someone with my temperament. What is even more mysterious is the content of the speech I composed and delivered. I entitled it "An Accident of Birth", and in it discussed the terrible inequalities endured by African Americans simply as a consequence of being born black.

I finally understood what prompted my decision to choose and speak on a subject about which I had no knowledge or personal experience. My sole connection to the few African Americans who lived in Harrisburg at that time derived from an image etched in my consciousness of a particular street not far from my house and on which only black people lived. I can still see them sitting on their porches or front steps, speaking in hushed tones among themselves. I had no idea what they were talking about. Or thinking. Or feeling. This image, however, was powerful and the more I reimagined it, the more it stirred within me profound sadness. I realize now many years later that what I saw in the faces of those people was what it must mean to spend an entire lifetime separated from the larger community, a kind of isolation that I was always feeling and dreading. The initial image of black people sitting among themselves on their street and its impact through recollection were undoubtedly for me a creative connection.

Winning the contest opened the doors to what seemed like unlimited possibilities for developing a new persona. It led first and foremost to being invited to join the debate team. Public speaking and debating were completely new to me. The only prior experience I had speaking before an audience was during my Bar Mitzvah but that hardly counted because it involved rote memorization.

Now, despite preparation in forensics and learning how to employ facts in support of arguments, I developed confidence in being an extemporaneous speaker. I had acquired the skill to think on my feet. Winning debates led to newspaper articles and a certain amount of campus fame. This kind of success contributed to honing a new self, a public self, or what I would one day realize as a "false self". I was becoming more and more adept at being effective in the real world which alleviated the suffering I had always felt, and which still plagued me. I had always possessed the intellectual prowess to get good grades and win the favor of my teachers. What was new, however, was the way I could navigate a successful social life. Dating was fun, but a serious romance was out of the question, not for any practical reasons, but rather because my emotions never led me there.

What I did become passionate about was attending football games on fall weekends. Cheering for Penn State with my fellow undergraduates was a visceral experience, primal in nature. It was exhilarating to be caught up in the frenzy of victory or the despondency of defeat. In either case, the vicarious thrills of being a spectator fed and nurtured the false self I was in the process of perfecting. Marlin Brenner was evolving into a minor celebrity on the campus and as my success as a debater increased, so did my public reputation. Milton Eisenhower, the president of the University, even invited me into his office to compliment my performance on the debate team.

During my junior year, I was tapped to become a member of Lion's Paw, an exclusive society of only twelve prominent leaders of the senior class. Being a member of such an elite group was the pinnacle of social acceptance. The twelve of us met once a week to discuss matters that affected the student body or newsworthy issues of national or international interest. Our opinion mattered, at least to us and sometimes to the students at large, our professors, and even administrators. I wondered if being a member of Lion's Paw was a harbinger of what life would be like beyond the university. For many of my fellow leaders, I am sure that it was. Success in one realm assured success in all future realms. That was not my fate, though I tried to sustain a feeling of wellbeing by remaining at Penn State for another year where I earned a Master's degree in economics.

THEORETICAL FRAMEWORK

Although the future looked bright, I could never completely erase the past. During my college years, I had gone home regularly for holidays and vacations. These visits are for the most part forgotten, except for one time, I cannot recall the date or occasion, but I vividly remember walking through the front door of an empty house. As I entered the living room, I was struck by the sight of an old threadbare easy chair that was there for as long as I could remember. It was where my father sat while reading the local newspaper or listening to Walter Winchell on the radio. Or just waiting for dinner to be called. The sight of that chair on that particular day triggered a flood of emotions that overwhelmed me. The emotions were mixed because the chair brought to my mind the reality that I had had a family, a father, a mother, and a brother. That this was home. My home. A place where I grew up.

The old chair was inviting in its familiarity. I could not resist sitting in it and allowing myself to feel the comfort it provided. It also evoked tears, for here I was, the renowned Marlin Brenner, top debater at Penn State, member of Lion's Paw, friend to the University President, who had returned to a home which never generated many happy emotions.

Attaching significance to that specific chair on that occasion, I am sure, had a great deal to do with the formative experience of my life, sitting in a different armchair in my New York apartment years later when I began to develop the capacity for self-reflection and becoming my own therapist. Am I making too much of an ordinary piece of furniture? Perhaps I am. But we all have favorite chairs that offer rest and relaxation, a comfortable place in which to read, listen to music, sip a brandy, or merely unwind. As you certainly surmise by now, such a chair is perfect for silent contemplation, a place for deep thinking and meditation, a portal to psychological understanding and healing. It is where I discovered what happened to me during the years of my education. I had to explain how for over a decade I had been able to function successfully in the real world as a vibrant, fully alive human being while repressing the intimidated boy who was fearful of the dark. The exploration of my two contradictory selves led to my discovery of what I call the "Symbiotic-Compensatory System".

I experienced these two contradictory selves as split-off parts of who I am. However, I did not recognize that I was dominated by these parts of self as they remained active within my dynamic unconscious. It is almost as if two or more dissimilar psychological entities, separate from each other existed in my mind. They may share the same ever-present experience of "this is me" because my divided self attempted to unite them in order to function with others.

It is the symbiotic-compensatory system that facilitates the amalgamation of the unconscious parts of the self, and culminates in a person's conscious awareness of a unified self. The unification process is not always perfect or entirely complete. The incompleteness of this process can appear in various degrees. Namely, the person without a unified self will experience intense negative emotions, such as severe anxiety, crippling depression, and/or the tormenting anguish of unmet needs. Hence, the person suffers greatly when divided, but does not understand why.

For example, when I was at Penn State and gained social status within the university community, I was able to appear happy, even though I was concealing my injured self from the public's eye. Nevertheless, the amount of mental anguish I suffered remained alive, although not totally recognized by my conscious mind. I just did not know why I was periodically experiencing bouts of unhappiness.

Despite the suffering, I was functioning relatively well within, what I call, the "Realm of Existence". The realm of existence is the reality I was born into, and where all social interactions and activities take place. How well I could participate in the realm of existence was determined by how unified my true self really was at the time.

At the same time, the symbiotic-compensatory system is faced with the problem of serving two masters: the screaming unmet needs of the injured self trapped within a pathological structure, and the healthy parts of the self that have developed normally. To attempt a successful entry into the realm of existence, my symbiotic-compensatory system created several invisible barriers that prohibited the expression of certain emotional states and/or behaviors. These invisible barriers also blocked the experience of positive emotions, making it difficult or impossible, for me to express creativity, love, and affection, and to gain knowledge of my own personal truth. The invisible barriers allowed me to live with some sense of safety as I tried to meet the perceived unconscious demands of significant others. I assumed that my inner, hidden emotions and behaviors would be unacceptable to the powerful authority figures in my life, namely my parents and older brother.

Consider one of my patients, Michelle, who at thirty-nine entered therapy with a history of romantic failures, unable to understand why the pattern persisted. During treatment, a few invisible barriers became apparent, namely Michelle's inability to express love and appreciation for her partner. It emerged that Michelle, as a child, was forbidden to express honest love toward her parents, and was made to feel humiliated and disparaged by having such feelings in the first place.

In this example, the unmet needs trapped within the patient's pathological structure are alive and active, alongside the mature desire to seek a mate. The patient's inability to fully amalgamate these two selves resulted in repeated romantic failures, and perpetuated continual suffering in her current life.

Just like Michelle, many of my patients enter therapy not knowing that a personal pattern of behavior has been established by their inability to form a cohesive self. Usually, the individuals I am observing are unaware of the division within the self, and they believe they are functioning in their usual, normal way. They are aware, however, of feeling mental disturbance and emotional distress, such as anxiety, fear, or sadness, but they have no working knowledge of the interactive effect that the dissimilar parts of the self have upon them.

I now look at all my patients from this "two selves" perspective. If the person appears weak and vulnerable, I understand that it is the split-off part of the amalgamated self, powered by the strong force of pathology, that is currently in ascendancy. But I am also aware that it is the unencumbered self, motivated by the creative, weak force that is telling me the story. The individual has amalgamated the split, and due to the work of the symbiotic-compensatory system, I can hear both sides at the same time. It is important for therapists to know the strength of the person, and the vulnerability and suffering that appear before them when a patient communicates.

As previously stated, the symbiotic-compensatory system aims to amalgamate and create a unified self that can function well with others in the world. Nevertheless, these forces remain powerful and influential within the mind, making self-unification difficult, if not impossible, and will result in the development of a false self. The false self empowers the individual to engage effectively in the realm of existence, even though it suppresses personal honesty. The individual's false self can gain some degree of gratification within the world, although it prohibits the person from living an authentic life. The invisible barriers that block a person's true self from emerging remain active throughout life. This may be a small psychological price to pay for appearing to be a fully functioning person. Specifically, the false self allows the individual to emerge as mature and age-appropriate to others, while still seeking infantile gratification.

My false self was very well-developed by the time I completed my academic studies at Penn State. I had all the effective interpersonal skills to engage and even charm others. Unfortunately, those invisible barriers that prohibited the expression of my true emotions also prevented me from living life fully.

The cost-benefit ratio can be illustrated in this way. The false self made it possible for me to interact successfully within the world, and at the same time, it severely distorted my ability to accurately perceive reality. Distortions in thinking will negatively influence a person's ability to form sound judgments and make rational decisions. Our choices in life can be grossly limited due to the narrow focus of our distorted perceptions. Moreover, many of the obstacles that interfere with healthy interpersonal relationships stem from perceptual distortions. The false self may offer a compromised existence within the interpersonal world, but it allows for an existence with others, nonetheless. For those able to forge a long-term intimate relationship, guided by the symbiotic compensatory system and aided by the false self, they may eventually develop a deep sense of disappointment in that relationship. Unfortunately, the disappointment could never really be spoken of, or even whispered aloud. Regardless, the individual will remain connected to that disappointing relationship for fear of experiencing what could be an even more unbearable loss and disillusionment without it.

When I was a young child, my parents did not value nor did they foster a creative connection with me. As a result, a constant inner state of isolation was created, and it became a fixed underlying part of my functioning mind. I was a lonely child, unable to really connect with family or friends. It was not until I turned 9 years old and my family moved to another part of town that I found a way to reinvent myself. I developed an elaborate compensatory strategy capable of effectively engaging with others and participating in social groups at school and later at the university. My bent-over, needy, psychological posture was leaning towards those that I perceived to have power and status in the peer group. I was anxious to please and accommodate the wishes of those powerful peers, and I soon entered the popular Jewish group at school. My invisible barriers were firmly established from a home life where no emotions, other than my father's anger, could be expressed. So, I was perfectly suited to become everyone's friend at school and on the playground. I had an exquisite ability to acquiesce to everyone's wishes, and I even had the ability to anticipate the needs of others so as to promptly supply them with what they needed before they asked. I guess contemporary society would call me a "people pleaser" but in my estimation, this was my constructive false self at work.

I was able to rise to the top of the social hierarchy of my peer group, excel academically in school, become a leader at the university, and behave as a very successful person. Yes, for a long time, my effective false self, with accompanying effective compensatory strategies and symbiotic pathological attachments to others in power, helped suppress my inevitable psychological suffering. However, when I was 24 years old, the internal game was up.

At that time, I entered the armed services and true panic attacks periodically came over me. I could no longer contain the screaming unmet infantile needs lodged deep in my pathological structure, and I seemed unable to keep my false self-image from crumbling. I yearned for relief and to understand what was going on inside. More importantly, I yearned to be real, alive and truly myself. This is where the long road of my heroic journey of self-discovery began. This journey started in earnest as I began to study psychology.

While at Columbia University pursuing my doctoral degree in psychology, one day I happened to enter the wrong office and needed to ask the student worker for direction. That young woman eventually became my wife. It was love and lust at first sight. We could not resist the basic primal urges of chemistry, and we were married shortly after meeting each other. I was well-known at Columbia and knew I was very popular among the women, but it was Marcia I would ask to marry. Looking back now, I could see that it was her unconditional acceptance of me that made her safe for me to join my life with hers. Furthermore, her idealization of me caused me to believe I was somebody special. I guess you could say that my false self was so polished, that at times, especially with Marcia, I believed I was the inauthentic person I was projecting to the world. It was not until much later in my marriage that I would have to find a way to encounter my true self behind my masterful persona.

Everyday life with another human being can become a litmus test, measuring what a substance is made of. I could not maintain my charming demeanor in such close quarters. I am sure Marcia sensed some negative emotional signals, but we never talked about the root cause of my moodiness. I found a way to shelter her from my rageful, injured self by spending long hours in my office, journal writing.

The therapy had disappointed me twice, once when I was in the Navy experiencing panic attacks, and then early in my marriage. My second therapist probably was helpful at first, but because he was traditionally trained as a psychoanalyst, he felt a need to provide me with intrusive interpretations. I thought to myself, if he only would "shut up", I could explore the contents of my own mind in his presence. Nonetheless, I was not able to hear my thoughts because his analytic interpretations invaded the necessary silence.

I did find that the silence and privacy of my own office were crucial if I were to contemplate and encounter my own mind productively. Marcia knew to leave me alone when I was in that sacred room. I was guaranteed the aloneness to think, meditate, and, finally, to journal write. Sometimes, I would leave my family, who lived upstairs, in the middle of a social activity to sit for hours in my office, just to listen to my thoughts. Other times, I would fiercely write in my journals, while rage poured out of me, breaking many pencils with the force of my negative emotions. I was so surprised to encounter this angry, vengeful, infantile self.

I literally filled up many hundreds of journals with my rage. No one in the family knew of this split-off self of mine. Even I did not know this other self very well, but I was slowly getting acquainted with my personal truth, and it was very painful to encounter. Over the years, I needed to destroy those journals, afraid that people I cared about would see what I wrote. Ironically, I could only throw out those anger-filled journals which contained parts of my true self, as my symbiotic-compensatory system became known to me. I could see my need to appear like a charming, considerate, and caring individual, and, finally, I became strong enough to confront and accept those aspects of my false self, and slowly try to relinquish the mask.

Journal writing and meditating on the content helped me convert my emotions and visceral reactions into words. Words are containers, and without an extensive language for human experiences, we are left to react rather than to think. Even now, when creatively connecting with my patients, I help them find the words. One precisely placed word in the dialogue miraculously transforms the patient's confusion and distress into personal understanding and relief. That sense of being understood by another is not only an aspect of the healing process in therapy, but it also provides patients with the tools necessary to heal themselves.

4

PATHOLOGICAL STRUCTURES

My journal writing has been essential to my ability to see my hidden personal truth. It is the receipt of a message from one part of my mind created by my self-reflection system. My ability to receive, accept, and encounter the message helps strengthen my true self. However, one must be courageous enough to see the truth hidden in plain sight as the writing unfolds.

Our past trauma seems to find a way to express itself in everyday circumstances with significant others. They become our own personal drama repetitively activated throughout life. To protect my marriage with Marcia, and my relationship with my sons from my troubled past, I regularly separated myself from them to become brutally honest with myself through my journal writing. Even when this habit served me well in many ways, the past can find paths to disguise itself in contemporary relationships. I remember one vivid incident with a student supervisee when I almost destroyed her trust in my professional work.

As you know, many psychologists work with other psychotherapists to help them identify issues with their clients and suggest new treatment

PATHOLOGICAL STRUCTURES 27

strategies. Supervision is an important part of training and enriching a psychotherapist's work with clients. The psychologist-supervisee relationship is a very personal and confidential one between two professionals. Nicole, my supervisee, had been working with me for over five years, and she had shared many of her apprehensions and insecurities of her therapeutic approaches with her clients. Nicole trusted me and allowed me to guide her work, even when she expressed her doubts about the therapeutic direction.

During one supervision session with Nicole, I found myself drifting away from the conversation and feeling a deep sense of isolation. As Nicole presented her client's case material, I felt like I was all alone and lonely, as if I had no one to care for me. I wanted to reach out to someone, anyone, maybe even Nicole, to find a personal and deep connection to alleviate my sense of loneliness.

While talking to Nicole and feeling so isolated, I could experience my emotional mental posture as being bent-over like a beggar, yearning for connection. I was tempted to try to turn Nicole into an attentive listener, a motherly significant other, a nurturer, a caregiver. I wanted her to enter my isolation and eliminate my sense of being unloved and unlovable. My fantasy was that she would empathically understand my woundedness and supply me with what I had missed all my life. Acting on this impulse would have been disastrous. I would have used Nicole for my own infantile needs at the cost of destroying our professional relationship. It was only through controlling my impulses at the time, and journal writing after that session, that I realized the cause of my intense feelings of isolation. Through self-reflective writing, I was able to shift mentally from a bent-over needy posture of a child to an upright mental position of a professional man. You see, Nicole had started to talk about how she could not bear the emotional distress of being a therapist for very long periods of time, and how her teaching while maintaining her private practice was very therapeutic for her. Nicole was describing to me how sensitive she really is, and how she often ends up identifying with the pain and suffering of her clients. I heard her say, "The pain and suffering of others can be excruciating for me to cope with". At that time, I must have unconsciously realized that if I acted out the needs expressed within my bent-over, child-like needy, mental posture, I would have caused her great emotional harm as well as injuring our professional relationship. So, during that supervisory session, I straightened up emotionally and discussed her client's case material from a less needy and more independent mental position.

This relational example with Nicole illustrates how powerful my past trauma, my personal drama, can be in my contemporary life. Through my self-reflective journal writing, I was able to encounter my childlike neediness as it related to my session with Nicole. It is important to notice that it felt like an instantaneous moment of mental change from the previous bent-over posture of neediness and isolation to a more self-reliant position with emotional independence. It seemed to happen magically. How did it happen, and what did I learn about myself and the transformative process of journal writing through this experience?

In that needy state, pathological trauma from my past dominated my mind. My impulse to repeat my personal drama with her seemed to be an overarching theme. However, I am Nicole's supervisor, and I must camouflage those childish needs and present a more professional emotional conversation within the supervisory session. Yet, those screaming needs contained within my mind yearned for expression. Journal writing with honest self-reflection helped me see the truth behind my camouflaged conversation. I could see how my emotional independence was lost momentarily, and my mental maturity was suppressed. I became very acquainted with my repetitious and rigid thinking about needing someone to empathically understand and rescue me from my internal isolation. That fantasied repetitive drama of wanting to be magically understood and rescued from isolation has been captured within my contemporary pathological structure in my mind. It then plays out in everyday life, specifically in this situation with Nicole.

I often saw examples of my pathological neediness played out late in the middle of the night when I would wake up in a deep sweat, trembling and fearful. To say that I had suffered from "night terrors" suggests a fear of the kind of violence often depicted in ghoulish horror movies. These bedtime experiences, however, were hardly like that. There were no weapons involved, threatening villains, or bloodshed. In fact, they were silent, so much so that while I woke up in a cold sweat, my wife Marcia, lying next to me, slept peacefully and undisturbed. Her presence never offered me comfort, but then again, I would have never awakened her to share my anxiety.

What I would do during the day in the privacy of my office was write about those episodes in my journal. The more I wrote about them, the more I began to discover that they were related to the overwhelming fear of abandonment that dominated so much of my boyhood. It felt as if I were reliving the painful traumas I suffered while sharing a bedroom with my brother Lennard.

Writing about the feelings that disturbed my sleep ignited memories of the past, both real and imagined. The bedroom itself entered my imagination as a blurred impression. I could not make out the color of the walls or any of the furnishings. Even the sleeping presence of Lennard escaped any clear perception. What did emerge in sharp focus was the doorway, which was slightly opened so that I could get a partial view of the hallway. It was that dimly lit opening which riveted my attention as I lay still awaiting the sound of footsteps, those of my mother and father, as they approached the doorway and passed by without looking in. I knew they were only going out to socialize with our neighbors in the next apartment, yet the sound of the outside door opening and then closing shut left me terrified. The frightened child within me believed I would never see them again, that I was doomed to endure my life all alone. Is it any wonder then that getting into bed at night for so many years was fraught with dread, even as an adult, a married man with children, and as a practicing psychologist?

Years later, through self-reflection, I experienced a vision of being suspended above a roaring fiery caldron. I was paralyzed as I experienced the vision. I said to myself, "I can't endure it...no one can". It took me some time/months/years to encounter the personal truth revealed by this vision. The caldron contained the infantile rage I have been storing up within my mind when I would periodically experience over again the wounded child, lying in bed, terrified that his parents would abandon him. With each encounter with the caldron vision, a new strength of self was achieved. With more insight about the trauma that created my original pathological structure, I gained more freedom from that repetitive pathology. With more mental freedom, the less likely I was to replay my pathological drama in my present life.

Some need a psychotherapist as a guide to the inner pursuit of one's personal truth. I, on the other hand, felt that "no one can see me as clearly as I can see myself". Nevertheless, if we use the tools discussed in this book (journal writing, self-reflection, meditation, dream analysis), with or without the help of another, we will have the capacity to be our own inner guide and encounter our own mind.

30   THEORETICAL FRAMEWORK

Children with positive creative connections to significant others develop healthy psychic structures that prepare them for subsequent steps in psychological development. On the other hand, children who experience repetitive, unsatisfactory connections, run the risk of creating lifelong, injurious mental structures. For children experiencing unfulfilling attachments to caregivers, the stage is set for the creation of a pathological structure. These unfulfilling relationships can cause the child to become trapped in a damaged or ruptured creative connection with the significant other. If the damaged relationship is continually unloving, then the development of a pathological structure is more likely to occur.

Failed creative connections can be traumatic, and if severe enough, they will require the child to withdraw from that frustrating and disappointing relationship. This withdrawal process is abnormal for the young child, and it is another major wound for the immature ego of the child to endure. The child is then forced to cope with his/her unmet needs alone and unprepared. The child's entire self does not withdraw however, and parts of the self remain connected to the significant other. Moreover, these negative influences produce the unsettled and unsatisfactory process of psychological growth and development of the child. Consequently, the child's self becomes permanently divided.

The withdrawn parts of the child's self contained in the pathological structure exist psychologically isolated from others, unable to form a positive creative connection. The pathological structure that contains the withdrawn parts of the child is appropriate for the age at which the child suffered the ruptured attachment. The immature ego, now isolated from the outside world, is inadequate to repair the breach. Thoughts, feelings, and memories of the separated significant other and the vital life-sustaining contributions from that needed person are unavailable, except through the child's memory. It seems as if the memory or fantasies of the lost significant other become encased within the child's pathological structure as well. Leaving the child and later, the adult, longing for a perfect "other" who will magically fill the aching separation.

As a result, the pathological structure of the child contains a repetitive circular drama of disappointment. The drama usually contains elements of the child experiencing the need for, and the desire to recapture what was lost, only to inevitably fail in that attempt, a never-ending repetition of loss. That drama will also include a search for an empathic significant other which was not initially realized and obtained within the original failed creative connection. The fault of the loss can be attributed to either the failure of the significant other or the failure of the child. In either case, painful emotions from the unmet needs are frequently experienced and amplified. It is within this repetitive drama that suffering erupts within the person and will be painfully relived throughout the life cycle.

These disturbing feelings and unyielding emotional states become embedded in the pathological structure of the person. Such structures become the foundation of personal suffering. The suffering will probably be experienced as one of the following: the insatiable longing for a lost love, unmet desires and urges that scream for satisfaction, agonizing feelings of deprivation, anger and rage, and/or fear, and distress. In addition, a distorted mental representation of the significant other or others who are in part responsible for the traumatic failure may also develop. When these threatening emotional states appear to break through to awareness, the isolated individual may become extremely anxious and possibly terrified, even though all the mental processes occurring within the pathological structure remain unconscious. They are only consciously known by the distressful, emotional experience of suffering, and the appearance of repetitive, self-defeating, and unsatisfying behavior patterns.

I believe that these pathological structures become "hardwired" within the person's mind and can be triggered throughout life by contemporary events. Continued developmental changes occur throughout the life cycle, and this also includes developmental changes within the pathological structures. Contemporary pathological structures contain the original failed connection with the original significant other, and it also contains the developmental changes due to current experiences with others in everyday life. The intense emotional states within the pathological structure occupy the mind of the individual and compel the person to continue to repeat the rigid, original drama in a contemporary revision. Similarly, the person's ego trapped within the pathological structure remains relatively immature, threatened, and incapable of handling the excessive energies of emotional stress in ordinary life.

The sense of living successfully in the world and doing things that are in themselves gratifying can alleviate, for a time, the suffering caused by the pathological structure. However, if the needs and fears trapped within the pathological structure become too strong and demanding, the so-called "successful" actions in the world will not adequately provide the person with enough protection against the erupting psychological distress. The only choice the person has, at that moment, is to find a source of gratification similar to an extreme "high". These highs are, in fact, attachments in one form or another, to fill the emptiness and dispel the terror that is part of the isolation contained within the pathological structure. The person may be driven to seek continuous human contact or superficial sexual contact to alleviate the isolation and abate the terror. Perhaps the excessive drive to accumulate more money can produce the compulsory high needed to gain momentary relief of the psychic pain. The person may even be compelled to seek greater power and dominance over others to fill that isolation void. These approaches may work adequately enough, if not very well, for decades. But the threat of severe suffering or even mental breakdown may be lurking in the shadows of the person's mind.

Most individuals are unaware of how they are keeping their emotional pain and psychological suffering at bay. But time itself and the incessant changes that take place as one matures can shift the high-seeking behaviors to meaningless pursuits. Unexpected changes in the environment, such as changes at work, disruptive love relationships, loss of money, or loss of power can shake up the person's equilibrium, thus exposing the person to the inherent suffering that was ever-present but ignored.

The idea of an emotional "mental posture" may clarify a bit more about the cause of personal suffering. Mental posture simply means the degree to which the mind is "bent over" and hyper-attentive to the outside world in order to get what are deemed to be essential supplies. The person seeking more money or power over others will have a mental posture to those aspects within the society that can provide them with the sources of money or power. The screaming and incessant needs within the person's mind for money or power will take precedence over everything else in that person's life. That individual's mental posture will cause one to ignore or overlook the opportunities to connect to their child, their spouse, and others within the family. The result will be a failed empathic envelope with their own child, causing that child to develop a pathological structure.

The failure of the mother-child relationship probably will result in the child experiencing isolation as well. The potential isolation in this case is produced by the mental posture of the caregiver for their unremitting need for money or power. Preoccupied with the outside world, this caregiver has little, if any, time to support their child's emotional development. A special word must be said about the power of isolation and failed relationships.

As stated above, the child's pathological structure is formed in isolation, and it is this isolation that motivates a great deal of maladaptive behavior and exacerbates personal suffering. There is, of course, a continuum in the amount of isolation individuals experienced in their early life. It is the very relationship with a significant other later in life that immediately helps dispel the isolation and create an atmosphere in which a "potentially" reparative empathic envelope can emerge. However, there are no guarantees that this newly found significant other is equipped to deal with the hidden pathological structure that the wounded individual brings to the new relationship. It is highly possible that the attempt to alleviate the original isolation within the individual compounds the isolation and increases the number of failed attempts to seek a creative connection with another.

Pathological structures are so damaging to the person's development because they divide the inner self. The part of the self encased in the pathological structure contains the trapped intense emotional conflicts stemming from the demands for an empathic significant other, and the aftermath of a failed creative connection. I find myself, as I conduct therapy with patients, recognizing what must be contemporary re-enactments of the drama contained within the original pathological structure.

I am surprised at how often I can see that drama in the very first session. I also find myself elaborating upon the contemporary enactment of the original drama to the patient in the first few sessions. The approach of educating the patient on what I see seems to be very helpful, even though it is expressed very early in treatment. An important part of contemporary pathological structures is the repetition of action, with similar beginning, middle and ending to the drama. These are not identical, but structurally, there is a great deal of similarity. A couple of brief cases might help illustrate how the contemporary pathological structure reveals the original drama.

A man I see in therapy, a successful lawyer, who is a skillful public speaker, must overprepare for every speech he gives. He spends long hours endlessly going over his scripts to make sure he is confident before speaking. His need to overprepare protects him from reliving an early emotional trauma of failing before an audience and suffering devastating humiliation. It seems that in his very early life, he suffered humiliation within his family without the protection from an empathic significant other. This early trauma became part of his original pathological structure and produced his repetitive drama. Recently, Jack became aware of the fact that he is also afraid to speak spontaneously without a script. In addition, he recognizes some block, an "invisible barrier", within his mind that inhibits his spontaneity and creativity.

Pathological structures age and mature along with the rest of the person's development, and pathological structures produce a contemporary personal drama that is adaptable and influential in current life situations. Jack acts appropriately for his age, yet he is unconsciously influenced and oppressed by the original failed connection with the original significant other from his past.

I mentioned the presence of an invisible barrier operating in Jack's mind that inhibited his spontaneity and creativity, causing him to remain stuck to a script when speaking in public. Invisible barriers are needed by the child in early life to control the expression of certain thoughts and feelings that would result in personal suffering, loss, and/or punishment. Invisible barriers serve the function of containing unmentionable anger and rage and providing a shield against punishment, but they can also inhibit loving and creative thoughts and feelings. In Jack's case, his invisible barrier prevented him from experiencing the freedom of expression in public.

My male patient, Henry, serves as another example of how an original pathological structure can influence contemporary life. Henry works in finance and does very well until his female supervisor sends for him to discuss his work. He describes his supervisor as "always angry and judgmental", ready to criticize him for what he calls "nothing". He finds himself provoking her by being a bit disorganized with his work product, and late for her meetings. After ten years at this company, she finally fires him. In our sessions, we were quite readily able to see the past feelings he had toward powerful women, including his mother, reenacted in a contemporary drama with the angry supervisor. It appeared that this was not the first angry woman supervisor he has had trouble with at work. His rage is clearly hidden in plain sight. However, because of his powerful invisible barrier stemming from his past difficulties with his mother, he cannot acknowledge to himself or express to me his rage for women supervisors directly. Rather, he indirectly expresses the rage by being disorganized at work, and creating clutter at home, which currently seems to infuriate his wife.

Now that Henry is no longer employed at the company, he is actively seeking employment. As a result of his job searching, Henry has managed to create a mess in the house by piling up mounds of papers around the table, job listings on the floor, and other paraphernalia propelled throughout other rooms in the home. His wife is in a rage at him for creating the clutter. Henry reports to me that he is constantly working on removing the mess but finds he cannot make much progress. Henry is enacting a contemporary version of the original repetitive drama, but this time, his marriage may be in jeopardy.

It is important to understand that pathological structures are rigid, unyielding, and inflexible. The content and actions within pathological structures inevitably age and develop by the laws governing development and the passage of time. Therefore, the pathological structure of the past becomes the contemporary pathological structure of the present. Although the contemporary version contains the regressed, fragile self of the child that suffered, it also contains the healthier aspects of the self which developmentally matured with age. Yet, each part of the self is attempting to satisfy its own set of needs. The contemporary regressed self seeks to fulfill the unmet needs trapped within the contemporary pathological structure, and the more mature self seeks to satisfy age-appropriate needs and desires. Again, we see how divided the person's self has become, and the conflicting motivations actively operating within the mind. These structures in the mind are extremely difficult to eliminate, but individuals can become equipped to deal effectively with them by incorporating the therapeutic tools discussed in the second part of this book.

Strong Force and Weak Force

Once the human mind is divided from childhood, it will remain so throughout life. The division within the mind operates by certain processes which I call the "strong force" and the "weak force". Pathological structures contribute greatly to the strong force within the mind. The strong-destructive force is an elaborate set of fundamental motivations for most actions in the world that are rigid, repetitive, and genetically predetermined. In contrast, the weak-creative force is a more innovative and flexible set of motivations. The strong force has the power to infuse the mind with powerful thoughts, feelings, and desires, and can seize control over the executive decision-making function of the mind and overwhelm the weak-creative force.

There is a struggle throughout much of life between these two great forces within a person's mind. The strong-destructive force operates by several seemingly inherited centers of power. Instincts, one contributor of the strong force, are inalterable tendencies to act without reason. Ancient evolutionary demands, such as an involuntary response to an enemy and rigid group identification, are another. The strong force can be seen in group identification with political, religious, and fanatical causes that can precipitate extreme groupthink leading to group action, which sometimes can lead to violence.

Moreover, the strong-destructive force is motivated by the unmet needs trapped within contemporary pathological structures. The strong force is also influenced by the unfolding of responsive behavior and thought patterns that are age-specific to lifecycle developmental demands. Think about how teenage adolescents begin to experience age-specific peer group behavior filled with competitive thoughts. These thoughts and behaviors do not appear earlier in the life cycle, and they dissipate in later stages of development.

The weak-creative force, on the other hand, is dependent upon the revelation of the "self-reflective system", and the growing capacity for self-reflection. The self-reflective system is the individual's source of wisdom, truth, strength, generosity, and creativity. I use the verb "revealed" rather than "developed" to denote that the self-reflective system exists in the mind from birth and evolves, and we do not develop it. It is through self-reflection within the weak-creative force that the person has the capacity to contemplate the influences of contemporary repetitive drama and the motivational pull of the destructive strong force. I am convinced that all human beings possess the potential to strengthen their own weak-creative force and encounter their contemporary pathological structures. Unfortunately, they may be so consumed by the noisy demands resounding within their own mind by the strong-destructive force that they may be prohibited from doing so in their present circumstance.

Patrick's marital conflict can illustrate how rational thinking can be considerably affected by his contemporary psychological structure, his repetitive drama, and the motivational pull of his strong-destructive force. He is married to a very loving woman, but he is plagued by thoughts that she is having an affair. Patrick confronts his wife periodically and conversations get quite heated. Nevertheless, Patrick's wife denies the allegations and tries to comfort him with her deep feelings of love and desire for him. Recently in sessions, Patrick's thinking became flooded with mental images of his wife with other men. He was most concerned with her time spent at work and his hyperattentiveness to her time out of the house became dominate in our sessions. It is important to note that all his accusations are uncorroborated. I believe the wife is telling him the truth.

In our most recent session, an extremely important episode of being dominated by sexual jealousy and conviction of his wife being unfaithful to him reached a tipping point. As Patrick cooperated with me to explore his contemporary pathological structure, he was able to see a familiar and a repetitive pattern that he experienced in various forms in his past. We were able to identify an elaborate and enduring drama, where Patrick was continually left feeling inferior and inadequate in relationships with women. This hidden drama trapped within his contemporary pathological structure flooded his conscious mind, occupied much of his current thoughts and perceptions, and affected his ability to think clearly about his marital relationship and the trustworthiness of his wife. The strong-destructive force of Patrick's pathology left him little room for rational thinking. When we slowly quieted those relentless thoughts and feelings by uncovering the hidden drama, Patrick's weak-creative force became strengthened, and he achieved much clarity of thought and insight.

Patrick's struggle as well as the story of humankind, in general, is the struggle for dominance between the strong-destructive force and the weak-creative force. Violence and destruction in a war between nations can be attributed to the operation of the strong force while great wisdom found in philosophy and literature demonstrates what can be produced by tapping the potential of the weak-creative force. The nature of each person is greatly determined by the interplay of these two great forces. The nature of the world, I believe, is also regulated by the interplay of the strong and weak forces.

The future of the world may be dependent upon the outcome of this struggle. Never have the dangers or the opportunities of the world been greater. The magnificent possibilities revealed by science and technology as well as the widespread opportunities for education have never been more promising. The very factors that offer us these opportunities also can support the negative forces that may make it possible for the destruction of the species. The atomic and hydrogen bombs were enabled by the advancements in science. The technological developments permitted us to access a vast amount of useful material that may also create the conditions resulting in destructive climate change.

Above all, the great human adventure of self-discovery consists of the difficult life task of revealing the untapped power of the weak-creative force within. Once unlocked, the weak-creative force can assume the executive decision-making function within one's mind and reduce the irrational grip of the strong-destructive force. This task is very difficult for us to undertake because we must face the internal fear, terror, anxiety, and loneliness captured within the contemporary pathological structure as greater awareness is revealed.

Yet, humanity has provided aids in reducing the grip of the strong-destructive force if we are encouraged to use them. Through education, we are given the opportunity to develop our critical thinking skills and analytic abilities; through the study of ethical standards, we can gain the knowledge of identifying which instinctual desires should be confronted and why; and by fostering self-reliance, we can enhance our individuality in order to resist the blind group behavior and conformity.

5

ENCASING WORLDVIEW

We know that at any time, our minds can shift attention from one thought to another, and from outside events to internal decision-making processes. Even though we are not consciously aware of the shifts, we experience ourselves in a world that seems stable and relatively understandable. Our understanding of the world permits us to navigate through it with some degree of purpose. At any given moment, we have some sense that we know who we are, where we are, and what we are doing. We do not realize, however, how much of what we experience as "reality" is really a distorted creation of our own minds and the complex influences shaping our thoughts. I call this an "Encasing Worldview".

We can regard all mental content, and certainly, that which appears in consciousness, as derivatives of the "deeper aspects" of mind contained within our encasing worldview. Several factors contribute to the formation and functioning of encasing worldviews, including perception, societal and environmental pressures, beliefs, ideologies, and religious and political perspectives. We usually see the world and behave in it in accordance

THEORETICAL FRAMEWORK

with our encasing worldview and the way we were shaped first by family and close individuals and, ultimately, by society itself.

In addition, pathological structures formed in our past and other deepseated unconscious processes affect our encasing worldview in particular ways. They impinge upon our consciousness by constricting our perception and causing our thinking to become more rigid, fixed, and less adaptable to ever-present reality. Therefore, our capacity to see beyond our encasing worldview becomes extremely limited, and we find our thoughts and behaviors less free.

Much of the task of development in general and psychotherapy, in particular, is to enlarge the individual's capacity to perceive reality more accurately and to expand the limits of consciousness as far as possible. In fact, the purpose of spiritual practices like meditation is to break through the illusions created by the encasing worldview and to free the individual from the automatic actions of limited thought patterns. We are intrinsically motivated to seek this freedom of thought, yet we may be terrified to do so. As we know, to break free of the rigidity of our mind can be hard and painful. The powers attached to the primitive parts of the mind that help create encasing worldviews are great and seem to seek mental domination. Even if we cannot be totally successful in achieving mental freedom from our fixed encasing worldview, we can be pleased to make some small but significant progress along the way.

Encasing worldviews can change over time. The encasing worldview of a five-year-old child is quite different from the very same person thirty years later. That boy may experience his fighting parents as the end of his security, a loss of his parents' love. As the boy matures and becomes a teenager, the encasing worldview he once had morphed into one where the original trauma he experienced seeing his parents argue is no longer debilitating. That experience may have caused fear or even a depression in the past. But his sense of reality has expanded now. Having contentious parents may no longer be so disturbing. He perceives a world where other parents can be loving. He has friends and meets their parents. He reads books about families, sees them in movies and TV shows, all of which widen his worldview even more, so much so that the anxiety he once felt in a household of conflict no longer dominates his mind. His encasing worldview has widened, and it will continue to do so the older and more experienced he becomes. There is a process of development that is fundamental to the life process and its evolution changes the basic nature of an encasing worldview in almost unnoticeably incremental ways throughout life.

Encasing worldviews give us something important, and they take something vital away from us as well. They offer us a sense of security, often illusory and with artificial boundaries, and they block out of consciousness more terrifying realities and more internal forces. What if the boy I described earlier cannot move beyond the early trauma of coping with arguing parents, and his encasing worldview has not expanded with his maturation? At the same time, he is paralyzed, afraid to challenge the illusions and false securities formed by the mental encasement. For him, external reality has not provided any reassurances that perhaps his original trauma can be overcome or that his initial fears can be conquered. In fact, the boy, now a young man, will insist that his version of reality is, indeed, the truth, the only truth that really exists. Believing and accepting this false truth, no matter how much his rational mind tells him it is false, is what I call "Cognitive Conviction". The more the patient subscribes to this view of reality, the more he becomes helplessly lost in a sea of confusion, anxiety, and distress. The psychotherapeutic goal is to loosen the bonds of the more limiting encasing worldviews by confronting the strongholds of cognitive convictions and permit expansion into a greater sense of reality with a broader, more realistic personal understanding of the truth.

I can best illustrate this shift in encasing worldviews leading to therapeutic success by presenting a vivid case example. David, a middle-aged patient, suffered throughout much of his adult life with haunting, sometimes devastating, anxieties. Late at night, he would often suffer anxiety attacks during which he would sweat, tremble and feel the deepest, darkest despair. His encasing worldview, during these attacks, was filled with the cognitive conviction that he had somehow destroyed vital relationships with significant others; it could be his wife, his relatives, his closest friends, and/or his colleagues. He was sure that whatever he had done was irreparable and unforgivable.

David would characterize his distressing experiences this way: "I am living within a threatening world unprotected by anything other than my feeble self". In the throes of the attack, according to David, "These feelings can reach a crescendo". In such a state, David said, "I feel torn, weak, and unable to do much about the situation. I know my efforts to change things

THEORETICAL FRAMEWORK

will fail and I can become convulsed with guilt because I am the cause of these awful feelings, feeling powerless and separated from those who might help or in danger of being lost forever". For David, "The overall feeling was suffering, just suffering, unending suffering".

It is within David's encasing worldview that the anxiety exists as well as the motivation to seek some form of desperate action, such as texting, calling on the phone, and emailing those he believed he injured by his very thoughts. He desperately needed to undo the damage he may have caused to others. In his case, the intensity of the anxiety was matched by the intensity of the motivation for action. In the past, he would seek out those individuals that represented comfort and security for him, only to find that his actions were misguided, ineffective, and more likely, misplaced attempts at a solution for earlier childhood trauma.

After working with David and introducing him to one of the tools of Reflective Therapy, he turned to journal writing the next morning after a disturbing anxiety attack. You may wonder why writing in a journal is so effective in a patient's therapy. The kind of journal writing I advocate is nothing like keeping a diary or a log that simply records experiences. What I encourage is more of a personal confrontation between aspects of a patient's mind. The rational side of the mind – an awareness of what is real – the circumstances of living in the here and now, which include the people and places of one's daily life involving family, friends, and colleagues begins the writing. That self will find the words to express thoughts and feelings that may touch on all kinds of painful emotions: fear, longing, sadness, loss, alienation, rage, betrayal, and despair. As these "unspoken" emotions find expression on the blank page, the patient is experiencing a creative connection with himself, his true self – discovering and facing harsh truths about the self that he has been repressing and denying and which have caused the underlying, festering malaise. He may have been asking himself, "Why do I always feel so depressed or sad or angry?" One aspect of journal writing is the technique of "free association". I encourage the patient to write about anything that comes to mind, with little attention to sentence structure, cohesion, or grammar. Can the journal writing go back to childhood traumas? Can the writing open doors and shed some light on those shady places that the patient was too afraid to even acknowledge? The journal is not the record but the tool by which self-reflection is actualized. It is how two parts of the mind can communicate – when the rational mind encounters the wounded self. It is a moment of truth and the first step in healing the suffering within.

Through journal writing, David saw the need to shift his encasing worldview from a horizontal – external flow of energy of childlike yearning, desire, loss, and fear, into a more vertical – internal flow of energy of self-determination. He reported to me in the following session, "I felt relief by the simple prospect of writing, as I logged on to my computer. My body became relaxed, and it was like falling into the arms of a loving presence".

We can see in this case example that the anxiety David experienced in the night seemed then to be the truth. No other truth existed for him. He felt as if a force of darkness slowly, persistently, and relentlessly moved against his every effort toward safety, and he would eventually be lost in the despair. He would be so lost that there would be no chance of reuniting with someone for security and protection and no chance of restoration or reparation. It was all too late. His encasing worldview contained the terrified childlike self embedded deep within its structure. The responses of the child traumatized are often wordless, primitive, violent, conflicted, and filled with primitive thinking that remains within the foundation of David's encasing worldview. The problem with early trauma is that the primitive thinking reaches extreme levels, greater than the mind of the child can or should be required to handle. David, however, is an adult in therapy and he could and does now handle the primitive thinking more successfully.

Once he began to journal write, David was able to form a creative connection with himself, his true self. He encountered his pain, confronted the strong-destructive power within his own mind, and uncovered a deeper degree of personal truth. As a result, previously held illusions fell away, and a more expansive worldview that allowed David a greater degree of mental and emotional freedom was forged. We can see in this case example that David's sense of self was encased in a worldview of being feeble and helpless amid the remnants of the crippling anxiety. Yet, there was a part of him that could reach a mental state free of the domination of the crippling emotions with journal writing. This shows us that the entire space of one's mind is not totally dominated by the encasing worldview, no matter how disruptive the present experience of reality seems to be.

It is the undominated part of David's mind that has the capacity to seek the truth and resist the demands of the trapped self lodged deep in his primitive encasing worldview. Through psychotherapeutic intervention,

THEORETICAL FRAMEWORK

David can continue to gain the strength and wisdom needed to obtain greater psychological freedom. We must keep in mind that encasing worldviews exist essentially to assist and protect the individual. The sense of security that was derived from David's encasing worldview was provided by an image of his parents or present-day surrogates. Consequently, major resistance to the progress of psychotherapy is the fear of relinquishing the false security that encasing worldviews provide.

The world beyond an encasing worldview can be isolating and potentially dangerous. Taking steps to challenge and possibly relinquish an existing worldview may make one feel like a lost child, parentless, and in some cases, in mortal danger. The original encasing worldview had created a trusted sense of security, even if it is mixed with pain, frustration, rage, and anxiety. It offers the person a primitive sense of completion about oneself in the world, a sense of conviction that one understands the nature, meaning, and purpose of one's existence.

I envision an encasing worldview within a person's mind like the image of a dog in the backyard tied to a pole by a leash. The mind seems to need a central pole around which the organization of an encasing worldview would coalesce. At the beginning of development, the central pole is the presence of another person. There may be several other poles consolidated as the person matures, such as leashes to teachers, friends, and relatives. With each new pole, an expansion of the radius of the leash increases, giving the individual greater psychological freedom to move about the backyard, so to speak.

The importance of a central pole and the expansion of the leash continue throughout life. Eventually, nonperson poles begin to appear in the backyard of the person's mind. These nonperson poles could be ideologies, like patriotism, capitalism, egalitarianism, or democracy. In addition, as we pursue a career, certain intellectual philosophies may become central poles within the mind, helping to expand our psychological reach. In order to find greater psychological freedom, some of our leashes must be severed, while others should be extended beyond its original distance allowing us to contemplate larger truths.

I have stressed in this chapter the importance of the encasing worldview as it influences everyday human behavior, our thinking, feelings, and course of action. The next chapter will discuss how functional structures and our social environment continue to affect our encasing worldview and our behavior.

6

FUNCTIONAL STRUCTURES

To formulate my ideas about "Functional Structures", I had to recall my own psychological history – one that took me from being a frightened young boy growing up in Harrisburg, Pennsylvania, to becoming a successful psychologist with a thriving practice on the Upper West Side of Manhattan and having a loving family, the esteem of colleagues, and a highly regarded reputation in my field.

When individuals enter the world, they enter an already existing social system. The social systems are composed of functional structures. Since humans are social animals, these functional structures are interpersonal in nature. It seems that individuals are probably genetically predisposed to exist within several functional structures at one time. They are part of, most likely, the evolutionary unfolding of humanity. We identify with functional structures and adhere to those "others" we consider members of our own functional group.

The original functional structure is, of course, the nuclear family. Functional structures have specific organization and purpose and are

46 THEORETICAL FRAMEWORK

arranged in a hierarchical format. Functional structures are best illustrated as a pyramid. The pyramid accommodates the hierarchy of individuals assuming certain roles within the social systems. Authority and power are usually concentrated at the top of the pyramid with an increasing number of individuals participating in the lower tiers of the structure. Members of functional structures have similar attitudes, thoughts, feelings, and motivation toward action. What is unique about membership in a functional structure is the shared mistrust of most others outside that structure. The purpose of all functional structures is to provide its members with the illusion of collective power, security, status, and position.

Remember our discussion of encasing worldview and the image of a dog in the backyard tied to a pole by a leash? Our functional structures provide us with another central pole and a leash for our internal mental stability. Once a person becomes a member of a functional structure, by entering a certain profession, a whole set of behaviors, attitudes, and norms are expected to be embraced and adopted by that individual. The person now knows how to dress, how to act, what to say and to whom to say it, as well as how others in the society will perceive them. One's position in the hierarchical structure is, therefore, known and accepted, and a sense of comfort, relief, and respectability within that structure is achieved. Life becomes predictable, and our place in it is understandable and secure.

The first time I experienced a functional structure occurred when I bonded with a group of Jewish boys in the third grade. Of course, I did not have a name back then for what I was experiencing. But I can now confidently affirm the way that the external world helped define me. The boys, the Rabbi, the synagogue – all gave me a social context within which I could feel secure – a sense of belonging that included others, a greater sense of an "I" that also included an awareness of a "we". This functional structure compensated for the lack of a strong family identification in my earlier years. While it sustained me throughout high school, it was also a happy prelude to the psychological wellbeing I enjoyed at Penn State. I didn't give up my Jewish identity entirely, for I joined a Jewish fraternity, dated only Jewish girls, and had no close non-Jewish friends, but I also began to feel a connection to the larger academic community thanks to my success as a debater. Over time, my victories on the debate stage led to my being elected captain of the team, which contributed to the esteem I was accorded from my fellow students, teachers, and even the President of the University, Milton Eisenhower.

Acquiring fame and status on any campus is to enter a functional structure that is to be envied. Is it any wonder that so many cling to that identification long after they graduate, wearing clothes adorned with the name of the university, attending alumni reunions, making contributions, all of which perpetuate the pride many have for their alma mater? These are ways to keep alive one of the most powerful functional structures to occur in the course of a lifetime.

Leaving Penn State after five years with a BA and an MA in economics and a solid reputation, I spent the next three years in the Navy, which for many young men and women serves as a meaningful functional structure. The military with its traditions and hierarchies is for some a perfect functional structure, one that provides instant recognition by simply wearing the uniform. Just consider all of the positive terminology associated with military service: pride, valor, sacrifice, victory, and honor. The sense of belonging to a brotherhood or sisterhood of dedicated individuals pursuing a common purpose in the service of their country is a functional structure like no other. For some, it may be a brief stint of two or three years, while many make it a lifetime career.

Examples of other functional structures of which the individual may become a part are: extended family, playgroup, school and peer groups, work environments, cultural, political, and religious group memberships, including social-economic group status. These social groups are where people meet, form friendships and love relationships, and will eventually marry, procreate, and perpetuate further functional structures that support the society.

The organizational design within functional structures can be complicated. A single individual can participate in several overlapping functional structures at the same time. For example, a person may belong to a religious functional structure, have a political affiliation, and simultaneously be a part of an extended family. The creation of wisdom, generosity, sympathy, and charitable action can be encouraged, emphasized, and supported within certain functional structures. There is a sense of "we" or "us", and often an unspoken sense of trust when one becomes a member of a functional structure. Those outside the functional structure are viewed as "them" and "different", and, to one degree or another, must be approached cautiously if approached at all. Our sense of self is strengthened and often defined by membership in our functional structures. We operate within the structure securely, assuming the roles and expectations required to maintain our good standing within the hierarchy.

For me, being in the Navy, despite the sense of belonging and security it afforded, did not give me the psychological wellbeing I was lacking. Emotions associated with my earliest years began to recur. That is when I knew I needed help and sought a therapist for a brief period.

From the time I left Penn State until I was accepted as a Ph.D. student in the Psychology Department at Columbia University, I was essentially without the safeguard of a functional structure. Ironically, nautical terms come to my mind probably because of my time in the Navy. I was now "adrift", "unmoored", and psychologically "at sea", needing more than ever a "safe harbor".

At Columbia, I once again experienced the benefits of a functional structure. I comfortably belonged to the academic world. Here I could fit in as a student, a teaching assistant, and a young man of promise who was considered by the bright pretty women on campus as a desirable catch. In some ways, it was Penn State Redux, but I knew that the stakes now were much higher. I was slowly but surely initiated into the world of psychology, a very complex realm that included graduate students, professors, and therapists, some of whom identified as Freudians, Jungians, Strict Behaviorists, Cognitive Behaviorists, and Humanistic Psychologists. It was a kind of "club" whose membership was highly desirable. After all, to be in this club meant that you were fully committed to a lifetime study of the whole person and that you were perceived by society as an intellectual devoted to understanding and healing emotional disorders. For the student, teacher, therapist, or patient, the human mind was paramount.

Possessing a Ph.D. from Columbia was indeed a badge of honor for it provided both self-esteem and the respect of others. Within this complex world, there were multiple ways to enhance one's reputation even further through fellowships, grants, department promotions, and requests to speak at or join institutes. Of course, there were eventually the financial rewards that come with opening a private practice.

That transition for me was doubly rewarding, for I was lucky enough to have fallen in love with a woman I married and began seeing patients almost simultaneously. Now I had another functional structure to graft onto the wider structure associated with psychology. The personal and the professional became conjoined. Being a husband and then becoming a father while also seeing patients seemed as if I were living a charmed life. The apartment Marcia and I lived in was on a floor above our offices. Domestic life and professional duties were carried on quite comfortably in an attractive building near Riverside Drive.

I have a wonderful memory that supports the idyllic nature of this time in my life. Although I played some baseball and basketball during my high school years, I would never consider myself athletic. I did not play any sports in college, but I was an avid biker. Living so close to Central Park now gave me a great opportunity to get some exercise pedaling through the many roads of the park. After Danny, my first son, was born, biking alone was interrupted for a time. As a new father, I was attentive and loving, though I admit I did not do much of the essential caregiving. When Danny was about three years old, however, I would place him in a secure seat on the back of my bike and ride through the park as I once did, but this time with a feeling of great pride. There is something emblematic in the image of a happy father with a budding psychotherapy practice cycling in the park with his son in tow. It is an indelible photo in my mind of a moment in time when I felt the power and pleasure of a perfect functional structure.

Functional structures can facilitate family life as well as community life. Various structures create a degree of uniformity of thinking, feeling, and action. Cooperation is expected and structural hierarchies are naturally formed with the shared purpose of self-protection. Although covered by the illusion of protection and security, functional structures may also expose us to unanticipated dangers. The dangers lie in the fact that functional structures are capable of moving millions of individuals in directed action either for better and worse, as seen in social activism and/or mob behavior.

Consider the biblical story of Moses after he led the Israelites out of Egypt. The people needed a functional structure. So, they appointed Moses as their leader, expecting to be guided and cared for by him alone. However, when his father-in-law, Jethro, came to visit and saw all the people swarming Moses and wearing him out by their continual need for direction, he told Moses that what he was doing was not good for the people. His father-in-law then proceeded to show Moses how to create a hierarchical pyramid of collective power, a workable functional structure that would serve the people and their needs. Jethro told Moses to select capable and trustworthy leaders who would act as judges and to only handle the most difficult cases

THEORETICAL FRAMEWORK

himself. In addition, Jethro suggested he appoint other governing officials to handle smaller groups of people, each with their own jurisdictions, duties, and authorities. As a result of following his father-in-law's suggestions, life in the wilderness became much more manageable for Moses and the Israelites. In other words, each member of that society now had a defined place and a secure role within that functional structure, and societal order was instituted.

The concept of the wilderness in the Exodus story is important to consider for several reasons, some of which we will discuss in more depth in the next chapter on the self-reflective system. But now, to further illustrate the "herd" mentality, it is essential to note that the Israelites preferred living in the highly developed culture of Egypt as slaves than to become lost in the unknown wilderness. Sure, life was hard in Egypt, but the Israelites had the security of the functional structure within the slave encasing worldview of their circumstances. Without the illusion of a secure functional structure, the multitudes, those in the herd, would experience mental chaos in the form of terror and helplessness in view of the dangerous outside forces. It seems to me that to become truly free, we must confront our own wilderness experience. The main way to accomplish that growth step is by relinquishing the illusion of security found in our dominant encasing worldviews and dare to leave a familiar functional structure in order to courageously enter new and uncharted psychological territory within our own minds.

Even so, there is a system for security within all functional structures that maintains and reinforces itself and the hierarchical pyramid. There is also a psychological mechanism working within the members on all the various tiers of the pyramid that ensures that both the organization and levels of power and protection remain the same. People may come and go, but the social roles within these tiers remain fixed.

Sometimes the assigned role in one's early life, our family functional structure, conflicts with the adult role within a work environment forcing that individual to sabotage a newly achieved hierarchical position. Jerry, a young man, who I saw in therapy, is a good example. He is an extremely bright technologist working in a large New York corporation. Over and above that, Jerry is often given very important projects with strict deadlines. It seems that he repetitively pushed those deadlines and frequently worried his project managers. Eventually, he would succeed in getting the

FUNCTIONAL STRUCTURES   51

work done in a superior manner but not without causing his managers a great deal of anguish. After much exploration in therapy, we found out that in his family's functional structure, Jerry was the child who always worried his father by his chronic procrastination. What became apparent was that even though Jerry has a high position of responsibility in his work environment, he needed to repetitively reduce his status within the hierarchy and among his coworkers. Jerry was driven to resume his familiar, low-status position within his family's functional structure by appearing to be the undisciplined, unreliable worker who could humiliate his father/manager at any time by not meeting an important deadline. For Jerry to change his behavior at work and gain greater psychological freedom to be a successful technologist, he would have to untether his mental leash from the functional structure that once assigned him the unreliable child role in the family. By severing the leash to that central pole in his mind, Jerry would be able to expand his encasing worldview to include being a more responsible, reliable, and disciplined coworker.

Functional structures can either be hateful and destructive to society or used for creative and positive purposes. The uprising of hate groups, whose purposes are prejudice, racism, and religious discrimination, are examples of the destructive use of functional structures. War is another example of the strong destructive functional structure operating within societies whose members aim at annihilating each other.

All "isms" create functional structures for individuals to become affiliated with and join as group members. However, Nazism is one of the most vivid examples of how an "ism" or functional structure can result in the very annihilation of others outside that designated group. The goal of the Nazi party was to create a racially pure society where all Aryan members could enjoy the right to territorial expansion, more "living space" for all. By being attached to such a charismatic and powerful leader as Hitler, each member of that functional structure vicariously obtained his power, status, and found a firm and secure position within his hierarchical organization.

Within all functional structures, those seeking positions at the top tier of the pyramid are driven by a dominant need to achieve extraordinary power, that is, an attempt to establish superiority over others within the functional structure. Sometimes a commitment to this influential goal will consume individuals throughout their entire life, at the cost of losing family and friends along the way. The functional structure itself can become the most pre-eminent, organized force in a person's life, driving that individual to perform acts they might never have done alone.

Think about the story of Citizen Kane, a 1940's film by Orson Welles. The main character was Kane, based in part on the larger-than-life newspaper mogul, William Randolph Hearst. Kane, as the wealthy and successful newspaper publisher, rises to the top from an impoverished beginning. His relentless drive for power gained him fortune, fame, and influence. He was feared by many, and his journalists, staff, and political acquaintances were easily manipulated by him. The top position in his self-created hierarchical functional structure allowed him total control over all those within his range of influence. Yet, Kane's marriage eventually failed, his affair with his mistress caused him a lost election bid, and he finally died alone, isolated from all those that were significant to him. Kane was consumed with absolute power and was able to achieve it only to find out how futile his entire life was in the end.

Functional structures, as stated earlier, are a part of the evolutionary unfolding of our humanity within our social environment. We are probably genetically predisposed to exist within a number of these functional structures throughout our life in order to fit into society. It only becomes harmful to our individuality when our membership within these functional structures demands too much rigidity and conformity of thoughts, attitudes, and behaviors, leaving us very little room to be our true self. Part of our psychological growth requires us to identify and question our participation in these functional structures. We must decide how much of our psychological freedom has been compromised by being tethered to the leashes of certain functional structures within our mind. Then, we should attempt to free ourselves from those encasing functional structures by either expanding or severing those leashes in pursuit of greater psychological freedom.

We must also take into consideration individuals who do not seem to fit into normative functional structures within the society, most of whom will suffer isolation, ridicule, and shame. The negative consequences of not "fitting in" will be discussed in future chapters in Part 2, the psychotherapy section. We will now proceed to discuss our most liberating of all mental structures, our self-reflective system.

7

SELF-REFLECTIVE SYSTEM

The self-reflective system is a quiet presence within the mind that is gradually revealed as strength of character, wisdom, capacity for generosity, compassion, and a deep and profound understanding of the nature of life. The self-reflective system is essential to what makes us human but is the most elusive part of the mind. I believe we are born with the capacity to self-reflect. This evolutionary developmental process is the necessary and requisite foundation for all creativity and self-knowledge.

When the self-reflective system gains ascendancy within our mind, it will facilitate the strengthening of our capacity to encounter our pathological structures and our infantile attachments. Through these encounters, our creative capability incrementally increases and becomes stronger. This may be a long, slow process but it is the beginning of the human heroic journey.

I can recall when self-reflection became the foundation of my own therapy. It was a discovery that ultimately informed the psychotherapy I offered my patients over the years. I was living alone on 52nd Street and

Park Avenue. By then, I had a Ph.D. in psychology from Columbia and had been seeing a therapist to talk about the fears of isolation that had been plaguing me since childhood. What I recall most about the last session with my analyst is that I wanted him to stop talking – to be silent – that the more he talked, the less relevant his words became. Feeling discouraged and somewhat defeated, I entered my apartment and sat in a chair – the one I had described earlier. Sitting quietly and then going deeper and deeper into my thoughts, I knew then and there that I would become my own therapist. To alleviate the persistent terrors lurking in my mind, I would have to embark on what I have come to call the heroic journey, an adventure not dissimilar to what Joseph Campbell (1949) describes in *The Hero with a Thousand Faces* and many of the great myths.

Before self-reflection can achieve its therapeutic goals, it requires an honest confrontation with the past. As we know, memory can be elusive. Painful experiences are often repressed, and happy ones can be exaggerated and overblown. What is the truth, after all? That question is a challenge to historians, scientists, philosophers and – yes – to psychologists as well, who strive to cut through conscious illusions and unconscious motives and dreams to arrive at some semblance of reality, without which healing cannot occur. From the moment I settled into that memorable chair, I embarked on my own self-reflective heroic journey which, over the years, encompassed an interpretation of my dreams, careful scrutiny of my meditative visions, and extensive journal writing.

The heroic journey requires that the person seeks a solitary path for exploration leading to self- knowledge. The communal nature of life, on the other hand, dictates social affiliation and shared social interactions. The aloneness required by the heroic path can reveal surprisingly unexpected infantile anxieties within one's mind that may still be very active, and disruptive to a person's sense of wellbeing.

One day, in the early years of my marriage, I decided to remain alone at home while my family went away for a short vacation on Fire Island. Saying goodbye to my wife Marcia and two young sons, Danny and Evan, was easy because their absence would give me some precious time to write. As that hot July day receded into the late afternoon, a mere five hours since their departure, I found that my resolve to do some serious work also waned. It became increasingly difficult for me to think, much less write. I knew that this feeling was not brought on by the usual writer's block. More than anything I wanted, not desperately needed, to be with my family. I was overcome with a severe, unendurable anxiety emanating from a deep sense of loneliness. It was the same loneliness that had characterized my early childhood and every other phase of my life, even from the time I had acquired friends among the Jewish boys in the third grade to the years I had experienced some degree of popularity at Penn State and Columbia and up to the present after I became a husband, a father, and a young therapist with a burgeoning practice on the Upper West Side. I have since learned that this fear of being alone stemmed from an unidentified infantile and unresolved pathological attachment still active within me. I quickly packed a bag, caught a train, and felt a wonderful relief knowing that I would be shortly reunited with my family in Fire Island.

That deep sense of loneliness I felt shows us how powerful a pathological attachment can be. The mind seems to be in frequent conflict between the destructive strong force of the pathology, and the creative weak force found in our self-reflective system. These two forces can vary almost daily in terms of their relative strength. It seems to work like a hydraulic pump, whereby the reduction in the amount of one force is matched by an increase within the other. At best, the hydraulic movement will result in a consistent dominance within the mind of our self-reflective system. It appears that the ascendancy of the self-reflective system fortifies the creative weak force and produces the necessary authority and power within the mind to dare approach and confront the derivatives of residual pathology.

Through these encounters, true insight and psychic ability required to confront the formidable and destructive aspects of the strong force can also occur. After a number of these courageous encounters, a person becomes able to embrace the newly revealed truth presented by one's self-reflective system. This inner guide, the voice of our self-reflective system, leads us along our solitary heroic journey to arrive at a profound sense of wisdom and understanding of our personal life. We find peace of mind in that quiet place of our self-reflective system, and a purposeful knowing of why we are and who we are.

A crucial aspect of this road toward self-knowledge can be illustrated with an image that may have occurred in a dream or had come to me while I was writing in my journal. I am not entirely sure of its origin, but I believe it can help clarify how self-reflection and memory can lead to a positive psychological outcome. I used the image of a "leash" before when discussing the encasing worldview and functional structures. Now I want to elaborate on that image.

Let us call this elaboration "severing the cord". I used the image of the stake with a tethered rope/leash before when describing the limitations of psychological freedom one may experience. At the beginning of our lives, the distance from the stake to the end of the cord is close to infinitesimal, allowing little movement from the center. An infant has no freedom to make choices. Whatever movement occurs is dictated by the child's instincts and the decisions of significant others who constitute the empathic envelope. The range grows wider with maturation as life becomes increasingly complex. Familial and social ties deepen, and functional structures expand. So, how much freedom do we have as these complications continue? There is a paradox here. While we may have more latitude, there are also more demands from others that need to be met. We take on relationships in our families as spouses, parents, and the caregiving children of those who raised us. At work, colleagues and coworkers place expectations on us that we may have never foreseen in seeking to fulfill our ambitions. We may become more involved in our communities, religious institutions, and political affiliations. While we may have moved a long way from the stake in the ground, how much personal freedom have we really acquired considering all these demands and expectations imposed upon us by others?

During the early years of my practice, I experienced anxieties that went as far back as my boyhood. It was that perennial fear of isolation which caused me to maintain ties to individuals and institutes that I believed I needed to confirm my reputation in the field of psychology. I found myself making phone calls to people I really had little respect or affection for simply because I needed to court their esteem. It was only through deep self-reflection that I began to understand that what was really important was my own self-esteem and not their affirmation. A crucial stage of my heroic journey was gaining the courage to "sever the cord" that tethered me to the illusion that a professional functional structure was necessary for my personal success. The word "sever" connotes a rupture that is sudden and forceful, and that vigorous approach within my mind was needed to strengthen my self-reflective system.

One of the best examples of the inner workings of the self-reflective system is illustrated in the efficacy of our dreams. Our dreams are elaborate dramas created by our mind to show us the specific encounters we should be having with certain content contained within our pathological structures. The self-reflective system invites us to look at the drama within the dream and to relate to the powerful representations and pathological derivatives found in the dream's story, characters, dialogue, and ultimately, the theme of the drama. This process reminds me of what often appears in great myths when the "gods" point the way, but the adventure must be taken by the individual alone. Our self-reflective system can point the way by presenting us with the dream, but only we alone can encounter the dream. Furthermore, through the process of encounter, we eventually find the revealed meaning and hidden truth contained within.

Not only does the self-reflective system produce our dreams, but it also allows us the opportunity to engage in the originality of thought or what I refer to as "creative thinking". Creative thought is not necessarily tied to what is commonly called creative product, such as poetry, art, or literature, but it is an ongoing process of living creatively in life. It is a free form of thinking in which original, adaptive, and purposeful thoughts arise in consciousness and guide our behavior and influence our awareness of feeling alive. Encumbered thinking, on the other hand, leads to conflictual and habitual patterns within the mind, causing the individual to experience a great deal of distress with episodes of repetitive suffering. The wisdom revealed by our self-reflective system can continue to unfold throughout our life if we learn to strengthen our creative thinking, and free ourselves from encumbered thought and repetitive behavioral patterns by "severing the cord".

We have seen in previous chapters that the functional structures exert great pressure upon us to be conforming in thought and action, in order to fit within the world. Even though our capacity for creative thinking exists, it remains dormant. Instead, we become overwhelmed with the encumbered demands of thought and action emanating from our social identification with our functional structures, and contemporary pathological structures. We simply must engage in those familiar and habitual patterns and suffer the painful failure those restrictions of thought impose upon us. A deep sense of unhappiness results from the repetitive failure and suffering is experienced by the person as unknown in origin.

In addition, our contemporary pathological structures shape our thinking in such a way that the process of self-reflection seems out of our reach, possibly non-existent. We experience ourselves as under the control of a powerful, restrictive, and demanding strong forces within the mind that causes us to act and think robotically. In psychotherapy, I aim to incrementally decrease the power of the restrictive strong force of the pathology while simultaneously strengthening the patient's ability to self-reflect, which will promote creative thinking. This is done by helping the patient become more aware of the conforming, habitual, and encumbered thought patterns contributing to the person's internal suffering. In other words, it is through the direct encounter with the restrictive strong force embedded in the person's pathological structure that incremental insight through the self-reflective system is revealed. An increase in creative thinking is the direct result of the decrease of influence and domination of the functional and contemporary pathological structures operating within the mind of the individual.

A few years ago, a disgruntled member of a therapeutic group that I ran asked, "What are we supposed to be doing here?" I instinctively said, almost immediately, "To tell the truth. We should try to do that within ourselves, with this therapy group, and, most importantly, as we interact with others". Telling ourselves the truth and creative thinking are intertwined and intimately connected. I believe these processes are products of the self-reflective system and are motivated by the same psychological energy. When one self-reflects, creative thinking is permitted, and the mind receives that wisdom revealed as truth.

That same group member, who asked about the purpose of our group sessions, a few weeks later brought us a very personal and powerful dream. Sharon apparently had been held back throughout her life by forceful invisible barriers that prohibited her ability to think freely and voice her opinions in public. Her early pathological structures greatly contributed to her inability, and now her contemporary relationships were stifled and restrained. She often said it was like living behind a mask, having a false self. The thought of disagreeing with significant people in her life would create anxiety and distress.

Yet, Sharon's dream centered on an argument between a wife and her husband. The woman in her dream had important political issues to take care of, and she was going forth to deal with those issues in public. However, her husband, in the dream, seemed to be attempting to stop her. Interesting enough, the woman could not be stopped. Instead, the woman kept looking straight ahead, and she was determined to move forward. The argument with her husband continued for a time, with her husband consistently attempting to stop her. In the final scene, despite his attempts, the wife in the dream became stronger, and she finally moved forward with greater determination.

After much discussion in the group and personal self-reflection, Sharon was able to see that she, indeed, had the potential to move forward in the world. She could, if she chose to, express her opinions publicly, and challenge her husband and others who may try to stop her. The encounter Sharon had in the group with the dream material and with her self-reflective system provided her with a transformative degree of wisdom about herself. She began to understand the motivations, drives, and forces prohibiting her creative thinking. In addition, she could identify those forces interfering with her ability to self-reflect and encounter the pathological structures within her mind. With each new encounter, Sharon incrementally integrated that newly found self-knowledge and found freedom of thought and behavior.

For most people, both their dreams and the flow of energy from the knowledge revealed by their self-reflective system could ultimately become accessible. However, few people recognize its value, and few people invoke self-reflection to gain the self-knowledge necessary for creative thinking. My entire creative life has been devoted to practicing what is necessary to gain this personal freedom and to understand the mechanisms involved in the process. I was fortunate enough to uncover many substantial tools that, when implemented, will contribute to one's personal growth and psychological freedom. In the next part of the book on psychotherapy, I will share those tools with you.

Part Two

PSYCHOTHERAPY

Part 2 will apply the previous concepts to the new approach of psychological treatment, Reflective Psychotherapy. The essence of this therapy is the person's experience of a creative connection with "the therapist within".

This section will illustrate, through case studies of clients, dream analyses, and personal interviews, how one's uncensored personal truth is revealed through the therapeutic methods of reflective therapy, specifically, journal writing, meditation, and self-reflection, to gain a degree of psychological freedom from suffering.

8

PSYCHOTHERAPEUTIC PROCESS

Psychotherapy, as I define it, is the process through which encounters are made between a person's self-reflective system and the derivatives of the pathological strong force. These courageous encounters can be very difficult for the patient and will require many attempts before the person is able to embrace the truth that is revealed by the process. The mind of a patient knows what it is doing, and it is our job, as psychotherapists, to create the conditions to receive what a patient's mind, the inner wisdom or inner guide, is trying to convey.

I asked a former patient of mine, William, to consider being interviewed by my colleague to gain a personal account of how Reflective Therapy affected him. William enthusiastically agreed to participate in a series of phone sessions with Michael, my colleague. By using William's perception of his experience in treatment, I will illustrate some of my psychotherapeutic processes.

William revealed to Michael that he sought therapy because he was experiencing serious psychological conflicts stemming from the death of his father which had occurred two years earlier. What Michael knew before their phone sessions had begun was that William had recently opened a second veterinary practice, had married and was eagerly and nervously anticipating the birth of a son this summer. William initially told Michael that he had started working out in a gym regularly, an indication that he cared about his health and appearance. From William's perspective, "he was currently in a good place", primarily the result of five years of therapy with me. It was clear to my colleague that William both needed and wanted to continue seeing me, but due to his heavy workload that was becoming increasingly difficult. Because of William's initial enthusiasm, Michael thought that weekly phone sessions would be a good plan. However, Michael soon learned that William was not always so available or forthcoming and he worried that perhaps William was having second thoughts.

My method of beginning therapy is to awaken a patient's ability to use self-reflection. I simply tell my patients that they are under no obligation except that we, together, try to hear what their mind really wants to tell us. I encouraged William to listen to his mind in a way that he probably never did before. He was unaware of how to be self-reflective, and it was strange for him to report everything that came to his mind in my presence. I particularly emphasized to William how important it is to listen carefully and to encounter in a very receptive way those invisible barriers that prevented him from talking. I think the old invisible barriers emerged again when William began his phone conversations with Michael. He had to give himself permission to express his mind freely to Michael without censorship.

Even though my initial instructions to my patients are simple enough, this does not mean that I only listen to what the patients say. I know a lot more than the patient does about the functioning of the human mind, and I listen for the periodic and powerful periods of domination of the patient's pathological structure prohibiting open communication. When Michael became concerned that William might be having "second thoughts" about talking to him, I reassured him that the ambivalence would pass. Michael's second attempt at a phone interview with William seemed to fail, so he thought because William was caught up with business issues on what was supposed to be his day off. Michael suspected that William does not ever really take time away from the demands of his practice. However, by the third interview, William was more accessible. My hunch was that William had begun to experience some anxiety by talking to Michael about the death of his father. Since that event was so traumatizing, Michael tried to learn more about the relationship William had with his father growing up. It started to become more and more obvious that William did not want to talk about that. When pressed, William said, "It was a good one – just like any father and son relationship you'd see in the movies". I needed to teach Michael that for William to talk about his father would be like asking him to rip open an old wound. I suggested that it would be better to encourage William to talk about our therapy together, not his personal childhood history.

After years of working with patients, I could see what was happening between Michael and William. The structure of the pathology that dominated William for so long must be allowed to unfold naturally over time within a creative connection with a valued other. William was able to work through the loss of his father with me, but it took a great deal of time, care, and an empathic relationship. Because of the strong creative connection I had with William, I was able to express for him what he could not for himself. Most of the time, the knowledge I gained within the creative connection I directly shared with my patients. Ultimately, I will know whether my creativity is in tune with the creativity of my patients by their response. William confirmed that I was hearing the unspoken truth within his mind by sharing with me the many ways his father provided him with the necessary security and love he now lost.

When Michael allowed William the time to reflect, he did open up and share a memory when his father took him fishing off a pier in the Rockaways. William enjoyed the time they spent together and then added, "But it was a pain in the ass to be awakened at two in the morning just to catch some fish". According to Michael, from the way William said this, he could detect his real affection for his father, who at that time was a cab driver. However, Michael felt that William seemed not to really know his father and he had some regrets about that as well.

According to Michael, two months after the initial interview, William, without being asked or prompted, recalled something about his relationship with his father that he had never told me about. William said that the sound of jangling keys evoked a memory from his boyhood when he would anxiously await his father's return home after completing his evening shift as a cab driver. Alone in his room, William listened for the cab to pull up and park on the street, but he remained uneasy until he heard the sound of those keys jangling from his father's hand. Then he was assured that it was his father who had arrived home. William told Michael that he felt great relief, even comfort, though he found it difficult to put that feeling into words. Recalling the sound of a set of keys brought it back to life.

My use of a creative connection with my patients helps me see disparate parts of their mental functioning that they could never put together by themselves. It may move them forward more quickly than they could on their own. William, because of our work together, was able to tell Michael the following ways certain events contributed to his emotional suffering. It was the unforeseen death of his father that concluded a painful year in which his beloved dog was killed when a reckless driver crushed it as it was sleeping on a patch of grass off the road. William was so devastated by the loss that to this day, he has not acquired another dog despite working as a veterinarian. Later, that same year, his Grandma died, causing another emotional setback. The final blow was the shock of losing his father who had died suddenly of a heart attack.

Psychotherapy is a unique process established between two people motivated by the patient's suffering. The suffering is usually caused by the powerful effects of contemporary pathological structures based on the original traumas from early life. Current life factors, such as the death of a loved one or a divorce or separation from significant others can also contribute to the patient's suffering, which brings the patient into therapy. Most patients are unaware of their own minds, and they only know that they are suffering. Suffering is based on the repetitive power of an inner story that has a great influence on the mind of a patient, yet the patient has not revealed it to himself or others. There is always a story that must be told, and only the patient can tell that story.

Almost always, the patient expects the therapist to be wiser, more experienced, and have the understanding needed to help alleviate the suffering. This is a contemporary recreation of an ideal relationship between a parent and a child. The ideal relationship may never have existed between the patient and early significant others, but the need for the perfect relationship remains active and powerful in the therapeutic relationship. The idealization of the therapist is tainted by the inner expectation within the patient that failure will indeed ensue because past relationships have repeatedly failed. This type of complexity between a therapist and a patient usually exists at the onset of therapy.

In addition, the patient may present repetitive patterns of ambivalent attachments with supervisors, bosses and/or within intimate relationships. The patterns may vary in type and nature, but the drama enacted within them will have the same fundamental failing and unfortunate ending. Repetitive "acting out" always supersedes self-reflection.

A patient can recognize the repetitive behavior that causes trouble, loss or failure, and can understand the purpose of the drama embedded in the suffering by the collaborative work done through the therapeutic process. It is within this collaborative work that true self-reflection, that is, the patient's ability to hear his own story, emerges. For William, the repetitive drama of loss was observed and eventually understood. He began having recurrent dreams of always looking for his father, and William brought those dream scenes to our therapeutic sessions for analysis.

Initially, the dream would take place in an empty space and William didn't recognize the background or context of the setting. But as the dreams continued over time, the background became more defined and more populated with other people whom he did not recognize. William said that what made the dream so disturbing was that he wanted his father to acknowledge him – or at least recognize him. But that never happened, even when he was close enough to touch him.

I never interpreted the unconscious meanings of William's dreams. Instead, I would simply ask him to "let his mind speak". William told Michael that "recounting the dreams was therapeutic enough" because he had felt burdened by them. He never told anyone else, so merely talking about them in the presence of a therapist he trusted and revered gave him the psychological relief he needed. William concluded his discussion with Michael by telling him that he "always entered Dr. Brenner's office feeling a heavy weight on my shoulders but left feeling as if that weight had been lifted".

According to Michael, whenever he asked questions about me, William became "uncharacteristically expansive and talkative". What William seemed to admire most about me as Michael states is my "taciturn presence – a near-silent reserve" that clearly appealed to William's own quiet temperament. Once William proudly said to Michael, "What are you going to do? I'm quiet – I'm a quiet guy". Michael said to me, "So, it isn't any wonder that it was easier for William to talk about you than his own father?" About me, William said to Michael, "Don't judge the man by his silent manner. He looks like he is not paying attention or that he is daydreaming, but he hears everything you are saying. He is a powerful man, not threatening, but friendly, and looks like a close uncle. In his calming presence, you feel comfortable". Summarizing his impression of my work with William, Michael said, "Apparently, the creative connection between you and William was a perfect match".

The psychotherapeutic process progresses slowly, from the knowledge of the power of the repetitive drama trapped within the contemporary pathological structure to a slow incremental decrease of the automatic and habitual behaviors stemming from the suffering as well as an increase in the power of self-reflection. As therapy continues, suffering is eventually reduced, and the patient gains more freedom of thought and choice.

Most patients only seek to eliminate the pain and suffering that brought them into therapy. Few go on to pursue the heroic journey of self-discovery past the original mental anguish. Therapy may be essential to provide the conditions leading to the ability of the suffering person to identify and hear from their "therapist within".

William was able to locate his father in his dreams which indicated that he had arrived at a deeper understanding and acceptance of his loss. He had gained enough mental freedom to choose to embark on his heroic journey. At the beginning of therapy, William was working for a veterinarian as an associate. By the end of five years of treatment, William had bought the practice and opened a second office. He worked hard in therapy to free himself from the initial suffering and distress, and he harnessed the necessary mental energy for a significant, intimate relationship. He, eventually, married a very successful woman, became a loving husband, and now eagerly awaits to assume his newest, most heroic role yet – becoming a father.

9

DREAMS AND VISIONS

To delve deeper into my own dreams and visions and how I work with them, I asked my colleague, Mike, to read over some of my previous dream journals and to ask me about them.

MIKE: You stated in one of your journal entries, "Dreams and visions are more complex than I initially thought. Most dreams and visions that I encounter in myself and in my patients reflect powerful aspects of the operation of pathological structures, and many other important processes as well".

MARLIN: Should I give you my theory of it?

MIKE: Yes, that would be helpful.

MARLIN: When you think about a dream, it is created out of one's unconscious mind. Now, a lot of things are created out of unconsciousness. But when you are in a dream, it seems as if you are experiencing it consciously. Right now, you and I are talking. It seems as if we are consciously involved in our talk and we are bringing up things that

70 PSYCHOTHERAPY

are important to us. Communication is interpersonal and seems more connected to reality right here, right now. Dreams were often regarded as messages or warnings from the gods, a form of communication. They appeared in unconsciousness, as we sleep, and could either be ignored and forgotten or they could raise our curiosity. I view a dream as a dramatic form, a creation of our mind that, if examined closely, will communicate to us our immediate concerns. Dream interpretation, in general, is the ability or interest in trying to have the dream reveal itself more than it has. Historically, there were many such efforts before Freud to interpret one's dreams. Freud, as you know, came to the idea that a dream is an expression of an unfulfilled wish. A desire, a wish. And that wish is at the heart of the dream. Whether Freud was right or not, I am not sure. But he felt that the dream was exclusively a wish and you must interpret it based on a wish.

MIKE: So, dream interpretation is to find out what the person is wishing for?

MARLIN: The dream, according to Freud, would almost always be a sexual wish for the parent of the opposite sex. There is something important here to consider. If you are a Freudian therapist, then you will have in your mind a kind of a template, a structure that you will be looking for in the patient's dream content. This template may cause you to see certain sexual meanings in your patient's dream that may be there but be of lesser importance than the actual communication the person is having with one's self.

MIKE: Do you have a template or structure in your mind that allows you to formulate an interpretation of your patient's dream?

MARLIN: Yes, I do. The patient can have a dream and not even pay much attention to it, or the patient can have a dream and bring me the dream content to discuss in a session. I would tell him or her, "Let the dream speak to you". That is my invitation to the patient to help expand their thinking to hear what the dream is saying. The communication between the self and one's mind could be about early experiences, or it may be about something that just happened to the person yesterday. And if we, the patient and I, listen carefully to the dream's communication, the message will begin to unfold incrementally to us. Then I ask the patient to simply absorb what the mind is telling us about the dream.

MIKE: So, this is then another example of the self-reflection process?

MARLIN: Yes, very well put. The self-reflection process does not just tell you something. It also listens. It allows you to attentively hear and understand the unspoken message within the dream. At first, the patient may take a passive approach and simply let his mind reveal whatever it wants about the dream. As the patient and I talk about the dream more, the interplay between the contents of the dream and the message of the dream begin to be revealed. The contents of the dream are always in a dramatic form with mental pictures of experiences occurring within the dream story or drama. And, most importantly, there is a story behind the story of the dream.

MIKE: A story behind the story of the dream?

MARLIN: Yes, a story in the dream. For example, I had a dream that I was in a war, a real war. I was a soldier in a trench, and the enemy was running toward the trench. It seemed like World War I. The enemy was trying to take the trench. To gain a bit of ground, we would have to sustain some casualties. There would then come time for hand-to-hand combat. The attacking forces went over the trench and that is when the bayonets came out which meant there could be much blood spilled. In the dream, I was in the trench as a soldier and the enemy was approaching to attack. They began to come around to the end of the trench, and unable to get over it, they had to go around it. An enemy soldier started to come around the end of my trench. His face was higher than mine, around the height of my eyes, and I soon realized that this person was my father.

MIKE: And you recognized him by his face?

MARLIN: Yes. There were certain characteristics of his face that compelled my attention. It was a dead face. He had no recognition of me and no recognition of us. He was just determined to get into a position to kill me.

MIKE: He did not recognize you?

MARLIN: He did not show any sign of it, but he proceeded and as he came over, I had no alternative but to fight. He was coming around the trench on his belly – sort of slipping around.

MIKE: In other words, he was crawling? The way a soldier would crawl on the ground with his elbows.

MARLIN: Yes. He came toward me. I had a knife and as he came closer, I stabbed him. He had a fat belly. And the knife sort of went into his belly and I felt my hand in his fat.

MIKE: So, you felt your own flesh penetrating his flesh?

MARLIN: Yes, and I do not remember much more of the dream. I cannot remember if anything occurred after the stabbing. I remember the trench. I remember walking in the trench. It seemed as if the stabbing occurred before the attack.

MIKE: So, you woke up at the point of feeling that flesh on your hand?

MARLIN: Yes, pretty much. But when I saw the face of that man, I had no doubt that it was my father. And the flesh was his too because he was a fat man and, essentially, I killed him.

MIKE: But now you said that this exemplifies that there is a story behind the story of the dream. That is intriguing. I want to hear about that.

MARLIN: Well, the story behind the story is that by recognizing his face, I realized it was my father. I was revealing to myself the hatred I had for him. A good father would come to save or protect me, but the man in the dream did not come to save or protect me. I believe that man would have killed me. I remember that the belly fat was familiar to me because of my many violent encounters with him in real life. He had a strap that he would hit me with. He would huff and puff as he followed me up the stairs, and I would go on to my bed, and when he leaned over to hit me with the strap, I could feel his belly fat.

MIKE: In other words, in the dream, you were attempting to protect yourself.

MARLIN: Yes. The dream shows a kind of violence in him, that I felt all my life. I think he probably would have killed me in the dream if I had not killed him first.

MIKE: So, in the dream, your father is the aggressor and you're simply defensive.

MARLIN: That's right — that's absolutely right. He is dangerous.

MIKE: And this is the way you are going to protect yourself, defend yourself.

MARLIN: Yes, that's right, absolutely right. However, in real life, my father died when I was a young adolescent. The dream I just discussed with you occurred about 20 years ago. So, to ask myself "what the story behind the story of the dream was", I must also look at my contemporary life (20 years ago). What was going on 20 years ago when my mind produced this dream? What communication was my mind trying to convey to my self-reflective system? Here lies the type of dream interpretation template I would use with a patient.

DREAMS AND VISIONS   73

MIKE: I see in your dream journal that you had another dream in a military setting. In this dream, you assumed a leadership position, and when we talked about that, you connected that to a time when you were a boy in Harrisburg and part of a group of young Jewish boys. You recalled that your group was attacked around the school building by another group, and all your friends ran away, but you stood your ground. You were the one to stand up to them.

MARLIN: Yes, that's right.

MIKE: Now is it possible that that kind of defensiveness or need to protect yourself is connected to this dream too?

MARLIN: That is a really good point, I would say yes. It shows how I was trying to work something out...a similar dramatic story.

MIKE: In other words, the dream would have been recurrent, not just a one-timer.

MARLIN: That's right.

MIKE: The other dream was about you assuming leadership... trying to get your fellow prisoners to be more defensive, but you were the only one to take the active role. It seems that in the dream in the trenches, and this other military dream, you are doing something that is frightening but you are doing it alone, with no help from others.

MARLIN: All of those instances in my dreams are part of, what I call, a person's heroic journey. The heroic journey is not talked about much in psychotherapy or psychology. It is talked about in myth and literature. I don't know how much Jung talked about it but I'm sure he did. For me, I relate it to Joseph Campbell's book "The Hero with a Thousand Faces".

MIKE: Jung talked a lot about it.

MARLIN: Did he talk about the heroic journey?

MIKE: Oh yes, he may have used different terminology, but it is very similar to this concept. It is definitely part of discovering the darker side of the self, a confrontation, and an encounter with the shadow figure. It is a rite of passage, a coming of age. You have got to go through it to reach any kind of enlightenment.

MARLIN: I think that it occurs in many of the great myths too. The important part, for my work, is that the heroic journey must be taken alone.

MIKE: I think that is universal in all the depictions, even the Australian walkabout. It must be done alone even if there is some kind of aid or

74 PSYCHOTHERAPY

acolyte. That person is not integral to it, it would help, but you do not do it with a partner.

MARLIN: The thing I read in these books is that a god or aide could be with you. It is so interesting, isn't it?

MIKE: Yes, it is fascinating. We could talk about these dreams as part of your heroic journey. They enable you to go deeper into discovering a greater sense of who you are.

MARLIN: Let me just elaborate on that a little bit because it is absolutely true. These dreams have a similar theme to them, a familiar drama. They are like a story. In other words, they are produced when you are meeting an obstacle that is too great and then you retreat, but the meeting with the obstacle is a very crucial encounter. Because you did it, even though you may have retreated initially.

MIKE: What do you mean?

MARLIN: Let's look at my military dream in more detail. The dream content had stayed in my memory for quite a while. I call it the "Prisoner Dream". In it, about one hundred or so American soldiers and I were being held captive by what I assumed were Japanese forces because of the jungle-like setting. Although I could not actually see them, I was certain of their menacing presence lurking behind the thick foliage. This dramatic situation was unusually surreal, for I was in the Navy during the Korean war and never experienced combat. Nor was I ever a prisoner. My unarmed fellow prisoners sat passively on both sides of a clump of trees which divided us up into two groups. They had the look of defeated resignation in their eyes and body language. What made the dream so remarkable, however, was my spontaneous assumption of leadership. There were no officers or high-ranking sergeants present. It was up to me to take charge and inspire the men to resist the unseen enemy who would surely inflict on us the harshest form of torture or death. My authority was not challenged, and I was able to recruit two or three others who followed my orders. When a vicious fight broke out between two soldiers, I stopped it before they caused any physical damage to each other or endangered the precarious position we all were in. It was at that point that I woke up.

When I reflect on the dream, I viewed it as an encounter with my own fears. I had become someone who felt empowered not only for myself but for others. It was not a sensation that was in keeping with

DREAMS AND VISIONS 75

my usual temperament. There was a real experience in my boyhood that you mentioned earlier, which suggested that at one time, I possessed a capacity to stand up to the threat of danger. Among my Jewish friends in high school, I was hardly a leader. But I would not have considered myself as a meek follower either. I was pleased simply to be a member of the group. However, there was a time when four or five of us were accosted by a band of teenage boys who were not Jews. I do not recall if any anti-Semitic threats were hurled our way. What does remain in my memory is that my buddies took off while I stood my ground. I had no experience as a street fighter, nor did I possess the kind of physique that would be regarded as intimidating. For some inexplicable reason, I was willing to fight back. Encircled by the bullies, I eagerly anticipated exchanging blows with one or all of them if need be. What did happen, however, merely intensified the mystery. They pushed the smallest member of their group into the circle to take me on. We never exchanged punches; I was able to subdue him simply because I was taller and slightly heavier. When I think about the Prisoner Dream now, my boyhood "act of courage" inevitably comes to mind. I was able to meet the challenge in real life back then and I took a step along my heroic journey. Having the "Prisoner Dream" in midlife reawakened my need to take another step along my heroic path of being my true self.

MIKE: I think another fascinating dream you wrote about in your journal had to do with Atlantic City. I think in that situation, again you were alone but somehow you needed to retreat to Atlantic City.

MARLIN: Yes, that dream is very complex. As in most complex dreams, there is a progressive and a regressive crossroad for the dreamer to encounter. I think of the regressive part of the dream as the strong force of one's pathology pulling us along that path, while the progressive direction, if chosen, will lead us along our heroic journey of self-discovery. The dream is created by us so we can encounter that choice. The drama within the dream will get us to the crossroad, and it may warn us that beyond this point, we cannot go. The drama either stops and we wake up at that point or we choose the regressive path of retreat. The Atlantic City dream shows me retreating.

I believe that the function of the dream is to carry us psychologically to a new frontier and to invite us to encounter as much as possible

76 PSYCHOTHERAPY

the adventure within the dream. If we are successful, then we broaden and strengthen our ability to function in the world. We may have to encounter similar dramas and adventures in our dreams until we are able to courageously choose the progressive path. This kind of internal growth happens in small incremental steps with the help of a guide or a therapist.

MIKE: Well, how exactly did the Atlantic City dream show both the regressive and progressive choices?

MARLIN: Before I regressed to Atlantic City, I was with my friends, Fred and Howie, in an English village in the country. We had gone into a beautiful and classy British men's store, yet I chose to walk out the back door of the store alone. I found myself walking along a stream leading to a forest. I see in front of me deep woods that were not far away from the stream. Next to the stream was a boardwalk. I go down to the boardwalk and begin to walk in the direction that the stream was flowing. Eventually, the boardwalk becomes narrower and narrower. It soon ended. The beautiful stream continued to flow though. I could see in the woods ahead a figure like Peter Pan flying from tree to tree. We do not acknowledge each other, but he was clearly there, and I do not know to this day what the significance of that figure was. I realize that I must get into the stream if I wish to go further. I stand there and I ponder about my situation. I soon determine that I cannot do it. I cannot enter the stream. I then turn around and follow the same boardwalk back. But as I walk back, I soon find myself in Atlantic City. I was approaching a sleazy hotel and casino, which I am now going to enter, and I am feeling insecure about whether I will be accepted in the sleazy hotel. That is the end of the dream and I wake up, troubled.

MIKE: You went from a beautiful English countryside to a sleazy hotel? How did you make sense of this?

MARLIN: The drama in the dream is quite apparent to me. Once I relinquished my necessary pathological attachments to Fred and Howie in the dream, I could go it alone. That is a progressive step for me. However, I can only go as far as I can once I meet a crisis (the stream), and then I can go no further. I chose to retreat, to turn back, to give up the adventure into the stream and the forest. My mind entered a regressive state, which landed me in front of a sleazy hotel in Atlantic

DREAMS AND VISIONS 77

City. Even there, I do not think I'm worthy enough of being accepted to enter the place.

MIKE: So, ending up in front of a sleazy hotel in Atlantic City, that you did not think you were worthy of entering, is the regressive part of the dream? What is the progressive part?

MARLIN: We can look at the stream entry as an opportunity to encounter the Buddha adventure. In Buddhism, entering a stream is the first of the four stages of enlightenment. The dream invites me to go forward into the stream to encounter the adventure. However, I could only go as far as I could go. And I assume that the same crisis presented in this dream also occurred in many other dreams, inviting me to choose the progressive path until, hopefully, I could move forward. But in this dream, I clearly made the regressive choice as illustrated by my behavior to retreat to Atlantic City.

MIKE: What about Fred and Howie, you mentioned they were "necessary pathological attachments"? How are they related to the regressive and progressive parts of the dream?

MARLIN: When I said I had to relinquish my necessary pathological attachments to them in order to leave the British shop and follow my heroic path alone to the stream, I encountered strong obstacles to my ability to move forward. At that time in my professional life, Fred and Howie, represented the many colleagues I interacted with frequently. We presented papers at conferences together, we discussed our therapy practice, and we supported each other professionally. By relinquishing them in the dream, I showed courage to do it alone, to be my true self. You see, much of my professional life was linked to my status in the therapeutic community, my functional role in the social hierarchy, and my continual need to preserve my successful false self-image.

MIKE: Was the dream successful in helping you develop courage?

MARLIN: I believe that the dream, perhaps all dreams have the function of trying to expand our psychological capacity and increase our psychological strength. Along with it may come some revealed truth, a perceived wisdom. However, the dream itself may not be sufficient to accomplish the complicated task of psychological growth alone. We need to cooperate with the process, engage with the content of the dream, encounter what is offered, and, hopefully, move incrementally further along the path of self-knowledge and growth.

MIKE: I see you also analyzed some of your visions in your journal. Maybe you should explain what you mean by a vision. How does one have a vision? Seems mystifying to me.

MARLIN: A vision is a mental image that you experience in consciousness. I had two vivid visions while meditating, that I still intensely remember. One was about a cauldron. I found myself dangling over the top of a large, boiling cauldron. Somehow, I was suspended over it. I could see down into the cauldron and I could feel the heat from the boiling liquid coming up as steam. I said to myself, "I can't bear this", "Nobody can bear it". I was terrified but I stayed with the vision and found myself down on the ground in front of the cauldron. I finally decided to walk around the cauldron because I noticed a narrow walkway there. At the end of the path, I found a room full of people mingling with each other, like at a cocktail party. I was able to join a small group as I entered the conversation.

Another vision was about a comatose young man on the gurney. He was at the bottom of a dry well, surrounded by black stones. Not far from his head was a profoundly dark entrance to what I assumed to be death. For a long time, I ignored that part of the vision. In the vision of the boiling cauldron, death was right there within the cauldron. The death within the cauldron would be violent. However, in the man on the gurney vision, death was inevitable but quiet. As I stayed with this vision, even though I was experiencing a great deal of despair, important insights flooded my mind.

MIKE: So, are you saying that in meditative states, you experienced these visions?

MARLIN: Yes, I would enter a meditative state as I would begin to write in my journal. Although I only had a few visions throughout my journal-writing practice, I must say the two I experienced were so vivid and powerful. In fact, it took me months to reflect on the visions and to fully encounter what they were communicating to me. I could say, now, it took me years to truly understand them.

MIKE: Would you discuss what you finally understood about yourself by having these visions?

MARLIN: The content in both visions frightened me. I realized that the comatose man on the gurney and the terribly threatening cauldron of boiling liquid both contained entrances to death. Both were about death, frightening and final. This was very difficult for me to confront when so much of my personal journey had been with much exuberance, a strong sense of success, a feeling of increasing strength of body and mind. These visions, on the other hand, caused me to encounter the absolute opposite of what I found before in my meditative practice. My self-reflective process led me to the realization that my mind was preparing me for my future reality and my place in the biological life cycle.

I believe there is an "inner guide" within our self-reflective system and dreams and visions are the main tools for its expression. Those who allow themselves to encounter the messages coming from their inner guide are achieving in small part an incremental increase in wisdom. It is this process of uncovering the wisdom within one's self that transforms us. We can then become stronger and more psychologically free.

10

JOURNAL WRITING AND MEDITATION

Once I began psychotherapy on my own, I discovered the value of journal writing. After engaging in a period of meditation and deep self-reflection, I felt compelled to put down words that expressed my thoughts and feelings. A lined yellow pad and a pencil became powerful tools in this process. The tactile experience of forming words on paper brought me closer to what I had experienced. It helped me understand more fully what the encounter within my mind was all about. The act of writing, a deliberative search for words, allowed for the experience to become meaningful.

I had never kept a journal before. Nor had I ever written in a diary. Let me explain what for some may be an obvious difference between the two. A diary for most is a record of what happened, from the most trivial and mundane events to those of momentous consequence. Writing in a journal for me was never about keeping any kind of historical record. But it was also different from the kind of journal kept by writers who want to record ideas, fragments, possibilities for stories, and character sketches that may one day evolve into fully realized works. From what I know of many literary artists, the notebook, journal, or sketchbook is a necessary component of their creative efforts. In the case of many writers, such workbooks have artistic merit in and of themselves and are invaluable sources for scholars and literary critics.

I also know of high school English teachers who advocate journal writing as warmups for writing personal essays, especially those that are part of an applicant's resume and transcript in seeking admission to college. That piece of writing is often viewed as a crucial barometer for future academic success primarily because of what it reveals about a student's sense of self. It seems ironic and rather perverse that such self-awareness, which eludes most human beings throughout a full lifetime of experiences, should be expected of an 18-year-old even before stepping foot on a college campus. Nevertheless, there is something to be said for having a sense of who you are at any age.

Journal writing, quite naturally, has been a valuable aid in therapy. Like painting, sculpture, and composing, writing is another outlet for confronting and overcoming many of the psychological obstacles that inhibit healing.

So, while I recognize and applaud all the ways a journal can be of value, I must explain how I define and incorporate journal writing in my personal psychotherapy and in my practice. But first, let us consider some fundamentals. The mind of a newborn produces thoughts, feelings, images, and memories in relationship to its main caregiver. Thus begins an interpersonal process. What happens is that like a therapist – a mother, father, or anyone who was part of the empathic envelope becomes attuned to the needs and pains as well as to the joys and pleasures of what is going on in the child's mind. As time goes on, the child develops the strength not to need as much contact with those others as it once did. This steadily evolving independence is characterized by the ability to receive from the self what it thought it desperately needed from another. At a certain time in life, for some, it may occur very early while still young, and for others, after many years and with greater maturity, there is a realization that one should have a relationship to what is authentic in one's own mind. What that relationship entails is an ability to receive and encounter what the mind reveals. Journal writing becomes an act of training to become better at receiving what the mind is saying. It is a matter of learning to listen to another part of your own mind. The more honest you are, the better you become at receiving whatever the mind tells you and you can then put it down on paper. Whatever you feel, write. You can explore your mind through these encounters, but it must always be with complete honesty, which facilitates the process. Most people lack any kind of relationship with their minds. They have a need to create a self in accordance with what they believe specific others want them to be. Inevitably, they become conformists and dissatisfied as individuals, no matter how successful and happy they appear to be. Through serious journal writing that accompanies self-reflection, one can become receptive to the voice within. By being honest in the journal, I become my own therapist. Saying the words is not enough. They must be written.

Writing on the pad is important in the same way that talking to a therapist is important. With the journal, you have a way of talking to yourself with absolute honesty. As you write the words down, you feel their power. The experience is visceral. So much so that there were times when I broke my pencil as I was writing. As you write your thoughts down, you realize that you are feeling, not just thinking. It is a chain reaction, from thinking to writing to feeling, which ignites more thinking and thus more writing. It is an amazing phenomenon. The written words act as containers of those thoughts and feelings I needed to encounter. Once received and encountered, a transformation within my mind takes place. I become freer, less burdened by those thoughts and feelings, and more importantly, I gain wisdom from my inner guide, my therapist within. As a container functions to store items, my journal writing stores my authentic thoughts and feelings that perhaps I could have never verbalized to myself or others. In addition, as a container provides a place for stored items, my journals supply me with a repository of those painful aspects of my true self that would have remained split off from my consciousness but subtly tortured me from within. Through the mediation and journal writing process, I creatively connected to those split off parts of self and began to feel whole.

If I am in therapy, I can assume my analyst will listen and respond to my thoughts, so that my thoughts as I speak them become the content of his thoughts. If the therapy is working well, the analyst will then have associations to my life experiences from what I have shared, and it will probably stimulate in the analyst memories of what I had once told him, and this will reinforce the creative connection between us. To clarify, by committing to the journal writing process, I hope to create a state of mind that allows me to hear myself openly, honestly, so that a creative connection to my true self can occur. I can record, confront, and meditate upon what I have received by writing it down, feeling what then comes up, and writing that down as well. That facilitates the transformative process and is the essential way to know oneself. I must be as honest with myself during the process as I want my patients to be with me.

Remember, the journey toward becoming my own therapist began on a fateful day when I sat in an easy chair and started a process of deep self-reflection. The idea of writing down what transpired in my mind seemed so natural, especially if I wanted to gain some understanding of my thoughts. Writing is inevitably slower than speaking, and that slower pace led to my making powerful associations to experiences, and the dreams and visions, that I discussed earlier. Doing this is the opposite of thinking on one's feet, which is a great skill in the right situation. Writing in the journal is more deliberative – even if I record only what has entered my mind without any agenda. I do not create those thoughts. I encounter them. I receive them.

There was a time when writing in a journal became a regular part of my daily routine – sitting in the chair, entering a deep meditative and reflective state, then picking up the pencil and yellow pad, writing down the date and recording my thoughts and feelings as spontaneously as possible. As I wrote down the words that expressed the experience, I did not consider whether they were the best words. Perhaps my phrasing could have been more precise or more elegant. Such concerns were of no consequence. What mattered most were the words, the containers, that unconsciously captured the workings of my mind. I am sure that the journal of a professor of literature would sound very different from that of someone with high school education. Despite the obvious differences in verbal skills, the results of having engaged in the process of journal writing could have invaluable therapeutic benefits for anyone.   -

Although I have stacked and stored these journals on shelves over many years, I have rarely reread them. As I stated earlier, these journals were never meant to serve as a chronicle, but as a repository. However, there was a time when I did look at approximately twenty yellow pads from an especially troubled period of my life. My curiosity overrode any qualms I had about revisiting the journals. My mental wellbeing necessitated their being read. As I suspected, these journals were striking evidence of the rage I had felt toward people I had and still loved. I can vividly recall breaking pencils when I put words to paper expressing my emotional turmoil. The language was powerful – but it was also hurtful. And so, I destroyed those pads primarily because I did not want anyone ever to see them and discover the depth of my anger. I do not regret having written the journals, for, at the time, they served their purpose. But I am pleased that I chose to destroy them.

There were days when writing in my journal had a cathartic effect analogous to what Aristotle described in his definition of tragedy as "arousing terror and pity". Another analogy comes to mind. Some patients have said that after leaving an intense session with me, they felt great relief as if a heavy burden had been lifted from their shoulders. By committing to the journal, you, in a way, become your own therapist, receptive to a part of your mind that may have been silenced by those early invisible barriers, but is now beginning to emerge with your resolve to engage in self-reflection.

Earlier, I had written about the empathic envelope and how the child becomes increasingly self-reliant, steadily overcoming the absolute dependency experienced in infancy. Acquiring independence is not without its perils. Significant others like parents and teachers may subject the young mind to their own versions of reality. Most of us are trained to be conformists, to be compliant, which often means to be dishonest to the truth of ourselves. It is easier to be what others want us to be than to be assertive and rebellious. Dependency on others is often contingent upon formulating a false self, one that becomes increasingly compromised or repressed into silence. Doing the "right" thing according to social norms and going along with what parents or friends or society expect(s) can lead ultimately to despair, anxiety, and depression.

The key question becomes – who am I? When the answer to this question is problematic, or even traumatic, therapy can provide a solution. The therapist is your guide in what I have called the heroic journey. He or she can help you navigate the complex difficulties of a lifetime of being defined by others. He or she participates in the search for your true self.

Writing in the journal is another way to rediscover the self that has been buried in the thickets of conformity, compliance, and compromise and all the other ways we are trained to be dishonest to self. Thanks to the meditation and journal writing, I encountered the anger and rage underlying the conformist personality I had been performing for my family, friends, and colleagues. Self-reflection and journal writing stripped away the illusory personas that I believed made up the real me; Marlin Brenner, Ph.D. from Columbia University, captain of the debating team at Penn State, successful psychotherapist, loving husband and father, and esteemed colleague. I wore my credentials like a bright new shirt, seeking and receiving compliments for something that was not entirely me. I did not design or make that shirt. I only wore it because it looked good on me, or so I was told. As a result of conscientious dedication to honest journal writing, I eventually discovered some painful truths about myself which were unattractive, but were, in the final analysis, liberating and productive.

11

THE HUMAN ADVENTURE/ HEROIC JOURNEY

During my life as a psychotherapist, and after many years of self-analysis and intense journal writing, the idea of "truth" became more important to me. If we compare communication with ourselves or others while burdened with prohibitions, such as invisible barriers, then "the truth" is sacrificed. As I discussed in earlier chapters, invisible barriers are created by our pathological structures to limit our expression of genuine thoughts and feelings. Invisible barriers can not only block our negative feelings and actions, but they can also block loving, creative, and generous feelings and actions as well.

What then is the truth? Simply stated, it is the product of creative connection. A creative connection is essentially the deep, empathic understanding of what is communicated between self and others, as in an interpersonal relationship, and from self to self, through meditation, journal writing, and psychotherapy. Truth, under ideal conditions, is the inner knowledge and revealed wisdom that incrementally unfolds to our awareness.

The truth revealed through creative connection stimulates creative thought and creativity. What I mean by creativity can be great and large, such as receiving inspiration to create a poem, or less so, such as a bit of understanding that did not exist before. If we think deeply about the product of creative connection, it flows from a deep unknown source within the mind, and it is received by the self-reflective system. Creative work is often done in solitude, and it is in that solitude that one may easily become creatively connected to the revelation of one's personal truth.

The self-reflective system already exists within the person, but it will only increase in strength and dominance if we exercise our ability to pursue the knowledge and wisdom within. By using self-reflection, we can encounter the power of the pathological drama with its invisible barriers that block our growth and psychological freedom. A series of successful encounters, through deliberate effort on our part, will reduce the power of the invisible barrier, and the powerful motivations arising from the drama that are so destructively active within our contemporary pathological structure. The degree of freedom that we receive is directly related to the degree of truth uncovered by our self-reflective system. As our personal truth is slowly revealed to our conscious mind, the negative influences of our pathological structure decrease, and we achieve relief from emotional suffering.

As I see it, patients enter therapy unable to express to themselves their personal truth. They are experiencing the painful emotions resulting from the deprivation of unmet needs historically experienced and trapped within their mind. The deprivation and the limitation of being unable to speak the truth result in intense anguish and suffering. It is the suffering that brings patients to psychotherapy.

When I begin work with my patients, I tell them that there is a story to be told, and neither of us are aware of it at the start. I encourage the patient to relax and awaken to his/her own capacity for self-reflection. By this process, we will receive what the patient's mind is trying to communicate to us. A dramatic story will become evident and we, through our creative connection, will be able to hear it and reflect upon it. The therapeutic relationship is the door that opens to the unfolding of the story that was originally hidden.

Each of us has a part to play in the unfolding process of revealed truth. The main part for the patient is to allow the creative connection to the therapist, and eventually to the self, to develop and flourish through the empathic relational experience. The capacity to be self-reflective is taught to the patient by the psychotherapist. The patient is asked to "get closer toward your true self" and "receive what your mind is trying to tell you". Additionally, I say, "You and I will begin to reflect upon the story, the hidden drama, that your mind wishes to tell us about". As we become more creatively connected emotionally, the more the patient will uncover the personal truth communicated through his/her dreams, memories, fears and anxieties, and burning unmet needs.

The patients learn that during early development, many mental structures have been created by the symbiotic compensatory system to reduce their inner pain and emotional suffering. This system created the pathological attachments to the outside world that the patients find themselves trapped in at the present. It is important to reassure the patient that these pathological attachments helped reduce the unbearable anxiety associated with previous emotional deprivation. When recognized, the patient may be able to slowly give up the pathological attachments only to encounter the original powerful negative emotions associated with the revealed truth. The original content of the pain and suffering must also be encountered leading to the incremental reduction of the power of the pathology. This entire process, through self-reflection, contributes to the patient's ability to gain more psychological freedom from mental distress. The revelation of our personal truth is potentially possible for all of us.

Not many patients have the initial intention or interest in embarking on their own human adventure and heroic journey to uncover their personal truth. Most people will stop therapy when their suffering has been reduced, and their self-reliance has increased. They have begun to find a creative connection with their true self, and they gained the ability to function successfully in the world. These skills are enough for many seeking psychotherapeutic help and support.

However, there is so much more to experience and achieve by progressing along the heroic path of the true self. Once an individual develops a creative communication within, he/she will find they can tolerate and appreciate an expansive state of aloneness. The solitary journey seems to be a necessary condition of the human adventure toward one's authentic life. As one becomes accustomed to and prefers more aloneness, a greater sense of independent thought is achieved. The probability of discovering the hidden wisdom emanating from the inner guide is also highly possible. As we hear and listen to our inner guide, we are well on the way toward

THE HUMAN ADVENTURE/HEROIC JOURNEY   89

the human adventure of becoming our true self. You find you can let go of false attachments, compensatory relationships, and illusions and begin to depend on "the therapist within" for wisdom and truth. As the relinquishment of the false self begins to take place, a newfound personal strength is experienced. My own heroic journey taught me to trust the process of shedding the symbiotic compensatory solutions of a false existence and dare to pursue the adventure.

Once I had the courage to leave the domination of my professional functional structure of classical psychoanalysis, and risk losing those colleagues I so needed for acceptance and admiration, I began to embark on my search for truth. I gained independence of thought and started reading ancient Zen Buddhist texts seeking to find wisdom and knowledge. But it was not until I began journal writing and meditation that I could finally identify the potential of my self-reflection system. Through reflection, the very slow process of encountering the power of my ancient pathological structures led me to see how the construction of my false self began. As the abandonment of my false self-image incrementally took place, I uncovered my personal truth.

I realize now that our inner guide does not lead us along the path of self-discovery by random, haphazard encounters. On the contrary, we encounter what we need to encounter at the right time in our mental development when we can receive that wisdom. Repeatedly in psychotherapy, I witnessed many patients' inner guide direct them to encounter what seems most pressing and important at the right time in their life. It was the mind of the patient, not mine, that controlled the timing and nature of the necessary encounters that eventually revealed the liberating insight.

I also noticed that the patient's inner guide determines how much elaboration that person could handle at the moment, how far the patient could go with a particular encounter, and ultimately, when to stop the encounter to return to a safer, more comfortable state of mind. We, as psychotherapists, must trust the tempo and depth of exploration that a patient's inner guide determines for each session.

The person in a solitary self-analysis should do everything within his or her power to accept what the mind wishes to bring forth. Effort should be made, without exceptions, to accept all that appears. If the self-analysis begins with a journal, then the writing should be determined by what comes to mind at the present moment. It has been my experience over many years of journal writing that the mental productions are self-regulating, and that even the confrontation with very difficult material is usually determined by my inner guide. I trust that my "therapist within" will reveal to me the awareness without destruction. If the encounter seems too much to handle, I found I could always avoid it and visit the material later. I respect and value my self-reflective system, and I teach patients to trust theirs as well. We do not tell the mind what to do or say. It tells us as it unfolds. As therapists, we can encourage patients to open a bit more to what is being revealed through incremental steps of small encounters with their true self.

When it is safe, the inner guide of the patient will present us with a dream and/or vision. Different therapeutic approaches use dreams in different ways and, surprisingly, find them valuable and mysteriously productive within their particular perspective. I know of various ways of interpreting dreams, but I find the most useful way is to assume that the dream is presenting to us, in its own language, what we must encounter next in life in order to move along our heroic journey. In fact, the dream may simply be an opportunity to attempt that encounter. If we can courageously meet the task of the drama in the dream, we have gained the necessary personal strength and mental ability to tackle those challenges in real life.

The dream always takes us to a point of the encounter and leaves us there. As the dreamer and the receiver of the message, we arrive at a crossroad. We have a choice to make. Should we go boldly toward the progressive path, or retreat to safety? The encounter to go forward may not be possible at the time of the dream, but our inner guide is preparing us for this challenge in the near future.

For example, many years ago, I had a dream I was holding on to a rope. I then noticed that the rope, which was previously attached to a secure mooring, had been severed. What was curious about the drama was that I did not feel any anxiety or distress by the severed rope. I had a sense that I really did not need it to maneuver to safety. As I reflected upon the dream content, I could immediately see the connection between my newly achieved freedom from the severed rope in the dream, and my real-life attempt to distance myself from certain colleagues and professional organizations. I no longer needed those pathological attachments that reinforced my false professional self-image. My inner guide revealed to me, through my dream, that I was ready to go it alone professionally. I was ready to sever certain professional relationships that prevented me from moving forward on my heroic journey.

To begin your own human adventure, you will need to create the essential conditions in which your personal truth can be uttered verbally and through journal writing. Through self-reflection, meditation, and journal writing, you will become acquainted with your inner guide. Continue to communicate with your own mind as your "therapist within" slowly reveals the wisdom needed to progress along the path of your heroic journey of self-discovery. Create that empathic envelope you always looked for in others, but now found deep within yourself. And live life courageously, authentically, creatively connected to your true self.

INDEX

adventure 10, 38, 54
Alger, Horatio 17
Aristotle 84
authority 46, 55

Brenner, Marlin 19, 20, 85

Campbell, Joseph 54, 73
cauldron 78
children 6, 8, 13, 29, 30
child's mind 8, 81
child's self 15, 30
"Cognitive Conviction" 41
communication 70, 72, 86
contemporary pathological
    structures 28, 31, 33, 35–38, 57, 58,
    66, 68
cooperation 49
cost-benefit ratio 23
creative connection 9–15, 42, 43, 65,
    66, 68, 82, 83, 86–88
creative thinking 57–59
creative work 87

disturbances 14, 15
drama 30, 33, 56, 57, 67, 71, 75, 76,
    87, 90
dreams 54, 56–59, 67, 69–79, 90;
    content 70, 74, 90; interpretation
    70; journals 69, 73

Eisenhower, Milton 19, 47
emotional anxiety 5
emotions 20
empathic envelope 3–8
encasing worldview 39–44
Exodus story 50

false self 19, 22–25, 58, 84, 89
Fitzgerald, F. Scott 17
friendship 9
functional structures 44–52, 56, 57

Hayden, Robert 12
Hearst, William Randolph 52
heroic journey 84, 86–91; of self-
    discovery 24, 75, 91

INDEX

"The Hero with a Thousand Faces" 54, 73
human adventure 86–91

ideal empathic envelope 6
invisible barriers 21–23, 34, 64, 86, 87
isolation 4, 5, 7, 8, 10, 15, 18, 27, 28, 32, 33, 52, 54, 56
Israelites 49, 50

journal writing 25, 28, 42, 43, 80–85, 90, 91
journey 24, 53–56, 68, 73–75, 83, 84, 88–91

leashes 44, 46, 51, 52, 55
life factors 66
Lion's Paw 19

marital conflict 36
meditation 25, 80–85, 91
mental functioning 66
mental posture 27, 32

Nazism 51
"Newness" 9
nomad child 7

pathological structures 15, 21, 22, 24, 26–38, 40, 57–59, 86, 87; strong force and weak force 35–38
patient's dream 70; content 70
patient's mind 5, 42, 63, 87
personal drama 26, 28
personal truth 21, 25, 29, 43, 87–89, 91
person's mind 15, 31, 32, 36, 44
power 36, 46, 51, 55
Prisoner Dream 74, 75
psychological distress 32

psychological freedom 44, 51, 52, 56, 59, 61, 87, 88
psychological wellbeing 48
psychologist-supervisee relationship 27
psychotherapeutic healing process 1
psychotherapeutic process 63–68
psychotherapy 61

rational mind encounters 43
realm of existence 21
reciprocity of feeling 6

self-analysis 5, 7, 89
self-knowledge 53–55, 59, 77
self-protection 49
self-reflective journal writing 28
self-reflective system 5–6, 13–14, 16, 29, 36, 50, 52–59, 61, 63, 68, 70, 71, 79, 84, 87–91
sense of orderliness 6
social activism 49
strong-destructive force 35–38
supervision 27
sure-fire career path 11
symbiotic-compensatory system 16–25, 88

"Those Winter Sundays" 12
traumatic states 14
truth 13, 14, 26, 36, 37, 41, 43, 44, 54, 55, 58, 86–89

unification process 21
unified self 21, 22

visions 29, 69–79, 83, 90

weak-creative force 35–38
wilderness 50

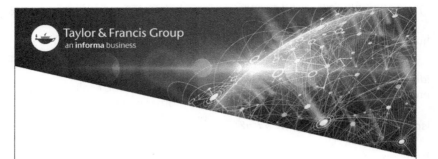

The Risk of Regional Governance

Creating metropolitan regions that are more efficient, equitable, and sustainable depends on the willingness of local officials to work together across municipal boundaries to solve large-scale problems. How do these local officials think? Why do they only sometimes cooperate? What kind of governance do they choose in the face of persistent problems?

The Risk of Regional Governance offers a new perspective on these questions. Drawing on theory from sociology and anthropology, it argues that many of the most important cooperative decisions local officials make—those about land use planning and regulation—are driven by heuristic, biased reasoning driven by cultural values. *The Risk of Regional Governance* builds a socio-cultural collective action framework, and supports it with rich survey and interview data from hundreds of local elected officials serving in the suburbs of Detroit and Grand Rapids, Michigan. It is a story of the Rust Belt, of how local officials think about their community and the region, and—most importantly—of how we might craft policies that can overcome biases against regional governance.

Thomas Skuzinski is Assistant Professor of Urban Affairs and Planning at the School of Public and International Affairs at Virginia Tech University. He holds doctoral and master degrees from the University of Michigan, and a law degree from Michigan State University. His work uses a sociological institutionalist lens to examine how the rules, norms, and cultures in which local government actors are embedded shape metropolitan governance.

Routledge Research in Urban Politics and Policy

1 **The Cultural Contradictions of Progressive Politics**
The Role of Cultural Change and the Global Economy in Local
Policymaking
Donald L. Rosdil

2 **Securitization of Property Squatting in Europe**
Mary Manjikian

3 **Local Politics and Mayoral Elections in 21st Century America**
The Keys to City Hall
Sean D. Foreman and Marcia L. Godwin

4 **The Risk of Regional Governance**
Cultural Theory and Interlocal Cooperation
Thomas Skuzinski

The Risk of Regional Governance

Cultural Theory and Interlocal Cooperation

Thomas Skuzinski

LONDON AND NEW YORK

First published 2018 by Routledge

2 Park Square, Milton Park, Abingdon, Oxfordshire OX14 4RN
52 Vanderbilt Avenue, New York, NY 10017

Routledge is an imprint of the Taylor & Francis Group, an informa business

First issued in paperback 2019

Copyright © 2018 Taylor & Francis

The right of Thomas Skuzinski to be identified as author of this work has
been asserted by him in accordance with sections 77 and 78 of the
Copyright, Designs and Patents Act 1988.

All rights reserved. No part of this book may be reprinted or reproduced or
utilised in any form or by any electronic, mechanical, or other means, now
known or hereafter invented, including photocopying and recording, or in
any information storage or retrieval system, without permission in writing
from the publishers.

Notice:
Product or corporate names may be trademarks or registered trademarks,
and are used only for identification and explanation without intent to infringe.

Library of Congress Cataloging in Publication Data
A catalog record for this book has been requested

ISBN: 978-1-138-23575-5 (hbk)
ISBN: 978-0-367-37198-2 (pbk)

Typeset in Times New Roman
by Wearset Ltd, Boldon, Tyne and Wear

To Michael and Elvira, and to my parents, for making this possible

Contents

List of Figures	xii
List of Tables	xiii
Preface	xiv
Acknowledgments	xviii

1 Introduction — 1

Opting Out 1
Governing Metropolitan Regions 5
The Legitimacy of Reform 8
Reform as a Transaction 11
The Limitations of Economizing 12
Theoretical Perspectives on Metropolitan Governance 16
The Goals of the Book 20
Evidence from Metropolitan Michigan 22
The Plan of the Book 25

2 Governing the Region through Cooperation — 34

The Manchester Community 34
The Difficulty of Structural Reforms 37
The Limitations of State and Federal Intervention 41
Distinguishing Cooperation 42
Enabling Cooperation 43
Awareness of the Law 45
Conclusion 46

3 Beyond Economizing — 51

Transaction Cost Economizing 51
Cooperation as a Transaction 53

x   *Contents*

The Individual in the Local Government Organization 59
Some Conceptual Issues 61
Maintaining Systems Versus Creating Lifestyles 62
When Reform Seems Irrational 66
Conclusion 71

4   Sociocultural Collective Action   75

Introduction 75
Revisiting Rationality 75
Individuals and Institutions 79
The Appropriateness of Regional Reform 82
An Illustration 84

5   Normative Legitimizing   91

Introduction 91
Economizing and Reciprocity in Preference Formation 92
The Norm of Responsiveness in Local Government 96
The Treatment of Responsiveness in Economizing Studies 98
Evidence of Political Legitimizing 101

6   Cultural Legitimizing   109

From Gay Rights to Gun Control to Governance 109
Grid-Group Cultural Theory 111
Reconciling Cultural Theory with Rational Choice
*   Institutionalism 114*
Connecting Dispositions to Governance 115
The Cultural Dispositions of Local Elected Officials 119
Dispositions and Partisan Identity 123
Evidence of Cultural Legitimizing 125
Conclusion 126

7   Conclusion   129

Avenues for Policy Reform under Legitimizing 132
Dealing with Cultural Pluralism through De-Biasing 133
The Prospects for Regional Governance through Voluntary
*   Interlocal Cooperation 139*

Contents   xi

Appendices   142

*Appendix A Local Governments and Local Elected Officials in
   Michigan 142*
Appendix B Survey of Local Elected Officials 144
Appendix C Data Sources and Variable Specification 151
Appendix D Summary of Hypotheses 158
Appendix E Estimation Technique 161
*Appendix F Preferences about Interlocal Land Use
   Cooperation 163*
Appendix G Results Tables for Quantitative Analyses 171

Index   179

Figures

1.1	Study Area Municipalities	23
2.1	The Original Manchester Community Municipalities	35
4.1	The Sociocultural Collective Action Framework	83
5.1	Perception of Residential Support	102
5.2	Perceptions of a Norm of Political Alignment	103
5.3	Perceptions of a Norm of Discretion	103
6.1	Grid and Group Dispositions and the Four Cultural Types	111
6.2	The Values and Preferred Social Relations of the Four Cultural Types	113
6.3	Cultural Dispositions and Preferences about Interlocal Cooperation	118
6.4	Cultural Dispositions of Respondent Local Elected Officials	122
6.5	Cultural Dispositions by Partisan Self-Identification	123
F.1	Preferences about Partial Area Cooperation	164
F.2	Preferences about Full Coverage Cooperation	166
F.3	Preferences about Governance under Partial Area Cooperation, by Metropolitan Area	168
F.4	Preferences about Governance under Full Coverage Cooperation, by Metropolitan Area	169
F.5	Preferences about Governance, by Extent of JMPA Coverage	169

Tables

4.1	Comparison of Townships near Manchester Village that Considered Adoption of a Joint Land Use Agreement	85
7.1	Support of the Hypotheses	130
B.1	Detroit Region, Institutional Representativeness of Sample of Local Elected Officials by Government Type and County	145
B.2	Grand Rapids Region, Institutional Representativeness of Sample of Local Elected Officials by Government Type and County	146
B.3	Detroit Area, Demographic and Fiscal Representativeness of Municipalities Represented by Elected Officials in Sample	146
B.4	Grand Rapids Area, Demographic and Fiscal Representativeness of Municipalities Represented by Elected Officials in Sample	147
D.1	General Hypotheses Based on Different Types of Rational Legitimizing	158
D.2	Hypotheses Based on Measures and Estimation Techniques Used in the Current Study	160
E.1	Share of Variance Attributable to Municipal Level in Multi-Level Ordinal Logistic Models	163
G.1	Preferences for Partial Area Land Use Cooperation, For All Respondents across Both Metro Areas	171
G.2	Preferences for Partial Area Land Use Cooperation, Comparing Respondents by Metropolitan Area	172
G.3	Preferences for Full Coverage Land Use Cooperation, For All Respondents across Both Metro Areas	173
G.4	Preferences for Full Coverage Land Use Cooperation, Comparing Respondents by Metropolitan Area	174
G.5	Preferences for Authoritative Versus Advisory Structure, For All Respondents across Both Metro Areas	175
G.6	Preferences for Authoritative Versus Advisory Structure, by Metropolitan Area	176

Preface

Around the time I was nearing the completion of the manuscript for this book, a student commented to me that there was no point anymore in learning about what local governments can and cannot do. "It's not like they can really make a difference now," she said resignedly. The conversation was in the middle of November 2016, shortly after a presidential election that had stunned even the most sage observers. I knew the student through a class I teach on land use law, and in it the dominant theme is the constraints faced by general purpose local governments—the tens of thousands of cities, towns, counties, villages, townships, and other units that comprise the crazy-quilt of sub-state government in the U.S. In one sense, then, the comment was not surprising because of the highly structuralist perspective from which I had presented the material. Local government actors had to navigate a space of legal limitation filled with constitutional provisions, statutes, regulations, and common law. They could only behave in the ways states dictated. I frequently emphasized to my students that local governments were, in the final analysis, "creatures of the state." And their decisions were further circumscribed by resource scarcity. I had encountered many theorists in political science, public administration, and the law who imagined the local actor as existing in an institutional space of very limited discretion. My own experience growing up in Michigan and seeing first-hand the decline of the Rust Belt made this conceptualization quite easy to accept. It seemed that my student had picked up on my native impulses, and I suppose I should have been pleased.

But I had also taught about theories of state–local fiscal federalism. I had lectured about the ways in which a quite expansive autonomy had been granted to many local governments through home rule constitutional and statutory provisions, and how land use planning and regulation were—along with public education—the functions that were most strongly localized in the United States. My students and I had started to unpack, too, some of the clever ways local governments had attempted to deal with problems that the state and federal governments could not or would not effectively address. America's cities and towns were, indeed, places of constraint, but they were also places of innovation and opportunity—a notion of freedom that also had its scholarly adherents. In the wake of a federal election that was poised to fundamentally change the

Preface xv

administration of national environmental and social policies, I found myself—much to my own surprise—touting the virtues of the empowered local government in the face of my student's frustration and despondency. Local government officials, I insisted, *could* make a difference—really—even under conditions that seemed constraining.

Students can often be a vital source of scholarly inspiration, and it was this conversation that helped me appreciate the timeliness of the theorization and empirical investigation at the heart of *The Risk of Regional Governance*. Allow me a few moments to unpack that title and the basic argument I make in the book. When I write about regional governance, I am referring specifically to formal, voluntary cooperation among general purpose local governments, a seemingly small action that has the ability to dramatically rescale and reform metropolitan policymaking. In the book, I propose that the geography of cooperation cannot be mapped fully with the tools of rational choice institutionalism, as they have been for the last few decades. Rather, the landscape is in significant part shaped by values and ideology, and its contours can be best appreciated from the perspective of a cultural theoretic variant of sociological institutionalism.

Competition and cooperation are formal outcomes of a process of social legitimizing, which is most simply defined as the holistic degree of support for an organization, to paraphrase John Meyer and William Scott from their work in the early 1980s. Legitimacy can come from legal mandates (its clearest etymological interpretation), but also from the norms that develop within and among organizations, and—most relevantly for the purposes of this book—from the cultural dispositions that align individuals with a social "tribe" that exists beyond these organizations. Applied to local governments, we would expect cooperation to be most likely where, for example, state enabling legislation allows it, where it is built on an existing network of cooperative relationships, and where its relative costs and benefits are evaluated in a way that is consistent with professionally accepted practices. But beyond this regulatory and normative legitimacy, we would also expect cooperation to be more likely where it aligns with the values of the individuals charged with its adoption and maintenance—i.e., where it is also culturally legitimate.

The real conceptual power of a sociological institutionalist framework for making sense of interlocal cooperation is that it can accommodate the surface logic of rational choice institutionalism by regarding it as a set of socially constituted norms that will *sometimes* dominate decision-making processes. We would, for example, expect decisions about water treatment or garbage collection or snow removal to be guided by considerations of efficiency and transaction cost economizing, for reasons that—if not evident now—will become so later in the book. For other targets of cooperation, however, rules permit a wide range of discretion, costs and benefits are highly uncertain, information is lacking, and norms of reciprocity are weak, creating what Elinor Ostrom would refer to as a sparse setting. The standard menu of rules and norms may be unable to signal a clear logic of instrumentality, but in their absence culture can still afford the logic of appropriateness on which local officials can draw.

xvi *Preface*

To my student, I had presented two competing visions of local governments as places of constraint and places of opportunity. These were also descriptions, respectively, of the contexts in local policymaking when elected and administrative officials would and would not rely on heuristic reasoning—the gut instincts, intuitions, moral codes, ideologies, and biases that are bound up in cultural worldviews. If we know when this reasoning is most likely to dominate, and we additionally know the cognitive processes that translate worldviews into policy preferences, then we are afforded two policy moments—an institutional one and a cognitive one—at which we can try to leverage or mitigate the operation of cultural worldviews. *The Risk of Regional Governance* can be read as a guide to divining those moments.

If we instead continue to imagine the local official as a rational, instrumental functionary strategically interacting with other like-minded actors in an institutionally rich setting, then I propose we are left with surprisingly few tools, and many of them rely on intervention by the state that has proven historically unpopular and politically untenable. Certainly not one of these tools is capable of dealing with the messiness of ideology. The election of 2016 will likely impart many lessons, but perhaps the most immediate one is that there is real value to be gained from respecting the power of heuristic reasoning. By developing a culturally grounded sociological institutionalist framework for metropolitan governance—what I refer to more simply as *sociocultural collective action*—and providing a preliminary test of it, I hope to demonstrate the value of cultural worldviews as a cognitive institutional tool for making sense of and perhaps even improving metropolitan areas.

The book is written with several audiences in mind. Anyone interested broadly in the function and dysfunction of metropolitan areas should find relevant the arguments and evidence presented in *The Risk of Regional Governance*, and that statement applies to academics, students, and lay readers. The book provides a primer on how we currently think about interlocal cooperation—an essential pathway to regional governance—and it offers an alternative perspective. The book also tells a story of Detroit and Grand Rapids, Michigan, and in doing so speaks to the dynamics that have shaped so many Rust Belt cities and that continue to fascinate so many of us, including many social scientists and other academics. It is a story about the suburbs of these two large cities, and how the local elected officials serving them think about reaching across boundaries to engage in cooperative land use planning and zoning.

The Risk of Regional Governance should be of some use to the political scientist or scholar of public administration working at the boundary between rational choice institutionalism and sociological institutionalism, as many have in recent decades. It injects cultural theory, which remains an underused way to theorize about the presence of culture in sociological institutionalism. And, along those lines, it uses a method for operationalizing culture—cultural cognition—that could prove highly useful. More broadly, the book focuses attention on local elected officials, who continue to be regrettably ignored. I have attended many conferences in which the panels that deal with local government

Preface xvii

are few, and within those most authors tend to skirt very close to committing an ecological fallacy by treating the individual and the organization—the local elected official and the local government—as synonymous. This may be true sometimes, and may be quite often justifiable for local administrative officials, but I do not believe based on my own observations that it is often true of local elected officials. The book also deals not with the big city mayors that so often garner attention when a study does focus on local government leadership, but rather with the suburban legislators who so often go unnoticed. In part this has been driven by a persistent view, traceable to Charles Tiebout, Paul Peterson, Gerald Frug, and others, of local governments as highly constrained and rational. This position is often warranted, but it should not preclude us from further investigation of these jurisdictions or the officials in them.

The Risk of Regional Governance is also written for theorists interested in the cultural and cognitive turns in the social sciences. If you ever looked at a policy or planning process, or participated in one, and felt there was some explanatory power for values, beliefs, and ideology, then you will likely find much of the material in this book resonant. Many scholars have surveyed and described the social world from this perspective. In the field of planning, my disciplinary home, theoretical work by Patsy Healey, Judith Innes, John Forester, and Frank Fischer, among many others, has helped us recognize how pervasive values are, even in the supposedly rational, objective, and value-free work of public officials. Planning, particularly in its intersection with policy analysis, has taken an argumentative and communicative turn, and that certainly helped push me toward the theoretical turn toward sociological institutionalism and cultural legitimacy I am advocating in this text.

Lastly, *The Risk of Regional Governance* is for those working to make local and metropolitan governance better—not just more efficient, or more effective, but more equitable. In the field of planning, theory and practice are inextricable. In 2016, I taught a class with the title *Theory and Practice of Planning*, and I found that only in making a conscious effort to weave the two together could any real lessons be learned—more often by me than my students, I suspect. We have many tools that are directed at improving participation and cooperation, but at least in the subfield of metropolitan governance we have not had a theory able to explain *why* and *when* such tools might matter in the context of interlocal cooperation. This book attempts to lay a few bricks in that foundation.

Acknowledgments

In life we are not often given the opportunity to properly give public recognition to the people who have been instrumental in allowing us to transform our ambitions and dreams into reality. Even if we express gratitude repeatedly in private, this somehow seems not enough. Writing acknowledgments seems like a good start toward remedying this inadequacy.

As with any project completed over many years and hundreds—I'll be honest: thousands—of hours, a book requires a vast quantity of practical assistance and an even greater measure of emotional support and patience. I was fortunate to have one or the other, and quite often both, from many people. I was also fortunate to have a ready supply of friendly faces and caffeine at the Starbucks on University City Boulevard in Blacksburg, Virginia.

First, I must thank the Editorial Board at Routledge, and Natalja Mortensen, Senior Acquisitions Editor in Political Science Research, for having the willingness to publish work by a junior scholar, and for having the patience to shepherd me through the process. Maria Landschoot and Lillian Rand provided exceptional support. Routledge published many of the books I have returned to again and again in my academic career, and I am proud to be part of their tradition of scholarship.

Next, I acknowledge some of the truly outstanding mentors I have had. Many of them were at University of Michigan, and are part of the strong tradition that university has in political science, policy, and planning. All treated me as colleagues long before I was one, and that is a rare thing. Elisabeth Gerber provided essential motivation and a critical eye for my ruminations, even when they likely held little of substance. Without exaggeration, I can say that I would have had neither the intelligence nor the confidence to write a book without her support. Whatever positive reputation I have as a scholar and teacher in the future will be directly attributable to her sound advice, probing questions and comments, and exemplary work ethic.

Scott Campbell gave me a deep appreciation for the value of a good theory grounded in real lives. I realized only after completing the book that my impulse to focus on individuals and how they think was in part due to his approach to theory. His knowledge was expansive, and he was willing to push my thinking in new and better directions. He also asked a question early on—*But does this really inform the field of planning?*—that forced me to make some connections I might not have otherwise, and that encouraged me to think frequently about my audience and my theoretical framework. Richard Norton became a mentor late in the development of the ideas behind this book, but he always showed a willingness to be available, even when I transitioned into the professoriate. His background in law and planning meant that our conversations were often especially resonant—to use a colloquial expression, he seemed to "speak my language." Jonathan Levine has always been a thinker who manages to be challenging and complex but also exceedingly lucid, and I hope that my writing one day approaches the quality of his. Jonathan was the first planning scholar I met and the first whose work I read, and despite never formally being his student the clarity and rigor of his scholarship have taught me a great deal already. I also owe a unique debt of gratitude to his wife, Noga—another stellar thinker and writer—who encountered me as a law student, at a time when I had interests in environmental, land use, business, and tax law (an unusual combination, I am sure). Somehow these all cohered around a general concern with how governments work and how they create our lived realities through institutions. Noga had the wisdom to suggest that I consider graduate studies in planning at University of Michigan, where her husband was at the time the departmental chair.

Several other faculty and staff were influential or inspirational during my years at the University of Michigan. Lan Deng encouraged me to pursue doctoral studies, and gave me some of my first opportunities to experience research and teaching. Rob Franzese, Megan Reif, and Giselle Kolenic provided me the serious guidance I needed in quantitative methods—something that long intimidated me. Ann Lin trained me in implementation and governance, and my ability to be nimble and interdisciplinary in my approach to understanding how local governments and metropolitan governance function must be credited both to what she taught and how she thought about it. Several other people in the Urban and Regional Planning Department, in Taubman College, and at the University of Michigan made my life a little easier. Lisa Hauser, Stacey Shimones, Laura Brown, Janice Harvey, Jeanette Turner, and Beverly Walter deserve a thank you for helping me navigate the bureaucracy of academia and—remarkably, I think—for always being friendly while doing so. Nicole Scholtz made solving seemingly complicated GIS and spatial data problems an odyssey that was fun; I do not use that term lightly. The same was true of all the library staff members who tolerated my questions.

The work that started in Michigan was finished at Virginia Tech, where I was fortunate to enter a department, college, and university peopled with colleagues who I already count as friends. I felt welcome from the start. Anne Khademian, the director of the School of Public and International Affairs (SPIA), has consistently been a gracious and accessible leader. In the Urban Affairs and Planning program, I have been lucky to work with outstanding senior and junior faculty (in alphabetical order, for the sake of equanimity): David Bieri, John Browder, Ralph Buehler, Maggie Cowell, Ralph Hall, Steve Hankey, Ted Koebel, Shelley Mastran, Shalini Misra, Elizabeth Morton, John Provo, John xx *Acknowledgments*

Randolph, Tom Sanchez, Todd Schenk, Max Stephenson, Kris Wernstedt, Diane Zahm, and Yang Zhang. If my work is anywhere nearly good as your contributions, I will be happy. Leigh Bower, Chris LaPlante, Krystal Wright, Leslie Day, Han Le, and Gale and Caleb all provide essential support—often including very fun conversations—that can easily get overlooked. Patricia Nickel and Joyce Rothschild, faculty in SPIA, helped me ease into my first year. Tripp Shealy and Travis Mountain started at Virginia Tech at the same time I did, and have been both friends and collaborators across disciplinary boundaries. Hopefully the grant funding will soon flow abundantly to our many ideas. I was also welcomed not long after joining Virginia Tech as a Faculty Fellow at the Global Forum on Urban and Regional Resilience. I owe Jennifer Lawrence for connecting me with this group of fine scholars, and I owe Jim Bohland for having the faith to take me on and include me in interesting projects that I hope will bear much fruit. The students, staff, and other faculty at the Forum have created an environment for innovative, collaborative, and applied scholarship that is remarkable. My thinking is already better for being part of it.

My students—both at Michigan and at Virginia Tech—have been a constant source of inspiration and ideas. I did not come across the insights of cultural theory by spending countless hours in a library or happening to see a conference presentation by an anthropologist or sociologist. Rather, I was discussing the early ideas for my theoretical framework with a public health student who happened to be reading Mary Douglas' classic *Purity and Danger*. From that conversation I would quickly make the leap to Douglas' work with Aaron Wildavsky, and eventually construct a bridge from these concepts to sociological institutionalism. This book would likely look much different, and might not even exist at all, if not for that conversation. I always found it enjoyable to talk to students, but that exchange gave me a steadfast appreciation for the synergy of teaching, advising, and research. I have had countless interactions with students that tweaked my thinking in ways big and small, and I hope to have many more.

Being a rather private person, I was never the type to pass drafts of chapters around for comment and critique, and I am sure that many will be surprised to learn I did not use my students as research assistants in this effort. Assuming I have more than one book in me, I plan to attempt to travel a less isolated path next time. There were a few exceptions to my hermit-like approach to the project. One was Sarah Pybus-Elmore, an undergraduate student assigned to work with me during my first summer at Virginia Tech through the university's Multicultural Academic Opportunities Program. She was diligent, thoughtful, and affable, even when given tasks that were probably not very stimulating. I am excited to see where she directs her talents and ambitions. Another was Alex Berryman, a 2017 graduate of the Master of Urban and Regional Planning program, and an excellent legal researcher and student. Lastly, a quick mention of the Urban Affairs Association (UAA), which helped me get out of my scholarly bubble and test my ideas in a broad community of scholars. The annual conferences have been uniformly stimulating and enjoyable experiences. This was

Acknowledgments   xxi

true when I was a student, and it became even truer once I transitioned into life as an assistant professor. Through UAA I have come to know a group of scholars that exemplifies what it means to be interdisciplinary and supportive.

Before I turn to the acknowledgments of my friends and family, I want to quickly mention some people who have provided motivation at a time it was sorely needed. I am sure they did not realize their impact, but this should not diminish it. A few have already been mentioned above. Martin Murray went above and beyond to offer encouragement and insight at a critical juncture, and I am still deeply grateful for that. Jered Carr, Annette Steinacker, and Antonio Tavares, during their time as editors at *Urban Affairs Review*, showed interest in my work that gave me a big boost of confidence. Jack Lucas, who I refer to as my "conference buddy" at the annual UAA gatherings, entered the academy at the same time I did, in the Department of Political Science at University of Calgary (I will also use this space to give a shameless plug to his research, which is both methodologically and theoretically interesting, and completely accessible). He suggested that a book was not the daunting task I had always imagined, and that same day I contacted Routledge to inquire about the possibilities of publishing with them.

These last few years I have started and maintained (miraculously!) friendships I hope will continue long into the future. They have enriched my life with unexpected happiness, kindness, and fun. Matt, Nghi, David W., Cooper, Nick, Ian, David E., Wonhyung, Neha, Paul, and Deirdra: you and your families made academic life bearable with commiseration, hospitality, and conversation. Nina David, your work helped spark my interest in regional governance in Michigan; thank you for clearing a lot of the path for me. Nolan, Kimiko, and Lisa: distance and life have meant that we sometimes go months without communicating, but I always feel when I see each of you that no time has passed at all. In the future I hope the quantity of our time together matches the quality. Rick and Tara, Susan and Brandon, Sarah and Ken, Alexis, Jason, Jessica and Ezra, Diana and Matt, and members of The Book Club That Shall Not Be Named: you have all been thoughtful and generous and hilarious and just basically wonderful these past several years, and being able to think about our happy times together often made writing a little more bearable.

Lauren and Adam, and Laura and Stephen, and all your children: as I get a little older and a little wiser (but still not much) I'm realizing just how rare it is to find people you can just be yourself around and to have friends who feel like family, and how much that makes all the other parts of life better. I never expected to have that, and it has meant more than you probably know. I realize I have not been good at reaching out across distance, but I doubt you'd hold that against me.

Finally, and most importantly, I acknowledge my family. Since this is my first book, I am going to be unrepentantly sappy and readers are welcome to move along to the first chapter (if they have not already). My father, Thomas Richard Skuzinski, passed away several years ago, and never had the chance to see me become a doctor, or an assistant professor, or an author. I know each of

xxii *Acknowledgments*

those milestones would have meant a great deal to him. He never scoffed at my long and tortuous educational road. He never discouraged me. I like to think he knows what is happening in my life, and is content about it. Rita Carolyn (Huber) Skuzinski, my mother and the original Dr. Skuzinski, always understood me better than anyone, and many times gave me the inner resolve not to give up even in the face of difficulties that seemed insurmountable. I understand better now how hard it can be to know your life is not just for yourself but for the people you love, and I have a deep respect for how well she managed being so much to so many people, especially her family. Being able to help take care of her during the past several years was unexpected and has not been easy, but it has helped me to appreciate what matters most in life. Elvira Skuzinski, my sister, has made far too many sacrifices for family in her life, and many of those were for me. I hope the future brings her many rewards, that I can be instrumental in helping her realize them, and that I get to see her enjoy them. My mother, father, and sister all inspired me to dream big while letting me know I would never be a failure no matter the outcome. This is no easy task, and I will always live with a sense of gratitude for having that kind of support.

And I acknowledge Michael Wise, my husband, my best friend, my better half, my most steadfast anchor, my strongest support, my inspiration, and my future. You have brought a sense of happiness and calm to my life that I never had, and you have helped me be a better person and scholar just by being present. The next time we're at the beach, I won't be working on a book!

1 Introduction

The township ... possesses two advantages which strongly excite the interest of mankind: namely, independence and authority.

— Alexis de Tocqueville (2000)

Opting Out

In late January 2015, Detroit once again made the news. Michigan residents, and soon after people around the world, heard the story of James Robertson, the "Walking Man." The nickname was well-earned. A resident of Detroit, nearly half of his commute to a factory shift at a suburban industrial park 23 miles away was made on foot: roughly 21 miles of the 46-mile round trip. The last miles on the return trip were traversed on foot from 1:35 a.m., bringing the 56-year-old home near 4 a.m. The next day's commute started with an 8 a.m. bus ride. Placed end-to-end, his daily commutes could have taken him from Detroit to Los Angeles each year, and nearly half of the trip would have been trekked (Graham, 2015; Laitner, 2015). Despite the daily obstacle, Robertson had a perfect attendance record over a dozen years, a record maintained through the rain, heat, and the often-brutal Michigan winters. He was the embodiment of perseverance.

Part of the short-term fix for Robertson was, perhaps not surprisingly in the Motor City, a car. This was the quintessential "band-aid" solution—the easy fix that deals with a symptom without addressing the underlying disease. Many residents of Detroit do not have a car: the city is ranked consistently in the top ten in the nation in the share of households without access to a vehicle (Laitner, 2015). Robertson now had a way to get to and from work, but many other Detroiters were still commuting to the suburbs from a city hemorrhaging jobs. Like Robertson, they often had to traverse transit "dead zones," waiting for infrequent bus connections, or trying to piece together a commute from public services that were continually pared down and restructured (Didorosi, 2015).

Robertson was front-page news and his story, even viewed in isolation, was compelling. But it was made more salient because his journey, and the journeys of others like him, were a symbol of all that was broken about Detroit—a distillation of the inequities that had resulted from race and class segregation, the massive disinvestment and spatial relocation of industry, and the crippling of a

2   *Introduction*

public sector with declining own-source and intergovernmental resources. Robertson's story highlighted a harsh question that had been asked for decades: how could it be that one of America's great cities and metropolitan areas, whose history was tied to the dream of conquering spatial barriers through mobility, had become so broken that a working-class Black man was spending hours every day traversing to and from work via a patchwork of busing and his own foot power?

Like many Detroiters, Robertson had to rely on a transportation system that lagged far behind those of other major cities in its coverage and reliability. Detroit has no metropolitan transit system. The Detroit Department of Transportation provides busing within city borders, while the Suburban Mobility Authority for Regional Transportation (SMART) covers Macomb County, Oakland County, and non-Detroit suburbs in Wayne County with fixed route and small bus services. But SMART is unique: unlike every other metropolitan transportation system in the United States, it allows suburban communities to opt out of participating (Henderson, 2015). In 51 suburbs, households do not have SMART bus service within the local boundaries, but they also do not have to pay a millage that amounts to $100 a year for a household with a home worth $200,000 (Lawrence & Gallagher, 2015). Of course, in a highly fragmented region with more than 200 general-purpose local governments, a resident could easily live in one location and ride from another. But the system, as a whole, was made highly inefficient and ineffective because of the patchwork of service. It was also inequitable. James Robertson's commute was a prime example of this: it required crossing through five suburbs, and the final suburb where his job was located was the opt-out suburb of Rochester Hills.

The story of Walking Man was, from a political and policy perspective, well-timed. The next year, 2016, would have a presidential election in November, and Michigan's Regional Transit Authority (RTA) could use the higher turnout to push a vote on a millage for a new metropolitan transit plan—a plan that would remove the option for opting out. The millage would add an additional tax of $120 per year for the family with a $200,000 home, atop the taxes paid already to fund the SMART system. The RTA had been created in 2012 to coordinate and improve transit in Wayne, Oakland, Macomb, and Washtenaw counties. Over the next 18 months, RTA officials would finalize a comprehensive transit plan focused mainly on bus rapid transit, and attempt to sell it to voters in the suburbs. As November neared, polling showed that the vote on the RTA millage would be a dead heat. It was: voters in the four counties barely rejected it, by fewer than 20,000 votes (Witsil & Lawrence, 2016). James Robertson had even participated in a documentary to encourage people to vote "yes," but it was not enough (Laitner, 2016).

Mere days before James Robertson's extraordinary commute hit the news, a crowd of concerned residents of Flint, Michigan—a city an hour north-northwest of Detroit that was the birthplace of General Motors (GM)—brought bottles and jugs of discolored drinking water to a public forum (Stafford, 2015). For the past nine months, residents had been complaining of rashes, nausea, and other health

Introduction 3

problems from the water since the city had started using the Flint River as a source—a river that had been for decades an industrial dumping ground for GM (Guile, 2015). The protest was not just the culmination of months of frustration, but was a direct response to Jerry Ambrose, a state-appointed emergency financial manager, turning down an offer from the Detroit Water and Sewerage Department (DWSD) to reconnect to its water (Err, 2015). Less than two years earlier, another emergency manager, Ed Kurtz, had pushed for the city to abandon its long-term DWSD contract and join a new regional water authority, the Karegnondi Water Authority (KWA), as a cost-cutting measure. There was one problem: the KWA pipeline was not finished. In the interim, Kurtz unilaterally decided the city would treat its own water from the Flint River (Fonger, 2015a). Workers neglected to change the additives used to treat the water after the switch; the additives were designed to prevent highly acidic water from corroding the legacy lead pipes common not just in Flint but in countless cities nationwide (Kennedy, 2016). Pipes that were benign conduits for water from DWSD would, with improperly treated water from the Flint River, become sources of highly toxic lead and other contaminants. The world would, over the ensuing months, once again learn of a crisis from southeast Michigan, but this time the effects were being felt by the residents of an entire city instead of just a single man, and they would compound long into the future. Policy decisions made, ostensibly at least, as an attempt to save costs had resulted in one of the most notorious and costly public crises in U.S. history.

Multiple national, state, and local actors—from city elected officials and emergency managers to bureaucrats in Michigan's Department of Environmental Quality and the U.S. Environmental Protection Agency—could claim part of the blame for the tragedy. But Flint's demography and history meant the water crisis quickly became about much more than a problem of ineffectual public administration, a flawed state–local relationship, and the failure of regulatory oversight. In a city with a history that made it the quintessential boom–bust, single-industry town of the Rust Belt, the water crisis was the latest unfortunate chapter in a decades-long story of decline permeated with themes of social injustice.

The non-response to all the warning signs in Flint was viewed, rightly, as the most visible symptom of pervasive, structural inequities in the implementation of federal, state, and local policies. In January 2016, Democratic presidential candidate Hillary Clinton remarked, "if the kids in a rich suburb of Detroit had been drinking contaminated water ... there would've been action" (Acosta, 2016). Michael Moore, the documentary filmmaker who had first gained notoriety for chronicling the rapid rise and tragic decline of the city—his birthplace—through the lens of corporate abandonment, noted that the water crisis simply would have never happened in Bloomfield or Ann Arbor or any of the Grosse Pointes, all municipalities considered part of Detroit's expansive suburban fabric (Moore, n.d.).

But Moore and Clinton did not even need to look that far away to make such assertions. The water crisis was not happening in places like Grand Blanc, Swartz Creek, or Flint Township, which are a few of the more than two dozen

4   *Introduction*

suburbs ringing Flint in Genesee County (Fonger, 2015b). A short five- or ten-minute drive from the Flint River could carry one to neighborhoods outside Flint's municipal boundaries where the water was still supplied through the DWSD. When GM became concerned about the water from the Flint River being too corrosive for manufacturing processes, it switched to suburban Flint Township's water, which was still from the DWSD. When residents in the localities surrounding Flint became concerned, understandably, that they were also drinking toxic water, the commissioner for Genesee County—the county in which Flint and its 26 suburban neighbors sit—was quick to point out that all the suburbs were still being supplied by the DWSD or wells (Fonger, 2015b; Gould, 2015). These suburbs had never been assigned an emergency manager, and they were not being forced into austerity policies. The suburbs are not all stable or growing bastions of the region's white, upper-class residents, but they were places of relative stability and wealth. Genesee County as a whole has suffered over the past quarter century, but Flint bore the brunt of this decline.

As often as the twin problems of racism and neoliberalism are brought up as explanations for Flint's troubles, another "-ism"—localism—has to bear some of the load. Localism is, most simply, the normative commitment to affording local governments—especially municipalities—a well-defined sphere of authority and territorial integrity. It is a commitment that was made in Michigan, as it was in many states, through the loosening of incorporation requirements, the provision of "home rule," and incremental statutory reforms that would make it difficult for one local jurisdiction to impose boundary changes on another. To appreciate how localism was at the root of Flint's woes, we must head back in time to the mid-twentieth century. Sixty years before the water crisis, an unusual collaboration between academics, city officials, and big business pushed hard for local government reform in Genesee County (Highsmith, 2014). The proposal was audacious: Flint would join with several of its municipal neighbors and incorporate as New Flint. Except for some major victories in the nation's largest metropolitan regions in the late nineteenth century, such large-scale territorial restructuring was as rare in that era as it is today. The reform would not be the joining together of one city and one county, a common form of centralization, but would instead require that multiple local governments merge together.

According to Andrew Highsmith, who has extensively chronicled the history of Flint (2009; 2014; 2015), the motivation for New Flint was simple. GM had in the past decade pursued a suburban strategy because of the lack of sufficiently large tracts of land for the new factories that would continue to modernize operations. Scholars in recent decades have been trying to understand the nature of city–suburb interdependence, with the classic view of suburban dependence on the central city being challenged by those who assert the relationship of dependence runs in the opposite direction (Post & Stein, 2000; Hill, Wolman, & Ford, 1995). But there was no question about this relationship for Flint and its suburbs in the first half of the twentieth century. Flint's water—water that came from the same river at the heart of the crisis decades later—was once the lifeblood of suburban economic development and rapid growth in Genesee County. All the usual

Introduction   5

culprits—the expansion of mortgage credit, the national security-based promotion of decentralization, the subsidization of basic systems infrastructure expansion—would encourage suburban development. But it was the provision of city water beyond city boundaries that provided a fortuitous resolution to the intractable suburban tension of trying to assert independence from the city while providing quality services in the absence of scale economies and higher tax rates. City officials, adhering to an understandably pro-GM policy stance, were unfortunately also encouraging the flight of capital and residents from the city. Flint's water was a source not only of corporate welfare but also suburban welfare. Throughout the early twentieth century, the suburbs were the place from which one hoped to escape, while the city was home to the metaphorically greener pastures. At the time of the New Flint proposal, the suburbs—aided by GM's investments and Flint water—were finally emerging from their history as rural slums (Highsmith, 2014).

The regional moment was extinguished, unusually, by a court ruling that found technical fault with the language of the consolidation proposal. We can never know how a public referendum would have played out, but polling at the time suggested defeat was inevitable (Zimmer & Hawley, 1956). The New Flint effort and its organizers had been so battered by suburban opposition that subsequent attempts at expanding Flint's territorial footprint were never made again. Had New Flint actually come into being, GM's newer plants would have still been centrally located economic assets within the larger consolidated metro. Even if the exact same out-migration had occurred in Genesee County over the next half-century away from Flint's central neighborhoods, a regional government would have meant that the movement of firms and households would not have been also a loss of tax base. The Flint region may have declined eventually with global economic restructuring intensifying in the 1980s, but the central city likely would not have had to travel the same steep and irreversible path toward concentrated unemployment, poverty, insolvency, receivership, and—eventually—public health crisis. Highsmith goes further in emphasizing the importance of the New Flint moment for the future of the region:

> had area residents succeeded in their quest to implement a metropolitan government, then the city of Flint would have remained an industrial powerhouse through the close of the twentieth century and beyond. The decision to reject New Flint ... had extraordinary implications for the city's economic fate.
>
> (2014, p. 33)

Governing Metropolitan Regions

The resistance to New Flint and the struggles to achieve regional transportation in Metro Detroit are both examples of failures in metropolitan governance.[1] In each narrative, the local motivation to "opt out" would have serious short-term and long-term consequences for the health and welfare of citizens in the broader

6 *Introduction*

region. Many problems stem from local governments planning and making policy decisions irrespective of broader regional interests, and scholars have been tracing these since the early twentieth century. In recent decades, the tension between local and regional interests has shown through in literature on jobs–housing imbalance (Cervero, 1989; Holzer, 1991; Horner, 2004; Ihlanfeldt & Sjoquist, 1998), the spread of property devaluation during the foreclosure crisis (Wassmer, 2011; Li & Morrow-Jones, 2010; Immergluck, 2011), the potential dependence between suburbs and central cities (Savitch, Collins, Sanders, & Markham, 1993; Blair & Zhang, 1994; Hill et al., 1995; Post & Stein, 2000), persistent race and class segregation (De Souza Briggs, 2005; Jargowsky, 1997; Marcuse, 1997), and the more generalized notion of impaired metropolitan resilience in response to crisis (Swanstrom, Chapple, & Immergluck, 2009). While the stories from southeast Michigan can be read as chapters in the distressingly long novel of metropolitan problems and impaired city–suburb and suburb–suburb relationships that have long plagued the region—and many other regions—they can also be read as illustrations of many of the institutional dynamics that characterize government in metropolitan areas in the U.S.

First, metropolitan areas are characterized by a high degree of balkanization. Simply put, they have many local political jurisdictions within their boundaries. While some metropolitan regions in the western U.S., such as Las Vegas, only have a handful of general-purpose local governments, these are exceptional; most regions have hundreds. The three most urbanized counties in the Detroit region—Wayne County, Oakland County, and Macomb County—contain 133 municipalities that enjoy well-defined autonomy over a wide range of public services. In the seven-county Detroit–Warren–Dearborn metropolitan statistical area, land use is fragmented among 211 general-purpose governments. In the 11-county Detroit–Warren–Ann Arbor combined statistical area that number grows to 327. According to 2016 census estimates, the 15 largest U.S. metropolitan statistical areas contained one-third of the national population—nearly 108 million people—and had almost 3,000 municipalities.[2]

Fragmentation is a reality even in metropolitan areas that have been touted as successes of regional governing. The highly elastic cities praised by David Rusk, where liberal annexation laws and an abundance of unincorporated land have encouraged rapid growth and continued dominance of the central city, still have enclave or island municipalities within the central city boundaries, and a growing number of incorporated suburbs at the municipal edge that can more readily resist annexation (Rusk, 1993). San Antonio, for example, was 36 square miles in 1930, 160 square miles by 1960 (outstripping Detroit despite having less than a third of that city's population at the time), and 465 square miles in 2015—with plans for continued expansion.[3] Despite this growth, the city still has more than 50 suburbs, seven contained within its municipal boundaries. New York City, which achieved a territorial scope roughly consistent with its economic and social imprint through a massive, five-county consolidation in 1898 that brought about the familiar five-borough system, would in a matter of years develop suburbs outside even its new boundaries. Today it has more than 600 suburbs

Introduction 7

across three states that have a high degree of social and economic integration with it. Indianapolis, the last major city to consolidate with its surrounding county, Marion County, has four "excluded municipalities" that exist as islands within the consolidated area; several other municipalities retain some of their government functions. In Portland, which is well-known for its regional Metro Council and urban growth boundary meant to curb sprawl, a Metropolitan Study Commission in 1966 did not originally recommend merely a metropolitan services district with some ability to coordinate planning, but rather a charter for a single municipality scaled to a greater Portland Urban Area. The goal, at that juncture, was a three-county consolidation akin to what had last happened six decades earlier in New York City, but this was strongly resisted by Salem and other suburbs. All these metropolitan areas are regularly looked to as exemplars of the waves of regionalism that have swept through the U.S. (Wallis, 1994), but in all fragmentation remains.

Second, the local units into which metropolitan areas are splintered tend to have a well-defined sphere of authority and territorial integrity. Scholars have long debated the actual extent of local autonomy, which is "the ability of people within distinct small areas to decide for themselves by democratic means the matters that fall within the competence of local authority" (Briffault, 1996, p. 1115). Some suggest local autonomy is quite expansive (Briffault, 1990a; Cashin, 1999) while others propose local governments are actually quite constrained in the policies they can choose and have been pushed into a practice of defensive localism (Barron & Frug, 2005). While these discussions provide some necessary nuance to our understanding of the state–local relationship, it is indisputable that most municipalities—and in particular the small suburb—enjoy a vastly superior legal position to the one they would have had a century ago. The sheer number of municipalities and the success of their resistance to regional reforms is itself supportive of this assertion.

No unbreakable constitutional commitment has been made to the primacy of local governments, or even to their existence. Their strength and integrity, rather, is the result of decisions made by state governments over the last 150 years to prioritize a vision of the U.S. as a confederation of small towns that could serve as a refuge from the perceived or actual negative qualities of the big city. States determine the legal ability of communities to incorporate, to attain home rule status, to annex nearby land or guard against annexation by a neighboring jurisdiction, to exercise jurisdiction outside their territorial boundaries, to form special single- or multi-purpose governments to fund the provision and production of specific public services, and to consolidate or merge with other communities. States also specify the ability of their constituent local units to raise own-source revenues, the way in which state-level revenues will be shared with these units, and the list of mandated services a local jurisdiction must provide or produce.[4] Local governments may, legally, remain creatures of the state, but the states have been highly solicitous of their independence.

Despite the commitment to polycentrism and localism in state laws, and despite the evident willingness of many local governments to use their autonomy

8 *Introduction*

to "opt out" of the region, many find ways to "opt in." They might do this through fiscal and administrative participation in broader regional planning and policy initiatives, or through acquiescence in structural reforms such as consolidation or annexation, or through working jointly with neighboring local jurisdictions on an ad hoc basis. It is this surprising persistence of opting in that is the third dynamic of metropolitan areas highlighted in the stories from southeastern Michigan.

Even in institutional settings that would seem to discourage large-scale planning and policymaking, we can discern spaces carved out in state law for regional governance—usually through piecemeal statutes that enable consolidation, annexation, and interlocal cooperation, or the incorporation of these into home rule provisions—and we see ongoing attempts by the public and their local representatives to take advantage of these spaces. The impulse to opt-in might be faint, but it is almost always present.

Consider consolidation. Successful consolidations are infrequent, the referendum campaigns are often rancorous, and the evidence is mixed about whether consolidations yield efficiency or accountability or a civic ethos. Still, citizens and local officials continue to attempt to put consolidation on the agenda, and are sometimes successful in their efforts (Marando, 1979; Carr & Feiock, 2004). Even in the failures, consolidation rarely loses decisively. Margins of victory are often ten points or less. Or consider annexation: it continues apace wherever it is allowed to thrive, exceeding by orders of magnitude the land area of the municipalities that are able to resist it. Large-scale regional land use and environmental planning efforts have occurred for decades in many metropolitan areas. Voluntary interlocal cooperation is quite common, and while it is most often used to target systems maintenance functions it is sometimes used to reach beyond these to lifestyle services such as land use regulation.[5] Contrary to the more negative assessments of the potential for regional governance (Downs, 1994; Norris, 2001), I view it as an impulse that arises remarkably persistently given the current state–local legal landscape.

Metropolitan governance, then, is shaped directly by local governments and the decisions made by their residents and public officials about how to use the grants of authority provided through state laws. While we could readily characterize the metropolitan areas in the U.S. as exceedingly polycentrist and localist, attempted and successful voluntary regional reforms remain a prominent feature. The question is: why? Why do the elected and administrative officials and residents in some municipalities readily participate in regionalizing reforms while others resist them?

The Legitimacy of Reform

In *The Risk of Regional Governance*, I propose that a local offical is driven by the logic of *appropriateness* to develop preferences and choose actions that are most legitimate according to the institutional characteristics—the regulative, normative, and cultural[6] characteristics—of the context in which the local actor

Introduction 9

is embedded. The desire for appropriateness leads to a *rational legitimizing* cognitive process, in which the chief concern is *not* solely with balancing material gains and losses—whether to the jurisdiction, the public, or to the local official individually. Sometimes the desire for legitimacy *will* lead the actor to economize: in other words, to opportunistically choose the government form that provides the greatest net joint and selective gains relative to the costs of transacting with other jurisdictions. This would seem especially likely, for example, when a local administrative actor is confronted with a decision about whether to contract with a neighboring jurisdiction for basic service provision, such as wastewater treatment or snow clearance.

But for some policy domains under some circumstances, the logic of appropriateness will allow an actor's values and beliefs—what we can term their *cultural worldview*—to dominate. This will occur where the actor's ability to internalize clear prescriptions from regulative and normative institutions is diminished, either because the signal from these institutions is weak or because the local official is not capable of being an effective receiver of these signals. However, no matter how imperfect that regulative and normative signaling, the local official will still be able to draw on cultural prescriptions that an actor can bring into any social situation. These prescriptions—which at base indicate the actor's biases about solidarity (as opposed to individualism) and equality (as opposed to differentiation)—provide strong heuristics with which to determine whether a policy is culturally right and good.

Under this logic, some actors will, as de Tocqueville posits in the opening quote of this chapter, be "strongly excited" by the independence and authority of the township, city, village, or other local jurisdictional unit. But those with affinities for solidarity and equanimity will be strongly excited by the prospect of treating boundaries not as fortress walls but as "picket fences" across which to extend a neighborly hand (Chen & Thurmaier, 2008; Thurmaier & Wood, 2002). And other local officials will fall somewhere between these extremes, finding only weak cultural excitement in the organization of government. But even that may be enough to predict their preferences about and behavior toward cooperation if it is strong enough to dominate regulative and normative signals.

I refer to this framework as *sociocultural collective action*. The use of the term "collective action" signals that my concern is not with mere coordination among local governments but rather with cooperation used to address true dilemmas in which the interests of a single individual or organization are in tension with group interests. It is the same articulation of collective action employed in the rich theoretical and empirical work of Mancur Olson and Elinor Ostrom, among many others.

Readers familiar with the evolution of institutionalism over the last several decades will recognize the logic I describe as being grounded in sociological institutionalism, a branch of new institutionalism. For the sociological institutionalist, change (or stasis) is guided not by a technical or material rationality that forms and reforms institutions—such as local and metropolitan governance—as instrumental means leading to certain ends. Rather, a social rationality based

10 *Introduction*

on values and interpretation is what will provide the most explanatory purchase in making sense of policy decisions, or any decisions in a social setting. As described by DiMaggio and Powell, "[t]he new institutionalism in organizational theory and sociology comprises a rejection of rational-actor models, an interest in institutions as independent variables, [and] a turn toward cognitive and cultural explanations" (1991, p. 8).

Developing a cultural explanation is critical. As I describe in the next section, and at other points in *The Risk of Regional Governance*, the prevailing model for how regionalizing reforms occur has a well-articulated normative narrative grounded in rational choice guided by transaction cost economizing. But if the communication of normative economizing signals to local officials is hindered, and if we can reasonably assume that local officials will only choose legal actions that have literal regulative legitimacy, then officials will have to rely on internalized prescriptions drawn from their cultural worldviews. These worldviews are not simply ad hoc subjective beliefs or values. In the same way that rules and norms are institutional expressions of social relations that occur in a specific organizational setting, such as a local government, cultural worldviews develop from social relations that occur over a lifetime and across a wide variety of settings. This understanding of culture comes from cultural theory, which "rejects … the isolated actor in the social science literature" and "argues that discrete beliefs cannot float freely because they are too closely tied to the social relations they legitimate" (Grendstad & Selle, 1995, p. 10).

Thus, I do not just insist that cultural worldviews matter or treat them as exogenous, immutable affectations. Rather, I treat them as institutional constraints that develop over a lifetime of socialization and provide powerful heuristics capable of interjecting in any reasoning process. Actors do not just occupy positions within organizations; they occupy positions within their cultural tribes, the broad social "organizations" which provide internalized prescriptions about what attitudes and behaviors are normal and good, regardless of—and perhaps in opposition to—our calculations of expected material utility. Importantly, internalized cultural prescriptions are discoverable through careful empirical investigation, whether through survey, interview, participant observation, or document analysis, in the same way that regulative and normative prescriptions are.

I highlight the *risk* of regional governance in the title of the book to help clarify the difference between legitimizing and economizing. Both modes of rationality can accommodate a view of risk as a subjective manifestation of uncertainty.[7] Economizing incorporates risk as a factor that diminishes net benefits in the calculation of utility, primarily through the unknowable future behaviors of other actors. Legitimizing recognizes that actors engage in amplification and diminution of risks based on whether those risks flow from actions that legitimate the institutions actors have internalized. For example, an actor would be more accepting of a political or economic risk that attaches to a policy reform if that reform is consistent with that actor's cultural dispositions.

Stated most succinctly, in *The Risk of Regional Governance* I propose that the driving question motivating a local actor's decisions about metropolitan

Introduction 11

governance is not *How do I optimize my material interests in this situation?* but rather *What is the appropriate response to this situation?* Sometimes that appropriate response will be grounded in material optimization because normative legitimizing provides the dominant institutional signal, but other times the response will be informed by different sources of legitimacy.

I have offered so far only a very brief sketch of the sociocultural collective action framework; I expand on it much more in Chapter 4. In the next section, I distinguish the sociocultural collective action framework from the prevailing explanation of metropolitan regionalizing reforms.

Reform as a Transaction

Most contemporary regionalists now start with governance rather than government as the goal (Feiock, 2007; 2009; Savitch & Vogel, 2000). "Gargantua"— the metropolitan area unified under a single government across all policy domains—is no longer the guiding construct for regional reformers as it once was (Wood, 1961; Gulick, 1957; Jones, 1942; Studenski, 1930). It has been replaced by a vision of the fragmented metropolis connected by an organizational network built through voluntary interlocal agreements, with these agreements capable of creating structural change or simply formalizing cooperative relationships.

These agreements are analogous, conceptually, to transactions in a metropolitan marketplace being made among highly rational decision-makers who are proxies for an organization. If we were to position this narrative in the broader landscape of social science theory, we would say that it is consistent with a rational choice institutionalist perspective (as opposed to the sociological institutionalist perspective I follow). Rational choice institutionalists, most simply, imagine a world in which individuals follow the logic of instrumentality with preferences and behaviors directed toward attaining well-defined material goals. The logic of instrumentality is grounded in transaction cost economizing and mediated by the formal rules and informal norms of the institutional environment. This perspective is at the heart of a theoretical framework most often termed *institutional collective action*, and I use this phrase as a referent throughout the book because it contrasts well with the name of my own framework.

Rational choice institutionalism departs sharply in its model of individual cognition from earlier thin rational choice models. As described by Feiock, a leading progenitor of the last two decades of regional reform scholarship,

> [s]econd-generation rational choice models explicitly take the context of collective decisions into account. Simply saying context matters is not a satisfactory approach. In order to generate testable propositions, a rational choice explanation must systematically address how context matters in specific choice situations. ... How officials understand ... costs will depend on the context of the decision setting, including the characteristics of the good

12   *Introduction*

or service being considered, the configurations of political institutions under which they operate, and the networks of existing relationships among local government officials.

(Feiock, 2007, p. 48)

In accord with this recognition of the importance of the institutional context, in the paradigmatic study of interlocal cooperation as an economizing activity the unit of analysis is the local government and reform is determined by a wide array of *intra*local and *inter*local characteristics that we would reasonably expect to shape institutional dynamics. Local officials are modeled as boundedly rational optimizers (or possibly "satisficers," in the tradition of Herbert Simon). As much as environmental and cognitive limitations allow, actors will appraise the institutional setting and choose the form of governance that will bring the most net material benefit to the local government organization and, by extension, to them.

Ecological inference is critical in making the connection between decisions that are made by individuals but that bind the organization—here, the municipal corporation—to a specific policy path. We generally assume the individual decision-maker who will support or oppose cooperation—a city manager or city council member, for example—aligns his interests with those of the local government organization. As an agent of the local government organization, whatever is best for it will likewise be best for him. If he holds elected office, he would anticipate re-election or other political reward from his intelligent efforts to better municipal conditions. If he serves in bureaucracy, his actions should enhance job security or open up opportunities for promotion.

The institutional collective action theoretical framework has much to recommend it. It generates hypotheses that are highly testable, and—like the broader new institutionalist tradition in the social sciences—attempts to chart a path between methodological individualism and methodological collectivism. It differs from my framework mainly in how it characterizes the rationality of the actor (transaction cost economizing versus regulative, normative, and cultural legitimizing), in how it conceptualizes the relationship between individuals and institutions (mediation versus internalization), and in how it deals with the connections of the individual to the organization (a model of the organization as a proxy for the individual versus investigation of variation among individuals within the organization).

These are subtle theoretical differences, but they are not inconsequential. In the metropolitan governance context, reliance on an economizing model has left us in a position in which forward progress is highly difficult.

The Limitations of Economizing

If the metropolitan region is purely a product of economizing, then our cities and suburbs are faced with a bleak future and no clear path out of it. Rational choice institutionalism predicts that regionalizing reform will simply not be feasible or durable in many of the policy domains that are most directly tied to persistent

Introduction   13

metropolitan problems—domains like land use planning and regulation, economic development, or even public transportation that can be grouped under the umbrella of *lifestyle policies* (Williams, 1971). Instrumental, material rationality does not abide reform that is merely symbolic or hopeful or visionary. It demands the prospect of clear, divisible joint gains accruing to the local fisc. For local officials, economizing rationality would require not only a joint benefit that cooperating municipalities could not otherwise access, but also a benefit that flows divisibly and distinctly to their own jurisdiction, plus some well-founded prospect of individual-level benefit such as career gain, perhaps through re-election or promotion. In the language of collective action, working together requires both collective and selective incentives (Olson, 1965).

Even if the actors making decisions about regionalizing reforms are somehow convinced in their bounded, satisficing utilitarian world that these incentives will obtain, a further hurdle must be jumped. The gains must not be outweighed by the anticipated Coaseian costs of transaction (acquiring information, negotiating terms, and monitoring and enforcing compliance) (Coase, 1937; 1998), or the local officials must be reasonably sure that their formal agreements will, through the terms of the agreements, reduce transaction costs over time so that net benefits will accrue. These costs of working together are shaped both by rules and by the past informal and formal relationships between local governments and local officials that create powerful norms of exchange.

Lifestyle policies like land use planning and regulation do not fare well under this kind of calculus. In the absence of revenue-sharing (which is exceedingly rare), the gains from cooperation are tenuous, distant, diffuse and indivisible. Transaction costs are high because the stakes are high: negotiating over the appropriate diminution of autonomy in policy domains that are foundational to local fiscal health is quite difficult. Trust established through easier forms of cooperation—over activities like wastewater treatment, fire protection, or snow plowing—may not readily translate to more difficult forms. Reformist collective action in lifestyle policy domains is also often meaningful—in the sense of addressing trenchant metropolitan problems—only when it occurs among heterogeneous actors that vary in their socioeconomic or physical attributes. To really matter, regionalizing reforms must be able to happen among jurisdictions that are wealthy and poor, fiscally strong and fiscally weak, minority and White, low-density and high-density. This heterogeneity is thought to add significantly to transaction costs.

Moreover, the transactions made in lifestyle policy areas are not de-politicized administrative actions in which local elected officials are mere veto players. Political actors are typically central to the decision-making process, and this adds the burden of norms of political responsiveness to the utility calculus. For a local elected official, supporting cooperation—in a rational choice institutionalist perspective—likely requires taking a long view with regard to the gains of collective action because short-term benefits may not be highly visible. It demands, further, having significant trust in how peers in prospective partner local governments will behave, or that those partners can be persuaded to agree

14   *Introduction*

to substantial behavioral constraints as a substitute for trust. And, additionally, a local actor must believe constituents support reform (or would support it), or are at least indifferent about it, even in the face of highly uncertain gains.

The confluence of all these conditions is highly unlikely, and this renders voluntary reforms a rather weak species of regional governing. They flower only in the most hospitable of circumstances, and fade at the slightest adversity. Such reasoning supports the distinction regularly made by scholars of metropolitan governance between lifestyle functions and systems maintenance functions I have already noted (Williams, 1971; Norris, 2001a; 2001b).

This distinction has hardened over time into conventional wisdom, but it is not wisdom completely supported by empirical observation. If you are trained in planning, you know that regional planning, regional transportation, regional economic development, and other "regionalized" lifestyle functions are not passing fancies. These planning efforts can even sometimes translate into regulations that are also regionally oriented. Lifestyle services, I will grant, do *tend* still to be more localized than regionalized, but we should not as scholars be satisfied with explaining away regional gestures as irrational or aberrant (or, worse, inexplicable). They have endured as a feature of the metropolitan landscape for far too long to be dismissed so easily. Similarly, we should not be satisfied with becoming more and more adept at charting the landscape of metropolitan governance over systems maintenance functions, which is much of what has been occurring in recent decades. These functions are, obviously, part of the quality of life of metropolitan residents, but they are secondary to lifestyle functions. Arguably, the need to reach across jurisdictional and sectoral boundaries to maintain basic systems is, in fact, a result of the failure to rationalize lifestyle functions to a regional scale.

One part of my dissatisfaction with the rational choice institutionalist perspective, then, is that it suggests a metropolitan future in which the enduring problems of localism and parochialism are, even in theory, almost certain to endure in all but the most basic of public service domains. But regionalizing reform *does* happen even when there is no strong evidence to suggest it will be the most efficient or effective option, and it often endures without any ongoing system in place for monitoring whether its original goals are being met. This has happened with structural reforms such as consolidation, and it has happened with cooperation; I review some of this evidence in Chapter 3. The long history of regional reform is marked by occasions when residents and their local representatives showed support for experimenting with reforms that would be inexplicable or irrational under instrumental logic. The converse is also true: people sometimes oppose cooperation and other reforms when all available evidence suggests it would be advantageous. Opposition can even persist when cooperation is the only responsible way to provide for critical public services.

Moreover, when reform is put to a vote—whether among members of a legislative body or among the general public—the margins are often close, and the demographics of support and opposition do not readily fit into an economizing narrative. We cannot say, for example, that the wealthy, White homeowners in a

Introduction 15

jurisdiction—those who might rationally fear redistribution of resources or suffer the most dilution of political power under regionalizing reform—will be uniformly opposed to it. The more typical outcome is for preferences and behaviors to be quite mixed across demographic categories. The evidence provided in this book shows that local elected officials are similarly heterogeneous: even those from the *same* community serving in the *same* kind of position can vary in their preferences about governance reform.

The other limitation in the economizing account of regionalizing reforms is that it provides no ready policy recommendations. The institutional collective action perspective *does* have the advantage of acknowledging that institutions matter, but even if we know rules and norms—the extent of institutions in the economizing narrative—are preventing cooperation in a specific policy domain, experience suggests changing these institutions is either difficult or impossible. The rules of the game, crafted by state legislation and constitutions and their judicial interpretation, do not readily change. If we find that norms matter, these can often prove similarly difficult to overcome. Consider the problem of homophily—the normative tendency for like to cooperate with like because transaction costs are lower when two organizations or individuals are quite similar. In the metropolitan governance context, we expect regionalizing reforms to be more likely among similarly situated local jurisdictions with a similar portfolio of costs, benefits, and risks. But if we know homophily is key to cooperation, what is the policy response? Do we efficiently target efforts at encouraging reform only among those local government neighbors that exhibit homophily? If we do this for lifestyle functions, we chance simply rescaling and reifying the differentiating dynamics that have led to a pattern of income polarization and racial segregation. The wealthy, White, growing suburbs that happen to share boundaries, for example, should all be willing to cooperate with one another, under the logic of homophily. Certainly we cannot demand the redistribution of households and firms to create stable homogeneous jurisdictions among which homophily will exist, as the disparate spatial organization of the metropolitan area is part of *why* we need interlocal cooperation in the first place.

Other policy levers are similarly confounding, and those who study interlocal cooperation have occasionally recognized this reality (Feiock, Steinacker, & Park, 2009). While this state of affairs should lead to louder calls for centralizing interventions—or at least the provision by state governments of incentives for cooperation—such reforms would be an open acknowledgment of the limitations of abandoning government (the vision of gargantua described earlier) in favor of governance (which accepts polycentrism and localism).

In short, rational choice institutionalism and the economizing view of the metropolitan future have left us in a tricky spot. We can accept the status quo and hope that regional governance arises by happenstance—against all instrumentally rational odds—to conquer our most enduring metropolitan problems by targeting lifestyle services more persistently. Or, we can attempt to craft a theoretical framework that provides a more positive account of why regional reform that infringes meaningfully on local autonomy *does* sometimes happen,

16   *Introduction*

and that also provides us a menu of policy recommendations for fostering such behavior.

Sociocultural collective action, as I described earlier in the chapter and will elucidate and empirically defend in subsequent chapters, is my attempt to do just that. It is a framework designed, through its expansive conceptualization of institutions, to help us explore more thoroughly what happens when voluntary reform targets services for which economizing signals are unclear but other normative and cultural prescriptions are expected to be strong.

Theoretical Perspectives on Metropolitan Governance

Sociocultural collective action may also breathe new life into decades-old debates about metropolitan governance. Political scientists and scholars of public administration have long debated the optimal governance of metropolitan regions, and the battle has often been waged on ground that is more normative and theoretical than empirical. The evolution of the academic debate, which has been traced most recently by Norris (2016), has been mostly in-step with the changes to the state–local legal relationship that are the focus of Chapter 2.

I begin this section in the post-World War II era, a time in which suburbs, like those ringing Detroit, Michigan, were enjoying a heavily fortified position thanks to pre-war reforms in the state–local relationship and a concomitant population explosion due to an array of demographic, economic, and political factors (Jackson, 1985). Small suburban governments—which by that decade had started to dominate the regional landscape in number if not also in population and territory and whose acquiescence or even support now were necessary to any regionalizing efforts—became the focus of those concerned with metropolitan health. Regional reformers, many of whom still hoped to achieve metropolitan unity, refocused their attack at a key normative justification for the Progressive vision of small, administrative local units: they claimed that this small size and the fragmented metropolitan region it promoted were inefficient and ineffective, and that any one unit was too small to take on the burden alone of providing public goods on which the broader region could free ride (Jones, 1942; Gulick, 1957; Wood, 1958; 1961). Briffault (1996, pp. 1116–1119) provides a brief but excellent summary of the history of reform advocacy in the U.S. By one critical measure the reformers lost: full dissolution of pre-existing local autonomy at a metropolitan scale was rare (it remains so), and was always outpaced by subsequent metropolitan area growth. Even moderate reforms outside basic systems maintenance functions remain exceptional and politically unpopular (Danielson, 1976; Teaford, 1979; Rusk, 1993; Norris, 2001a).

Those who opposed the vision of the single metropolitan general-purpose government coalesced around the work of public choice theorists at Indiana University—the so-called Bloomington School of public choice, in contrast to variants developing in Rochester and Virginia (Mitchell, 1988). Led initially by the work of Vincent Ostrom and Charles Tiebout, and later by Elinor Ostrom

Introduction 17

and numerous other colleagues and peers (Tiebout, 1956; Ostrom, Tiebout, & Warren, 1961; Ostrom, Bish, & Ostrom, 1988), the public choice position is built on a foundation of economic competition as a driver of efficient and effective local public service delivery. Competition produces variety that can match the highly heterogeneous preferences—and ability to pay—of residents who are mobile "consumer-voters" (Tiebout, 1956, p. 419). It also creates efficiency by encouraging local governments to offer their unique bundles of services and goods at the lowest tax price possible. The primary mechanism linking residents to local officials, according to public choice theorists, is the threat of exit.

Public choice served as a rejoinder to the assertion that a single organization form—the unitary, general-purpose metropolitan municipality—would optimally serve all metropolitan areas. As described by Ostrom and Ostrom (1971, p. 211), the public choice perspective seems eminently reasonable:

> [T]he public choice tradition would anticipate that no single form of organization is good for all social circumstances. Different forms of organization will give rise to some capabilities and will be subject to other limitations. Market organization will be subject to limitations which will give rise to institutional weaknesses or institutional failure. Bureaucratic organization will provide opportunities to develop some capabilities and will be subject to other limitations. Those limitations will in turn generate institutional weakness or institutional failure if they are exceeded. A knowledge of the capabilities and limitations of diverse forms of organizational arrangements will be necessary for both the future study and practice of public administration.

The appeal of this perspective, in the context of metropolitan governance, is that the organization of governance in a specific policy domain could only endure as long as enough consumer-voters were satisfied with its efficiency and effectiveness (1971, pp. 211–212).[8] Public choice theorists also had remarkable faith in the capacity of the judiciary to intervene where a local unit's decisions were causing adverse consequences for neighbors or the region. Using California's regional water provision as an example, Ostrom and colleagues (1961, p. 841) remark:

> [t]he heavy reliance upon courts for the resolution of conflicts among local units of government unquestionably reflects an effort to minimize the risks of external control by a superior decision-maker. Court decisions are taken on a case-by-case basis. The adversaries usually define the issues and consequently limit the areas of judicial discretion. This method also minimizes the degree of control exercised following a judgment. [State] courts, in particular, have accepted the basic doctrines of home rule and are thus favorably disposed to the interests of local units of government in dealing with problems of municipal affairs.

18   *Introduction*

This faith in state courts, an outgrowth of the broader program in law and economics, is still promoted within legal scholarship (Gillette, 2001; 2005). I use the word "faith" because, as I discuss more in the concluding chapter and as will become clearer in Chapter 2, there is no evidence supporting a widespread willingness among jurists to rein in local autonomy.

The public choice theorists' reliance on the state judiciary and on a well-informed and highly involved public should not be diminished, but it often is as the theory is reduced to the simple mechanism of efficient foot-voting and preservation of efficiency-inducing local autonomy. What is overlooked is that much of metropolitan governance—the proliferation of special-purpose districts, the highly variable role of county governments, the cooperative interlocal and cross-sectoral agreements, and even the homeowner associations that together determine the quality of public services and the regional lived experience—remains invisible to the public. The assumptions of the Tiebout model are often questioned and shown to be flawed, but these were highly stylized, simplifying assumptions of a model that even Tiebout did not ardently defend as reflective of metropolitan reality. The more important and potentially flawed components of the public choice argument, in my view, are the assumptions about the capacity of the public and the judiciary to serve as gatekeepers who can monitor and reform poorly performing governance structures.

Such a system is most likely to break down where public services are tightly bound up with questions of interlocal differentiation and inequity. Swanstrom remarks that

> [t]he Achilles' heel of the public choice approach to metropolitan governance has always been the problem of inequality. Critics have long contended that the proliferation of local governments in metropolitan areas has reinforced segregation by income and race, resulting in unequal provision of local public goods and services.
>
> (2001, p. 482)

While some public choice theorists will respond by suggesting that this inequality is a function of preferences, it seems disingenuous to assert that those who are left living in ghettoes have been fully able to exercise their consumer vote (Frug, 1998; Cashin, 1999; Briffault, 1990a; 1990b). Others have suggested that these inequalities inevitably require redistribution, a function that has long been allocated in the fiscal federalism literature to higher levels of government. Apart from these mild responses, however, public choice has not adequately addressed its Achilles' heel.

The most recent development in the long academic engagement with the metropolitan region has been the rise of a "new regionalist" perspective beginning in the 1990s. The new regionalism has never acquired a steady core of central tenets. Parks and Oakerson describe it as a "mixed bag of old prescriptions and new remedies to address problems both new and longstanding" (2000, p. 169), and Neil Brenner, in attempting to "decode it," echoed this sentiment (2002).

Introduction 19

Reynolds (2003, p. 112), similarly, describes new regionalists as not having "a cohesive ideology with a well-accepted policy agenda." Still, a few consistencies can be discerned. First, new regionalists accept the endurance of local governments and fragmented metropolitan areas; they promote regional govern*ance* rather than regional govern*ment*. While they reject many of the normative arguments of the public choice theorists, most accept the local political and territorial landscape as it applies to general-purpose municipal governments. The preferred regionalizing reform is voluntary cooperation through intergovernmental and interlocal agreements.

New regionalists also chart a normative middle ground by attempting to appeal to both economy and equity at the same time. They tend to be concerned with the stronger place a healthy and resilient metropolitan region could have in a global economy (Barnes & Ledebur, 1997; Peirce, 1993). For them, this strength hinges on a reduction in interlocal disparities, especially between central cities and suburbs. Several scholars have attempted to promote a suburb–city dependence or interdependence hypothesis, albeit with mixed success (Blair et al., 1996; Savitch et al., 1993; Ledebur & Barnes, 1993). The city–suburb dependence and global competitiveness pieces of new regionalist scholarship attempt to show how the equitable region—the one without income polarization and race and class segregation, or more pointedly the one without ghettoes and enclaves—will also be a more economically efficient and effective region. Recalling the stories from earlier in this chapter, the region in which opting out occurs—a place like Metro Detroit, for example—cannot be a successful region.

While the new regionalists helped to bring fresh thinking and renewed attention to the question of metropolitan governance, what they did not do was address how inequality and inequity could be dealt with by supposedly self-interested local residents and representatives acting voluntarily. The kind of preference formation and behavior anticipated under transaction cost economizing, as I stated in the last section, would not extend to lifestyle services. Voluntary cooperation over land use planning and regulation are the holy grail of the many theorists—regionalists and localists alike—who accept the endurance of polycentrism and local autonomy. Land use is the only policy domain that is capable of truly confronting the multiple collective action dilemmas that plague metropolitan areas.

Research within the sociocultural collective action framework is designed to test of the limits of the public choice and new regionalist perspectives. If voluntary cooperation is not a viable path to regional planning and regulation of land use, as some assert strongly it is not (Norris, 2016), then regionalists must once again push state-level reforms to the laws governing local governments, or a more extreme return to direct state intervention in local governance and local boundary reforms.

20   *Introduction*

The Goals of the Book

While advocacy for a theoretical turn is at the heart of *The Risk of Regional Governance*, the book is motivated by practical concerns. If the legitimizing model I offer through the sociocultural collective action framework is correct, it has the potential to reinvigorate the conversation about how we address trenchant metropolitan problems through governance reforms. Policy domains that have only rarely been targeted by cooperation may be able to be accessed more frequently. Local and interlocal contexts that we would never expect to be able to nurture cooperation may, in reality, prove fertile. Acts of regional governance that seem like inexplicable historical accidents or simple examples of path dependency may be explicable through the lens of rational legitimizing. Perhaps most importantly, evidence of sociocultural collective action would call for so-called "soft" policy reforms that rely on cognition-targeting tactics such as informational framing. These have the distinct advantage of being politically viable where structural reforms have proven difficult.

Second, my framework puts a renewed focus on the individual within interlocal cooperation, and on the linkages between the individual and the local government organization. Formal agreements legally bind the municipality, but they are organizational and institutional outcomes produced by individuals. Surprisingly, the individual is regularly overlooked in extant studies of interlocal cooperation. The theoretical linkages between the individual and the organization are rarely treated theoretically, and they are never questioned empirically. Part of the reason why the mechanisms underlying individual–organizational alignment have not been subject to testing—at least not for interlocal cooperative decisions—is that their *conceptual* strength is very high for cooperative provision of systems maintenance functions, which as noted earlier in this chapter are also the more common targets of interlocal cooperation and its study.

But consider the multiple mechanisms that must function properly for individual–institutional alignment to occur with regard to the local *elected* official, who is pivotal to cooperation over lifestyle functions.[9] One possibility is that a local elected official is a technocrat who defines serving the public interest as maintaining the municipality's fiscal and economic well-being. Such an actor would have to be remarkably well-informed about the municipality's fiscal and economic changes to recognize when a change in governance is leading to a negative outcome, or is likely to do so. Another possibility, probably more likely, is that a local elected official functions as a political animal who regards re-election as a high-powered incentive. An electoral mechanism requires first that residents be able to discern a clear difference in outcomes between cooperation and the status quo, and recognize these differences as imposing some net benefit or cost to their households. These residents must also be able to signal their approval or disapproval, either through voice (e.g., voting) or exit (e.g., moving away). The elected official must receive this signal clearly, and be able to sort it from competing signals. The preference of the median voter (or some variation on this hypothetical voter) must be clear and unambiguous. Whether

Introduction 21

primarily a technocrat or a politician, the local elected official must reconcile any conflict between an objective conception of the public interest (whether municipal well-being or the perceived will of constituents) and her own subjective cultural biases about the public good in favor of the former. Absent a theory that deals with culture and cognition directly, we will not be able to understand the potential for cooperation when this reconciliation favors subjectivity, or when the signal from constituents (or even the municipal budget) is unclear. Sociocultural collective action supplies a possible explanation, and I address how political responsiveness functions within the framework at length in Chapter 5.

Third, the study at the heart of the book gives overdue attention to local governments in counties that are both suburban and exurban. Many of the studies of interlocal cooperation have researched its occurrence among communities in highly urbanized counties with a central city and inner-ring suburbs. The local officials in my study frequently come from places that would be labeled "small towns"—places where there is "no sharp boundary between government and civil society, [and where] serving as an elected municipal official is little different from holding office in a civic association or local church" (Oakerson, 2004, p. 35). Career politicians who have strong ambitions for re-election or advancement upward into regional or state offices are a less frequent occurrence in such settings. Many of these local elected officials do not receive training or professionalization, serve part-time, and are minimally compensated for time spent in monthly meetings. Just as I have emphasized the need for attention to individual–organizational linkages because they may present gaps into which culture can interject forcibly (in the absence of strong regulative and normative pressures that inhere in an individual's position), I highlight here that these gaps are probably more common in smaller suburban and exurban jurisdictions.

The fourth goal of the book is to push toward an appreciation of cooperation as more than just a dichotomous outcome. The literature on interlocal cooperation has been justifiably concerned with behavior, and it has had to treat cooperation as an either/or proposition: adoption of a formal agreement occurs, or it does not. Because I am dealing with cultural worldviews and preferences, and because I am focusing on cooperative land use planning and regulation under a highly flexible state statute, I have the luxury of investigating the marginal support for cooperation as it changes in its scope and implementation. Such empirical investigation, to my knowledge, has not occurred.

Finally, *The Risk of Regional Governance* tells a story of Michigan, my home state. I have spent more than three decades—the vast majority of my life—in Michigan's rural, exurban, suburban, and urban communities. I was born and raised in a town with fewer than 3,000 people that served as a county seat and minor hub in a very rural part of the state. In my early 20s, I lived in a rapidly growing suburb of Grand Rapids in West Michigan that was farmland when I was born. I have been a resident of the state capital, and for a decade I lived in two mid-size cities in the periphery of the Detroit metro. I have journeyed in and through the Detroit region countless times. Observing Michigan first-hand from

22   *Introduction*

the 1980s through the 2000s, it was inevitable that I would become fascinated by local governments and by how their elected and administrative officials think about jurisdictional boundaries and the use of land within those boundaries. The book serves as yet another entry in the already long story of Michigan and Detroit.

In telling a Michigan story, the book also contributes to a well-developed body of literature on the process of interlocal cooperation within the state. Andrew (2009, p. 135) notes that "what is known about current patterns of [interlocal cooperation] mostly comes from comprehensive studies of agreements in just three states: Michigan, Iowa, and Florida." Work by several scholars has described and tried to explain this cooperation, both in the state as a whole and in southeast Michigan (David, 2008; 2015; Gerber & Loh, 2011; Carr, LeRoux, & Shrestha, 2009; Zeemering, 2008; Carr, Gerber, & Lupher, 2007; LeRoux & Carr, 2007). This body of scholarship suggests a widely held regard for Michigan as a setting from which findings and policy recommendations can be generalized.

Evidence from Metropolitan Michigan

Empirically defending the sociocultural collective action in a single volume would be a daunting endeavor. At a minimum, it would require drawing data from multiple states and policy domains in which we would reasonably expect the regulatory, normative, and cultural sources of legitimizing to vary. In *The Risk of Regional Governance* I take on a more modest, preliminary task.

I have already noted in this chapter the complexity of metropolitan governance, that voluntary reforms are—for better or worse—the easiest path for developing a functional region in any policy domain, and that voluntary reforms tend to be limited to systems maintenance functions. If sociocultural collective action works at all as a framework for metropolitan governance, then it would lead us to expect the rationality of economizing to play a minimal or non-existent role in explaining the preferences and behaviors about regionalizing reforms that target lifestyle services. This, indeed, is the most basic hypothesis of the theory I am developing, and it provides a logical starting point for empirical investigation. In particular, I expect to see cultural legitimizing dominate cognition about lifestyle services, such as land use planning and regulation: a highly significant correspondence between cultural worldviews and preferences about voluntary regionalizing reforms.

In the book I provide evidence, mostly in Chapters 5 and 6, that significant, systematic links exist between preferences about regionalizing reforms and cultural worldviews, and that these linkages persist even when controlling for attributes that would be consistent with an economizing narrative. Stated most strongly, the evidence suggests that even if two local elected officials with similar demographic attributes serve in the same local government, they can still diverge in their cultural worldviews, and this divergence should show up in discordant preferences about regional reform.

Testing for this relationship required a large sample of local elected officials in heterogeneous contexts from whom I could validly generalize to a broader swath of the population of local elected officials. The consolidated metropolitan areas of Detroit and Grand Rapids, Michigan, provided a familiar setting from which to draw such a sample. The two metropolitan areas have, among them, 17 counties with more than 500 general-purpose local governments (cities, charter townships, townships, and villages).[10] The final sample of 262 local governments with 538 local elected officials was highly representative[11] across a wide range of individual, intramunicipal, and interlocal attributes relevant to an institutional theoretical framework (see Figure 1.1). The study is novel in that it elicited multiple responses from the same jurisdictions. On average, two elected officials completed a survey for each local jurisdiction in the sample, and in some instances more than five local officials responded from a single community.[12]

Michigan provides an exemplary opportunity for testing the relationship between reform preferences and cultural worldviews. In 2003, Michigan's

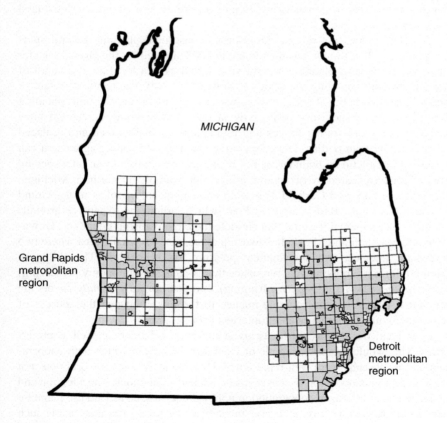

Figure 1.1 Study Area Municipalities.
Source: 2010 TIGER/Line Shapefiles (U.S. Census Bureau, 2010).

24 *Introduction*

legislature passed the Joint Municipal Planning Act (JMPA),[13] which allows all counties, cities, townships, and villages to work together on planning and zoning in a variety of ways. The JMPA is bare-bones enabling legislation that could be readily passed, likely without any objection, in any state; the prevalence of such legislation both generally and for specific public services—which I outline in Chapter 2—is supportive of this assertion. The JMPA allows local government actors—specifically the members of legislative bodies, such as city council members, mayors, village presidents, or township board members—the freedom to voluntarily negotiate with legislative actors in other jurisdictions to adopt a formal joint planning agreement. The JMPA—which had no incentives or mandates tied to it—has had minimal uptake,[14] and as I review in Chapter 5 the knowledge about the JMPA is also quite limited. The presence of this state statute allows hypotheses about interlocal land use planning and zoning to be grounded in the real world, which can be quite beneficial in the investigation of preferences. And the minimal formation of agreements under the JMPA— especially in metropolitan localities—and low general awareness about it meant that it was unlikely respondents had formed a prior opinion about interlocal land use cooperation.

The JMPA does not require abolition of constituent planning commissions and zoning bodies, though an amendment in 2008 allowed for the phased transfer of power from local planning commissions—and even a local zoning board of appeal—to corresponding joint bodies. Most of the JMPA agreements retain as much local jurisdictional autonomy as possible by structuring the joint planning commission as an advisory body; only in one joint planning agreement have local planning and zoning bodies and regulations been dissolved and replaced completely by joint bodies. The cooperative planning and zoning agreement can extend to jurisdictional boundaries, but it can also be tailored to target a specific area of concern shared by two communities. For example, in northern Michigan the Traverse City and Garfield Township agreement only applies to the Grand Traverse Commons Redevelopment Plan, which targets the expansive grounds of the old state mental hospital that straddle the city–township boundary. Downstate, the Marshall and Marshall Township agreement covers the area where two interstates intersect and development pressure has been high. The ability to choose a form of cooperative governance that is *advisory* (autonomy preserving) versus *authoritative* (autonomy infringing), and that *partially* or *fully* covers the municipal territory, adds valuable nuance to the links between the sources of legitimizing and preferences about interlocal cooperation.

In an ideal world, I would focus my attention on behaviors as well as preferences. This would require a sample of local jurisdictions in which both cooperation and its absence were well-represented. Unfortunately, such a world does not exist, except in cooperation over systems maintenance functions. The adoption and maintenance of interlocal cooperation in policy domains such as land use planning and zoning remain a rarity, as I have mentioned, even in states that enable such cooperation. This makes the study of the determinants of *actual* governance outcomes difficult, and requires initial attention instead to thought processes.

Introduction 25

While I acknowledge this limitation, fortunately we know from decades of psychological studies of planned behavior and reasoned action (Ajzen, 2005; Fishbein & Ajzen, 2011) that beliefs are quite predictive of attitudes and behaviors. Moreover, if interlocal cooperation is going to be a viable governance approach for confronting metropolitan dilemmas, then understanding how local officials *think* about cooperation over the lifestyle functions driving these dilemmas is essential. It is in cognition that we can interrogate the first imaginings and impulses about cooperation. Are preferences about cooperation determined by the laws and regulations that shape local officials' spheres of authority? Are these preferences based on a rational economizing appraisal of potential costs and benefits? Are they shaped by the social regularities of the organizational position an official occupies? Or are they an outgrowth of an actor's worldviews? We might reason that preferences are a combination of all of these. But if one of these institutional sources—rules, norms, or culture—is the dominant cognitive player, then encouraging cooperation will require a thoughtfully tailored set of policy responses. An exploration of preferences is a useful first step.

A final word on the research behind this book: the relationship between worldviews and preferences is *necessary* to the sociocultural collective action framework—if we cannot show that actors think in a culturally legitimizing way, then we cannot go much further on the sociocultural path I develop—but I recognize it is not *sufficient*. Future work will be needed to support the broader proposition that cultural legitimizing drives behaviors, and that it only does so under circumstances in which other institutional signals are weak. The book provides a first step on a much longer path, and I hope it offers an invitation to other scholars to join me in testing the sociocultural collective action framework.

The Plan of the Book

The remainder of the book is structured in six chapters. In Chapter 2, I discuss interlocal cooperation as a form of regional governance, and explain why it is legally the form of cooperation that is, arguably, the most feasible under the existing state–local legal relationship. The chapter begins with a vignette from Michigan that illustrates the basic dynamics of how interlocal land use cooperation is adopted and repealed. It then provides a brief history of the rise of polycentrism and localism in state laws governing local governments in the United States, and distinguishes cooperation from other regionalizing reforms. The goal of the chapter is to thoroughly justify for the reader why a book about voluntary interlocal cooperation—a reform which has been derided by some commentators for its inability to move beyond systems maintenance—remains essential.

Chapter 3 reviews in much greater detail the prevailing explanation for voluntary interlocal cooperation: transaction cost economizing, as developed in the institutional collective action framework and rooted in rational choice institutionalism. The chapter further explores how economizing, as explained in the extant literature, treats the role of the individual in the local government organization, and in which ways the analogy of cooperation to a transaction (and the

26 *Introduction*

local government to a firm) is conceptually strained. Building off themes from Chapter 1, I focus in Chapter 3 on how cooperation that targets lifestyle services and that flows through local elected officials is particularly incompatible with rationality based on pure transaction cost economizing. I discuss some of the existing empirical evidence that suggests regionalizing reforms do not always hew to explanations grounded in economizing, and conclude the chapter by discussing how governance decisions are often ideological exercises (i.e., they are products of cultural legitimizing).

In Chapter 4 I add some color and shading to the sketch of the sociocultural collective action framework I offered earlier. I first review how the framework shifts away from the institutional collective action perspective in its articulation of rational choice and the relationship of individuals to institutions. I show how the framework is grounded in the foundation of sociological institutionalism. I then illustrate how regionalizing reforms can be decisions based on the rationality of legitimizing, reflecting the logic of appropriateness rather than the logic of instrumentality.

Chapters 5 and 6 present evidence, drawn from surveys of hundreds of officials serving in suburbs in Michigan's two largest metropolitan areas, about the explanatory power of regulative, normative, and cultural legitimizing in the preference formation of local elected officials. Taken together, the chapters show that both cultural worldviews and a norm of political responsiveness have a strong influence, that the interpretation of this latter norm is itself highly subjective, and that economizing has, at best, a weak to mixed influence on preference formation.

The evidence suggests several pathways for encouraging regional governance that do not rely on structural centralizing reforms and that respect the need for voluntary reforms. I present these in Chapter 7. Overall, I am only cautiously optimistic about whether sociocultural collective action can help create a more viable pathway toward meaningful, voluntary regional governance via interlocal cooperation. But I hope in *The Risk of Regional Governance* that I have charted a path for future empirical investigation and future policy experiments that may help us discern, with a thoroughness and finality that is currently lacking, whether the polycentrist and localist tendencies we currently indulge in the U.S. are actually worth preserving.

Notes

1 The definition of metropolitan governance remains quite open. Fukuyama has described governance as "a government's ability to make and enforce rules, and to deliver services" (2013, p. 350). Peters and Pierre (1998), like many authors in recent decades, have not directly defined governance but have given it shape by comparing it with government. They note, consistent with most authors, that governance emphasizes the use of networks and partnerships (both within and across sectors) and a reliance on markets. Also see the definitions reviewed in Meier and O'Toole (2006). Although Hamilton emphasizes that some problems of regional development demand public–private coalitions, he acknowledges, "basic regional governance does not require private involvement. Regional services can be delivered and governments can

Introduction 27

cooperate among themselves without the involvement of the nongovernmental community" (2002, p. 404). Businesses can also be quite helpful in promoting regionalizing reforms (Kanter, 2000), but I am interested specifically in the local–local relationships within the public sector. Thus, unlike many scholars, I do not emphasize the involvement of the private sector in governing when I use the term governance in this book. I closely follow Oakerson by defining the term as, simply, the set of institutions "by which human beings regulate their interdependencies in the context of shared environments" (2004, p. 19). Governance, therefore, can be much broader than government. Metropolitan governance, by extension, is the process of interdependency regulation in metropolitan areas. The term metropolitan is open to many definitions but is perhaps easiest to define, particularly for research purposes, using the statistical approach of the federal government (Stephens & Wikstrom, 2000, pp. 14–17).

2 These municipalities vary widely in their characteristics, a reality traced by many scholars in recent years (e.g., Hanlon, Vicino, & Short, 2006; Lewis, 2004). Relative to central cities, most are small in size and population, serve primarily as residential commuter havens, and have homogeneous populations. But many do not fit this profile. Most metropolitan regions have suburbs that have become important economic sub-centers (Lewis, 2004), occasionally rivaling the dominant position of the central city. The variation in the density of fragmentation across space and per capita is generally thought to make working across local government boundaries more difficult because of the heterogeneity in interests between, at the extreme, a large suburban employment center and a small residential enclave.

3 The City of San Antonio can only pursue annexation in the land five miles outside its current boundaries—the area subject to extraterritorial jurisdiction under state law. In 2014, San Antonio had 518 square miles under extraterritorial jurisdiction, illustrating just how rapidly expansion could happen—at least legally—under state law.

4 The state judiciary, through its rules of statutory interpretation, shapes the narrowness with which the many grants of state authority are construed. As I discuss more in Chapter 2, this shapes the de jure space within which local governments operate.

5 As described in this chapter, a classic distinction in the literature on interlocal cooperation is drawn from Oliver Williams' Lifestyle Model of Urban Politics (1971), which posits that metropolitan area services can be categorized into systems maintenance functions and lifestyle services. The former relate to the infrastructure essential to maintaining public health and safety and include, for example, water treatment and solid waste disposal. They are considered easier targets of centralization or cooperation because they are politically benign and are not used to differentiate one community from another. Lifestyle services are those that can be used to shape social access. As he was writing at a time when the main regionalizing reform was centralization, Williams' main thesis is that "policies that are perceived as neutral with regard to controlling social access may be centralized, but those that are perceived as controlling social access will remain decentralized" (1971, p. 4). Whether this argument can be extended conceptually to interlocal cooperation is debatable, since cooperation can still allow differentiation among small regions within a metropolitan area and still retains local autonomy and the possibility of exit. Indeed, these features are why it is so readily embraced by many contemporary regionalists.

6 As I describe in much more detail in both Chapters 4 and 6, the use of the word "cultural" here is different than the reader might expect.

7 Risk is often regarded as a knowable probability of an adverse event that is somewhere between zero and one, while uncertainty arises where probability is unknowable. However, I view both as subjective constructs (Slovic, 1992).

8 Ostrom and Ostrom (1971, p. 212) were confident that public choice could create sustained, effective administration of metropolitan areas because of the rationality of administrators and a well-informed public:

28 Introduction

> [W]e should not be surprised to find rational, self-interested public administrators consciously bargaining among themselves and mobilizing political support from their clientele in order to avoid political stalemate and sustain the political feasibility of their agencies. Perhaps a system of public administration composed of a variety of multiorganizational arrangements and highly dependent upon mobilizing clientele support will come reasonably close to sustaining a high level of performance in advancing the public welfare.

Whether these conditions exist today, or indeed ever existed, is unknown. Certainly the state–local legal framework, described in Chapter 2, did not promote a regulatory structure that weighted the costs and benefits of competition and cooperation evenly.

9 Chapter 5 provides a much fuller treatment of the political mechanisms I touch on in this paragraph.

10 I do not strictly follow the census definition of the core based statistical area here since this includes some extremely rural counties that would be difficult to study and likely not that interesting for consideration of cooperation, but I do hew closely to it.

11 The appendices contain more detailed information on the representativeness of the sample.

12 This clustering necessitated the use of multi-level modeling, since multiple respondents could be nested within local governments. I describe the technique at length in the appendices.

13 Michigan Compiled Laws 125.135, et seq.

14 Agreements exist (as of December 2015) in Fremont, Dayton Township, and Sheridan Charter Township (Newaygo County); Suttons Bay and Suttons Bay Township (Leelanau County); Bellevue and Bellevue Township (Eaton County); Bear Lake, Bear Lake Township, and Pleasanton Township (Manistee County); Manchester and Manchester Township (Washtenaw County); Marshall and Marshall Township (Calhoun County); Quincy and Quincy Township (Branch County); Homestead and Inland townships (Benzie County); Thompsonville, Colfax Township, and Weldon Township (Benzie County); Traverse City and Garfield Township (Grand Traverse County); Hastings, Hastings Township, Rutland Charter Township, and Carlton Township (Barry County); and Norway and Norway Township (Dickinson County). This is less than 2 percent of municipalities in Michigan.

References

Acosta, R. (2016, January 17). Hillary Clinton addresses Flint water crisis during presidential debate. *MLive*. Retrieved from www.mlive.com (last accessed March 12, 2017).

Ajzen, I. (2005). *Attitudes, personality, and behavior*. McGraw-Hill Education.

Andrew, S. A. (2009). Regional integration through contracting networks: An empirical analysis of institutional collection action framework. *Urban Affairs Review, 44*(3), 378–402.

Barnes, W. R., & Ledebur, L. C. (1997). *The new regional economies: The US common market and the global economy*. Sage Publications.

Barron, D. J., & Frug, G. E. (2005). Defensive localism: A view of the field from the field. *JL & Pol., 21*, 261.

Blair, J. P., Staley, S. R., & Zhang, Z. (1996). The central city elasticity hypothesis: A critical appraisal of Rusk's theory of urban development. *Journal of the American Planning Association, 62*(3), 345–353.

Blair, J. P., & Zhang, Z. (1994). "Ties that bind" reexamined. *Economic Development Quarterly, 8*(4), 373–377.

Introduction 29

Brenner, N. (2002). Decoding the newest "metropolitan regionalism" in the USA: A critical overview. *Cities, 19*(1), 3–21.

Briffault, R. (1996). The local government boundary problem in metropolitan areas. *Stanford Law Review*, 1115–1171.

Briffault, R. (1990a). Our localism: Part I—the structure of local government law. *Columbia Law Review, 90*(1), 1–115.

Briffault, R. (1990b). Our localism: Part II—localism and legal theory. *Columbia Law Review, 90*(2), 346–454.

Carr, J. B., Gerber, E. R., & Lupher, E. W. (2007). Explaining horizontal and vertical cooperation on public services in Michigan: The role of local fiscal capacity. *Working Group on Interlocal Services Cooperation, Paper 34*. Retrieved from http://digital commons.wayne.edu/interlocal_coop/34 (last accessed March 12, 2017).

Carr, J. B., LeRoux, K., & Shrestha, M. (2009). Institutional ties, transaction costs, and external service production. *Urban Affairs Review, 44*(3), 403–427.

Cashin, S. D. (1999). Localism, self-interest, and the tyranny of the favored quarter: Addressing the barriers to new regionalism. *Geo. LJ, 88*, 1985.

Cervero, R. (1989). Jobs-housing balancing and regional mobility. *Journal of the American Planning Association, 55*(2), 136–150.

Chen, Y. C., & Thurmaier, K. (2009). Interlocal agreements as collaborations: An empirical investigation of impetuses, norms, and success. *The American Review of Public Administration, 39*(5), 536–552.

Danielson, M. N. (1976). *The politics of exclusion*. Columbia University Press.

David, N. P. (2015). Factors affecting municipal land use cooperation. *Land Use Policy, 42*, 170–182.

David, N. P. (2008). *Why cooperate? An evaluation of the formation and persistence of voluntary regional land use cooperative arrangements in Michigan* (Doctoral dissertation, University of Michigan).

De Souza Briggs, X. (Ed.). (2005). *The geography of opportunity: Race and housing choice in metropolitan America*. Brookings Institution Press.

Didorosi, A. (2015, February 10). Metro Detroit needs a transit revolution. *Detroit Free Press*. Retrieved from www.freep.com (last accessed March 10, 2017).

DiMaggio, P. J., & Powell, W. W. (Eds.). (1991). *The new institutionalism in organizational analysis*. University of Chicago Press.

Downs, A. (1994). *New visions for metropolitan America*. Brookings Institution.

Err, R. (2015, January 22). Who wants to drink Flint's water? *Detroit Free Press*. Retrieved from www.freep.com (last accessed March 12, 2017).

Feiock, R. C. (2009). Metropolitan governance and institutional collective action. *Urban Affairs Review, 44*(3), 356–377.

Feiock, R. C. (2007). Rational choice and regional governance. *Journal of Urban Affairs, 29*(1), 47–63.

Feiock, R. C., Steinacker, A., & Park, H. J. (2009). Institutional collective action and economic development joint ventures. *Public Administration Review, 69*(2), 256–270.

Fishbein, M., & Ajzen, I. (2011). *Predicting and changing behavior: The reasoned action approach*. Taylor & Francis.

Fonger, R. (2015a, October 13). Ex-emergency manager says he's not to blame for Flint River water switch. *MLive*. Retrieved from www.mlive.com (last accessed March 12, 2017).

30 Introduction

Fonger, R. (2015b, January 9). Drain commissioner assures Genesee County customers they aren't drinking Flint River water. *MLive*. Retrieved from www.mlive.com (last accessed March 12, 2017).

Frug, G. E. (1998). City services. *New York University Law Review*, 73, 23.

Fukuyama, F. (2013). What is governance? *Governance*, *26*(3), 347–368.

Gerber, E. R., & Loh, C. G. (2011). Prospects for expanding regional planning efforts in Michigan. *Urban Studies*, *48*(11), 2303–2319.

Gillette, C. P. (2005). The conditions of interlocal cooperation. *JL & Pol.*, *21*, 365.

Gillette, C. P. (2001). Regionalization and interlocal bargains. *NYUL rev.*, *76*, 190.

Gould, G. (2015, January 15). Flint water problems are not those of the city. *Grand Blanc View*. Retrieved from http://grandblancview.mihomepager.com (last accessed March 12, 2017).

Graham, D. A. (2015, February 2). The 21-mile walk to work. *The Atlantic*. Retrieved from www.theatlantic.com (last accessed March 10, 2017).

Grendstad, G., & Selle, P. (1995). Cultural theory and the new institutionalism. *Journal of Theoretical Politics*, *7*(1), 5–27.

Guile, J. (2015, January 20). Detroit offers to sell Flint water amid health concerns. *Detroit Free Press*. Retrieved from www.freep.com (last accessed March 12, 2017).

Gulick, L. (1957). Metropolitan organization. *The Annals of the American Academy of Political and Social Science*, *314*(1), 57–65.

Hamilton, D. K. (2002). Regimes and regional governance: The case of Chicago. *Journal of Urban Affairs*, *24*(4), 403–423.

Henderson, S. (2015, February 10). Awful transit policy fails everyone in metro Detroit. *Detroit Free Press*. Retrieved from www.freep.com (last accessed March 10, 2017).

Highsmith, A. R. (2015). *Demolition means progress: Flint, Michigan, and the fate of the American metropolis*. University of Chicago Press.

Highsmith, A. R. (2014). Beyond corporate abandonment: General Motors and the politics of metropolitan capitalism in Flint, Michigan. *Journal of Urban History*, *40*(1), 31–47.

Highsmith, A. R. (2009). Demolition means progress: urban renewal, local politics, and state-sanctioned ghetto formation in Flint, Michigan. *Journal of Urban History*, *35*(3), 348–368.

Hill, E. W., Wolman, H. L., & Ford, C. C. (1995). Can suburbs survive without their central cities? Examining the suburban dependence hypothesis. *Urban Affairs Review*, *31*(2), 147–174.

Holzer, H. J. (1991). The spatial mismatch hypothesis: What has the evidence shown? *Urban Studies*, *28*(1), 105–122.

Horner, M. W. (2004). Spatial dimensions of urban commuting: A review of major issues and their implications for future geographic research. *The Professional Geographer*, *56*(2), 160–173.

Ihlanfeldt, K. R., & Sjoquist, D. L. (1998). The spatial mismatch hypothesis: A review of recent studies and their implications for welfare reform. *Housing Policy Debate*, *9*(4), 849–892.

Immergluck, D. (2011). *Foreclosed: High-risk lending, deregulation, and the undermining of America's mortgage market*. Cornell University Press.

Jackson, K. T. (1985). *Crabgrass frontier: The suburbanization of the United States*. Oxford University Press.

Jargowsky, P. A. (1997). *Poverty and place: Ghettos, barrios, and the American city*. Russell Sage Foundation.

Jones, V. (1942). *Metropolitan government*. University of Chicago Press.

Kanter, R. M. (2000). Business coalitions as a force for regionalism. In B. Katz (Ed.), *Reflections on regionalism* (pp. 154–182). Brookings Institution.

Kennedy, M. (2016, April 20). Lead-laced water in Flint: A step-by-step look at the makings of a crisis. *National Public Radio*. Retrieved from www.npr.org (last accessed March 12, 2017).

Laitner, B. (2016, October 19). Story of Detroit's walking man, James Robertson, to be documentary. *Detroit Free Press*. Retrieved from www.freep.com (last accessed March 10, 2017).

Laitner, B. (2015, January 31). Heart and sole: Detroiter walks 21 miles in work commute. *Detroit Free Press*. Retrieved from www.freep.com (last accessed March 10, 2017).

Lawrence, E. D., & Gallagher, J. (2015, February 12). SMART's opt-out option gets blame for transit woes. *Detroit Free Press*. Retrieved from www.freep.com (last accessed March 10, 2017).

Ledebur, L. C., & Barnes, W. R. (1993). All in it together: Cities, suburbs and local economic regions. *National League of Cities*.

LeRoux, K., & Carr, J. B. (2007). Explaining local government cooperation on public works: Evidence from Michigan. *Public Works Management & Policy, 12*(1), 344–358.

Lewis, P. G. (2004). An old debate confronts new realities: Large suburbs and economic development in the metropolis. In R. Feiock (Ed.), *Metropolitan governance: Conflict, competition, and cooperation* (pp. 95–123). Georgetown University Press.

Li, Y., & Morrow-Jones, H. A. (2010). The impact of residential mortgage foreclosure on neighborhood change and succession. *Journal of Planning Education and Research, 30*(1), 22–39.

Marando, V. L. (1979). City-county consolidation: Reform, regionalism, referenda and requiem. *Western Political Quarterly, 32*(4), 409–421.

Marcuse, P. (1997). The enclave, the citadel, and the ghetto: What has changed in the post-Fordist US city. *Urban Affairs Review, 33*(2), 228–264.

Meier, K. J., & O'Toole, L. J. (2006). *Bureaucracy in a democratic state: A governance perspective*. Johns Hopkins University Press.

Mitchell, W. C. (1988). Virginia, Rochester, and Bloomington: Twenty-five years of public choice and political science. *Public Choice, 56*(2), 101–119.

Moore, M. (n.d.). How can you help Flint? Do not send bottled water. Retrieved from http://michaelmoore.com/ (last accessed March 12, 2017).

Norris, D. F. (2016). *Metropolitan governance in America*. Routledge.

Norris, D. F. (2001a). Prospects for regional governance under the new regionalism: Economic imperatives versus political impediments. *Journal of Urban Affairs, 23*(5), 557–571.

Norris, D. F. (2001b). Whither metropolitan governance? *Urban Affairs Review, 36*(4), 532–550.

Oakerson, R. J. (2004). The study of metropolitan governance. In R. Feiock (Ed.), *Metropolitan governance: Conflict, competition, and cooperation* (pp. 17–45). Georgetown University Press.

Ostrom, V., Bish, R. L., & Ostrom, E. (1988). *Local government in the United States*. Ics Press.

Ostrom, V., & Ostrom, E. (1971). Public choice: A different approach to the study of public administration. *Public Administration Review, 31*(2), 203–216.

32 *Introduction*

Ostrom, V., Tiebout, C. M., & Warren, R. (1961). The organization of government in metropolitan areas: A theoretical inquiry. *American Political Science Review, 55*(4), 831–842.

Parks, R. B., & Oakerson, R. J. (2000). Regionalism, localism, and metropolitan governance: Suggestions from the research program on local public economies. *State and Local Government Review, 32*(3), 169–179.

Peirce, N. R. (1993). *Citistates: How urban America can prosper in a competitive world.* Seven Locks Press.

Peters, B. G., & Pierre, J. (1998). Governance without government? Rethinking public administration. *Journal of Public Administration Research and Theory, 8*(2), 223–243.

Post, S. S., & Stein, R. M. (2000). State economies, metropolitan governance, and urban-suburban economic dependence. *Urban Affairs Review, 36*(1), 46–60.

Reynolds, L. (2003). Intergovernmental cooperation, metropolitan equity, and the new regionalism. *Washington Law Review, 78*, 93.

Rusk, D. (1993). *Cities without suburbs.* Woodrow Wilson Center Press.

Savitch, H. V., Collins, D., Sanders, D., & Markham, J. P. (1993). Ties that bind: Central cities, suburbs, and the new metropolitan region. *Economic Development Quarterly, 7*(4), 341–357.

Slovic, P. (1992). Perception of risk: Reflections on the psychometric paradigm. In S. Krimsky & D. Golding (Eds.), *Social theories of risk* (pp. 117–152). Praeger.

Stafford, K. (2015, January 21). Crowd outbursts cut Flint water meeting short. *Detroit Free Press.* Retrieved from www.freep.com (last accessed March 12, 2017).

Stephens, G. R., & Wikstrom, N. (2000). *Metropolitan government and governance: Theoretical perspectives, empirical analysis, and the future.* Oxford University Press.

Studenski, P. (1930). The government of metropolitan areas in the United States. *National Municipal League.*

Swanstrom, T. (2001). What we argue about when we argue about regionalism. *Journal of Urban Affairs, 23*(5), 479–496.

Swanstrom, T., Chapple, K., & Immergluck, D. (2009). *Regional resilience in the face of foreclosures: Evidence from six metropolitan areas.* Working Paper, Institute of Urban and Regional Development.

Teaford, J. C. (1979). *City and suburb: The political fragmentation of metropolitan America, 1850–1970.* Johns Hopkins University Press.

Thurmaier, K., & Wood, C. (2002). Interlocal agreements as overlapping social networks: Picket-fence regionalism in metropolitan Kansas City. *Public Administration Review, 62*(5), 585–598.

Tiebout, C. M. (1956). A pure theory of local expenditures. *Journal of Political Economy, 64*(5), 416–424.

Tocqueville, A. (2000 [1835]). *Democracy in America.* University of Chicago Press.

Wallis, A. D. (1994). The third wave: Current trends in regional governance. *National Civic Review, 83*(3), 290–310.

Wassmer, R. W. (2011). The recent pervasive external effects of residential home foreclosure. *Housing Policy Debate, 21*(2), 247–265.

Williams, O. P. (1971). *Metropolitan political analysis: A social access approach.* Free Press.

Witsil, F. & Lawrence, E. D. (2016, November 9). RTA millage rejected by metro Detroit voters. *Detroit Free Press.* Retrieved from www.freep.com (last accessed March 10, 2017).

Introduction 33

Wood, R. C. (1961). *1400 governments: The political economy of the New York metropolitan region.* Harvard University Press.

Wood, R. C. (1958). Metropolitan government, 1975: An extrapolation of trends: The new metropolis: Green belts, grass roots or gargantua? *American Political Science Review, 52*(1), 108–122.

Zeemering, E. S. (2008). Governing interlocal cooperation: City council interests and the implications for public management. *Public Administration Review, 68*(4), 731–741.

Zimmer, B. G., & Hawley, A. H. (1956). Approaches to the solution of fringe problems: Preferences of residents in the Flint metropolitan area. *Public Administration Review, 16*(4), 258–268.

2 Governing the Region through Cooperation

Assuming voluntary, cooperative action is possible ... will it be limited to solving easy problems with fewer conflicting interests and outcomes?
— Jimenez and Hendrick (2010, p. 266)

The Manchester Community

In 2007, four communities at the edge of metropolitan Detroit—Manchester Village, Manchester Township, Freedom Township, and Bridgewater Township—came together with a goal of managing future growth in their region. The area is a snapshot of small-town, rural America: a roughly two-square mile village of about 2,000 people, surrounded by townships with another 7,500 people spread across more than 100 square miles. Despite being an hour from Detroit itself, the threat of sprawl from the metropolitan suburbs and from nearby Ann Arbor—a major economic hub and home to the University of Michigan—was a very real threat to what local stakeholders described as the "Manchester Experience" of

> driving along country roads from any direction with rolling hills, old churches, historic barns and farmsteads, with countless beautiful vistas opening up as one rounds a curve on the road until one arrives in the quaint and historic Village of Manchester.[1]

An earlier regional plan adopted in 2003 noted that

> given current zoning and density regulations ... the Manchester area could experience intensive growth ... that is significantly inconsistent with what local citizens and officials desire for their community. ... [T]he continuation of agriculture as a viable economic activity and the preservation of open space could be at risk in the long term.

To forestall this threat to their way of life, the communities would enter into a formal joint planning agreement per which they would adopt a new regional plan and form a joint planning commission that would replace the administration of planning in the individual jurisdictions. This was a marked change from the status quo. In Michigan, the three basic forms of municipality—cities, townships, and villages—vary in their legal rights and responsibilities, but all share the ability to adopt and administer comprehensive plans and zoning regulations. Manchester Village and the three townships had all taken advantage of this grant of authority. In the absence of regional land use practice, if you were to walk straight north from Manchester Village's downtown, within a mile or two you would step on land planned and zoned by three different local governments. The same would be true if you headed due west or northwest (see Figure 2.1). The regional plan acknowledged, however, the artificiality of the corporate territory: "[f]ew land use, economic, natural features, or transportation issues facing the community, among many others, are contained within political boundaries."

Under the joint agreement, the jurisdictions would retain their own zoning ordinances and the joint commission's decisions would be advisory, but the presence of a regional plan—rather than four separate comprehensive plans—was not inconsequential. State law demands that the regulation of land use—through zoning ordinances, subdivision regulations, and the like—be made in accordance with the underlying comprehensive plan. A regional plan is not itself legally binding, but the land use regulations it supports and justifies would necessarily become more coordinated over time. The joint planning commission would also ensure the formalization of communication and decision-making about land use in the participating communities, and could help diminish competitive bidding among municipalities for new development.

The Manchester Community enjoyed several advantages that both practitioners and scholars would expect to encourage both the adoption and endurance of

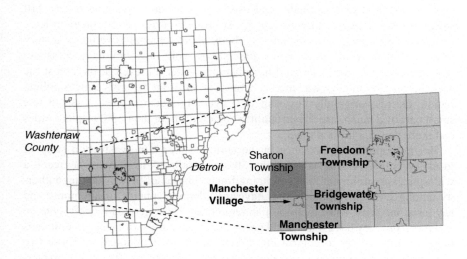

Figure 2.1 The Original Manchester Community Municipalities.
Source: 2010 TIGER/Line Shapefiles (U.S. Census Bureau, 2010).

36 Governing the Region through Cooperation

cooperation. The joint agreement was being built on a network of local officials who had, over recent decades, found ways to collectively tackle solid waste disposal, adopt a shared Mineral Extraction Ordinance, and an authority to manage building permitting and soil erosion control. Local officials who were members of the area Optimists Club had started informally gathering in the early 1990s, and this activity would eventually formalize as the Greater Manchester Area Council and, in 1997, the Southwest Washtenaw Council of Governments (SWWCOG). A non-profit third party actor, the Land Information Access Association, was providing start-up assistance for the regional planning efforts, both financial and administrative. The surrounding townships were highly homogeneous fiscally, politically, and demographically, and all were general-law townships facing many of the same constraints and opportunities. Perhaps most important, the village—while jurisdictionally distinct—had long served as a town center of the broader area. It was the hub of economic and social life for a region that was, according to the 2003 regional plan, "a clearly identifiable community, with strong ties and deep historical roots."

Despite these many advantages, the attempt at land use coordination in the Manchester area could not be sustained. Citing a perceived loss of local autonomy and the planned direction of future growth primarily to Manchester Village and Township, the Bridgewater Township supervisor moved for immediate withdrawal in March of 2011 (Veselnak, 2011). At the public hearing required under the exit provisions in the joint agreement, both residents and board members expressed mixed opinions about joint planning but the board would eventually vote four to one to adopt an ordinance rescinding its membership. Less than a year later, Freedom Township also left. By 2011, regional planning had been reduced from an effort among four communities that could have had the potential to coordinate land uses across an area spanning nearly 110 square miles to a two-community enterprise covering less than 40 square miles.

It may seem peculiar to include in a book about regional governance a story of a handful of local governments attempting—with only limited success—to work together to coordinate land use planning. After all, even at its largest the Manchester Community was merely a tiny corner of an expansive metropolitan region. Despite originally covering well over 100 square miles, it is but one small part of a much larger metropolitan region of more than 5,800 square miles and more than 5.3 million people.

But metropolitan governance in the United States *is* pervasively a story of local governments. The laws of the 50 states reflect—to varying degrees—a widespread commitment to encouraging fragmentation of policy-making authority among local governments that have well-defined spheres of autonomy and territorial integrity. Most metropolitan regions are characterized by *polycentrism* and *localism*: they have many local governments, and most of these governments have a robust power to control the affairs within their boundaries. These two characteristics have made regionalizing reforms difficult, and they are characteristics that have been directly encouraged by state and federal laws.

The Difficulty of Structural Reforms

In the nineteenth century, the hierarchy of metropolitan political power in the U.S. was squarely with central cities. Apart from a few exceptions outside the largest cities of the era—New York, Boston, Philadelphia, and the like—suburbs were generally places with limited, low-quality infrastructure (Harris & Lewis, 1998). Much of the area outside the core city's municipal boundaries was unincorporated. Even where suburban communities had incorporated, they often did not have the population or the resources to remain independent in the face of central city growth. Or, a majority of residents actively desired the improvement in services that would be possible if they were part of the central city.

One of the major avenues to expansion in that era was annexation of unincorporated and occasionally incorporated land. In the late nineteenth century, the tactic was widely available. Even major cities in the Northeast and Midwest, which are known for their mostly fixed boundaries today, were able to expand markedly in size. Take Detroit as an example. Detroit was less than one square mile in size when it incorporated in 1806, was roughly 40 square miles by 1915, and then exploded—largely through influence from real estate developers in local and state policies—to nearly 140 square miles by 1926. Annexation required simply taking the land of the townships, which were unincorporated subdivisions of the counties. While villages could occasionally successfully resist annexation if they had enough influence with the state—as occurred with Highland Park and Hamtramck in the late 1800s thanks to the corporate interests of Ford and Dodge[2]—few had the clout to pull off the feat. The Detroit "metropolitan district," the name once used for metropolitan areas by the census bureau, was in 1930 nearly 750 square miles with over 2.1 million residents. The 600 square miles of the district outside the boundaries of Detroit only had about a quarter of that population.

Consolidation—in which multiple units come together under the banner of a new government—had been another common way to rationalize the size of the city through structural reform. Originally it had to be pursued via special state legislation. Beginning with the consolidation between New Orleans and New Orleans parish (roughly the equivalent of a county in other states) in the first decade of the 1800s (Sheppard & Moak, 1940), there were nine consolidations over roughly the next century—usually of one central city and its surrounding county—that were enabled through legislative action.

But despite the powerful position they seemed to occupy as drivers of territorial expansion, cities did not have nearly the autonomy we now associate with municipalities. Before St. Louis in 1875, no city in the U.S. possessed the right to general legislative initiative or any de facto immunity from state interference—the sphere of autonomy we now roughly know as "home rule," a concept I discuss more in a moment. In the nineteenth century, the sense of local deference to the state was much greater than it is now. All local government rights and responsibilities—from the incursion of debt to the ability to collect refuse—traced to special legislative grants from the state. While one might imagine large

38   *Governing the Region through Cooperation*

cities holding relatively greater sway, they were not especially influential with their state legislatures in that era, despite having larger delegations. Though some commentators have noted large cities were successful in bringing so-called "district bills" to the floor (Allard, Burns, & Gamm, 1998) and even regularly securing their adoption (Monkkonen, 1990; Teaford, 1979), on balance the evidence suggests that in the latter part of the century larger cities tended to be *less* successful in getting special legislation passed (Gamm & Kousser, 2013, p. 666).

Home rule dramatically changed this state of affairs. Finding a single definition of home rule is made impossible by the variations on the home rule concept one finds among the states, and even within a single state among different types of local government. What *was* consistent about the mix of state grants and limitations from one state to another was its reaction against the prior system. Home rule was meant to eradicate the pursuit of special district bills by large city municipal delegations by creating broad grants of local autonomy through general legislative action (Krane, Rigos, & Hill, 2001). A home rule local government—a status initially available only to the largest and most urban of the cities in a state—was not entirely independent, but it enjoyed powers of initiative and a promise of immunity it had never before enjoyed; with the adoption of legislative and constitutional home rule provisions, there was an undeniable shift in favor of self-determination and independence. The state legislature could no longer act as a capricious *quasi*-city council, putting up unnecessary roadblocks to municipal reform or allowing special interests to take advantage of the municipal government. Home rule could effectively shackle the corrupting hand of the state. It could please the conservatives who longed for a return to "small government" municipal corporations that could not be forced to tax and incur debts and spend all in the name of a public good defined by faraway legislators. It could also, simultaneously, appeal to progressives who sought the "administrative city" free from political corruption (Barron, 2003).

Home rule, therefore, is not a synonym for local autonomy; the latter is a much more complex concept that requires careful investigation of all the grants and limitations on local initiative powers, the interpretation of these powers, immunity from state interference, and technical and fiscal capacities. It is also not an antonym for Dillon's rule, which is a tenet of statutory interpretation that requires local powers to be expressly or impliedly authorized by the state and resolves any statutory ambiguity in favor of retaining the power at the state level. Named for the jurist who developed it, the rule prioritized the view of the municipality as a corporate extension of the state: "[i]n many of its more important aspects a modern American city is not so much a miniature State as it is a business corporation" (Dillon, 1911, p. 34). Home rule and Dillon's rule *both* speak to the state–local relationship, but the two occupy entirely different space in the legal framework for local government (Richardson, 2011); many states, in fact, have both.

Home rule encouraged suburban jurisdictional reification by making the major avenues of reform discussed above—annexation and consolidation—easier to resist and further increasing the appeal of incorporation, the latter of

Governing the Region through Cooperation   39

which was often made available to communities with quite low populations and population densities. The effects of this change over time cannot be overstated, and Detroit once again can serve as an example. Michigan adopted home rule in 1909. This may seem curious since it was well before Detroit enjoyed its greatest expansion in 1926. But many of the communities around Detroit were still not incorporated or lacked home rule status, and those that had it either actively wanted to be annexed or lacked a strong anti-annexation residential base. Home rule would only gain real meaning for the suburbs when it was married to a growing tax base and became a tool with which differentiation from the city could be secured. By the time Detroit again sought expansion after World War II it was legally difficult and suburban dwellers no longer had the economic or cultural affinity for the central city they once possessed. The physical boundaries of Detroit have not changed in nearly a century, even as the metropolitan region outside Detroit has witnessed expansive growth in size and population. In 2010, the official Detroit suburbs—those in the metropolitan statistical area—covered nearly 3,800 square miles and were home to more than 3.5 million of the region's 4.3 million residents. Detroit was not alone in this fate. Annexation was severely limited throughout states in the upper Midwest and East, and boundary changes in many states became contentious and exceedingly difficult.

In the wake of home rule, consolidation would also prove only infrequently successful. Following the consolidation of Honolulu and Honolulu County in 1907, only one more major city consolidation would occur in 1969, between Indianapolis and Marion County. Since the first failed attempt at a referendum-based consolidation between Oakland and Alameda County in California in 1921, only 32 of 162 consolidations—a rate of less than one in five—have passed.[3] As Wallis (1994, p. 162) characterized the situation, home rule was part of a broader change in the game being played: "the balance of political interests no longer favored central cities. By then suburban interests in most states had gained sufficient influence to force amendments of state constitutions making consolidation without confirmation of a referendum virtually impossible." Marando, writing about consolidation by referendum, once described it as a "grand gesture" that provided an opportunity for major reform of governance (1979, p. 410). Over time, that gesture proved quite difficult.

Structural, territorial reforms were not completely foreclosed as home rule reforms progressed throughout the nation. Annexation continued to be quite accessible throughout much of the Sunbelt and West, and this remains true today thanks to large expanses of unincorporated land and liberal laws that allow major cities to aggressively pursue jurisdictional growth and even exercise some control outside their boundaries through extraterritorial jurisdiction. Atlanta's growth from three square miles to 130 square miles included a quadrupling in size from 1950 to 1970. San Antonio was 36 square miles in 1930, 160 square miles by 1960 (outstripping Detroit despite having less than a third of that city's population at the time), and 465 square miles in 2015—with plans for continued expansion into the city's large sphere of extraterritorial jurisdiction.

40 *Governing the Region through Cooperation*

Consolidations were still occurring, also in many states in the Southeast and lower Midwest, with a jump in such activity in the 1970s and again in the 1990s.

Metropolitan residents were also finding ways to improve public services while retaining their burgeoning autonomy. While the expansion and centralization of *general*-purpose regional governance seemed impossible, special purpose regional governance was both legally viable and popular. By 1952, the U.S. had more than 12,000 special-purpose districts.[4] New York, Illinois, and California—the states that were host to the most populous urban areas—led the way in district formation, highlighting the practical need for large-scale systems maintenance amidst fragmented political landscapes. In the 1960s and 1970s, multi-purpose districts were also becoming more popular, but these still only tackled systems maintenance.

Two truths are evident from the preceding discussion. First, even with structural reforms it has been impossible to achieve unitary metropolitan areas with a single, general-purpose government for all functions. Annexation came close to attaining this reality, a fact recognized by David Rusk in his work on "cities without suburbs" and the importance of elastic boundaries (1993). But even then many suburbs were able to resist annexation as the city grew outward. And consolidation was—with the exception of New York City's five-borough consolidation—a one-county affair that had largely become an activity of small- and medium-size cities (Carr & Feiock, 2001). It, too, often left independent, island municipalities, and would sometimes only tackle basic services. The steady rise in power of the suburbs in the first half of the twentieth century meant that annexation and consolidation—the bulwarks of structural reform—were all but abandoned by regional reform advocates by the 1950s.

Second, local governments continue to be, in a very real sense, "creatures of the state." They do not enjoy federal constitutional protection. The word "local" appears nowhere in the foundational legal document of the U.S., and the Supreme Court has referred to local governments as nothing more, legally, than "convenient agencies for exercising … such powers as may be entrusted to them."[5] An aggressive state legislature—ideally backed by enough popular support to prevent such action being political suicide—could dissolve incorporated municipalities. But in many states a majority of legislators represent suburban districts, or come from the suburbs. The laws of the 50 states reflect—to varying degrees—a widespread commitment to encouraging fragmentation of policymaking authority among local governments that have well-defined spheres of autonomy and territorial integrity. Most metropolitan regions are characterized, as I emphasized in Chapter 1, by *polycentrism* and *localism*: they have many local governments, and most of these governments have a robust power to control the affairs within their boundaries and maintain territorial integrity. This reality represents a political choice, and it is open to reform.

The Limitations of State and Federal Intervention

The continuing rise of home rule empowerment and limitations on structural reforms in the postwar era would promote a shift toward what Wallis (1994) described as the "second wave" of regionalism: one that respected local governments as they then existed and sought to encourage their coordination and cooperation rather than boundary reform. Intergovernmental incentives for comprehensive planning and coordinated action among existing sub-state units began to proliferate, and the first metropolitan Council of Government formed in Detroit in 1954. By the late 1970s over 90 percent of all counties were members of 660 Councils of Government (COGs), largely in response to the federal programs and grants that made cooperation and coordination all but essential for local governments (Wallis, 1994).

In two metropolitan areas, the drive for coordination across multiple service areas would result in forms of regional governance that have proved enduring. The Twin Cities Metropolitan Council was promoted by both citizens and legislators in response to a suburban wastewater treatment crisis and a need for regional transit, plus the general lack of planning coordination across seven counties and nearly 200 general-purpose local governments. The efforts in the Twin Cities would eventually expand to include regional tax-base sharing (which is still a rarity at the metropolitan scale in the U.S.) and a Metropolitan Housing and Development Authority. A metropolitan council appointed by the governor from distinct geographic districts would address regional planning efforts, though these would remain advisory. In 1970, Portland voters approved a Metropolitan Service District which, less than a decade later, would became the modern-day Metro, a body elected by metropolitan-wide voting that would be in charge of large swaths of planning and service provision. Both the Minneapolis and Portland efforts were built atop Metropolitan Planning Commissions that had been formed in the 1950s.

The 1970s also saw several states take back a modicum of control from local governments as part of a "quiet revolution" in land use planning and management (Bosselman & Callies, 1971). While a full survey of the eight growth management efforts from that decade is beyond the scope of this book (Gale, 1992), a few themes are worth highlighting. First, most included provisions to allow review of developments that would have a regional impact. Second, all contained consistency requirements, typically requiring that local comprehensive plans be consistent with county plans but sometimes going above this up to the state level. Thus, they were clearly an effort at least superficially to dampen the urge of local governments to use their land use autonomy to opt out of regional interests.

The progress made from the 1950s through the 1970s was short-lived. The changes were most immediate at the federal level. Under the Reagan administration, nearly every program that had incentivized coordination or cooperation was defunded or dismantled. COGs, once at the forefront of the second wave of regionalism, lost much of their value as intermediaries and retreated to

42 *Governing the Region through Cooperation*

technocratic consultancy and mild advocacy, a position that most still occupy today. Over time, the quiet revolution ultimately proved too quiet, with significant retention or return of local power in many growth management states.

When I say that state and federal interventions are limited in their ability to promote regional governance, I do not mean that they are limited in their *legal* ability. As noted in the previous section, local governments only exist at the pleasure of state governments and the behavior of local officials is shaped thoroughly by a regulative institutional structure created by states. And the federal government can prove hugely influential through intergovernmental grants. The problem is a lack of commitment by legislators at either level to promoting regionalizing reforms—whether through mandate or through incentive—either because it would create political costs or because it would offer no political rewards.

Distinguishing Cooperation

In light of the preceding discussion, it is evident that metropolitan regionalizing reform has been left to the voluntary collective action of local governments—i.e., to interlocal cooperation.[6] In the remainder of the book, I refer to all such cooperation as interlocal cooperation; others have used the term "intermunicipal cooperation," but I shy away from it because of the varying use of the word "municipality" in many state statutes. Some state statutes use the word even for those units that are not incorporated. Interlocal cooperation does not have a settled definition. I define it as discretionary action among the officials of two or more general-purpose local governments to address an issue that could not be addressed as well (in terms of effectiveness, efficiency, equity, or another criterion of importance to local actors) or at all without sharing and coordination of resources. *Local government* refers to counties, cities, townships, villages, and other units below the level of the state, or a similar regional government in a federal system, such as a province. Interlocal is not synonymous with intergovernmental, which typically means between federal and state governments; it also does not cover cross-sectoral arrangements between public and private entities, which have typically been the focus of governance scholarship.

Discretionary means that exit and entry are through the voluntary action of local legislative or administrative actors. The state and federal governments may offer incentives or impose penalties to influence this decision, but these do not create a de facto or de jure legal requirement. Interlocal agreements are typically established within a state statutory framework authorizing their creation, but not mandating it (Taylor & Bassett, 2007). Discretionary also means that while local residents may have strong opinions about the arrangement, they do not necessarily control its ratification or repeal through a referendum. This is a feature much more common to consolidation or other centralizing forms of regionalism in which a local government may be completely dissolved. The dramatic reorganization and rescaling of representation justifies, in such instances, a direct appeal to the public for approval.

Specialized means that while two local governments may have a variety of arrangements, some formal and others handshake deals, these are all discrete. The failure of one link might lead to the failure of another, or of the entire inter-local relationship, but this is not functionally inevitable. This piecemeal development is logical, since each agreement would be among a particular set of local officials dealing with specific circumstances, relationships, and interests (Thurmaier & Wood, 2002).

Interlocal cooperation is unique among forms of governance because it retains local boundaries and is a voluntary endeavor with the possibility of exit. Many modes of regional governance do not respect local boundaries, whether functionally, geographically, or formally. Full consolidation combines the local government with the county in which it sits (Carr & Feiock, 2004; Leland & Cannon, 1997; Lyons & Lowery, 1989). Merger, a less common variation that occurs between two horizontally aligned local units, such as two cities or a city and township, also reduces the number of governments. Annexation, whether consensual or involuntary depending on state enabling legislation, also redefines local boundaries (Fleischmann, 1986; Galloway & Landis, 1986; Liner & McGregor, 1996).

Interlocal cooperation is also unique because it can target policies—in areas like land use, affordable housing, and public transit—that bear directly on regional dilemmas. The formation of special districts as a method of governance has exploded in popularity, and can create occasionally powerful units with their own unique authority. However, these are only used for gap filling in service provision rather than regional problem solving (Foster, 1997; Hawkins, 1976; Bollens, 1986).

Enabling Cooperation

Every state has carved out an institutional path for regional governance through interlocal cooperation. Sometimes that path is made quite clear through explicit enabling legislation (Reynolds, 2003; Briffault, 1990a). Other times the path is poorly marked because the ability of local governments to cooperate is only implied in other grants, or in the general home rule legislation. Many local government officials are likely unaware they can cooperate, and many hail from states in which the use of Dillon's rule by state courts may make the lack of a clear textual commitment to cooperation quite problematic. But, in general, the residents and representatives of local jurisdictions have the ability to decide how they will use the autonomy they have. State laws provide a decision-making space within which action can occur, but it is local representatives or residents whose behavior animates that space. In short, if competition is possible, then cooperation is, too.

In Michigan alone, multiple pieces of state legislation have been passed over the last seven decades that touch on interlocal cooperation. The Regional Planning Act (1945; Act 281) allowed for the creation and funding of regional planning commissions among two or more municipalities to govern part or all or the

44   *Governing the Region through Cooperation*

land within their jurisdictional boundaries. The Intergovernmental Contracts Between Municipalities Act (1951; Act 35) authorized a municipality to contract with others "for the ownership, operation, or performance, jointly, or by any one or more on behalf of all, of any property, facility or service which each would have the power to own, operate or perform separately." More plainly, if a municipality could legally engage in a certain activity, then it could also contract to do so on behalf of one or more other municipalities. The 1967 session saw two key pieces of legislation passed: the Urban Cooperation Act (1967; Act 7) and the Intergovernmental Transfers of Functions and Responsibilities Act (1967; Act 8). The former authorizes Michigan public agencies (which includes any local unit of government, extending to municipalities of all type, special districts, and authorities) to enter into intergovernmental agreements with any other public agencies in Michigan, other states, and Canada. The latter act authorizes cities, villages, and other political subdivisions to enter into contracts transferring functions or responsibilities to one another. In 1984, the passage of Act 425 allowed for the conditional transfer of property by contract between governments for up to 50 years (Zeemering, 2008).

Most recently, and most pertinently for this book, in 2003 the passage of the Joint Municipal Planning Act (JMPA; Act 226) made explicit the ability of counties, townships, cities, and villages to cooperatively plan and zone, even allowing them to dissolve their own planning commissions and zoning boards of appeal and vest authority with joint bodies. The JMPA was the major legislative outcome from a push in the direction of growth management during Governor Jennifer Granholm's first year in office. The Michigan Land Use Leadership Council (MLULC), a bipartisan committee created by the Governor, had prepared a lengthy report on the state of land use in Michigan, including a detailed chapter on improvements to the legal framework for land use planning and zoning ("Michigan's Land, Michigan's Future"). The MLULC report noted that "Michigan's local governments are not required to coordinate plans, zoning, or infrastructure with adjoining units of local government or with the county, region, or state" and that "[t]here is no state statutory authority for joint planning or joint zoning for those cities, villages, and townships that wish to do so cooperatively" (pp. 53–54). The report recommended ensuring in the future that "[i]ncentives and tools (including existing tools and the creation of new ones) are available, and disincentives are eliminated to allow local governments to make better land use decisions and to improve intergovernmental coordination and planning" (p. 54). The report also spoke extensively about the competition encouraged among municipalities due to the combination of home rule authority, an overreliance on property taxes, and the negative effects of horizontal and vertical fragmentation. The JMPA, at the time of its passage, was therefore seen as an opportunity to adjust the decision space for land use planning and regulation. However, the lack of incentives and mandates, and even ongoing promotional or educational efforts, suggest a lack of commitment to the recommendations of the MLULC report.

Awareness of the Law

Before concluding this chapter, it is useful to address just how well-acquainted local officials are with the laws about cooperation. I briefly mentioned regulative legitimacy in Chapter 1 when I outlined the sociocultural collective action framework. I noted that this source of legitimacy is perhaps the most literal and simplest to understand: actors internalize prescriptions from laws, regulations, and other formalized rules, and act in accordance with these prescriptions. As a very basic example, we would expect that if a state were to ban cooperation among local governments the activity would not occur, at least not formally. But laws are complicated. To function well, the policy targets of a law must have an appreciation of the sphere of rights and responsibilities accorded by a piece of legislation. Regulative legitimacy is not simply about the *objective* reality of behaving in a legal way, although this is the most critical component of it. Rather, it is also about the *subjective* perception of legitimacy: what an actor knows and understands about the legal terrain. A prescription, even one grounded in the law, can easily become internalized in different ways by different actors.

There is evidence of this happening in Michigan. The first survey items asked whether a local elected official was aware of the JMPA. It also asked whether the official's municipality had a JMPA agreement and whether the municipality had some other interlocal agreement that affected land use decisions. Respondents were split in their awareness of the JMPA: 246 were aware of it (about 46 percent) while 292 were not. However, 238 respondents (44 percent) did not know if their municipality was part of such an agreement. About one-fifth (98) said their municipality was, even though only *nine* municipalities in the study area were, at the time, participating in a joint planning agreement and only six local elected officials from these municipalities responded to the survey.[7] This shows a large disconnect between local elected officials and state law, at least the law that addresses regional governance: while many respondents are aware of the JMPA, many do not know if their community has one, and they may be confusing a JMPA agreement with some other formal or informal coordinating activity.

More than a quarter of respondents (150 of 538) said their municipality had some other type of cooperative agreement that affects land use planning and zoning decisions. Such arrangements could come in a variety of forms, and it is difficult to accurately count how many exist with secondary research. About a fifth did not know if their municipality had such an arrangement (115 of 538). Whether a local elected official believed his municipality was involved in land use cooperation (through the JMPA or another piece of legislation) had no connection to the demographic or fiscal characteristics of the municipality. Some individual characteristics led to not being aware of the JMPA, or not knowing about land use cooperation in one's own municipality. As expected, those with awareness of the JMPA had been in office about two-and-a-half years longer (about 11 years versus 8.5 years). Elected officials who did not know whether

46 *Governing the Region through Cooperation*

their municipality had an agreement had been in office, on average, about four years less (about 11.5 years versus 7.5 years). For knowledge of other types of land use-relevant cooperation, the gap was closer to five years. Local elected terms in office in Michigan range from two years to four years.

JMPA awareness was similar among different municipal types—for example cities versus general law townships. When asked about the agreements their municipalities had, local elected officials from cities (either council-manager or mayor-council) and more densely populated municipalities were more likely to give an "*I don't know*" response than a "*yes*" or "*no*" than their peers in townships and villages, perhaps because elected officials in such contexts rely more on various administrative actors to maintain cooperative activity.[8]

Conclusion

I have demonstrated in this chapter that voluntary interlocal cooperation is, arguably, the most viable path to metropolitan regional governance under the current state–local legal framework. Under this framework, polycentrism and localism have been so clearly prioritized that infringements on either—whether through limitations on incorporation, diminution of home rule, or relaxation of the procedural and substantive hurdles to consolidation, annexation, and other structural and territorial reforms—are highly unlikely. These normative values have also been largely accepted in scholarship on metropolitan governance. Even those who are regionalists have accepted networked, cooperative governance in place of unitary government.

Interlocal cooperation can target any public service that local governments provide, from systems maintenance functions to lifestyle services. *The Risk of Regional Governance* focuses on interlocal cooperation in land use planning and regulation. This is because I expect it to be an area in which the logic of economizing is difficult and in which the logic of legitimizing—in particular cultural legitimizing—will show through. Land use is, intrinsically, about controlling social relationships, as are cultural worldviews. Dennis Coyle (1993, pp. 5–6) has observed:

> [a]s a laboratory for finding everyday people grappling with the great questions of social life in circumstances with direct impact on the participants, a hearing at the local land use commission is hard to beat. ... By joining together under the banner of government, individuals can extend their control beyond their private world.

Land use cooperation provides something of an extreme case: if we cannot discern the functioning of cultural worldviews in preferences about interlocal cooperation over land use policy, then we are unlikely to find it elsewhere.

Land use also matters, greatly, to metropolitan quality of life. Many of the most insoluble metropolitan problems, I have noted already, can be traced to the fragmentation of land use authority across dozens if not more than a hundred

Governing the Region through Cooperation 47

incorporated units, a reality noted by scholars advocating for regional reform (Rusk, 1993; Peirce, Johnson, & Hall, 1993; Orfield, 1997; 2002; Downs, 2004). As one observer remarked, "In fragmented governmental settings, the dice are institutionally loaded against policies designed to enhance desegregated housing location, the matching of fiscal resources and fiscal needs, and the effective management of growth and economic development" (Lowery, 2000, p. 73). The social, economic, and ecologic unity of the metropolitan area is politically and fiscally splintered by local boundaries. The scale of what Susskind and Hoben (2003) have coined "problem-sheds" rarely is bounded by or perfectly aligned with the boundaries of a single, general-purpose local government. Through land use regulation, communities can shape their future character, from the tax base that forms the backbone of municipal revenues to what types of residents are admitted. Land use policy represents a tension point between regionalism and localism because that which is best for the region may directly contradict what local residents and their public representatives hope to achieve through the planning and regulation of land use (Briffault, 1996).

This tension is at the heart of the question posed by Jimenez and Hendrick at the start of the chapter: "[a]ssuming voluntary, cooperative action is possible ... will it be limited to solving easy problems with fewer conflicting interests and outcomes?" (2010, p. 266). Advocates of the polycentrist, localist vision of metropolitan America have yet to articulate a convincing account of how local governments that have been gifted a high degree of initiative and immunity in land use planning and regulation—a sphere of autonomy that persists even amidst state growth management reforms that should directly diminish it—can possibly work together.

I propose that the potential of interlocal cooperation to address lifestyle services has never been fully interrogated because there have been no systematic attempts to target the multiple legitimizing logics that support local autonomy—regulative, normative, and cultural. The question moving forward is which narrative of local government decision-making has more explanatory purchase: one in which actors economize within the constraints of mediating institutions to find the best form of governance or one in which they have a wider latitude than we imagine to choose cooperation or competition, with their choice reflecting multiple legitimizing influences. The rest of the book can be read as an argument that the latter explanation is the stronger one.

Notes

1 The Manchester Area Joint Master Plan (2009) is available at http://swwcog.org/ regional_issues/chicken_broil_html/manchester_jpc/jpc_Master_Plan_Draft_ October_8_2008.doc (last accessed March 8, 2017).
2 The two villages became cities, and still remain landlocked municipalities within Detroit.
3 The first eight consolidations were successful, and none relied on referendum. The National Association of Counties tracks consolidations, and has data for 1805 through 2010. Following World War II, as the outlying areas in urban counties became home to

48 *Governing the Region through Cooperation*

more incorporated communities with more residents and more political clout, many states adopted constitutional reforms or changes to enabling legislation that allowed consolidation only through recourse to a local referendum. Still, consolidation remained an attractive option for many places. Even if it failed more often than it succeeded, the three decades from 1947 to 1977 would see 18 more city–county consolidations. The pace would slow slightly in the next four decades, with only another dozen consolidations passing. Harrigan and Vogel provide a history of consolidation's successes and failures (2000, p. 350).

4 Two states—Illinois and California—already had more than 1,000 by that decade, and another four states had more than 500.

5 *Hunter* v. *City of Pittsburgh*, 207 U.S. 161 (1907).

6 Interlocal cooperation is not the prevailing behavior by local governments. Internal, direct production and provision remain dominant for service delivery (Brown & Potoski, 2003, pp. 455–456; Warner & Hebdon, 2001). Still, the scope and variety of cooperation continue to expand. Many types of interlocal cooperation exist, including mutual-aid agreements, memoranda of understanding, intergovernmental fee-for-service arrangements, joint service agreements, equipment and facilities sharing, joint planning agreements, intergovernmental service transfers, and boundary agreements to share the costs and revenue of development and negotiate or coordinate other issues (Andrew, 2009).

7 This included one official from Sheridan Charter Township, three from Hastings Charter Township, one from Hastings City, and one from Rutland Charter Township.

8 A local elected official with awareness of the Joint Municipal Planning Act was more than 60 percent more likely to be in a more favorable response category.

References

Allard, S., Burns, N., & Gamm, G. (1998). Representing urban interests: The local politics of state legislatures. *Studies in American Political Development, 12*(2), 267–302.

Andrew, S. A. (2009). Recent developments in the study of interjurisdictional agreements: An overview and assessment. *State and Local Government Review, 41*(2), 133–142.

Barron, D. J. (2003). Reclaiming home rule. *Harvard Law Review*, 2255–2386.

Bollens, S. A. (1986). A political-ecological analysis of income inequality in the metropolitan area. *Urban Affairs Review, 22*(2), 221–241.

Bosselman, F., & Callies, D. (1971). *The quiet revolution in land use control*. Council on Environmental Quality.

Briffault, R. (1996). The local government boundary problem in metropolitan areas. *Stanford Law Review*, 1115–1171.

Briffault, R. (1990). Our localism: Part I—the structure of local government law. *Columbia Law Review, 90*(1), 1–115.

Brown, T. L., & Potoski, M. (2003). Transaction costs and institutional explanations for government service production decisions. *Journal of Public Administration Research and Theory, 13*(4), 441–468.

Carr, J. B., & Feiock, R. C. (Eds.). (2004). *City-county consolidation and its alternatives: Reshaping the local government landscape*. M. E. Sharpe.

Coyle, D. J. (1993). *Property rights and the constitution: Shaping society through land use regulation*. SUNY Press.

Dillon, J. F. (1911). *Commentaries on the law of municipal corporations*. Little, Brown.

Downs, A. (Ed.). (2004). *Growth management and affordable housing: Do they conflict?* Brookings Institution Press.

Fleischmann, A. (1986). The politics of annexation: A preliminary assessment of competing paradigms. *Social Science Quarterly, 67*(1), 128.

Foster, K. A. (1997). *The political economy of special-purpose government.* Georgetown University Press.

Gale, D. E. (1992). Eight state-sponsored growth management programs: A comparative analysis. *Journal of the American Planning Association, 58*(4), 425–439.

Galloway, T. D., & Landis, J. D. (1986). How cities expand: Does state law make a difference? *Growth and Change, 17*(4), 25–45.

Gamm, G., & Kousser, T. (2013). No strength in numbers: The failure of big-city bills in American state legislatures, 1880–2000. *American Political Science Review, 107*(4), 663–678.

Harrigan, J. J., & Vogel, R. K. (2000). *Political change in the metropolis.* Longman Publishing Group.

Harris, R., & Lewis, R. (1998). Constructing a fault (y) zone: Misrepresentations of American cities and suburbs, 1900–1950. *Annals of the Association of American Geographers, 88*(4), 622–639.

Hawkins, R. B. (1976). *Self government by district: Myth and reality.* Hoover Institution Press.

Jimenez, B. S., & Hendrick, R. (2010). Is government consolidation the answer? *State and Local Government Review, 42*(3), 258–270.

Krane, D., Rigos, P. N., & Hill, M. (2001). *Home rule in America: A fifty-state handbook.* CQ Press.

Leland, S., & Cannon, C. (1997, April). Metropolitan city-county consolidation: Is there a recipe for success? *Annual Meeting of the Midwest Political Science Association, Chicago.*

Liner, G. H., & McGregor, R. R. (1996). Institutions and the market for annexable land. *Growth and Change, 27*(1), 55–74.

Lowery, D. (2000). A transactions costs model of metropolitan governance: Allocation versus redistribution in urban America. *Journal of Public Administration Research and Theory, 10*(1), 49–78.

Lyons, W. E., & Lowery, D. (1989). Governmental fragmentation versus consolidation: Five public-choice myths about how to create informed, involved, and happy citizens. *Public Administration Review, 49*(6), 533–543.

Marando, V. L. (1979). City-county consolidation: Reform, regionalism, referenda and requiem. *Western Political Quarterly, 32*(4), 409–421.

Monkkonen, E. H. (1990). *America becomes urban: The development of US cities & towns, 1780–1980.* University of California Press.

Orfield, M. (2002). *American metropolitics: Social segregation and sprawl.* The Brookings Institution.

Orfield, M. (1997). *Metropolitics.* The Brookings Institution.

Peirce, N., Johnson, C., & Hall, J. S. (1993). *Citistates: How urban America can prosper in a competitive world.* Seven Locks Press.

Reynolds, L. (2003). Intergovernmental cooperation, metropolitan equity, and the new regionalism. *Wash. L. Rev., 78*, 93.

Richardson Jr, J. J. (2011). Dillon's rule is from Mars, home rule is from Venus: Local government autonomy and the rules of statutory construction. *Publius: The Journal of Federalism, 41*(2), 662–685.

Rusk, D. (1993). *Cities without suburbs.* Woodrow Wilson Center Press.

50 *Governing the Region through Cooperation*

Sheppard, S. S., & Moak, L. L. (1940). New Orleans leads in consolidation. *National Civic Review, 29*(11), 724–727.

Susskind, L., & Hoben, M. (2003). Making regional policy dialogues work: A credo for metro-scale consensus building. *Temp. Envtl. L. & Tech. J., 22,* 123.

Taylor, G. D., & Bassett, E. M. (2007). Exploring boundaries in governance: Intergovernmental boundary agreements. *State and Local Government Review, 39*(3), 119–130.

Teaford, J. C. (1979). *City and suburb: The political fragmentation of metropolitan America, 1850–1970.* Johns Hopkins University Press.

Thurmaier, K., & Wood, C. (2002). Interlocal agreements as overlapping social networks: Picket-fence regionalism in metropolitan Kansas City. *Public Administration Review, 62*(5), 585–598.

Veselnak, D. (2011, March 8). Bridgewater township: Board of Trustees approves departure from Manchester Community Joint Planning Commission. *The Manchester Enterprise.*

Wallis, A. D. (1994). Inventing regionalism: The first two waves. *National Civic Review, 83*(2), 159–175.

Warner, M., & Hebdon, R. (2001). Local government restructuring: Privatization and its alternatives. *Journal of Policy Analysis and Management, 20*(2), 315–336.

Zeemering, E. S. (2008). Governing interlocal cooperation: City council interests and the implications for public management. *Public Administration Review, 68*(4), 731–741.

3 Beyond Economizing

> *Individuals are ... "embedded" in so many social, economic, and political relationships beyond their control and even cognition that it is almost absurd to speak of utility-maximizing and rational behavior in a strictly economic sense. The very concept of rationality is dependent upon its environment.*
> — Koelble (1995, p. 235)

Transaction Cost Economizing

I noted in Chapter 1 that the prevailing theoretical framework used to explain cooperation and other voluntary regional governance reform analogizes the local government to a firm in a metropolitan marketplace, with local officials as the agents of that firm engaging in governance transactions. To better understand this analogy, it is necessary first to appreciate in more detail the nuances of transaction cost economizing.

Transaction cost economizing theory began development in the 1970s as part of a New Institutional Economics program—the form rational choice institutionalism took in the field of economics (Shepsle, 1989). It adopted the theory of the firm as an organizational governance structure in place of the theory of the firm as a production function; it is an approach that applies to any issue capable of formulation as a contracting problem (Coase, 1937; 1960; Williamson, 1996; Riordan & Williamson, 1985).

Williamson describes transaction cost economics as favoring bounded rationality, a term I revisit at length in Chapter 4, because "all complex contracts are unavoidably incomplete" (1999, p. 1089). Individuals are not myopic but have foresight, and are not simply self-interested but are strategically opportunistic. The *transaction* is the unit of analysis, as one would expect, and costs arise due to *frequency*, *uncertainty*, and *asset specificity* (1999, p. 1089). The *method of governing the transaction* (hierarchy, hybrid, or market) is the outcome of interest (Williamson, 1985, p. 1). *Market* governance occurs where there is no relationship of dependency outside the contract and the identity of the parties does not matter. The buyer and seller can both be replaced by others in the marketplace. *Hybrid* governance occurs when some degree of bilateral dependence is present, and identity matters because replacement with another buyer or

52 *Beyond Economizing*

seller would be costly. *Hierarchy* occurs with vertical integration, when governance is brought in-house within the firm.

If following a transaction cost analysis, one is attentive not to the actual buyer and seller but rather to the *relationship* between them with regard to a specific good or service. Therefore, one could not say *ex ante* that a transaction had high costs simply by knowing the characteristics of the buyer and seller, or the nature of the good or service. While Herbert Simon argues individuals exist in a pervasively organizational economy where failures are dealt with by resort to the market (1991), Williamson takes the prevailing view of organizations as a response to market failures, and sees opportunistic attitudes and behaviors as the driving failure. According to Williamson, "one productive way to think about economic organization is as a means by which to economize on bounded rationality and mitigate the hazards that accrue to opportunism" (1999, p. 1090).

The transaction cost approach regards the firm (the non-market) solution as a last resort. When investments made in a market transaction are *asset specific* (i.e., they cannot be redeployed to alternative uses or users), or infrequent or uncertain, this creates risks in the absence of security features provided by rules in the play of the game (Williamson, 1998, pp. 27–28). Williamson regarded asset specificity—how specific an invested asset is to a particular transaction— as the most important of three characteristics of goods. *Uncertainty* and *frequency* matter, but they matter *only if* asset specificity is not low. Asset specificity is about redeployability: can the investment (which can be physical, human, or even social capital) be invested *as efficiently* in another transaction on the market? It is not about how capital intensive an investment is. A small, nonintensive investment can be highly asset specific, while a large, intensive investment can have low asset specificity. Asset specificity is essential to the distinction of the transaction cost approach from a (neo)classical economic approach to understanding behavior.

The features of goods are viewed in combination with transaction costs. For example, one would only begin to look at the costs of negotiation and bargaining in the case of high asset specificity. If asset specificity is low, the investments in the transaction can be redeployed readily to another exchange relationship. If asset specificity is high, redeployment is foreclosed and the parties will incur the many costs of contract hazard to maintain the bilateral exchange relationship. But this will occur only up to the point when these costs—the transaction costs—are greater than the likely costs of moving the transaction in-house.

Thus, vertical integration within the firm is a solution, but *only if* the bureaucratic transaction costs of this mode (relative to the arm's-length contract transaction costs of markets or hybrid options) do not outweigh the benefits of risk reduction from no longer interacting on the market. The selection of governance is efficient if no feasible alternative can be implemented with expected net gains (benefits less costs). This core proposition is known as the *discriminating alignment hypothesis* (Williamson, 1991, p. 277): whichever governance type minimizes transaction costs is the preferred option.

Beyond Economizing 53

To summarize transaction cost theory, one can think about how the different pieces—the three characteristics of a good, the costs of maintaining a contractual exchange relationship, and the costs of producing a good through hierarchy (in-house)—interact to yield predictions about the selection of market, hybrid, or firm (David & Han, 2004, p. 41). First, as investments become more *specific* to a transaction, the risk of incurring contractual costs (renegotiation, legal recourse, and the like) necessary to maintain that relationship becomes higher, and eventually surpasses the risk of incurring bureaucratic costs (human resources, supervision, and the like) from in-house production. In other words, as asset specificity increases, the transaction costs of the market option increase, and hierarchy becomes the best option. Second, when specific investments have been made in a transaction, *uncertainty* at high levels will make in-house production preferable. If asset specificity exists, then increasing uncertainty will lead to preference for hierarchy. Third, when specific investments have been made in a transaction, increasing *frequency* of the transaction will require constant monitoring and eventually make market costs higher than in-house production costs. Note, again, that uncertainty and frequency do not matter with low asset specificity because the failure of a market contract is not costly in that situation—even a highly uncertain and frequent one will still be less costly than the costs of producing in-house.

Cooperation as a Transaction

The dominant approach in studies of interlocal cooperation is to analogize the local government to a firm in a marketplace considering the decision whether to deliver a service on its own (self-production and/or provision) or contract with another municipality (or private firm) for delivery. Feiock (2007, p. 48) developed "a rational choice explanation for interlocal cooperation ... in which agreements occur where net benefits exceed the transaction costs of bargaining." In a later paper he remarks, "the governance preference of local government actors will depend on the nature of the problem as well as transaction costs they face" (Feiock, 2009, p. 366). The *transaction cost* is something of an umbrella concept:

> [the] characteristics of goods, the geographic, social, and demographic position of communities, the structure of local government political institutions, and the structure of the policy networks determine the scope of ... transaction cost problems and the ability of local leaders to overcome them.
>
> (Feiock, 2007, p. 53)

These structural attributes are often grouped according to which type of transaction cost they are thought to affect, including information or coordination costs, negotiation or division costs, enforcement or monitoring costs, and agency costs (Feiock, 2007).

Other attributes describe the benefits—whether collective or selective—against which costs are weighed. Many authors concur with these ideas. For

54 *Beyond Economizing*

example, Andrew, in describing his use of the institutional collective action framework, notes it is a "perspective on the formation of contractual ties according to the transaction risks associated with specific kinds of goods and services" (2009b, p. 379). An earlier article on local government service production decisions, and one that continues to serve as a touchstone for studies of interlocal cooperation across many policy areas, states that "[a]lthough the transaction costs approach has traditionally been applied to private firms' decisions about internal production and outsourcing, it can also help explain governments' service production decisions" (Brown & Potoski, 2003, p. 443). Social network ties, too, are woven into the transaction cost framework. Feiock (2007) develops transaction cost propositions about bridging and bonding ties, and LeRoux, Brandenburger, and Pandey state the institutional collective action framework "posits that the transaction costs of cooperation can be mitigated by networks and networking among local government actors" (2010, p. 270). Carr, LeRoux, and Shrestha (2009, p. 404) remark, "networks of local government officials play an important role in reducing transaction costs. Moreover, some types of network participation may help offset risks created by service transactions with highly specific assets and measurement difficulty." While not every study of interlocal cooperation uses the terminology of transaction cost economics, the frequency of reference to it suggests the approach has been widely accepted.

A general proposition flowing from the logic of economizing is that the larger the gains to a jurisdiction from resolving a problem, the greater the likelihood of cooperation (Feiock, 2007, p. 49). In cooperation these gains must flow to all participant jurisdictions. The presence of a collective benefit is a threshold requirement—it is necessary for cooperation, but it may not be sufficient. As Feiock, Steinacker, and Park note succinctly, "[t]he necessary condition for any cooperative agreement is an increase in benefits, and the larger that gain, the more likely it will outweigh the transaction costs necessary to achieve it" (2009, p. 258). Gains include improving efficiency, accessing economies of scale, capturing positive spillovers, and avoiding negative ones. Feiock and colleagues (2009) refer to the possibility for joint gains, and reason that the larger the relative benefits from interlocal cooperation, the more likely it is compared to other options. Other authors speak simply of economic and fiscal gains, an approach consistent with the notion of collective benefits (LeRoux & Carr, 2007, p. 347).

To figure out whether interlocal cooperation over systems maintenance functions is more likely in a community based on collective benefits, the most common approach is to consider fiscal distress. Municipalities with low capacity or high distress are thought to have more to gain from cooperation, typically because of cost savings from scale economies. Andrew notes "[a] longstanding presumption among scholars is that adoption of [interlocal cooperation] is often motivated by fiscal stress in local government" (2009a, pp. 136–137). Studying joint ventures in economic development, which is the closest policy area to land use found in the extant literature on cooperation, Feiock and colleagues (2009) measured distress by whether a city is predominantly residential and has access to sales tax, and through three survey measures (perceived level of economic

Beyond Economizing 55

growth, self-rated emphasis on economic development, and targeting of large businesses). It is unclear how these measures capture the idea of a collective benefit, since nothing about working together is inherently an improvement over the status quo. Indeed, a municipality that cares about economic development (as these variables generally measure) might do better by working alone and retaining a competitive advantage. Other examples of variables capturing some dimension of fiscal stress are: income per capita and the share of expenditures devoted to public works (LeRoux & Carr, 2007); per capita own-source revenue and per capita intergovernmental grants (Shrestha & Feiock, 2011); and population growth and level of tax revenues (Carr et al., 2009). The explanatory power of these fiscal distress measures is mixed, as it is for those from earlier studies (Bartle & Swayze, 1997; Morgan & Hirlinger, 1991). Again, transaction cost economizing would also demand that a transaction afford some net benefits to offset transaction costs, so it makes sense that joint benefits appear so frequently in existing studies.

The characteristics of the goods or services under consideration for cooperation also matter. In accord with Williamson, the first is *asset specificity* and the second *measurability* or *meterability*. Brown and Potoski (2003) were influential in drawing these concepts into studies of interlocal cooperation. In their work, they described asset specificity as the "degree of specialized investments ... that apply to the production of one service but are very difficult to adapt for the production of other services" such that "if a government decides to contract for such a service, it is more likely that only the selected vendor will be available in future rounds of contracting" (2003, p. 466). A service was easily measurable if it was "straightforward to monitor the activities required to deliver the service and to identify performance measures that accurately represent the quantity and quality of the service" (2003, p. 466). Based on surveys from 36 city managers and mayors, the authors calculated the average asset specificity and measurability "scores" for 64 services. The most asset specific services were "disposal of hazardous materials" and "operation of airports," while the least asset specific services were "secretarial services" and "buildings and grounds maintenance." The most easily measured were "tax bill processing" and "payroll," while the most difficult to measure were "drug and alcohol treatment" and "operation of mental health programs." Brown and Potoski then used multinomial logistic models to estimate the probability of engaging in five different types of service production across variation in this score, controlling for other municipal attributes.

According to the authors, their findings "do not support the basic transaction costs hypothesis that *increases* in asset specificity increase internal production" but suggest that high asset specificity services (which, due to the authors' definition, equate to high fixed cost services) lead to more contracting with other governments relative to other options (Brown & Potoski, 2003, p. 464). This is more reflective of the logic of economies of scale than it is of asset specificity. The findings for measurability are not much stronger: the decision to engage in internal production increased only from 58 percent to 62 percent when shifting

56 *Beyond Economizing*

from the least measurable services to the most measurable. Nevertheless, the authors conclude that empirical analysis supports "that transaction costs risks play a key role in how governments decide to organize to produce services" (2003, p. 464).

Where asset specificity and uncertainty are variables in other studies of interlocal cooperation, the approach of Brown and Potoski has been adopted whole cloth. For example, Shrestha and Feiock (2011) hypothesize a transition from the private market option, to interlocal cooperation, then to joint contracting, and finally to direct provision as asset specificity and measurability difficulty increase (if one were to look at only the likelihood of interlocal cooperation against asset specificity, the function would be an inverted "U"). Despite studying only cities in Georgia, the authors use the survey-based measures from the 36 nationally sampled city managers and mayors in Brown and Potoski's study (2003). Carr and colleagues (2009) use a similar approach for 43 city services in Michigan, but with different control variables. The findings on both asset specificity and measurability are consistent with those from another study (Shrestha & Feiock, 2009) in direction but not in magnitude, and are inconsistent with the findings of Brown and Potoski (2003) and, most importantly, the general reasoning of Williamson presented earlier. In a footnote, the authors acknowledge "the practical difficulty in developing measures of asset specificity that are able to distinguish this concept from production characteristics," and further note that the distinction matters and that conflating the two contradicts Williamson's theory (Carr et al., 2009, p. 424). However, they go on to conclude that in most instances high fixed cost services will also be high in asset specificity, and vice versa. One is left to wonder, however, why the neoclassical logic of scale economies is not simply employed instead of transaction cost economizing.

Andrew attempts to merge a social network perspective with service characteristics by asking whether contractual ties can mitigate the risks of asset specificity and measurability problems. Specifically, he reasons, first, that measurement difficulties will promote the development of "a highly dense network structure … to mitigate the problems of shirking" (2009b, p. 383) and, second, that activities with high asset specificity will generate a "sparse network … dominated by a few highly centralized actors … to reduce the costs of crafting and monitoring multiple agreements with other localities independently" (2009, pp. 7–8). The measurement of asset specificity and measurability relies, once again, on the prior work of Brown and Potoski (2003), rather than on investigation of the actual *transactions* under study consistent with transaction cost theory, and the results are mixed.

I have described so far how collective benefits and the characteristics of the services targeted for cooperation are thought to affect interlocal cooperation. What about contracting costs—the costs that are at the heart of a transaction? These come in several forms. A common approach is to roughly follow the classic Coaseian categories: agency, information, and division of gains (Feiock et al., 2009). However, most other authors do not follow this typology in

Beyond Economizing 57

discussing the many demographic and economic factors thought to affect cooperation. I use the following breakdown, which tracks more closely the extant literature: *homophily*, *network ties*, and the *density of governments*.

Homophily—usually defined as socioeconomic similarity among cooperating entities, such as local jurisdictions—was included as a determinant even in early studies and this continues into recent work. "Economic and demographic homogeneity across cities ... indicates common interests and service preferences, narrowing the range of acceptable outcomes and making cooperative agreements more probable ... [and] tends to equalize bargaining power" (Feiock et al., 2009, p. 259). Examples of variables used to test this kind of homophily include: categorical population size (as an indicator of asymmetric bargaining power) and differences between metropolitan statistical area averages and those of a local jurisdiction (2009, p. 263); and dyadic ties among local governments rather than higher-level governments (Andrew, 2009b, p. 388). Gerber, Henry, and Lubell (2013) test for *political* homophily, finding that regional planning networks are more likely to arise among local governments with politically similar constituents.

While the socioeconomic and fiscal differences *among* communities matter, heterogeneity *within* a community can also be important as a source of transaction costs. The reasoning here is drawn from principal–agent theory. If local officials are attuned to the interests of constituents, then they will better be able to aggregate the preferences of the many residents they serve. Consider an extreme example: every household in a community is exactly the same, with the same income, home value, service usage, and tax payments. Finding the median voter or discerning the public interest is simple, and since all interests are the same there is also no risk of special interest capture that may shift in subsequent bargaining. When representatives of this community come to the bargaining table, other parties will know those representatives are true agents. Thus, homogeneity

> reduces agency costs for officials negotiating interlocal agreements on behalf of citizens. Interests are less likely to be less uniform and it is more difficult to aggregate preferences and hold agents accountable in heterogeneous communities ... [where] communication costs will also be higher.
> (Feiock, 2007, p. 55)

Race is a common dimension of intralocal heterogeneity, often measured through a dissimilarity index (Shrestha & Feiock, 2011) or share of population that is non-White (Feiock et al., 2009), though it is unclear why decisions about local services would relate to race. Economic heterogeneity is more conceptually sound and has been measured by the ratio of mean household income to median household income, such that higher value indicates a more skewed distribution (Feiock et al., 2009). The study by Feiock and colleagues also used a direct survey measure about the degree to which economic development issues—the policy area under study—were controversial, and a land dissimilarity index to proxy for conflict between business and residential interests. However, the

58   *Beyond Economizing*

literature as a whole shows little consistency in measures of intralocal heterogeneity, or in findings.

Another aspect of the interlocal context is the presence or quality of network ties among local governments or local government officials, though these two levels are typically conflated (i.e., government ties proxy individual relationships). The two most used hypotheses are about bonding and bridging, which correspond roughly to the importance of strong and weak ties. Examples of strong tie variables include the frequency of interlocal contact as measured with a survey item and centrality as measured by number of mentions of a target city by other cities with regard to policy interaction (Feiock et al., 2009, p. 264). Weak ties are sometimes interpreted as membership in a common organization, such as a council of government (COG) (Carr et al., 2009, p. 416) or other regional organization (LeRoux, 2008; Feiock et al., 2009, p. 264).

However, a gap exists between why these variables matter theoretically and how they are measured empirically. For example, Shrestha and Feiock (2011) discuss the importance of mutuality and reciprocity, and the trust that evolves from this, referencing classic work by Granovetter (1985, p. 576), who notes "[r]eciprocity helps minimize opportunism and foster cooperation through predictability and repeated exchanges." Although the dynamic of trust is interpersonal (actors do not breach trust because of "reputational damage" and fear of community sanction), the authors employ a binary variable based on the presence of interlocal expenditures and interlocal revenues (Shrestha & Feiock, 2011, p. 577). However, the measure tells us about the interactions between local governments as organizations; it tells us nothing directly about trust or reputation, and this is a common problem in the literature.

Another way to incorporate the logic of network ties is to consider the role of professionalization. For example, because city managers have an administratively conjoined epistemic network (Frederickson, 1999), this is thought to reduce information costs. Studies frequently use a dichotomous measure of whether a municipality has adopted the council-manager form or not (e.g., Shrestha & Feiock, 2011). Using similar reasoning, Carr and colleagues (2009, pp. 413–414) propose positive effects on cooperation from city managers' professional networks, and include dichotomous variables for whether the form of government is council-manager and whether the city manager has a public administration professional degree and is a member of the major professional organization for city managers.

Lastly, the pool of potential partners could conceivably affect information gathering, bargaining over the division of gains, and monitoring or enforcing behavior. Confusingly, having more available partners has been viewed as both an aid and challenge to interlocal cooperation. Shrestha and Feiock (2010) view it as negative because of the potential for greater conflict of interests, and measured it as the number of general-purpose local governments divided by land area in the county in which a municipality was located. Others view having many neighbors as a positive because "[a] city is likely to have more and better information about its neighboring communities, increasing trust among them and

Beyond Economizing 59

enhancing reputational effects" (Feiock et al., 2009, p. 264). As with the other dimensions of the interlocal context, findings are mixed.

The purpose of this long sojourn into the economizing model served a few purposes. First, as the dominant model of interlocal cooperation and regional governance reforms and the referent against which I contrast my own model, it is deserving of careful attention. Second, my own research incorporates many of the variables from the rational economizing perspective to control for the possibility of normative legitimizing following this model. Lastly, much of the empirical literature flowing from this literature suffers from a lack of standardization in measures of key variables. This is not a fatal flaw, and it is one common to many bodies of research that grow out of important theoretical perspectives. But I hope that my own variable specification, described in detail in later chapters and in the appendices, is an improvement that will help provide a template for future research.

The Individual in the Local Government Organization

Now that I have described how cooperation is treated theoretically and empirically as a transaction and explored the effects of intramunicipal and intermunicipal characteristics on these transactions, I can turn to how the institutional collective action framework treats the connection between the actor (such as a local administrative or elected official) and the organization (the municipal corporation).

The literature on interlocal cooperation only mentions the question of shifting from individual to organization twice. Feiock (2009, p. 357) states:

> Only individuals are capable of action, yet individuals often act in the name of a group or organization. Thus, it is meaningful to investigate collective action among composite actors defined by position, authority, and aggregation rules. ... These rules solve the problem of matching empirically observable individual behavior with the institutionally defined unit of reference on whose behalf action is taken ... [Institutional collective action] implies capability for intentional action above the level of individuals. This requires us to focus on interactions between and within institutional units.

A similar discussion can be found in the preface to an edited volume with John Scholz (Feiock & Scholz, 2009). The literature neither theoretically nor empirically attempts to consider how variation in position, authority, and aggregation rules affects interlocal cooperation. More importantly, when explaining the link between context and outcomes the variables are always gathered at the municipal level even when the underlying mechanisms are supposed to be individual. Whether such inference is justifiable is never treated. Stated most simply, the brushing over of the *micro–macro* links—those connecting individual to organization—has allowed insight into the *circumstances* in which cooperation arises and endures. This is valuable information, but it obscures the individuals within these settings who make policy decisions.

60   *Beyond Economizing*

One reason why the individual actor seems to get so little attention is because the unifying idea of studies of interlocal cooperation is that the logic of collective action can be extended from the individual to the institutional level. However, in the careful framework building of Ostrom (2005) and Scharpf (1997), whose work is foundational to institutional collective action, the links between individual actor and organizational actor were carefully drawn. Both authors noted as necessary considerations the method of aggregation from individual to organization and the degree of alignment between individual interests and organizational interests. In short, individual–organization linkages may not need to be given much attention, but this conclusion requires empirical investigation. "[F]or some purposes, one may ignore the linked situations—especially, when the interests of the organization, and thus the strategy it will follow, are very clear and unlikely to change. ... Alternatively, one may self-consciously examine the linked structure" (Ostrom, 2005, p. 38).

Part of this linked structure is the attributes of individual participants, who "bring a diversity of ascribed or acquired characteristics to any situation. These characteristics may not influence their actions in some situations, while having a major impact on others" (Ostrom, 2005, p. 40). Some characteristics may affect the processing of information, such as "feedback from the world and the shared culture or belief system in which an individual is embedded" that shape an individual's "mental model" (2005, p. 105). Others may affect valuation, including emotions and norms, and "little empirical support exists for an assumption that all individuals value only the material outcomes that flow only to them" (2005, p. 110).

Situations can have incomplete or partial information, the distribution of information may be asymmetric, the extent of repetition may vary, and individuals may cycle in and out. Because of this, a researcher investigating institutions must often carefully investigate "how individuals view risk, uncertainty, and information asymmetries and how they react to the actions and perceived attributes of other participants" (Ostrom, 2005, p. 102). Scharpf confronts divergent "actor orientations" directly:

> [i]t is not in the real world but in the actor's mental image of the world that the attribution of causes and expected effects must be located; and actions are motivated not by actors' objective interests but by their subjective preferences.
>
> (1997, p. 60)

He treats at length the circumstances when one may adopt the assumption that a plurality of individuals can be treated as an actor (1997, pp. 51–60). For a composite unit to have the capacity for *strategic action* one must find "preexisting convergence ... of (policy-relevant) perceptions and preferences among the (policy-relevant) members ... [and] capacity for conflict resolution" (1997, p. 59). Knowing the role of an individual actor can allow inferences about the rules and norms that actor would follow, but one

Beyond Economizing 61

must remain alert to the possibility that individual self-interest, or the idio-syncratic orientations of individuals (which are never quite absent in any case), may in fact become so important in the case at hand that our explana-tions will fail if we do not take them into account.

(1997, p. 62)

The unpacking of the nature of the individual actors within a corporate "actor" follows the reasoning of Simon, who remarked in a discussion of the role of rationality in organizations "that it is sometimes possible to say a great deal about aggregate components without specifying the details of the phenomena going on within these components" (Simon, 1991, p. 126). The same point has been made more pointedly by Elster: "If we think of institutions as individuals writ large and forget that institutions are made up of individuals with divergent interests, we can be led hopelessly astray" (1989, p. 154).

Some Conceptual Issues

A narrow transaction costs approach faces some obvious conceptual difficulties. Granted, some appeal exists in the use of transaction cost theory: the rigor of an economic approach explicitly about the selection of different governance forms, and an analogy of market-hybrid-hierarchy to private-interlocal-direct provision that aligns well with the tradition of viewing the metropolitan area as a market of local governments. But the application of transaction costs logic is strained for a few reasons.

One difficulty is that the market is not the dominant default condition in the interlocal context. Most local governments have certain responsibilities, and begin in the position of hierarchy in the market-hybrid-hierarchy typology. Ver-tical integration within the firm (hierarchy) is, therefore, not a last resort. There are many services a government will have to provide, even if it does not have another government or a private partner with which to contract. Firms might very well resort to in-house production only after failing to find an economically satisfactory exchange relationship on the market or within a hybrid arrangement, as transaction cost theory predicts. But local governments resort to a hybrid structure only after failing to be able to provide an acceptable level of service under their current revenue structure.

Second, while public–private partnerships may be characterized by market-like qualities—a large number of buyers and sellers and high information—for interlocal arrangements the number of potential partners is limited. For many services adjacency is required to make interlocal delivery even remotely efficient and allow access to scale economies. And private service provid-ers may simply not be available, or not at the scale necessary to make an exchange worthwhile. A related difficulty is that local governments are argu-ably never in a market-like relationship. Rather, their interdependencies place them in the position of being in a constant condition of interdependent, hybrid governance.

62 *Beyond Economizing*

Finally, some goods and services are fundamentally different when provided locally versus cooperatively. A single government *cannot* provide regional land use planning, or protect a natural resource that spans municipal boundaries, or create a regional transportation system. Williamson's firms might find an exchange relationship adds value, but the good being produced on the market and the one produced in house are substitutes. The transaction cost approach might work well for the decision whether to engage in a public–private transaction over wastewater treatment because the service is the same regardless of the scale—the quality might improve slightly or the cost might decrease, but there is no substantive difference in the nature of locally versus cooperatively provided treatment.

Once we begin to more carefully consider the differences between market, hybrid, and hierarchy, and the nature of the goods produced and invested in Williamson's work, it is quite evident the transaction cost approach is an awkward fit for local governments. One might object the transaction cost approach is meant to simply impart insights about the dynamics of interlocal cooperation. But throughout the interlocal cooperation literature, we see struggles to make variables fit within the unified transactional logic, stretching Williamson's concepts almost beyond recognition. If the search is for insights, then much better sources seem to exist for how we might describe local governments and the actors in them.

Because the logic of economizing relies substantially on analogy, these conceptual difficulties are not insuperable. The bigger problem, however, is that economizing is likely to be completely inaccessible as a logic model in areas of cooperation that go beyond systems maintenance. At times, rationality may have to come from other sources. In the remainder of this chapter I explain why cooperation over lifestyle services likely requires moving beyond economizing.

Maintaining Systems Versus Creating Lifestyles

There is no Democrat or Republican way to pick up garbage.

The quote, most often attributed to New York City's Mayor LaGuardia in the 1930s, conveys an image of local governments as primarily administrative units where all that matters, or at least what matters most, is the effective and efficient delivery of goods and services. Residents, the maxim suggests, do not really care how well a local elected official aligns with the platform of one party or another. Opinions about access to abortion or gun regulation or marriage equality might matter when voters decide who should hold state or federal positions, but these viewpoints are largely inconsequential to voters determining who should be a mayor, city council member, or county supervisor. The engine of local politics— what drives people to give voice at the voting booth or city council meeting, and perhaps even exit by moving to another community—is not partisanship, but rather the level of satisfaction with goods and services, something over which local leaders have at least some modicum of control, and often quite a bit more

Beyond Economizing 63

than that. Do the streets have potholes? Are sidewalks cleared promptly after a snowstorm? Is the drinking water safe? Are parks accessible and well-maintained? Do buses run on time? Is the garbage being picked up?

For many of the functions of local government, LaGuardia's quip is appealingly logical. Democrats and Republicans and those of other political stripes would undoubtedly agree that efficient and effective garbage collection, as just one example among many public services, is critical to the public health, safety, welfare, and comfort that a local government is charged with advancing. No clear partisan divide exists about the need for snow plowing or treatment of drinking water or the reliability of public transit, but all are susceptible to evaluation using efficiency and effectiveness criteria. A local actor can know, often with a great deal of certainty, what the costs are of the different ways of doing the business of local government. Many goods and services are highly measurable, and require specific investments whose fixed and variable costs can be reliably estimated. There is little mystery to waste management and the like.

These characteristics also make decisions about the governance of a service relatively straightforward. Local government elected officials and administrators, faced with scarce human, capital, technical, and fiscal resources, must often turn to privatization or cooperation with neighboring local jurisdictions to meet their responsibilities. The stable, highly certain cost structures of many services make contracting, monitoring, and enforcement remarkably straightforward, whether it is with a private sector or public sector partner. The local policy actor can confidently estimate payoffs and their associated transactional risks, and try to maximize utility accordingly. From the perspective of both the resident and the local policy actor, it should matter little whether garbage collection or an array of other services are privatized, or are handled by another government, so long as value and quality are optimized.

I have noted a few times in the book already that much of the testing of inter-local cooperation hypotheses has been in the policy domains related to public works and public safety. Here, an economizing model built on a rational choice institutionalist framework seems highly applicable, for the reasons I have already articulated. While some uncertainty will always exist because the actions of a partner producer or provider are never fully predictable and because conditions may require future renegotiation, much of this can be dealt with through institutions, such as the language of a formal contract or the normative pressures of past and future dealing.

What this means is that the linkages between the individual and the organization—the local elected official and the jurisdiction she serves—do not need to be investigated for many cooperative endeavors, and that reasoning that local actors engage in market-like behavior, particularly in repetition over time, may be sound. Sometimes, measures of structural attributes and municipal level behaviors *should* correspond to the mental processes of the individual local actor and rational choice institutionalism is defensible, even if empirical evidence has not quite caught up to justifying it.

64 *Beyond Economizing*

But local governments are not simply managers of systems maintenance services. They do not just deal with the picking-up of garbage, or with the filling of potholes or clearing of sidewalks or treatment of water. They are not just in the business of systems maintenance that can, at least in theory, be offered through the private sector or another local jurisdiction. More importantly, scholars of interlocal cooperation have never limited the frameworks they use and propositions they develop to only certain types of cooperation. The promise of interlocal cooperation has never been *just* about service provision efficiency and government effectiveness, as important as those might be, and has always been touted for its potential to confront truly regional dilemmas.

As I outlined in Chapter 2, local governments have control over many functions for which boundaries and scale matter a great deal. Chief among these are land use planning and regulation, interdependent tasks that are at the heart of local autonomy in the U.S. (Briffault, 1990a). Because of the close link between autonomy and land use, local governments are typically seen, and perhaps their officials regard them, as self-determining of municipal character. Many scholars hypothesize that land use policy behavior can be predicted by municipal fiscal and demographic characteristics because zoning is an inherently fiscal and exclusionary process. Research into the determinants of land use regulation shows that many such characteristics do play a significant role (Pogodzinski & Sass, 1994; Bates & Santerre, 1994; Glaeser & Ward, 2009). Ample evidence suggests interlocal stratification by both income and race (Briggs, 2005; Logan, Stults, & Farley, 2004; Swanstrom, Dreier, & Mollenkopf, 2002). Exclusionary zoning is commonly found in higher status municipalities (Rothwell & Massey, 2010; Massey, Rothwell, & Domina, 2009; Gyourko, Saiz, & Summers, 2008). In the midst of a foreclosure crisis and recession, with a vicious cycle of vacancy, out-migration, declining property values, and decreasing revenue, the ability to differentiate may mean the difference between fiscal health and distress.

But the word *may* in the last sentence is critical: empirical evidence shows it is unclear whether the desire to zone to improve fiscal futures or exclude actually works. Consider the firm location decision, often stylized as the result of rational consideration of the total bundle of goods available in a community or region plus the subsidies offered by the local government. The evidence is mixed about whether such offers make a difference in firms' decisions (Peters & Fisher, 2004; Fisher & Peters, 1998; Logan, Whaley, & Crowder, 1997; Feiock, 1991), and even measuring success (or failure) can be difficult (Reese & Fasenfest, 1996). One of the risks of *not* cooperating is that competitive economic development policies may distort location-based decisions. A local government may lose out on new investment it would otherwise gain while other governments make concessions that diminish the revenue a development may have generated. This competition may also distort the relationship between firms and local governments, amplifying costs and muting benefits to the public sector, even as a firm may end up in roughly the same location within a metropolitan area that it would have otherwise occupied.

Beyond Economizing 65

A similar problem arises in the location decisions of households. Peterson (1981) asserted that local governments are inherently competitive, have an incentive to avoid redistributive policies, and are uniformly oriented toward economic growth. Tiebout-style sorting, described in Chapter 1, is a well-known model of responsive household migration that has motivated municipal reasoning for half a century. But it is unclear whether this competition does any good, especially when controlling for the larger scale social and economic forces that drive household moves (Percy, Hawkins, & Maier, 1995; Besley & Case, 1992; Schneider, 1989; Lowery & Lyons, 1989).

Partly this is because so much of goal realization in land use planning requires that myriad actors comply with a planning vision. Planning is an attempt to manage the uncertainty of the future, but even within a single government limitations exist as to how successful this management can be. When we move beyond the dynamics within a single municipality into the interlocal sphere, multiple jurisdictions are working together on a regional vision and uncertainty multiplies. Interlocal cooperation might enable site assembly that draws a major new industrial or commercial development, integrated parks and trails, or the preservation of a natural resource such as a watershed or green belt. But these benefits all depend on a common vision, and an outcome in which all the gains accrue to a single municipality is just as possible.

Individual elected officials, therefore, would face considerable uncertainty about the potential collective and selective benefits of cooperation. While some economies of scale might result—for example, everyone paying one consulting firm, or relying on a larger municipality's planning staff—the major results are not usually measurable or visible, or may be years away. What residents prefer may be unclear. Presumably, cooperation is "good" if it is locally beneficial, but "bad" if it is locally detrimental. Knowing this in advance, however, is impossible. Knowing how residents define the locality may also be tricky. The lives of residents in a metropolitan area rarely operate within municipal boundaries, and quality of life may link just as strongly to the region outside the municipality as it does to the smaller community within the municipality.

In short, the institutions that structure decisions about interlocal cooperation—the rules and norms conveying which patterns of action will yield the highest net benefit for the municipality, and determining the links between the interests of the municipality and the interests of the individual administrative or elected official—are likely to be weak for land use planning. One could object that the transaction costs framework is meant to describe situations with strong institutions—situations where the analogy to the firm and the reliance on rational choice institutionalism is supportable. But the ambitions of the framework have never been so limited. As noted in the discussion of the debate between public choice localism and reform regionalism, resolution hinges on the viability of interlocal cooperation not only over systems maintenance functions where efficiency is often the driving concern, but also in policy areas where equity, sustainability, and other contentious measures of success come into play. Land

66 *Beyond Economizing*

use—and other lifestyle policies that bear directly on who can live in a community and how the built environment interacts with the natural one—is one of these policy areas.

When Reform Seems Irrational

So far I have dealt largely in theory, but empirical evidence also suggests the economizing model may be incomplete in providing an account of the dynamics of interlocal cooperation. A persistent but under-emphasized finding in the literature on regionalizing reforms is that economizing—either in the transaction cost or neoclassical sense—is not always a satisfying explanation.

Most pertinently, Thurmaier and Wood (2002, p. 587), studying interlocal agreements as social exchange networks by interviewing chief administrative officers and chief financial officers in a case study of local governments in the Kansas City metropolitan area, found that "economizing value is not the predominant rationale for [interlocal agreement] participation." The authors continue:

> [a]lthough there is surely a definable set of [interlocal agreements] that have developed from desires for direct economizing activities, with few exceptions, cost reduction was seldom the primary reason for [interlocal agreements]. The overwhelming lack of evidence that economizing is a continuing aspect of [interlocal agreements] ... suggests to us there are one or more alternative values that better explain the existence and continued propagation of interlocal agreements.
>
> (2002, pp. 593–594)

Alternative values included, for example, "help[ing] smaller neighboring jurisdictions," or needing a program to run more effectively even if it meant no cost savings (2002, p. 594). In later work with Chen, this time using data from a decade-long statewide survey of local officials in Iowa municipalities, the analysis reinforced the earlier findings, and careful interview work by Zeemering (2008) leads to similar conclusions. LeRoux and Carr (2007, p. 355) also find that "despite the expected cost advantages of collaborating on public works services, many local governments do not collaborate." To paraphrase Herbert Simon (1991), the distribution of organizational forms does not always mimic what we would expect under a transaction cost mechanism that is well functioning.[1]

The idea that interlocal cooperation might be more than an exercise in economizing had its genesis not in secondary literature review but rather in several unstructured interviews with local elected officials in northern Michigan communities. In the spring and summer of 2013, before I had even thought about doing large-scale surveys or began to sketch the shape of the sociocultural collective action framework, I wanted to simply explore why Michigan's Joint Municipal Planning Act (JMPA)—described at length in Chapter 2—had been so unpopular. Recall that the act was a bare-bones enabling act: it simply assured

Beyond Economizing   67

municipal actors explicitly that land use planning and regulation could be done cooperatively. The formation of joint planning agreements was minimal, and I assumed the lack of promotion and incentives was partly to blame. Later survey results would, indeed, bear this out. As I review in more detail in Chapter 5, most local elected officials had never heard of the JMPA, and another large group confused it with other types of cooperation. But this lack of knowledge was useful: I could present the possibilities of joint municipal land use with whatever framing I wanted. I could simply provide the text of the statute, or I could accompany it with stories of success and failure. The JMPA, in my stylized scenarios, could be something residents supported or opposed. It could be a source of great cost savings, or none at all. Communities that had used it could have had large increases in their tax base, or could have experienced the problem of all new growth going to their neighbors with no redistribution back to them.

Researchers always enter a situation with expectations of some form, and what I expected to encounter were rational economizers. Specifically, I wanted to get an initial response to the JMPA and then see how this changed as different facts were presented. I assumed the biggest motivator for local elected officials would be the "results" of an artificial poll of residents, and that fiscal information might also have some influence. I also expected that current intramunicipal and intermunicipal characteristics would matter, as the institutional collective action framework suggested.

Instead, the conversations presented me with a puzzle. When I spoke about joint municipal planning and zoning, the initial sentiments being expressed had no grounding in any of the ideas about efficiency I was anticipating. I would usually start the conversation by explaining, in very bare terms, what I wanted to talk to them about, being careful not to use words like local and regional: Michigan had passed an act several years earlier, and I wanted to figure out what local officials thought about it both in general and for their community. I would allow them to read the act, ask how they felt about it (*"on a scale of 1 to 10, 10 being most favorable ..."*), and then ask them to explain why. I was used to elected officials pinning their preferences to what was best for their constituents or what was best for their jurisdiction, and theory had taught me to expect this kind of language. It rarely happened. Instead, the justifications for preferences were highly abstract. One township supervisor, a Democrat, noted that she "just never liked this big government idea." A city council member—who also identified as a Democrat and hailed from a nearby community—remarked, "I just always believed two heads were better than one."[2]

I could discount some of these comments as kneejerk reactions. I was, after all, asking officials to form preferences and justify them in the span of a few minutes, with no information. What happened next, however, was even more peculiar: the initial negative or positive response to cooperation persisted, even as I introduced scenarios that depicted highly skewed costs and benefits from cooperation—extreme cost efficiencies, tales of massive tax base loss, polls and conversations with residents about wide margins of support or opposition. Sometimes these would budge preferences, but never enough to change them. Those

68 *Beyond Economizing*

who opposed cooperation were ready to disregard or diminish information touting its many benefits. Those who favored it were just as willing to ignore information portraying cooperation as a uniformly costly idea. One off-the-record comment was particularly telling: "I'm here to serve the people, but sometimes they're not that smart about how things work."

I also discovered that these views only became more entrenched as I presented different forms of JMPA cooperation. Recall that an agreement can be structured to cover a shared part of two jurisdictions, or can extend to the jurisdictional boundaries. It can also be drafted in an advisory or authoritative way, with the authoritative option requiring a phased dissolution of the local planning commissions and zoning boards. I expected those opposed to cooperation to become more resistant as the scope and impact of cooperation expanded. But those who tentatively favored cooperation—initially, before any information was presented beyond the statutory text—persisted in their support, too.

At the end of the interviews, when I revealed the information was false, the officials were often quick to point out that they were onto my game. One exchange is memorable. A township board member, upon learning that I had made up poll results and that the residents did not in fact *support* joint planning and zoning by a 65:35 margin in her community, exclaimed, "I thought that must be bogus! I knew people here wouldn't feel that way." What made the comment so striking was that her fellow township board member had said almost the exact same thing about the township's residents—but I had presented her "false" information that the residents were *opposed* to joint planning by a 65:35 margin. Both board members, *serving in the same community*, were so utterly convinced about whether land use cooperation was or was not in the public interest that they were willing even to discount or ignore statistics about their own constituents. This inconsistency within the exact same institutional setting fit with the overall distribution of preferences. Opposition to cooperation did not arise in only one type of community. The same was true of support. It seemed to be scattered around randomly, and at the time it was utterly confounding. I could only assume—for several weeks—that dealing with preferences was a dead end.

I would later recognize that most of these officials were engaging in rational *legitimizing*, and that they were looking to their own cultural worldviews as the source of that legitimacy because all the other institutional signals were failing them. The JMPA itself was not telling them what was appropriate. It had no mandate or incentive attached. And even if their position in government supported rational economizing for fiscal or political gain, in the *initial* assessment of the JMPA they had no cues to help them toward this end. The only appropriate thing to do was make a cultural judgment.

The interviews would lead, months later, to the large-scale survey at the heart of the research in this book. While I reserve further discussion of the survey findings for Chapters 5 and 6, a few observations about the preferences toward interlocal land use cooperation deserve emphasis. First, these preferences *did* vary, even in a large group of heterogeneous elected officials from widely varying settings. I present the data on preferences in Appendix E. Respondents had the option of expressing a neutral sentiment about joint municipal planning, but they overwhelmingly did not. This was true even though many respondents knew nothing about the act and had no direct experience with it.

Second, preferences did exhibit some consistency across different types of interlocal cooperation. Someone who supported a very strong form of cooperation—one that required dissolution of local planning and zoning functions and a complete scaling up to a regional level—would almost always support a weaker, advisory form of cooperation. But the reverse did not always hold: many who supported advisory cooperation would oppose authoritative cooperation. Similarly, support for cooperation that covered the full territory of all participating jurisdictions usually meant the respondent also supported partial area cooperation, but the reverse was not always true. Some respondents, in other words, were comfortable with weaker forms of cooperation at a smaller scale, but not stronger forms at a larger scale. Those who felt favorably toward the latter were usually uniformly positive about all forms of cooperation. And some were opposed to all forms of cooperation. This consistency gave me some confidence that the responses to scenarios about cooperation were not just random and had some thought behind them.

The third point about the surveys is the most important: in almost two-thirds of the jurisdictions that had at least two respondents, preferences were divergent for at least one of the land use cooperation scenarios. By divergent, I mean that one official would express support or strong support for cooperation, and that another—from the same jurisdiction—would express opposition or strong opposition. Not only was there no tendency for a certain type of jurisdiction to consistently produce support or opposition, but the same exact jurisdictional setting could be home to very different views about cooperation. In terms of sociocultural collective action, the logic of appropriateness seemed to be tied to something outside the organizational setting. As I show in Chapter 6, that something else was the cultural worldview of each elected official.

We can also infer evidence of non-economizing legitimization at work in the stories that opened this book. It is easy to frame the decision to opt-out of suburban transit as an expression of rational choice. Indeed, this is often how local elected officials defended the opt-out decision: constituents simply did not want regional busing because the annual cost of participation was too high, and the buses were not needed where everyone had personal vehicles. Other piecemeal programs could help serve those few older residents or poor households who might not have ready access to a car. But even in the consideration of an efficiency criterion we can see the imposition of subjective frames. If an actor focused on short-term, jurisdictionally bounded costs and benefits and past rates of ridership, she would easily conclude that regional transit was a losing proposition. Focus on the potential for long-term gains, positive economic spillovers, and increased ridership on an improved system, and she would—again, using an efficiency criterion—determine that regional transit would be a net boon. In the act of considering whether to opt-in or opt-out, an actor would have to be engaging in an act of imaginative economizing. The only party remotely

70 *Beyond Economizing*

capable of engaging in rational economizing in the RTA scenario is, I suggest, the individual voter. The voter would likely know what the millage would cost in annual property taxes. The voter would know, too, how much she would need transit. But even here the veneer of rationality wears thin. On the benefit side of the ledger, it is a question of values—not of utility—whether we include *only* the material benefits that are selective and personal and proximate flowing only to us as individuals and will do so only in the near term. Some voters were clearly doing this, as were some politicians.

The tricky thing with regional transit is that it requires a *vision* of potential benefits, many of which will only flow to the individual indirectly and diffusely. The only way to explain the closeness of the vote for the RTA is to recognize that many voters were able to imagine such a vision. Planners reading this will surely recognize that much of their job is about persuading the public or stakeholders that one vision of the future is superior to others, and part of the RTA plan and the marketing of it, similarly, was about the envisioning of the future of the region.

The same was true in Flint in the late 1950s. New Flint was a proposal that could give the city needed land while providing the suburban residents the quality of life improvements they desired. It seemed to be that most rare of regional efforts: the structural reform that would be mutually advantageous for all its participants. Even its robust promotional campaign was tailored to highlight the specific benefits it could offer both the city and the suburbs. New Flint was framed not as a realization of normative arguments favoring centralizing government reform through annexation or consolidation (the terms were completely avoided in promotional campaigning), but rather as a joining together by all the area governments to create a new city that would benefit all with greater efficiency, economic growth, and improved infrastructure. It was sold as a dream of economic rationality. Those opposing New Flint, meanwhile, spoke of suburban identity, local democracy, and the prevention of subjugation to the central city—themes that resonate as being quite integral to the suburban consciousness.

The battle of messages being fought in Flint was, fundamentally, a battle *not* between logics of instrumentality but rather between logics of appropriateness. The residents of the many local governments in Flint never had the chance to have their voices heard at the ballot box, and so we cannot know how much actual support existed for New Flint in the suburbs, and we also cannot rely on historic exit polls to understand the attributes of those who opposed or supported the reform. Fortunately, as I noted in Chapter 1, suburban residents were the subject of an extensive survey about attitudes toward the city, its suburbs, and the relationship between the two. Amos Hawley and Basil Zimmer, the two sociologists who had been advocates of New Flint and wanted to explain the resistance to unification in Genesee County through surveys of the general public, found that opposition to New Flint was strong. This was true among residents in those suburban jurisdictions that had been the most dependent on Flint historically, and it even persisted among those residents who had higher levels of education. The resistance crossed class and race divisions. The researchers were

Beyond Economizing 71

confounded, and readily characterized the typical suburban resident as incapable of understanding the relationship between government form and their needs and desires. There was a

> general lack of interest in any cooperative approach to common problems on the part both of core city and of fringe officials. Much antagonism and suspicion has characterized their relations. It seems that each has sought, within his own domain, to preserve independent existence, even at the cost of inefficient service.
>
> (Zimmer & Hawley, 1956, p. 258)

Unfortunately for the prospects of regionalism in Genesee County, a strong spirit of localism had already taken root in the suburbs. It was not just rooted in race or class or housing tenure, because it crossed so many demographic categories and lifestyle circumstances. Recall that the reality of the suburban dream outside Flint for decades was one of rural slums and poor services, a reality that had existed in the early decades of the twentieth century and that persisted after the war. Part of the suburban identity was akin to a pioneer spirit—a willingness to endure roads, water, sewers, and other public goods and services that were far inferior to those in the City of Flint. Townships had limited taxing authority, and a limited tax base against which to use this authority. They had no easy way out of their circumstances without direct assistance from Flint. But despite the salability of a rational, economic narrative that could promote a unified New Flint, suburbanites and their representatives were strongly opposed to it.

Conclusion

The two stories from southeast Michigan, introduced in Chapter 1 and revisited in this chapter, highlighted the ways in which regional governance might not necessarily hinge on the logic of economizing, even if it is presented in those terms. The brief recounting of the interviews with local elected officials about interlocal land use cooperation, and the survey results that built on these interviews, showed that even with no or minimal information elected officials were capable of developing preferences about cooperation, and that these preferences proved consistent and remarkably durable. The lack of alignment between jurisdictional characteristics and preferences, and the ability of strongly divergent preferences to come even from local elected officials working in the same jurisdictions, further suggests that this heuristic reasoning was not simply being built on past experience or kneejerk rational economizing learned through experience. The extant literature, too, hints at the possibility that economizing might not be the primary motivation for explaining interlocal cooperation and other regionalizing reforms, even when targeting systems maintenance functions that should be amenable to such reasoning. In the next chapter, I develop the sociocultural collective action framework as a way to explain these peculiar findings as more than just irrational outcomes.

72 *Beyond Economizing*

Notes

1 While I do not address in this book the literature on general public attitudes about issues related to planning and cooperation, many scholars have studied attitudes about growth management and regional planning at the metropolitan and state level. Wassmer and Lascher (2006, p. 623) highlight the "lack of consensus about findings" in their exhaustive review of this literature.
2 All interview transcripts are on file with the author, with information about position and municipal characteristics included but all other identifying information removed.

References

Andrew, S. A. (2009a). Recent developments in the study of interjurisdictional agreements: An overview and assessment. *State and Local Government Review, 41*(2), 133–142.

Andrew, S. A. (2009b). Regional integration through contracting networks: An empirical analysis of institutional collection action framework. *Urban Affairs Review, 44*(3), 378–402.

Barron, D. J., & Frug, G. E. (2005). Defensive localism: A view of the field from the field. *JL & Pol., 21*, 261.

Bartle, J. R., & Swayze, R. (1997). Interlocal cooperation in Nebraska. *Unpublished report prepared for the Nebraska Mandates Management Initiative.*

Bates, L. J., & Santerre, R. E. (1994). The determinants of restrictive residential zoning: Some empirical findings. *Journal of Regional Science, 34*(2), 253–263.

Besley, T., & Case, A. (1992). *Incumbent behavior: Vote seeking, tax setting and yardstick competition.* National Bureau of Economic Research.

Briffault, R. (1990). Our localism: Part I—the structure of local government law. *Columbia Law Review, 90*(1), 1–115.

Brown, T. L., & Potoski, M. (2003). Transaction costs and institutional explanations for government service production decisions. *Journal of Public Administration Research and Theory, 13*(4), 441–468.

Carr, J. B., LeRoux, K., & Shrestha, M. (2009). Institutional ties, transaction costs, and external service production. *Urban Affairs Review, 44*(3), 403–427.

Coase, R. H. (1960). The problem of social cost. *Journal of Law and Economics, 3*(1).

Coase, R. H. (1937). The nature of the firm. *Economica, 4*(16), 386–405.

David, R. J., & Han, S. K. (2004). A systematic assessment of the empirical support for transaction cost economics. *Strategic Management Journal, 25*(1), 39–58.

De Souza Briggs, X. (2005). *The geography of opportunity: Race and housing choice in metropolitan America.* Brookings Institution Press.

Elster, J. (1989). *Solomonic judgements: Studies in the limitation of rationality.* Cambridge University Press.

Feiock, R. C. (2009). Metropolitan governance and institutional collective action. *Urban Affairs Review, 44*(3), 356–377.

Feiock, R. C. (2007). Rational choice and regional governance. *Journal of Urban Affairs, 29*(1), 47–63.

Feiock, R. C. (1991). The effects of economic development policy on local economic growth. *American Journal of Political Science*, 643–655.

Feiock, R. C., Steinacker, A., & Park, H. J. (2009). Institutional collective action and economic development joint ventures. *Public Administration Review, 69*(2), 256–270.

Fisher, P. S., & Peters, A. H. (1998). Industrial incentives: Competition among American states and cities. *Employment Research Newsletter, 5*(2), 1.

Beyond Economizing 73

Frederickson, H. G. (1999). The repositioning of American public administration. *PS: Political Science & Politics, 32*(4), 701–712.

Gerber, E. R., Henry, A. D., & Lubell, M. (2013). Political homophily and collaboration in regional planning networks. *American Journal of Political Science, 57*(3), 598–610.

Glaeser, E. L., & Ward, B. A. (2009). The causes and consequences of land use regulation: Evidence from Greater Boston. *Journal of Urban Economics, 65*(3), 265–278.

Granovetter, M. (1985). Economic action and social structure: The problem of embeddedness. *American Journal of Sociology, 91*(3), 481–510.

Gyourko, J., Saiz, A., & Summers, A. (2008). A new measure of the local regulatory environment for housing markets: The Wharton Residential Land Use Regulatory Index. *Urban Studies, 45*(3), 693–729.

Koelble, T. A. (1995). The new institutionalism in political science and sociology. *Comparative Politics, 27*(2), 231–243.

LeRoux, K. (2008). Nonprofit community conferences: The role of alternative regional institutions in interlocal service delivery. *State and Local Government Review, 40*(3), 160–172.

LeRoux, K., Brandenburger, P. W., & Pandey, S. K. (2010). Interlocal service cooperation in US cities: A social network explanation. *Public Administration Review, 70*(2), 268–278.

LeRoux, K., & Carr, J. B. (2007). Explaining local government cooperation on public works: Evidence from Michigan. *Public Works Management & Policy, 12*(1), 344–358.

Logan, J. R., Stults, B. J., & Farley, R. (2004). Segregation of minorities in the metropolis: Two decades of change. *Demography, 41*(1), 1–22.

Logan, J. R., Whaley, R. B., & Crowder, K. (1997). The character and consequences of growth regimes: An assessment of 20 years of research. *Urban Affairs Review, 32*(5), 603–630.

Lowery, D., & Lyons, W. E. (1989). The impact of jurisdictional boundaries: An individual-level test of the Tiebout model. *The Journal of Politics, 51*(1), 73–97.

Massey, D. S., Rothwell, J., & Domina, T. (2009). The changing bases of segregation in the United States. *The Annals of the American Academy of Political and Social Science, 626*(1), 74–90.

Morgan, D. R., & Hirlinger, M. W. (1991). Intergovernmental service contracts: A multivariate explanation. *Urban Affairs Quarterly, 27*(1), 128–144.

Ostrom, E. (2005). *Understanding institutional diversity.* Princeton University Press.

Percy, S. L., Hawkins, B. W., & Maier, P. E. (1995). Revisiting Tiebout: Moving rationales and interjurisdictional relocation. *Publius: The Journal of Federalism, 25*(4), 1–17.

Peters, A., & Fisher, P. (2004). The failures of economic development incentives. *Journal of the American Planning Association, 70*(1), 27–37.

Peterson, P. E. (1981). *City limits.* University of Chicago Press.

Pogodzinski, J. M., & Sass, T. R. (1994). The theory and estimation of endogenous zoning. *Regional Science and Urban Economics, 24*(5), 601–630.

Reese, L. A., & Fasenfest, D. (1996). More of the same: A research note on local economic development policies over time. *Economic Development Quarterly, 10*(3), 280–289.

Riordan, M. H., & Williamson, O. E. (1985). Asset specificity and economic organization. *International Journal of Industrial Organization, 3*(4), 365–378.

Rothwell, J. T., & Massey, D. S. (2010). Density zoning and class segregation in US metropolitan areas. *Social Science Quarterly, 91*(5), 1123–1143.

74 Beyond Economizing

Scharpf, F. W. (1997). *Games real actors play: Actor-centered institutionalism in policy research.* Avalon Publishing.

Schneider, M. (1989). Intermunicipal competition, budget-maximizing bureaucrats, and the level of suburban competition. *American Journal of Political Science*, 612–628.

Shepsle, K. A. (1989). Studying institutions some lessons from the rational choice approach. *Journal of Theoretical Politics*, *1*(2), 131–147.

Shrestha, M. K., & Feiock, R. C. (2011). Transaction cost, exchange embeddedness, and interlocal cooperation in local public goods supply. *Political Research Quarterly*, *64*(3), 573–587.

Shrestha, M. K., & Feiock, R. C. (2009). Governing US metropolitan areas: Self-organizing and multiplex service networks. *American Politics Research*, *37*(5), 801–823.

Simon, H. A. (1991). Bounded rationality and organizational learning. *Organization Science*, *2*(1), 125–134.

Swanstrom, T., Dreier, P., & Mollenkopf, J. (2002). Economic inequality and public policy: The power of place. *City & Community*, *1*(4), 349–372.

Thurmaier, K., & Wood, C. (2002). Interlocal agreements as overlapping social networks: Picket-fence regionalism in metropolitan Kansas City. *Public Administration Review*, *62*(5), 585–598.

Wassmer, R. W., & Lascher Jr., E. L. (2006). Who supports local growth and regional planning to deal with its consequences? *Urban Affairs Review*, *41*(5), 621–645.

Williamson, O. E. (1999). Public and private bureaucracies: A transaction cost economics perspectives. *Journal of Law, Economics, and Organization*, *15*(1), 306–342.

Williamson, O. E. (1998). The institutions of governance. *The American Economic Review*, *88*(2), 75–79.

Williamson, O. E. (1996). *The mechanisms of governance.* Oxford University Press.

Williamson, O. E. (1991). Comparative economic organization: The analysis of discrete structural alternatives. *Administrative Science Quarterly*, 269–296.

Williamson, O. E. (1985). *The economic institutions of capitalism.* Simon & Schuster.

Zeemering, E. S. (2008). Governing interlocal cooperation: City council interests and the implications for public management. *Public Administration Review*, *68*(4), 731–741.

Zimmer, B. G., & Hawley, A. H. (1956). Approaches to the solution of fringe problems: Preferences of residents in the Flint metropolitan area. *Public Administration Review*, *16*(4), 258–268.

4   Sociocultural Collective Action

> *What an individual will see as "rational action" is itself socially constituted. ...*
> *If rational choice theorists often posit a world of individuals or organizations*
> *seeking to maximize their material well-being, sociologists frequently posit a*
> *world of individuals ... seeking to define and express their identity in socially*
> *appropriate ways.*
>
> — Hall and Taylor (1996, p. 949)

Introduction

Institutions are the common thread between the institutional collective action framework, which currently dominates the study of interlocal cooperation, and sociocultural collective action, which I suggest could add considerably to our understanding of cooperation. The study of institutions has been central to political science since its inception. The debate among the various adherents of new institutionalism, among those who agree that institutions matter but disagree over how, is at the heart of that most fundamental of social science questions: how do we explain preferences and behaviors?

Building on the discussion in Chapter 3, I structure this chapter around two questions. First, how do individuals think and behave? In other words, what does it mean for them to be rational? Answering this question requires some preliminary grounding in rational choice theory, and so I begin the chapter with a brief tour of it before contrasting the economizing and legitimizing perspectives that describe rationality, respectively, under the institutional collective action and sociocultural collective action frameworks. Second, what is the nature of the relationship of the individual to *institutions*? To answer this question, I define institutions, and then distinguish between institutional mediation versus institutional embeddedness.

Revisiting Rationality

Theories of rationality are central to the social sciences. Simon once remarked, "Nothing is more fundamental in setting our research agenda and informing our research methods than our view of the nature of the human beings whose

76 Sociocultural Collective Action

behavior we are studying," and this nature includes their cognitive preference formation and choice processes (1985, p. 303). If we want to generalize about the individuals we study in one situation to those in other contexts or in the future, then we must be clear about how we are modeling those individuals. What are the assumptions we have made about how they think and behave?

My starting point is rational action, which is simply selection by actors among alternative courses of action in accordance with assumptions about rationality that depend on situational attributes. When I use the term *actor* in this section, unless indicated otherwise I am referring solely to individual human beings, not to aggregate, corporate, or collective actors, as these units are incapable of engaging in actual choice. Early on, rational choice theory was based on the principle of utilitarian *optimizing*,[1] per which actors are certain of the consequences of all *possible* actions and have perfect (i.e., complete) information about the linkages between actions and consequences. Actors have a consistent cardinal utility function in which utility is defined by material self-interest. The invariability of preferences—that they always orient to material self-interest and are unchanging—is not strictly necessary for rational choice, but it is a simplifying assumption adopted nearly universally.

We can regard the evolution of rational choice models away from this unconstrained or basic model as an attempt to bring the abstract rational actor closer to that existing in the real world—a series of relaxations of strict assumptions that were often unrealistic. For example, most situations of choice are marked by risk or uncertainty rather than complete certainty (Harsanyi, 1977), and so rational choice models began to incorporate these into the theory about utility formation. Another relaxation was in the area of optimization itself. Facing objections that the calculations necessary for true rational choice were prohibitive in light of the limited capacity of most decision-makers in real-world settings, Friedman and others advanced an "as if" hypothesis: individuals could not make rational choice optimizing calculations in most cases, but behaved as if they were doing so. This was the foundation of the Chicago (or American) school (Friedman & Savage, 1948; Friedman, 1953). Others promoted models of constrained optimization (Stigler, 1961; Anderson & Milson, 1989), in which actors do not look at the universe of all possible action but stop searching for information about alternatives once the benefits of continued search outweigh costs.[2]

While optimizing rational choice theory has loosened in some ways, it has remained quite consistent in its treatment of preferences, which are either unobservable, irrelevant, or both. However, utility, in its original Benthamic conceptualization, *was* a psychic reality—that which brought utility to one actor did not necessarily bring it to another. If one were to chart the process of taking an action, one would start within the mind and then finally arrive at the selection of an alternative as an expressed behavioral outcome. The process moves from preference formation to choice. The optimizing models offered by early rational choice theorists focused squarely on the logic of choice. For Friedman, individuals who failed to act as if they were optimizers would be excluded, in a natural selection-like process, from the market. Whatever happened *within* the mind was

Sociocultural Collective Action 77

only relevant in that it distinguished those who were rational from those who were irrational.

The turn from optimizing models and Friedman's Chicago school perspective began with Allais, who used an experimental approach to directly observe preferences that violated the assumptions of strategic expected utility. One response to these findings was adjustment of the utility function (Hey, 1991). The shift continued in the work of Simon (Cyert, Simon, & Trow, 1956) and Tversky and Kahnemann (1975; 1986), who explicitly included mental processes in their research. They used experimental methods to further test—and find questionable—the assumptions of strategic expected utility (Camerer, 2003).

The problem with optimization theory, in the view of this scholarship, was that it "finesse[d] completely the origins of the values that enter into the utility function ... [and] finesse[d] just as completely the processes for ascertaining the facts of the present and future states of the world" (Simon, 1990, p. 14). The alternative was a behavioral model of rationality as a mental process. The analytical focus, accordingly, shifted from the *logic of choice* to the *psychology of valuation* of the bounded processes of search and selection.

Under bounded rationality, we assume that individuals do not attempt to optimize or are not necessarily consistent across all situations and over time; even the actors within a single situation are not necessarily following the same model of rational choice (Simon, 1991). Simon's vision of bounded rationality has at its core two limitations: those of the human mind (cognitive), and those of the surrounding environment (ecological) (Simon, 1990). Regarding the first, people are serial processors limited in their time, energy, knowledge, capacity to learn, and the like; regarding the second, situations can be ill-defined, information can be imperfect, and links between actions and consequences can be vague. Actors, therefore, cannot optimize but "must use approximate methods" (Simon, 1990, p. 6). These methods can be generally thought of as heuristics, of which *satisficing* (a combination of satisfying and sufficing that involves setting a well-defined aspiration and taking actions to achieve it) is the most well-known and most often associated with bounded rationality (Simon, 1990). Other "rules of thumb" are possible. Cognitive and ecological limitations are related: heuristics tend to be adopted that have performed well in past iterations of the same situation or in similar situations. One can identify heuristics and understand why they work (or not) only with awareness of the attributes of the external environment.

For Simon, and for others following the logic of bounded rationality, the psychology of choice is inherently social: the values with which we focus attention, the alternatives of which we are aware, and our understanding of the links between actions and consequences "derive from our interaction with the social environment" (Simon, 1990, p. 75). It is this social environment that prevents bounded rationality from sliding into unbridled subjectivity and idiosyncratic explanations. Institutions are a key source of regularity and stability in the social environment. Even the market or quasi-market setting in which optimization occurs "takes place within an intricate environment of institutions" (Simon, 1985, p. 78). Rather than look to the assumptions of classic rational choice

78 *Sociocultural Collective Action*

models as a way to reduce variation, the investigator can instead look to institutions for this task (Scharpf, 1997). If the rules and norms are well-known enough to shape an actor's choice calculus, then they should leave evidence an outsider can observe. The preceding discussion demonstrates that the universe of what is *rational* continues to expand with improved understanding of the mental processes and real-world choices of actors. The boundary is not a Friedman-esque distinction between the rational and the irrational, but rather between different forms of rationality adjusted to best describe the actors in a situation.

For each model of rational choice, one must specify three assumptions. According to Ostrom, one must decide (1) "the way that participants acquire, process, represent, retain, and use *information*"; (2) "the *valuation* that participants assign to actions and outcomes"; and (3) "the processes (maximizing, satisficing, or using [other] diverse heuristics) that participants use for *selecting* particular actions or strategic chains of actions in light of their resources" (2005, p. 103). Any theory of the actor requires an *information-valuation-selection* specification.

The actual rational choice mechanisms behind economizing are only rarely mentioned directly in the literature on interlocal cooperation. In one excerpt, Shrestha and Feiock (2011, p. 584) state:

> *Self-interested* behavior together with *limited* rationality and the inherently incomplete nature of agreements make exchange risky. Actors, therefore, look for a governing mechanism that minimizes the transaction risks. Exchanges are also embedded in relationships. Relational structures such as mutual trust and mutual sanctions facilitate exchange by minimizing ex ante and ex post opportunism.

While the rational processes of information acquisition and selection are barely treated except to give a throwaway mention of limited—presumably bounded— rationality, the operation of valuation is fairly clear. Interlocal cooperation scholars "assume that institutional actors select the available strategy that most enhances their (generally short-term) interests, in the absence of mitigating institutions" (Feiock, 2009, p. 358). The actor is self-interested, boundedly rational, and opportunistic, and this makes the use of another government or firm for service provision or production a risky proposition. The many attributes of municipalities, their neighbors, and the services they target for cooperation (plus a handful of quasi-individual attributes still measured by proxies at the municipal or network level) shape the governance choices of the rational opportunist (Feiock, 2007; Shrestha & Feiock, 2011; Andrew, 2009; Feiock, Steinacker, & Park, 2009; Andrew & Carr, 2013).

Despite rationality for these actors being described as *bounded*, the interpretation of that term is prospective. It is not about the *present* cognitive limitations of serial processing, but about the inability to forecast the future and deal with this uncertainty in a contract. In other words, the meaning aligns with the work of Williamson rather than Simon. In the present, the actor still is presumed to be

Sociocultural Collective Action 79

able to know a rather large volume of objective information that enables choosing efficiently among difference forms of governance.

In the sociological institutionalist perspective, rational choice is thoroughly dominated by institutions, reflecting an old adage that economists are preoccupied with choice while sociologists are concerned with the lack of choice. Individuals are bounded in the sense described by Simon, and they do pursue utility, but the kind of utility function they use depends on institutions, which I discuss more in the next section.

Information acquisition is still very much bounded; at least at this stage the two frameworks imagine actors similarly. But valuation is quite different: in place of the opportunist who is uniformly self-interested and emphasizes material utility is an actor who values actions according to the degree to which they are appropriate to someone in his position, both viewed narrowly (within an organization) and broadly (within a cultural affiliation). Selection does not demand maximization but is rather based on heuristics drawn from the multiple sources of legitimacy. An actor will become highly familiar over time with which preferences and attitudes are the most appropriate, and develop regulative, normative, and cultural cues on which to draw. In short, institutions define the very nature of rational choice. Sometimes it will look exactly as it does, to the empirical investigator at least, under rational economizing, and yield the same pattern of preferences and behaviors. But the underlying reason is not because economizing is always how rational choice functions for all actors or even for a single actor all the time. Rather, economizing—in the sociological institutionalist perspective I follow—only occurs where it is cognitively feasible and is legitimate under the institutional circumstances. The logic of appropriateness requires careful, thoughtful reasoning. It is in no sense irrational. But the rationality is directed not to some instrumental end or future consequence. Rather than a concern with material utility, actors judge actions and preferences by how closely they align with the multiple sources of legitimacy (March & Olsen, 2004). I describe this more in the next section.

Individuals and Institutions

Institutions, then, are bound up with notions of how rational choice works in interlocal cooperation, but the way they matter in the sociological institutionalist perspective is different from how they matter in a rational choice institutionalist one.

Douglass North, working in the new institutionalist economics tradition, defined the term as follows:

> the humanly devised constraints that structure political, economic, and social interactions. They are composed of both formal rules (statute law, common law, regulations), informal constraints (conventions, norms of behavior, and self-imposed rules of behavior); and the enforcement characteristics of both.

(1992, p. 4)

80 *Sociocultural Collective Action*

Institutions are durable, surviving even after the circumstances that gave rise to them no longer exist. March and Olsen (2004, p. 21), similarly, define institutions as "rules of conduct in organizations, routines, and repertoires of procedures." As was true of North's definition, institutions can include formal rules, procedures, organizational standards, and governance structures, but also conventions and customs.

The concept of the institution is quite broad. Rational choice institutionalists suggest that individuals create institutions to foster their interests and encourage desired outcomes, and most existing studies of interlocal cooperation draw insights from this perspective by adopting insights from Fritz Scharpf's actor-centered institutionalism and Elinor Ostrom's institutional analysis and development framework (Feiock & Scholz, 2009; Feiock, 2007; 2009; Andersen & Pierre, 2010).[3]

Ostrom is clear that institutions matter, but that they are far from fully explanatory: "[t]he focus on the components of institutions ... should not be interpreted to mean that ... institutions are the *only* factor affecting outcomes in all action situations" (2005, p. 29). For Scharpf (1997), whose work was also influential for institutional collective action scholars, institutions receive a similar treatment: they provide stability and regularity, and much of what we would need to explain outcomes can be found in institutions. But the constraints are not absolute.

> Even binding rules may be violated by actors who are willing to pay the price of sanctions being applied or who subjectively discount their incidence. More generally, the influence of institutions on perceptions and preferences, and hence on intentions, can never be complete.
>
> (1997, p. 42)

Cognitive orientations, preferences, identity, and norms all play a role.

What Ostrom and Scharpf are describing is a role for institutions that is *mediating* in individual rational choice mechanisms. While room is left for investigating cognition, the institutional collective action theorists—as I noted in Chapter 3—view individuals in political decision-making processes as transaction cost economizers. Individuals seek to maximize attainment of goals from a specific preference function, and these are exogenous to any institutional analysis. The institutions provide information, enable monitoring and enforcement, and structure agency. They determine the structure of the choice situations in which actors exist, such as economic transactions among local governments.

The view of sociological institutionalists is somewhat different: institutions do not just intervene in a rational choice calculus, but instead are deterministic. The individual is embedded in a world of institutions (Granovetter, 1985). These do more than provide information to be used in calculation. Individuals are not free to choose among institutions, such as rules, procedures, and norms (Powell & DiMaggio, 2012, p. 10), and institutions also determine identity—who an actor is, and what it means for that actor to be moral or good or appropriate in a

Sociocultural Collective Action 81

situation (Powell & DiMaggio, 2012). Institutions are the sources of internalized prescriptions (Hall & Taylor, 1996). They are the sources, more plainly, of legitimacy.

The legitimizing perspective uses an expanded definition of institutions: they are not merely rules and organizational norms—such as procedures, standards, and governance structures—but also social conventions and customs (DiMaggio & Powell, 1991). Rules, as the reader can intuit by now, provide prescriptions that are internalized from structural legal constraints (for example, the enabling statutes discussed in Chapter 2 that shape local autonomy). Norms provide their prescriptions through the socialization of an actor within an organizational position (for example, a town planner or city council member). Any organizational change, such as a shift in the mode of governance from a non-cooperative status quo toward cooperation, can *only* survive if it comports with both formal institutions (rules) and informal institutions (norms).

The highly controlling nature of institutions may seem, on first impression, an awkward view of the individual—especially as a policy actor within the public sector. Surely we are not completely dominated by the rules and norms that inhere in the positions we occupy as we move through life. Surely there is some room for opinion and ideology and the interjection of the self. This tension between institutional constraint and individual action is reconciled through an expansion of the concept of the institution to include prescriptions grounded in *culture*, which is the third source of legitimacy (Scott, 2001). The inclusion of culture marks a significant shift taken by sociological institutionalists, and drove the research behind this book.

I save a more thorough definition and operationalization of culture for Chapter 6. At this early stage, culture can be adequately described as the aggregation of socializing experiences that create in us a worldview about how people should relate to each other (Wildavsky, 1987). If cues are not found readily in rules and norms, but individuals nevertheless have to decide where they will give limited, usually serial attention under bounded rationality (Simon, 1990; Ostrom, 2005), then they can rely on prescriptions internalized from cultural worldviews. We internalize these prescriptions from our broader social lives in the same way we internalize the various prescriptions from our organizational lives. If anything, cultural prescriptions are much harder to change, and may be harder to ignore. Cultural worldviews equip us with "rules of thumb" or heuristics that can be used in all decisions, including those about governance, and across all organizational contexts, whereas the heuristics developed from rules and norms are often unique to a specific organizational setting.

Because individuals are part of so many organizational contexts, each with rules and norms dictating what is appropriate and what is not, and because culture is always present in the background, individuals are so thoroughly embedded that the notion of a singular rational choice floating apart from institutions is simply not tenable. Indeed, the very concept of rationality is dependent upon its environment. What this means for the selection of organizational form—in this book, the selection of governance, and its attendant institutions—is that it will not

82 *Sociocultural Collective Action*

be chosen to minimize transaction costs but rather to maximize legitimacy. It will simply seem like the natural way, if not the only conceivable way, to do things. To survive, organizations must accommodate multiple institutional expectations, and these may have little to do with technical or economizing notions of performance (D'Aunno, Sutton, & Price, 1991; DiMaggio & Powell, 1991; Scott, 1987).

The Appropriateness of Regional Reform

We can now review the sociocultural collective action framework. The appropriate unit of analysis is the individual actor, such as a local elected or administrative official, and that individual is embedded in a rich institutional environment comprised of rules, norms, and cultural worldviews. These institutions do not mediate preference formation and behavioral outcomes, but are rather the source of internalized prescriptions.

We would expect, first, that all else being equal the local official would prefer and engage in behaviors that have regulative legitimacy. Stated most plainly, the official will attempt to behave in a way that is legal, to the best of his ability and knowledge. Regulative legitimacy might have only a weak role in some settings, but in the public sector in a small government it is reasonable to expect it to have a strong role. Of course, this expectation can be tested.

We would expect, second, that the local official would have prescriptions internalized as social norms from the organizational setting, conceived both narrowly and broadly. For example, a staff planner would want to follow the norms that inhere in her field, and would want to also follow the norms befitting someone in an administrative position in her city.

It is through the rationality of normative legitimizing that transaction cost economizing might enter into the preferences and behaviors we see in regional governance. Three norms, in particular, are relevant here. The first is, obviously, a norm of economizing that we would expect to be internalized specifically by bureaucrats—i.e., administrative but not elected officials—through the process of professionalization and the constraints of their position, especially when they are administering systems maintenance functions (Sonenblum, Kirlin, & Ries, 1977; Morgan & Hirlinger, 1991; Bartle & Swayze, 1997). Such a norm would also be consistent with a general ethos of duty and loyalty to the public (Heclo, 2002; Perry & Wise, 1990; Mosher, 1982). The second is a norm of reciprocity, which is well-known in social exchange theory as the foundation for relationships of trust (Coleman, 1988; Emerson, 1976) and has been applied to local government and governance (Frederickson, 1999; Maloney, Smith, & Stoker, 2000; Coffé & Geys, 2005). The third norm is political responsiveness: the notion that a political actor would want to represent voters or some abstract conception of the public interest, and not necessarily only because it instrumentally might provide political reward. I treat this norm at length in Chapter 5 because it has not before been incorporated into the literature on metropolitan governance.

Taken together, these three norms are suggestive of many of the components of the current institutional collective action framework (Carr & Hawkins, 2013; Feiock, Jeong, & Kim, 2003; Clingermayer & Feiock, 1997). However, viewing them through the lens of legitimizing can help make sense of situations when the norm of economizing by itself seems to offer little explanatory purchase. For example, some evidence exists that reciprocity norms can trump economizing in systems maintenance interlocal agreements (Thurmaier & Wood, 2002), and that economizing can be quite difficult even for administrators. The legitimizing approach would instead ask *for these administrative officials in this institutional context, what are the internalized prescriptions that are most dominant?* By contrast, most extant research on interlocal collective action tends to conflate the two norms and assume they carry equal weight. It also assumes that a norm of economizing is always available, even though—as I have shown—it is likely only available for systems maintenance functions.

Finally, we would expect legitimizing to also operate through a third type of institution: culture. Culture is the broader set of lifelong social experiences from which an individual develops dispositions about how relationships should be arranged. In the same way that rules and norms create prescriptions actors internalize, dispositions work together to create a worldview capable of generating heuristics that can function across organizational settings. Cultural dispositions are measurable, and they can be linked systematically to preferences about governance because, as I show in detail in Chapter 6, they speak directly to notions of independence and differentiation that are at the heart of local autonomy. All else being equal, we expect certain cultural "types" to support interlocal cooperation and other voluntary regionalizing reforms (see Figure 4.1).

When one starts to consider cultural worldviews, a valid fear is the slide into unbridled subjectivity and a constant embrace of idiosyncrasy. However, the incorporation of culture should not be read as advocacy for throwing out models

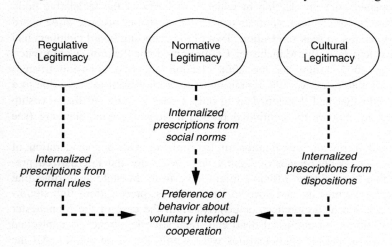

Figure 4.1 The Sociocultural Collective Action Framework.

84 *Sociocultural Collective Action*

and assumptions. It is the recognition, rather, of a need to examine more carefully whether propositions based on the current rational choice institutionalist assumptions about cooperation—those embedded in models of transaction cost economizing—are actually functioning well both conceptually and empirically for systems maintenance and can be extended to lifestyle services. In short, "[s]ubjectivity need not rule out regularity as long as different sorts of people feel subjective in similar ways with regard to similar objects" (Thompson, Ellis, & Wildavsky, 1990, p. xiii). A highly appealing feature of existing studies of interlocal cooperation is that they can promote both quantitative and qualitative study, and the sociocultural collective action framework is designed to retain that characteristic.

An Illustration

To show how legitimizing differs from economizing, I return to the story from the introduction to Chapter 2 about the rise and fall of the Manchester Community in southeastern Michigan. One township did not ratify (or even vote on) a JMPA agreement despite being a member of SWWCOG, one repealed its agreement with a split vote following a few months of negotiation (Bridgewater Township), one followed suit with a unanimous repeal vote within the next year (Freedom Township), and one continues to have the agreement in force (Manchester Township, along with Manchester Village). Adoption and repeal occur at two very different points in time, with the latter happening after exposure to the joint planning process. Focusing on Sharon Township and Bridgewater Township can provide insight into the limitations of institutional explanations, at least as currently studied in the literature.

Looking only at municipal-level data would obscure this narrative. The repeal by Bridgewater Township, the first domino to fall in the decline of the regional effort, happened after an election in which a majority of the legislative body changed, not due to electoral contests or partisan shifts but because three board members opted not to seek re-election. Two of the departing board members had voted to participate in the Manchester Community Joint Planning Commission (MCJPC) in 2007. Following the 2008 election, the two township trustees who were eligible to be MCJPC representatives did not want to serve due to a three–two split that had developed, with only a bare majority of the township board showing support for continued participation in regional planning (see Table 4.1).

We would begin an investigation of legitimizing with a consideration of regulations—i.e., with *regulative legitimizing*. What are the internalized prescriptions that local elected officials might have from the state-level rules that govern local governments, and does variation in these prescriptions link significantly to variation in preferences or behaviors? In the case of the Manchester Community, this is an empirical dead end; regulative legitimacy is controlled because all participating municipalities were within the same county. All the townships in the Manchester Community were general law townships, meaning

Table 4.1 Comparison of Townships near Manchester Village that Considered Adoption of a Joint Land Use Agreement

	Sharon Township		Freedom Township		Bridgewater Township		Manchester Township	
JMPA outcome	Never adopted		Repeal		Repeal		Adopted	
COG member	yes		yes		yes		yes	
Elections	2004	2008	2004	2008	2004	2008	2004	2008
# primary contests	0/5	2/5	1/5	1/5	1/5	2/5	0/7	0/7
# general elec. contests	1/5	1/5	0/5	1/5	1/5	0/5	0/5	0/7
uncontested turnover	1/5	**2/5**	2/5	**2/5**	4/5	**3/5**	2/5*	**0/7**
Demographic/fiscal measures	2000	2010	2000	2010	2000	2010	2000	2010
Population	1,678	1,737	1,580	1,330	1,646	1,674	4,102	4,569
% pop. ≥62	11.5	20.0	11.8	18.6	11.9	19.5	14.0	18.4
% White	96.7	98.0	93.1	97.8	99.1	98.8	98.1	97.4
Unemp. rate	1.2	4.2	2.6	5.5	1.9	3.7	2.3	4.5
Mean hh. inc. ($)	75,622	84,708	68,315	89,605	73,939	89,712	67,878	73,709
% hh owneroccupied	97.4	93.5	91.7	91.1	97.2	93.3	94.1	90.1
% units single family detached	96.0	99.6	89.3	92.8	93.0	99.5	75.0	79.8
Med. housing value ($)	170,900	248,500	203,600	266,900	158,800	240,400	147,600	195,400
% structures built, last 10 yrs	25.2	10.2	14.4	6.8	24.5	15.9	26.4	12.1
% hh moved in over last 10 yrs	50.5	19.8	47.9	33.6	55.1	35.1	57.5	50.9
Fiscal measures	2008	2009	2008	2009	2008	2009	2008	2009
Gen. fund revenue ($)	267,134	264,095	251,887	278,959	490,118	463,747	623,766	660,527
Gen. fund expenditures ($)	—	248,435	307,222	250,858	436,793	428,252	537,140	671,009
Taxable value ($1,000)	92,418	90,892	93,995	93,910	86,602	87,178	196,581	190,688

86 *Sociocultural Collective Action*

that all faced the exact same legal framework: the same level of autonomy, the same fiscal policy space, the same incentives and challenges with regard to what they could and could not do. While the master plans and zoning ordinances for each community reflect the unique natural and manmade geography and past settlement patterns, all work within the same basic system, defining what can happen and where with the same legal effect and similar terminology. Rules might work well as explanations for varying outcomes in a comparative context that spans multiple states or counties, but in this situation the rules that an investigator would have ready access to do not give us insight into why the officials in different townships behaved differently.

Normative legitimizing may prove more promising. Even where rules are constant, we would expect the relationships among decision-makers—the shared social environment within which they operate—to create a set of expectations about appropriate behaviors. The Southwest Washtenaw Council of Governments (SWWCOG), which existed well before the MCJPC, could have engendered norm development. The jurisdictions had even worked through SWWCOG to create a master plan in 2003, though it had no legal effect in a pre-JMPA world. At the municipal and intermunicipal levels, a history of cooperation and coordination existed in many service areas dealing with public works and public safety. If these experiences were capable of generating trust that would be supportive of a *norm of reciprocity*, then this should have occurred for the actors in *all* the Manchester Community municipalities.

What about a *norm of political responsiveness* as an explanation for variation in the behavior of the township officials? We would look for evidence that the constituents in Sharon Township, whose board members never considered participating in the Manchester Community, reward not cooperating either in general, or with regard to land use, or specifically with one or more other Manchester area communities. Electoral transitions on the township board, participation in SWWCOG, and votes for ratification of earlier cooperative agreements are all useful sources of information. In the case of that township, no evidence is available that suggests cooperative actions were penalized with a loss of board membership.

Using partisanship as a proxy for responsiveness does not get us any further toward explaining the heterogeneous outcomes among the townships. All the elected officials identify as Republican, and strong Republican majorities exist in each community. But joint planning seems to have little natural alignment with party affiliation. Its outcomes might tend to have some partisan dimension, and joint planning may have very different results among Republican officials in Republican-majority communities versus Democrat counterparts in Democrat-majority communities. However, this would not correspond necessarily to an *ex ante* partisan approval or disapproval of cooperation among highly politically similar townships. To the extent residents expressed opinions at public meetings, these were mixed. This may be because the joint agreement was voluntary and its effect on local decisions would be only advisory. While consolidation and other forms of regional governance that infringe on local autonomy—or

Sociocultural Collective Action 87

completely remove it—are contentious and can sometimes require public referenda, the Manchester form of cooperation seemed de-politicized. If an elected official wanted to curry favor or avoid punishment, a vote about the Manchester Community agreement would seem to provide little electoral value.

A *norm of transaction cost economizing,* in which officials attempt to legitimize their preferences and behavior through the kind of instrumental reasoning that currently animates interlocal cooperation theory, would be another option. To investigate this as an explanation, we would need to examine the socioeconomic, demographic, and fiscal attributes of the community that an elected official might consider in interpreting costs and benefits and deciding on strategies. As Table 4.1 shows, however, the townships are striking in their homogeneity. While Manchester Township is larger, among the four townships we see none of the class and race cleavages that stoke fears of redistribution or negative externalities such as property value decline or crime. If one consults the township master plans of the communities from the last decade and a half, one learns about four municipalities that all take pride in their rural agricultural character and natural resources, and want to strictly manage growth rather than encourage it. All such documents readily acknowledge Manchester Village as the commercial hub of the area. The repeated references to the communities as "ag(ricultural)" communities and emphasis of rural character in local and regional planning language make this clear. Regardless, since all townships are similar and have a similar perspective about their relationship to Manchester Village (and even the Ann Arbor area and Metro Detroit), municipal attributes do not help us understand what made officials in Sharon Township behave differently. The same is true of intermunicipal characteristics—the *relative* positions among the communities along fiscal, economic, and demographic dimensions changed hardly at all before and after adoption.

Lastly, and most uniquely, the sociocultural collective action framework would demand that we investigate cultural dispositions. While prescriptions internalized from the rules and norms may be influential, they might also come from the broader set of social relationships—those existing within and outside a specific organization—in which we are embedded. These could be discerned through the public rhetoric used by officials, through an analysis of the content of their communications, or through interview. Over time, we might be able to reasonably state that specific individual attributes are effective proxies for some cultural dispositions. For example, perhaps it really is the case that knowing if an individual identifies as Democrat or Republican can actually help us understand the view of that actor toward interlocal land use cooperation and other regionalizing reforms. In the study behind this book, I used a survey instrument to measure culture. Other techniques may be possible.

In any preference or behavior of a local elected official (or any official at any level of government) we should expect to see traces of legitimizing behavior, if the sociocultural collective framework—which draws from sociological institutionalism—is correct. Some institutional sources of legitimacy may have only been weakly internalized as prescriptions, while others may have been quite

88 *Sociocultural Collective Action*

strongly internalized. In any municipality (or any local government or any other jurisdictional unit) we would expect variation to exist in how individuals cognize different policy decisions. For some, normative legitimizing may dominate because the organizational setting has very well-articulated norms about that policy. For others, rules may matter most. For still others, cultural worldview may be the most important source of legitimacy. What is key for the researcher to understand is that the policy responses to these different institutional sources of legitimacy will be *very* different.

In the next two chapters, I present the evidence on normative and cultural legitimizing from a survey of more than 500 local elected officials in more than 200 communities. I demonstrate that, at least for interlocal land use cooperation preference formation, the dominant sources of legitimacy are culture, followed by some norms of political responsiveness. I then consider the policy implications of the sociocultural collective action framework and of the findings in this book in Chapter 7.

Notes

1 Many accounts of optimizing theory are available; I refer the reader to Harsanyi (1977) and Dixit and Skeath (1999) for highly detailed descriptions.
2 It is worth noting that even in the unconstrained model the external environment plays at least a theoretical role: it structures the decision situation and places limits on which actions are possible. However, the interpretation of possibility could still be wildly complex, since rules can be broken, convention contravened, and facts ignored. In other words, much of the external environment—particularly its institutional features—is not immutable.
3 The institutional analysis and development framework is most fully articulated in Ostrom's *Understanding Institutional Diversity* (2005).

References

Andersen, O. J., & Pierre, J. (2010). Exploring the strategic region: Rationality, context, and institutional collective action. *Urban Affairs Review, 46*(2), 218–240.

Anderson, J. R., & Milson, R. (1989). Human memory: An adaptive perspective. *Psychological Review, 96*(4), 703.

Andrew, S. A. (2009). Regional integration through contracting networks: An empirical analysis of institutional collection action framework. *Urban Affairs Review, 44*(3), 378–402.

Andrew, S. A., & Carr, J. B. (2013). Mitigating uncertainty and risk in planning for regional preparedness: The role of bonding and bridging relationships. *Urban Studies, 50*(4), 709–724.

Bartle, J. R., & Swayze, R. (1997). Interlocal cooperation in Nebraska. *Unpublished report prepared for the Nebraska Mandates Management Initiative.*

Camerer, C. (2003). *Behavioral game theory: Experiments in strategic interaction.* Princeton University Press.

Carr, J. B., & Hawkins, C. V. (2013). The costs of cooperation: What the research tells us about managing the risks of service collaborations in the US. *State and Local Government Review, 45*(4), 224–239.

Sociocultural Collective Action   89

Clingermayer, J. C., & Feiock, R. C. (1997). Leadership turnover, transaction costs, and external city service delivery. *Public Administration Review*, 231–239.

Coffé, H., & Geys, B. (2005). Institutional performance and social capital: An application to the local government level. *Journal of Urban Affairs*, *27*(5), 485–501.

Coleman, J. S. (1988). Social capital in the creation of human capital. *American Journal of Sociology*, *94*, S95–S120.

Cyert, R. M., Simon, H. A., & Trow, D. B. (1956). Observation of a business decision. *The Journal of Business*, *29*(4), 237–248.

D'Aunno, T., Sutton, R. I., & Price, R. H. (1991). Isomorphism and external support in conflicting institutional environments: A study of drug abuse treatment units. *Academy of Management Journal*, *34*(3), 636–661.

DiMaggio, P. J., & Powell, W. W. (Eds.). (1991). *The new institutionalism in organizational analysis*. University of Chicago Press.

Dixit, A. K., & Skeath, S. (1999). *Games of strategy*. W. W. Norton.

Emerson, R. M. (1976). Social exchange theory. *Annual Review of Sociology*, *2*(1), 335–362.

Feiock, R. C. (2009). Metropolitan governance and institutional collective action. *Urban Affairs Review*, *44*(3), 356–377.

Feiock, R. C. (2007). Rational choice and regional governance. *Journal of Urban Affairs*, *29*(1), 47–63.

Feiock, R. C., Jeong, M. G., & Kim, J. (2003). Credible commitment and council-manager government: Implications for policy instrument choices. *Public Administration Review*, *63*(5), 616–625.

Feiock, R. C., & Scholz, J. T. (Eds.). (2009). *Self-organizing federalism: Collaborative mechanisms to mitigate institutional collective action dilemmas*. Cambridge University Press.

Feiock, R. C., Steinacker, A., & Park, H. J. (2009). Institutional collective action and economic development joint ventures. *Public Administration Review*, *69*(2), 256–270.

Frederickson, H. G. (1999). The repositioning of American public administration. *PS: Political Science & Politics*, *32*(4), 701–712.

Friedman, M. (1953). *Essays in positive economics*. University of Chicago Press.

Friedman, M., & Savage, L. J. (1948). The utility analysis of choices involving risk. *Journal of Political Economy*, *56*(4), 279–304.

Granovetter, M. (1985). Economic action and social structure: The problem of embeddedness. *American Journal of Sociology*, *91*(3), 481–510.

Hall, P. A., & Taylor, R. C. (1996). Political science and the three new institutionalisms. *Political Studies*, *44*(5), 936–957.

Harsanyi, J. C. (1977). Morality and the theory of rational behavior. *Social Research*, 623–656.

Heclo, H. (2002). The spirit of public administration. *Political Science & Politics*, *35*(4), 689–694.

Hey, J. D. (1991). *Experiments in economics*. Wiley-Blackwell.

Maloney, W., Smith, G., & Stoker, G. (2000). Social capital and urban governance: Adding a more contextualized "top-down" perspective. *Political Studies*, *48*(4), 802–820.

March, J. G., & Olsen, J. P. (2004). The logic of appropriateness. In R. E. Goodin (Ed.), *The Oxford handbook of political science* (pp. 478–497). Oxford University Press.

Morgan, D. R., & Hirlinger, M. W. (1991). Intergovernmental service contracts: A multivariate explanation. *Urban Affairs Quarterly*, *27*(1), 128–144.

90 *Sociocultural Collective Action*

Mosher, F. C. (1982). *Democracy and the public service.* Oxford University Press.

North, D. C. (1992). *Transaction costs, institutions, and economic performance.* San ICS Press.

Ostrom, E. (2005). *Understanding institutional diversity.* Princeton University Press.

Perry, J. L., & Wise, L. R. (1990). The motivational bases of public service. *Public Administration Review,* 367–373.

Powell, W. W., & DiMaggio, P. J. (Eds.). (2012). *The new institutionalism in organizational analysis.* University of Chicago Press.

Scharpf, F. W. (1997). *Games real actors play: Actor-centered institutionalism in policy research.* Avalon Publishing.

Scott, W. R. (2001). *Institutions and organizations* (2nd ed.). Sage.

Scott, W. R. (1987). The adolescence of institutional theory. *Administrative Science Quarterly,* 493–511.

Shrestha, M. K., & Feiock, R. C. (2011). Transaction cost, exchange embeddedness, and interlocal cooperation in local public goods supply. *Political Research Quarterly, 64*(3), 573–587.

Simon, H. A. (1991). Bounded rationality and organizational learning. *Organization Science, 2*(1), 125–134.

Simon, H. A. (1990). *Reason in human affairs.* Stanford University Press.

Simon, H. A. (1985). Human nature in politics: The dialogue of psychology with political science. *American Political Science Review, 79*(2), 293–304.

Sonenblum, S., Kirlin, J. J., & Ries, J. C. (1977). *How cities provide services.* Ballinger.

Stigler, G. J. (1961). The economics of information. *Journal of Political Economy, 69*(3), 213–225.

Thompson, M., Ellis, R., & Wildavsky, A. (1990). *Cultural theory.* Westview Press.

Thurmaier, K., & Wood, C. (2002). Interlocal agreements as overlapping social networks: Picket-fence regionalism in metropolitan Kansas City. *Public Administration Review, 62*(5), 585–598.

Tversky, A., & Kahneman, D. (1986). Rational choice and the framing of decisions. *Journal of Business,* S251–S278.

Tversky, A., & Kahneman, D. (1975). Judgment under uncertainty: Heuristics and biases. In *Utility, probability, and human decision making* (pp. 141–162). Springer Netherlands.

Wildavsky, A. (1987). Choosing preferences by constructing institutions: A cultural theory of preference formation. *American Political Science Review, 81*(1), 3–21.

5 Normative Legitimizing

Introduction

In the last chapter, I presented the sociocultural collective action framework. In the framework, actors are dominated by the logic of appropriateness (rather than of instrumentality) and engage in rational legitimizing (rather than economizing). Their purpose is to have preferences and behaviors that accord with the regulative, normative, and cultural prescriptions they have internalized in their life, both within and outside a specific organizational setting. Individuals are expected to be heterogeneous in the regulative and normative and cultural prescriptions they internalize, and organizational settings are also expected to vary in how strongly they prescribe the different legitimizing institutions. It is an empirical question what the mix of the different prescriptions will be. To recall the stories from the opening of this book, the local official may find that in his local government organization—as in many—it is appropriate to serve the public interest by making economizing decisions that lead to opting out of regional governance, and that enough information is available to permit this calculative function to work. But at other times we may need to look to other normative and cultural sources of legitimacy.

This chapter focuses on normative legitimacy. I described in Chapter 4 how norms of economizing, reciprocity, and responsiveness might operate, and indeed dominate, in decisions about regional governance. I begin by considering the evidence from metropolitan Michigan on economizing and reciprocity. The theoretical mechanisms behind these norms have been thoroughly treated in the institutional collective action literature and were summarized in Chapter 3; I do not revisit them in this chapter. I find that even with careful and varied operationalization and measurement of the variables needed to test for the presence of these norms, there is scant evidence—at least for local elected officials functioning in metropolitan suburbs in Michigan—that they are at work in the preference formation of local elected officials about interlocal land use cooperation.

I then shift to a discussion of responsiveness. While a persistent thread in public administration scholarship is the false dichotomy between politics and administration (Demir & Reddick, 2012; Svara, 1999)—i.e., no one clings to an idealized image of the bureaucrat completely insulated from public

92 *Normative Legitimizing*

pressures—administrators are nevertheless kept secure from direct retribution at the ballot box. Because interlocal cooperation often does flow through elected officials, we must also consider how political norms of responsiveness might affect decisions about regional governance. Some scholars have already started in this direction (Zeemering, 2008; 2012; Ihrke & Newson, 2005), and further movement is warranted. I describe how a political norm might function with regard to decisions about regional reform made by local elected officials serving primarily in smaller suburban jurisdictions. I examine the theories and evidence regarding political representation in general and local representation specifically. I conclude the chapter with evidence that shows local elected officials do not uniformly tie their policy preferences to those of residents, that many perceive high levels of discretion in decisions they make about interlocal land use cooperation, and that variation in perceptions of residential support and discretion link to variation in support for interlocal land use cooperation. The evidence I have is not complete enough to craft a thorough narrative of political dynamics, and is limited by a focus on preferences and perceptions rather than behaviors. However, what becomes clear is that local elected officials, on balance, at least want to appear to have policy preferences that align with what they think residents desire.

Economizing and Reciprocity in Preference Formation

As noted in Chapter 4, we can conceptualize transaction cost economizing as a behavior that is an expression of normative legitimizing. My first task in this chapter is to explore whether the characteristics of the municipality an official serves and the relationship of the municipality to its neighbors serve as significant determinants of preferences about interlocal land use cooperation. Because of the uncertainty surrounding the joint gains, selective gains, and transaction costs in the area of interlocal land use cooperation—and likely in any lifestyle services cooperation—I do not expect that the typical local elected official will regard transaction cost economizing to be normatively legitimate behavior.

I begin the discussion of economizing and reciprocity by considering them as determinants of preferences about *partial area* cooperation,[1] in which two or more local jurisdictions use cooperative planning and zoning to target a shared area that is only part of the municipal territory. Examples would include a corridor improvement district, or a lakefront revitalization scheme. Surprisingly, the socioeconomic and physical attributes of a jurisdiction seem, at least based on this evidence, to have no significant effect on preferences. The same is largely true of the measures of interlocal similarity. Only one interlocal measure was significant: local elected officials from communities that were in the *bottom* quartile in the relative share of structures built since the year 2000 were much more likely to oppose cooperation. An example of a municipality in this group is Ann Arbor Charter Township, which has about 13 percent less of its structures built since 2000 compared to the 11 municipalities touching its borders—about 5 percent versus about 18 percent on average in its neighbors, which include many

Normative Legitimizing 93

townships that have developed quickly in the last decade. The finding speaks most clearly to physical heterogeneity, corresponding in most cases to a built-out, usually more established community surrounded by ones that are growing. However, social heterogeneity also tends to accompany such patterns: the more established community may also be the one with the strongest exclusionary impulse. Reaching agreement about a common vision for land use might be perceived as tricky. However, there was not a consistent pattern in the preferences of local elected officials from municipalities that had experienced more recent intense development than their neighbors, such as Canton Charter Township (the home of a recently developed major regional shopping hub). The lack of significance in any other indicators of heterogeneity that have to do with socio-economic characteristics, furthermore, suggests the stronger relationship, at least across the full sample of respondents, is between preferences and *relative* features of the built environment.

None of the variables corresponding to the presence of interlocal ties—such as membership in a voluntary regional association such as the Grand Valley Metropolitan Council or Downriver Community Conference, or number of interlocal agreements—was significant. This lack of a significant finding on any of these measures may suggest that interlocal agreements and memberships are not a reliable way to look at the issues of trust and reciprocity norms these links are thought to represent. These are, traditionally, what have been used as proxies in the existing literature. Rather, measures of positive and negative interpersonal relationships may be necessary, despite increased difficulty in gathering such data.

These variables tell very different stories when we consider each metropolitan region separately. In Detroit, the effect of having a very high share of owner-occupied housing is significant and sharply increases the likelihood of a local elected official have a less favorable preference toward partial area cooperation. These are places like Bloomfield Hills and many of the townships in the Detroit metropolitan area, all of which have upwards of 90 percent of their housing units occupied by owners (by contrast, those municipalities in the lowest quartile have no more than 70 percent). Note this does not mean that the municipalities have *relatively* more owner-occupied housing than their neighbors. The measure does not reflect heterogeneity among jurisdictions. It more likely captures the importance of a strong homeowner lobby in shaping local elected officials' preferences. As I discuss more later in the chapter, this might also explain the high magnitude for residential support in the Detroit metro and the lack of a significant finding for the discretion measure. At least for the adoption of *partial area* cooperation, a high rate of homeownership may have more of a bearing on the preference formation of the local elected official in a municipality in the Detroit area.

The narrative in the Grand Rapids metro area includes a curious finding about the role of race and fiscal distress. Elected officials from communities with a *relatively* low share of residents identifying as White compared to neighboring communities are overwhelmingly more likely to have a *more* favorable response to cooperation—more than three times more likely. But those elected officials

94   *Normative Legitimizing*

from municipalities under considerable fiscal distress compared to neighbors, as measured by relative change in taxable value, are also more than three times as likely to be in a *less* favorable response category. The results suggest that local elected officials in those places with *only* a relatively low White population (but not a high decline in taxable value) are more likely to favor *partial area* land use cooperation. However, the opposite situation is likely to yield opposition to cooperation. These results, of course, are *ceteris paribus* outcomes, and a careful inspection of the data reveals that the estimation is attempting to predict an association from a handful of data points. Studying preference formation more closely among the local officials in some of the communities with a more racially heterogeneous population but no fiscal distress (like the city of Grand Rapids or charter township of Allendale, a college town)—or the opposite situation, in a small farming community like Coopersville—may be enlightening at least on the west side of the state. Another municipal-level finding for the Grand Rapids area is that an elected official from a community with more secure operations funding (i.e., more of a surplus) than neighboring communities has a *less* favorable attitude toward cooperation. Being a half standard deviation higher would correspond to about seven percentage points, a roughly 37 percent increase in having a less favorable cooperation preference. The finding is consistent with the idea of heterogeneity being detrimental to cooperation.

We would expect preferences about *full coverage* cooperation to be more divided. Rather than cooperating over land use in part of the municipality, under a full coverage agreement a common vision with one's partners must be reached regarding the planning of *all* the municipal land—not just commercial or industrial uses of varying intensities. Such cooperation involves all current residents and their properties much more directly, and the risk calculus is likely to be markedly different under a full coverage scenario.

Population decline was the one structural attribute that played a role, and it did so in two ways which, when viewed together, yield an interesting result. A local elected official from a municipality with a very high *decline* in population had much higher odds of being in a more favorable response category regarding full coverage cooperation. But a local elected official from a municipality with very high *relative* decline in population compared to its neighbors had much lower odds. Thus, being in a rapidly declining community in a stable or growing region decreased the odds of a more favorable preference, while being in a highly declining community surrounded by more similar communities had the opposite result. The heterogeneity hypothesis is well supported by this finding, at least for this one dimension of heterogeneity for one type of interlocal cooperation.

As was the case with partial area cooperation preferences, the stories in each metropolitan area with regard to the factors that shape full coverage preferences are quite different. In the Detroit metro area, a local elected official in a municipality that has had high development in the last 15 years in a region that is also stable or developing, having a high median home value, and having a more racially heterogeneous population are all associated with increased odds of being

Normative Legitimizing 95

more favorable toward full coverage interlocal land use cooperation. The finding for structures built recently suggests the appeal of interlocal land use cooperation as a growth management device. The second finding (about high median home values) contradicts the standard hypothesis that economic distress leads to more cooperation. The latter finding about race is discordant with the prevailing view about heterogeneity impeding cooperation. The parameter estimate for having a high share of structures built *relative* to neighbors is well below one, which supports the notion that physical heterogeneity is more important than demographic heterogeneity for land use cooperation purposes. The only significant structural variable for the Grand Rapids metro area was that elected officials from municipalities with a *relatively* high general fund surplus have much higher odds of being in a more opposing preference category.

Lastly, we can consider preferences about how cooperation should be governed. Having a relatively high surplus is associated with more favorable attitudes toward an *authoritative* structure. While this seems to oppose the hypothesis about heterogeneity being problematic, the finding might simply mean that officials from such communities perceive a competitively advantageous position compared to neighbors. An authoritative structure might be seen as a way to help them secure this position through strategic use of land use cooperation in certain areas. The models for the partial area governance structure dependent variable were the only ones in which such a metropolitan effect occurred. Also, local elected officials from municipalities in the Detroit metropolitan area had higher odds of favoring an authoritative structure, all else being equal.

For preferences about the structure under a *full coverage* scenario, having a high share of homeowners greatly decreases the odds of having a response more favorable toward an authoritative structure. We would expect this result, especially since most respondents perceive residential opposition or neutrality. A strong homeowner lobby is generally thought to be anathema to cooperation, and this proxy measure provides some evidence in favor of that notion.

Lastly, we can consider the differences across regions. In the Grand Rapids metro area, the models for governance structure preferences are quite similar in the list of covariates and the magnitude and significance of parameters. Having a very low median home value relative to neighbors was associated with a much stronger likelihood of favoring an authoritative structure, and—curiously—increases in racial heterogeneity also were associated with greater odds of favoring an authoritative structure. Heterogeneity in this situation may have the curious effect of making a local elected official more accepting of the idea of needing a way to monitor and enforce agreement. A high share of homeowners, also counterintuitively, led to more support for an *authoritative* approach under full coverage. Also having a similar effect on structural choice under either partial area or full coverage scenarios was the number of neighboring municipalities. Having more was associated with a greater likelihood of favoring an *authoritative* structure. This may be the same dynamic at play as with heterogeneity. More voices at the planning table, and more different voices especially, may spur more willingness to have a strong form of governance.

96 *Normative Legitimizing*

Under a partial area JMPA scenario, a low share of homeowners was correlated with higher odds of preferences for an *authoritative* structure, while being much more racially homogeneous than neighboring municipalities had the opposite association, and quite strongly. For the full coverage scenario, the odds of favoring an advisory structure were better for elected officials from municipalities growing much faster but also declining in taxable value much more quickly than their neighbors.

While a few of the variables relating to norms of economizing and reciprocity had a significant correspondence with some preferences, when considering the very high number of variables reflecting economizing and reciprocity, the multiple ways in which they were measured, and that this was done across four different model specifications for the various preference outcomes, at best we can say that these norms have a weak, inconsistent role. This, again, is what we would expect under the sociocultural collective action framework because of the level of uncertainty that attaches to interlocal land use cooperation regardless of its geographic scope and governance structure. Knowing the socioeconomic conditions in a municipality, those in neighboring communities, and the regional bodies and agreements in which a municipality participates would give us very limited ability to accurately anticipate how officials from that municipality would respond to an opportunity for cooperation.

The Norm of Responsiveness in Local Government

If economizing and reciprocity do not get us very far, does responsiveness fare better? Perhaps not surprisingly for local *elected* officials, it does. Representation of the public interest, in its literal and most political form, requires responsiveness to the interests of those served by the goods and services of a jurisdiction: the residents.

The interest in re-election is one Frant (1996) refers to as a high-powered public sector incentive, analogous to the professional interests ascribed to city managers and other administrative officials. While few local elected officials are career politicians, many have long tenures and are often from small communities where incurring the wrath of even a few voters may be enough to lose their position on a city council or township board, or simply make their social interactions in the community less pleasant. This social mechanism may even make up for the lack of monetary compensation and low electoral turnout. Oakerson quips that "when there is no sharp boundary between government and civil society, serving as an elected municipal official is little different from holding office in a civic association or local church" (2004, p. 35).

If, on average, the local elected official is persuaded of the importance of working in the public interest, how does he define it? The homevoter hypothesis suggests local actors are motivated by the interest of resident homeowners in maximizing property values (Fischel, 1987; 2009). Direct tests of the full hypothesis are rare (Dehring, Depken, & Ward, 2008), but the components are well-supported and the logic is intuitively appealing. Because municipal characteristics and amenities are so efficiently capitalized into the values of homes (Fischel, 2009; Yinger, 1982; Hamilton, 1975; Oates, 1969) homeowners are driven to participate politically, including and especially in land use decisions, to protect the value of their largest asset (Schively, 2007; Nguyen, 2005; Fischel, 2001; Pendall, 1999; Lake, 1993). Municipal land use officials respond to this pressure, perhaps because they are elected and desire political reward from homevoters, or because they believe following the wishes of the polity is what it means to serve the public interest (Howe, 1992; Levine & Forrence, 1990; Klosterman, 1980). They are also, of course, resident homeowners interested in the value of their asset and any limitations on their use and enjoyment of it.

Another possibility is that policies might be decided according to partisanship—that local elected officials will choose the alternative most in line with what they think is the prevailing political ideology of constituents. In recent work, Tausanovitch and Warshaw (2014) found that variation in city policies tends to align with the variation in policy conservatism among residents of the cities. The finding informs a lengthy debate about whether the policies of municipal governments are responsive to what residents want based on political identity (Tausanovitch & Warshaw, 2014; Gerber & Hopkins, 2011). The evidence in this area, however, tends to draw on relatively large cities, and is generally mixed especially compared to the strong policy-partisan linkages at the state and federal levels.

The decision to cooperate over land use may be difficult not because of trouble discerning residents' interests or due to partisan ideological conflict but, more fundamentally, because it requires voluntarily yielding some of the limited control and authority over local affairs for which elected officials may have originally entered office. Gerber and Gibson (2009, p. 635) highlight the tension faced by a local actor:

> when contemplating a regional approach to policy, decision makers must consider the expected regional benefits and costs of the policy, the expected local benefits and costs, and how these net benefits compare to the likely political costs associated with delegating power to the region. ... [B]enefits may come at the cost of less control and greater uncertainty over policy outcomes.

Even if regional benefits from cooperation do occur, they may not allow for credit claiming, the mechanism that leads elected officials to prefer projects that have visible benefits directed at the short-term interests of their general constituency or a specific interest group (Feiock, Jeong, & Kim, 2003; Feiock & Clingermayer, 1986; Mayhew, 1974). This may be especially true with growth management, which has been a common motivation for the few interlocal cooperative agreements in Michigan. Calavita (1992) notes the political benefits of slowing or managing growth may be diffuse, while "the benefits of economic development are often highly visible and provide politicians opportunities to

98 *Normative Legitimizing*

claim credit and reward specific constituents or supporters that provide instrumental political resources" (Feiock, 2002, p. 131).

Long term maintenance of the status quo—the preservation of a community's character—may or may not be enough to garner electoral reward. If locally undesirable projects are being kept out of the locality and also not siting in neighboring communities where constituents may also work and live, then highly politicized not-in-my-backyard (NIMBY) responses may create a positive feedback loop between cooperation and re-election. But many benefits of land use cooperation may be longer term, relatively invisible, and spread across a large number of constituents. When narrowly targeted growth and economic development is a goal, then high visibility is less likely to be a concern, and short-term benefits may have a high ratio to costs. If the project is seen by enough constituents as improving local quality of life, then local elected officials may see some reward.

The Treatment of Responsiveness in Economizing Studies

In the literature on transaction cost economizing, political responsiveness has received limited attention. The general proposition is that selective benefits matter, consistent with a loose reading of Olson (1965): the larger the political incentives and career incentives from favoring cooperation, the greater the likelihood of cooperation (Feiock, 2007, p. 50). Feiock and Carr (2001, pp. 382–383) list as selective benefits for public elected officials the interest in "political power and reelection" and for public employees "job protection and greater autonomy." They argue that selective costs and benefits that accrue to individuals and groups are more likely than collective costs and benefits (such as efficiency or scale economies) to explain institutional collective action. This discussion of selective and collective benefit is similar to the distinction between particular interests and public interests by Bish (1971), who suggested the former was likely necessary for policy reform. Feiock also distinguished between benefits that are public (accruing to the local unit through "efficiencies and economies of scale in the provision and production of services") and private (accruing to the economic or political interests of an individual actor) (2008, p. 49). An individual cannot simply anticipate a collective or public good from interlocal cooperation for it to seem attractive, but must also have something personally to gain.

The calculation of individual actors about selective benefits and costs sometimes appears in the discussion of agency costs, which were already mentioned in the intralocal heterogeneity discussion. For example, some authors have reasoned that the short time horizon of mayors and their need to create visible positive impacts leads them to take more risks in negotiation, leading to the mayor-council form of government generating more cooperation (Feiock, Steinacker, & Park, 2009, pp. 263–264). The composition of the city council may also matter: a higher share of seats elected by district may lead to more parochial interests resistant to the loss of influence that can happen under cooperation. The mechanism behind both propositions is re-election (2009, p. 259). This dynamic

Normative Legitimizing 99

is similar to the manifestation of more local targeted behaviors by metropolitan planning organizations with a higher share of elected versus administrative local officials comprising their governing board (Gerber & Gibson, 2009).

Overall, the empirical evidence on selective benefits is quite thin. This is especially true for the local elected official. Andrew remarks in passing that "[e]ver since Frederickson ... described interlocal cooperation as primarily an administrative activity, scholars have largely ignored the role of local elected officials" (2009, p. 138). Interlocal cooperation is not typically a hot-button issue, and may not even be on the political radars of constituents. Zeemering's study of Michigan local elected officials found, in part, that officials reported receiving no public input about more than two-fifths of the projects subject to interlocal service arrangements. About a third of the efforts received positive feedback, and another quarter received negative feedback. While this general apathy about governance may suggest that local elected officials perceive an opportunity to exercise their own discretion, "officials run the risk that a small but mobilized group will express opposition" (Zeemering, 2008, p. 737).

Interlocal *land use* cooperation has not been subject to empirical study. Because interlocal land use cooperation is a relatively untested policy tool, it is hard to gauge *how* residents would respond to the cooperative act itself. Knowing what the median voter wants may be unclear to the local elected officials. Even in the limited archival data on public meetings held to address JMPA adoption, views among constituents about cooperation were diverse. Most elected officials are not part of a professional organization that can impart norms, and public meeting attendance is often low except for the most contentious of issues. Land use, of course, may be one of those issues and scholarship acknowledges this (Svara, 1999; Teske & Schneider, 1994; Forester, 1993; Fleischmann, 1989; Marcuse, 1976). Residents often care about land use at a very small scale, as is evident in the literature on "not in my backyard" attitudes (Tighe, 2010; Dear, 1992). And they care about it at a broader scale, such as the county or state. This is evident in the long-standing political contentiousness of attempts at metropolitan reforms such as city–county consolidation or centralization (Brenner, 2002; Norris, 2001; Lineberry, 1969). While many scholars have studied attitudes about growth management and regional planning at the metropolitan and state level, Wassmer and Lascher (2006, p. 623) highlight the "lack of consensus about findings" in their exhaustive review of this literature, as I noted in Chapter 3.

Suburban elected officials are not just different from state or federal legislative counterparts, but are likely to be quite different from "big city" politicians. The holding of office may be less about starting a career trajectory than about fulfilling a genuine public service ethos or functioning as a citizen-legislator. Most studies of political dynamics, even those relatively few research efforts that directly target the local level, consider only those localities with a population of at least 50,000. Such places are the exception in Michigan, in which only 30 of the nearly 2,000 local governments meet this population threshold. Set the threshold at 20,000, and the number of included localities only grows to about 100.

100 *Normative Legitimizing*

The same is true for most states. Less than 4 percent of New York's local governments have 50,000 people. In Missouri, the figure is only about 1 percent. In Florida, the number pushes up to about 15 percent. Even in highly urbanized California, the corresponding figure is just over one-third. From coast to coast, the regional governance of metropolitan areas in policy areas requiring contiguity (as most do) would by necessity engage "small town" political actors. The study of local politics has long been a study of urban politics, with semi-rural and rural suburban politics relegated to a lower level of theoretical and empirical importance. But the empirical reality in which metropolitics occurs demands knowledge of the local elected officials serving smaller suburbs.

It is useful to consider the local elected officials from the metropolitan local jurisdictions I studied for this book.[2] In my sample of local elected officials, only about 7 percent of the respondents were mayors, and only a handful were from cities using a mayor-council form. Most elected officials—about 60 percent— served in townships. On average, local elected officials in the sample had tenure of nearly ten years ($n = 529$), ranging from newly elected officials with a year or less in office (15.5 percent of respondents) to long-time office holders with 20 or more years in office (14.7 percent of respondents). Many local elected officials in Michigan seem to be static. A simple measure of tenure does not directly capture ambition, a future-oriented state of mind. Still, remaining in local office for a decade or more is reasonably interpretable as a strong commitment to serving at that level of government.

Though I did not ask for compensation information or the hours worked per week, anecdotal evidence and secondary sources suggest the vast majority of local elected officials statewide in Michigan—as in many states—serve only part-time. Wide variation exists in the income they earn. In Caledonia Charter Township in Kent County, a quickly growing locality within the study area in the present research with a current population around 13,000, the 2015 salary for the Township Supervisor was about $29,000. The Treasurer had an annual salary set near $40,000, while the Clerk's was about $54,000. A trustee would only earn about $4,000. The salary differences reflect the differing responsibilities accorded each role. The median household income in Caledonia Charter Township is in the low $60,000s. A 2011 article on compensation for Township Supervisors in the metropolitan counties around Grand Rapids showed that the vast majority earned less than $25,000 per year. Those earning more served in more populous townships that had not hired a professional manager. The per capita compensation ranged from less than $1 to about $10. In the suburbs of metropolitan Detroit, the City of St. Clair Shores Compensation Commission found in 2016 that 30 neighboring municipalities in southeast Michigan paid their elected officials an average of $7,500 for mayors and $5,250 for council members. Slightly more than half the local elected officials in my sample serve in a community that has less than 10,000 people, and an overwhelming 95 percent are from places with less than 50,000 people. Despite the supposed civic inculcation promoted by "small town" life, turnout in Michigan is very low— even among less populous communities.

Evidence of Political Legitimizing

I structure my discussion of the evidence on political legitimizing as follows. First, I describe the overall perceptions of responsiveness. As detailed in Appendices B and C, I considered this norm in three dimensions: support, alignment, and discretion. Respectively, I developed survey items that probed whether a local elected official thought residents would be supportive of a joint municipal planning agreement generally, whether an official thought it was important to make decisions that aligned with what residents wanted, and whether an official perceived she had the discretion to make decisions that were in the interest of the municipality even if residents were opposed to them. These survey items were meant to capture how respondents interpret their role as representatives of residents and/or the abstract, corporate public interest, since the two may not be identically defined.

Second, I consider whether these perceptions have individual-level determinants, such as time in office, age, and gender. Third, I turn to local determinants of perceptions, such as fiscal and demographic conditions in a municipality. In short, I want to explore whether a specific type of local elected official in a specific setting tends to adopt a predictable stance about responsiveness, or if instead the variation on these items is distributed more or less randomly throughout the sample of local elected officials. Lastly, I consider the bivariate and multivariate relationships between the three responsiveness items and the preferences about the hypothetical JMPA scenarios, the outcomes of interest in this study.

The residential support item read "*In general, residents would _____ a JMPA agreement.*" The measurement scale was similar to those described already: five-point, non-forced choice, and Likert-type, ranging from "strongly oppose" to "strongly support." Studies often use proxy measures of residential support based on municipal demographic characteristics. Because I have data on municipal characteristics, I can also consider the match between those characteristics and perceived residential support—in other words, I can gain direct insight into how well the proxy approach works.

A third of respondents (see Figure 5.1) thought residents would be opposed to interlocal cooperation, and another 10 percent perceived strong opposition ($n=538$). A quarter thought residents would be supportive, though only two anticipated strong support. Many respondents (about 30 percent) indicated residents would neither support nor oppose interlocal cooperation. Even though land use implicates local autonomy, the mix of perceived support and opposition and the high rate of neutral responses suggest local elected officials do not, in the aggregate, receive a clear signal about what residents want in this policy area. This supports the premise that interlocal cooperation in land use delivers weak instrumental signals.

I expected elected officials would exhibit high *alignment* and low *discretion* overall, because of the conventional wisdom that elected officials are attuned to the desires of their constituents above all else and are would feel compelled to do what residents wanted even if sub-optimal for the municipality. Responses,

102 Normative Legitimizing

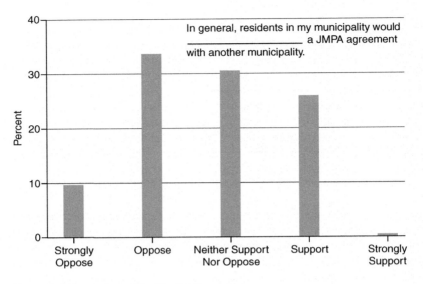

Figure 5.1 Perception of Residential Support.

however, showed perceptions of *both* high alignment and high discretion. The distribution of perceptions of alignment deserves some additional consideration (see Figure 5.2). Of the 538 respondents, nearly half strongly agreed that it is important to do what residents want, and another 160 strongly agreed (about 30 percent). However, this figure was actually lower than I expected: nearly one in five local elected officials *disagreed* or *strongly disagreed* with the importance of doing what residents want. What are the characteristics of this group of individuals who do not think it is important to follow resident wishes? This group has nearly identical individual attributes (tenure, age, gender, educational attainment, party affiliation, and position) to those who perceive a high need for alignment. Municipal attributes reveal those who exhibit low alignment are from municipalities that are slightly more populous and more densely populated with a higher tax base, but otherwise the two groups come from municipalities with very similar characteristics. Those from villages (which were slightly undersampled, with only 28 respondents) exhibited low alignment: 20 of them disagreed or strongly disagreed about the importance of doing what residents want. Overall, no stark distinctions exist between the officials who perceive high alignment and those who do not.

Contrary to expectations, half of elected officials agreed (about 43 percent) or strongly agreed (another 7 percent) that they had the ability to do what is best for the municipality even if it is unpopular with residents (see Figure 5.3). Roughly one-quarter of respondents disagreed and another 6 percent strongly disagreed. As with the alignment measure, we can compare the individual and municipal characteristics of the high discretion (agree or strongly agree) and low discretion

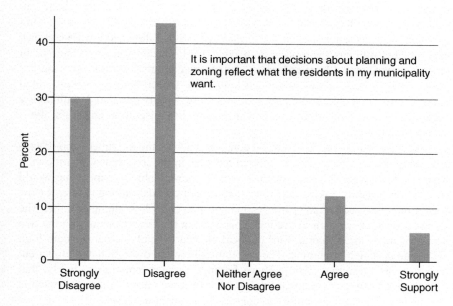

Figure 5.2 Perceptions of a Norm of Political Alignment.

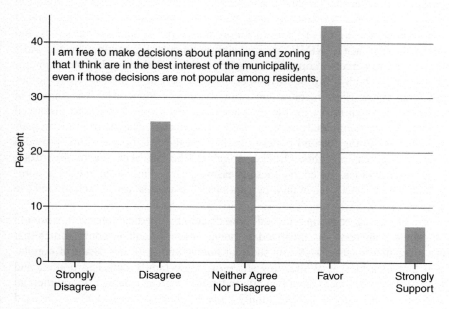

Figure 5.3 Perceptions of a Norm of Discretion.

104 *Normative Legitimizing*

(disagree or strongly disagree) respondents. Apart from some discrepancy in gender (the male/female split was 68/32 for those elected officials perceiving they had high discretion and 58/42 for those perceiving they had low discretion), local elected officials expressing both types of discretion were very similar in individual attributes. Elected officials who perceived high discretion were similar to those who perceived low alignment in one key aspect: both types represented municipalities that were more populous and more densely populated, with higher expenditures and expenditure burden than their low discretion and high alignment counterparts.

I expected survey responses to be consistent across the alignment and discretion measures: if a local elected official believes in the importance of following what residents want (high alignment), then it is reasonable to expect she would be less comfortable making decisions that are not popular among residents (low discretion). And, conversely, if a respondent perceives low alignment, then she should also perceive high discretion. This was not the case. Considering the two items together, more than a third of local elected officials perceived both high discretion *and* high alignment. The correlation between discretion and alignment responses was minimal (0.07). These findings suggest, counterintuitively, that many elected officials can regard doing what residents want as important, while also feeling they have the ability to contravene resident interests.

The literatures on interlocal cooperation and land use are unclear about which types of residents support land use cooperation. Homeowners, particularly those who are long-time residents or have high value homes in which considerable wealth is stored, are often viewed as more protective of land use autonomy and are the typical face of NIMBY and related sentiments. We might expect to see a higher rate of perceived opposition among local elected officials from municipalities with a high share of owner-occupied homes, high median value homes and median household income, and a low share of residents who have moved in recently—a rough proxy for the presence of a "homevoter" lobby, as discussed earlier. A very rough analysis, comparing local elected officials from municipalities that are in the top and bottom quartiles on the listed dimensions, provides some preliminary insights. Officials from jurisdictions with potentially strong homevoter lobbies, based on these measures, were similar to those in communities with weak ones in their perceptions of residential opposition to land use cooperation.

Preference aggregation—the ability to discern the median voter with whom to align one's interests—is theorized as being more difficult in communities that are more heterogeneous. A low share of homeownership, low share of population that identifies as White, low share of single-family detached homes, and high taxable value per capita (usually indicating a greater degree of commercial and industrial land use and potentially more active business sector) can be used as proxies for heterogeneity. Local elected officials from such municipalities should have a higher rate of "neutral" responses, perceiving neither support nor opposition from residents, because of the potentially mixed signal they would receive. The survey responses showed that officials from the most heterogeneous

Normative Legitimizing 105

municipalities did have higher rates of neutral perceptions about resident support than those from the least heterogeneous municipalities when looking at share of owner occupied homes (about 41 percent versus 22 percent), the share of single-family detached homes (35 percent versus 25 percent), and share of population identifying as White (38 percent versus 24 percent).

Overall, the evidence from this study suggests that using proxies for residential support may not always work. Assumptions that high rates of homeowner-ship, for example, are indicative of opposition to cooperation, or that a heterogeneous population is indicative of difficulties in preference aggregation, may not be well-supported. These assumptions may not provide a strong empiri-cal foundation with which to test hypotheses about norms of responsiveness.

We can now consider the relationship between norms of responsiveness and preferences about interlocal land use cooperation. Do they relate in expected ways? For the most part, yes. Let us start with preferences about interlocal land use cooperation over an area covering some portion of at least two municipalities—what I have been terming *partial area* cooperation.[3] We would expect higher per-ceptions of alignment—of the importance of doing what residents want in regard to land use planning and zoning—to correspond with less favorable attitudes toward cooperation generally. The evidence bears this out: a one-unit *increase* in the perception of the importance of alignment (on a five-point scale) is associated with a roughly 20 percent *decrease* in the odds being in a more favorable response category. By contrast, we would expect higher perception of the ability to make decisions that are good for the municipality but unpopular with residents—higher discretion—to correspond with more favorable attitudes toward cooperation. The evidence also supports this expectation. Perception of residential support, not sur-prisingly, was highly significant and strong in magnitude. A one unit increase in the perception of residential support for land use cooperation (on a five-point scale) corresponds to more than a doubling in a local elected official's odds of being more favorable toward partial area cooperation.

The three political variables were also significant and consistent with expec-tations for *full coverage* cooperation. A one-unit increase in the perception of the importance of doing what residents want with regard to land use planning and zoning (the alignment item) is associated with a roughly 20 percent decrease in the odds being in a more favorable response category. By contrast, an increase in perception of discretion (the ability to make decisions that are unpopular with residents but good for the municipality) corresponds with a roughly 20 percent increase in these odds. Perception of residential support for land use cooperation is strongly positive and highly significant, as it had been as a predictor for partial area cooperation. Those officials who perceive residential support in their muni-cipality or believe they can contravene what residents want should be more likely to support cooperation. Those who believe alignment with resident inter-ests is important should be more likely to oppose it. In general these expecta-tions hold up.

Lastly, I consider the relationship of responsiveness to preferences regarding the structure of governance under the joint planning agreement—from a more

106 *Normative Legitimizing*

advisory to a more authoritative structure. The advisory structure was described as having two features: an advisory joint planning commission, and a non-binding land use plan. The authoritative structure, by contrast, had a joint planning commission and joint zoning board of appeals, and the dissolution of municipal (local) level planning and zoning. Local elected officials who perceived lower levels of alignment (those who tended to put less stock in doing what residents want) tended to prefer advisory structures for partial area cooperation, but tended to prefer authoritative structures for full coverage cooperation. This suggests a peculiar relationship between norms of responsiveness, the scope of interlocal cooperation, and the governance of it that is deserving of further study in the future. Other relationships were not significant.

Overall, the evidence I have presented in this chapter suggests that political norms as measured through perceptions of support, alignment, and discretion have a stronger role in preference formation than do economizing and reciprocity norms as they have traditionally been measured. Multiple sources of normative legitimizing are possible in the sociocultural collective action framework, and it makes sense that a local elected official forming preferences about interlocal cooperation over land use would be dominated more by a norm of political responsiveness than a norm of economizing. Even if costs and benefits were uncertain, an elected official would, at the very least, probably seek to match his preferences to those of constituents. That being said, there is also evidence that local elected officials vary wildly in the weight they accord residents' wishes. As I discuss in Chapter 7, these insights about the norms of political responsiveness suggest some policy responses that can directly target the representative–resident relationship. But first, in Chapter 6, I discuss cultural legitimizing—the process of attempting to shape one's preferences to match socially formed dispositions about solidarity and equality.

Notes

1 The estimates supporting this discussion can be found in the tables in Appendix F.
2 They ranged in age from 24 to 88 years old, with an average of about 56 years old. About two-fifths of the local elected officials identified as Republicans, and another quarter identified as Democrats. Most of the remaining third indicated they were Libertarians or independents. Republicans tended to serve about three years longer in office, but on every other individual attribute—gender, race, educational attainment, and age—were highly similar to Democrats and all other elected officials.
3 A stylized accompanying diagram showed an area covering parts of three municipalities. See Appendix B.

References

Bish, R. L. (1971). *The public economy of metropolitan areas*. Markham Rand McNally.
Brenner, N. (2002). Decoding the newest "metropolitan regionalism" in the USA: A critical overview. *Cities, 19*(1), 3–21.
Calavita, N. (1992). Growth machines and ballot box planning: The San Diego case. *Journal of Urban Affairs, 14*(1), 1–24.

Normative Legitimizing 107

Dear, M. (1992). Understanding and overcoming the NIMBY syndrome. *Journal of the American Planning Association*, 58(3), 288–300.

Dehring, C. A., Depken, C. A., & Ward, M. R. (2008). A direct test of the homevoter hypothesis. *Journal of Urban Economics*, 64(1), 155–170.

Demir, T., & Reddick, C. G. (2012). Understanding shared roles in policy and administration: An empirical study of council–manager relations. *Public Administration Review*, 72(4), 526–535.

Feiock, R. C. (2008). Institutional collective action and local government collaboration. *Big Ideas in Collaborative Public Management*, 195–210.

Feiock, R. C. (2007). Rational choice and regional governance. *Journal of Urban Affairs*, 29(1), 47–63.

Feiock, R. C. (2002). A quasi-market framework for development competition. *Journal of Urban Affairs*, 24(2), 123–142.

Feiock, R. C., & Carr, J. B. (2001). Incentives, entrepreneurs, and boundary change: A collective action framework. *Urban Affairs Review*, 36(3), 382–405.

Feiock, R. C., & Clingermayer, J. (1986). Municipal representation, executive power, and economic development policy activity. *Policy Studies Journal*, 15(2), 211–229.

Feiock, R. C., Jeong, M. G., & Kim, J. (2003). Credible commitment and council–manager government: Implications for policy instrument choices. *Public Administration Review*, 63(5), 616–625.

Feiock, R. C., Steinacker, A., & Park, H. J. (2009). Institutional collective action and economic development joint ventures. *Public Administration Review*, 69(2), 256–270.

Fischel, W. A. (2009). *The homevoter hypothesis: How home values influence local government taxation, school finance, and land-use policies*. Harvard University Press.

Fischel, W. A. (2001). Why are there NIMBYs? *Land Economics*, 77(1), 144–152.

Fischel, W. A. (1987). *The economics of zoning laws: A property rights approach to American land use controls*. Johns Hopkins University Press.

Fleischmann, A. (1989). Politics, administration, and local land-use regulation: Analyzing zoning as a policy process. *Public Administration Review*, 337–344.

Forester, J. (1993). *Critical theory, public policy, and planning practice: Toward a critical pragmatism*. SUNY Press.

Frant, H. (1996). High-powered and low-powered incentives in the public sector. *Journal of Public Administration Research and Theory*, 6(3), 365–381.

Gerber, E. R., & Gibson, C. C. (2009). Balancing regionalism and localism: How institutions and incentives shape American transportation policy. *American Journal of Political Science*, 53(3), 633–648.

Gerber, E. R., & Hopkins, D. J. (2011). When mayors matter: Estimating the impact of mayoral partisanship on city policy. *American Journal of Political Science*, 55(2), 326–339.

Hamilton, B. W. (1975). Zoning and property taxation in a system of local governments. *Urban Studies*, 12(2), 205–211.

Howe, E. (1992). Professional roles and the professional roles and the public interest in planning. *Journal of Planning Literature*, 6(3), 230–248.

Ihrke, D. M., & Newson, R. J. (2005). Council member perceptions regarding representational and service delivery effectiveness in Wisconsin. *The Social Science Journal*, 42(4), 609–619.

Klosterman, R. E. (1980). A public interest criterion. *Journal of the American Planning Association*, 46(3), 323–333.

108 *Normative Legitimizing*

Lake, R. W. (1993). Planners' alchemy transforming NIMBY to YIMBY: Rethinking NIMBY. *Journal of the American Planning Association, 59*(1), 87–93.

Levine, M. E., & Forrence, J. L. (1990). Regulatory capture, public interest, and the public agenda: Toward a synthesis. *Journal of Law, Economics, & Organization, 6,* 167–198.

Lineberry, R. L. (1969). Reforming metropolitan governance: Requiem or reality. *Georgetown Law Journal, 58,* 675.

Marcuse, P. (1976). Professional ethics and beyond: Values in planning. *Journal of the American Institute of Planners, 42*(3), 264–274.

Mayhew, D. R. (1974). *Congress: The electoral connection.* Yale University Press.

Nguyen, M. T. (2005). Does affordable housing detrimentally affect property values? A review of the literature. *Journal of Planning Literature, 20*(1), 15–26.

Norris, D. F. (2001). Whither metropolitan governance? *Urban Affairs Review, 36*(4), 532–550.

Oakerson, R. (2004). The study of metropolitan governance. In R. C. Feiock (Ed.), *Metropolitan governance: Conflict, competition, and cooperation* (pp. 17–45). Georgetown University Press.

Oates, W. E. (1969). The effects of property taxes and local public spending on property values: An empirical study of tax capitalization and the Tiebout hypothesis. *The Journal of Political Economy, 77*(6), 957–971.

Olson, M. (1965). *The logic of collective action.* Harvard University Press.

Pendall, R. (1999). Opposition to housing NIMBY and beyond. *Urban Affairs Review, 35*(1), 112–136.

Schively, C. (2007). Understanding the NIMBY and LULU phenomena: Reassessing our knowledge base and informing future research. *Journal of Planning Literature, 21*(3), 255–266.

Svara, J. H. (1999). The shifting boundary between elected officials and city managers in large council-manager cities. *Public Administration Review,* 44–53.

Tausanovitch, C., & Warshaw, C. (2014). Representation in municipal government. *American Political Science Review, 108*(3), 605–641.

Teske, P., & Schneider, M. (1994). The bureaucratic entrepreneur: The case of city managers. *Public Administration Review,* 331–340.

Tighe, J. R. (2010). Public opinion and affordable housing: A review of the literature. *Journal of Planning Literature, 25*(1), 3–17.

Wassmer, R. W., & Lascher, E. L. (2006). Who supports local growth and regional planning to deal with its consequences? *Urban Affairs Review, 41*(5), 621–645.

Yinger, J. (1982). Capitalization and the theory of local public finance. *The Journal of Political Economy,* 917–943.

Zeemering, E. S. (2012). The problem of democratic anchorage for interlocal agreements. *The American Review of Public Administration, 42*(1), 87–103.

Zeemering, E. S. (2008). Governing interlocal cooperation: City council interests and the implications for public management. *Public Administration Review, 68*(4), 731–741.

6 Cultural Legitimizing

Cultural theory starts with one basic assumption: that the most important factor in people's lives is how they want to relate to other people and how they want others to relate to them.

— Grendstad and Selle (1995, p. 12)

From Gay Rights to Gun Control to Governance

It seems like blacks, women, homosexuals and other groups don't want equal rights—they want special rights just for them.

The first time I read that sentence I had a quite strong reaction. You probably did, too. It is not the sort of statement that one can respond to with subtlety, much less neutrality. It deals with how different groups relate to each other, and which fundamental advantages and disadvantages we find acceptable to tie to identity. It goes to the core of our social fabric, and how we think the world should work. If I knew how you felt about that statement, I bet I could guess how you feel about a wide range of policies. I could start with the policies that flow most directly from the statement—affirmative action, marriage equality, and equal pay. If you strongly agreed with the opening statement, I would expect you to be opposed to such policies. That reasoning does not require any great leap in logic, but what if I told you that your agreement with the opening statement also means that you likely oppose pollution controls in response to climate change? Or that you support policies to increase the oversight of nanotechnology development? Or that you are against restrictions on firearm purchases? Researchers have, indeed, made such connections in myriad studies of the general population (Kahan et al., 2012; Kahan, Braman, Slovic, Gastil, & Cohen, 2009; Kahan & Braman, 2003) There is, it seems, something in common between how one feels about gay rights and, say, gun control, and it is something deeper than simply political party affiliation. That something is *culture*: "shared values legitimating social practices" (Wildavsky, 1987, p. 6). We can see here the strong compatibility between the language of sociological institutionalists and cultural theory. Both are about rationality that functions through legitimacy. If an attitude or action violates a rule it will be illegitimate and

110 *Cultural Legitimizing*

unsustainable. The same will be true of a violation of norms. The same is also true of culture: we can only rationally support that which coheres with the cultural way of life in which we are embedded. Our attitudes and actions must be culturally viable, to use the language of cultural theorists.

Governance, of course, is at base a social arrangement. Regional governance through interlocal cooperation supports a much different social arrangement because it allows those who exist outside the community boundaries to have a say in how public (i.e., communal) goods and services are provided. Municipal incorporation has always required, at the very least, a pre-existing stable community. Once established, municipal territorial boundaries function as an institution of differentiation because of the power of land use regulation to help set the price of admission and general character for a community. Strengthening the independence and authority associated with that boundary—to recall the quote by de Tocqueville that started this book—would be appealing to someone with a cultural disposition that favors differentiation, in the same way that a traditional definition of marriage would also appeal to that person. Both viewpoints are bound up in the privileging of those with a specific identity or behavior.

Consider another statement: "The government should stop telling people how to live their lives." In the same way that the reaction to the earlier statement told us about a cultural disposition, so too does the response to this statement. For this statement, strong agreement would be expected to travel with preferring liberal firearm purchasing regulations, or opposing state-restricted definitions of marriage. But the underlying mechanism is not differentiation. Rather, it is autonomy. An individual who is strongly attached to autonomy would be expected to have many policy preferences that roughly correspond to a scaled-back role for government, at least in social policies. In the same way, we might expect that such an individual prefers local government to regional governance, and would therefore oppose efforts at negotiating voluntary cooperation. Indeed, the very idea of cooperation would be anathema.

In this chapter I expand on this logic and guide the reader through how cultural theory can fit into the sociocultural collective action framework, how cultural dispositions can be measured, and how these dispositions align with preferences about interlocal cooperation. I discuss how culture is defined in cultural theory, specifically the variant known as *grid-group cultural theory*. Cultural theory, in general, remains impactful in the social sciences because of the challenge it poses to traditional conceptions of rational choice. As outlined in Chapter 4, one relaxation of classic rational choice theory was the idea of bounded rationality in the appraisal of information. Rational choice theorists typically struggled to explain why some individuals are, for example, seemingly altruistic or other-regarding even in the absence of repeat play, and would either label the behavior as irrational or expand the definition of what counts as a material benefit to make altruism somehow appear materially self-interested. What cultural theory provides is a rational mechanism that explicitly accounts for information, valuation, and selection processes that seem contrary to what is conventionally understood as self-interest. When individuals search for information, they focus attention where risks to their cultural ways of life exist, value more highly those alternatives that help secure (or threaten least) their cultural way of life (with its corresponding values and social relations), and tend to select the alternatives that are most likely to be protective of this identity.

Grid-Group Cultural Theory

The specific form of cultural theory I use is known as *grid-group cultural theory*. The terms grid and group are drawn from the work of Mary Douglas, whose anthropological investigations formed the basis of the typology central to the last four decades of research applying the theory (Douglas & Wildavsky, 1983; Douglas, 2003). Grid and group do not have specific, consistent definitions. Rayner's (1992, p. 87) descriptions of the poles of the grid and group dimensions provide some of the clearest elucidation of the concepts.

> Weak-group individuals fend for themselves and therefore tend to be competitive. ... Strong group people depend on each other, which promotes values of solidarity rather than the competitiveness of weak group. ... Low grid indicates an egalitarian state of affairs in which no one is prevented from participating in any social role because he or she is the wrong sex, or is too old, or does not have the right family connections. A high-grid state of affairs is one where access to all social activities depends on one or another of these kinds of discriminations.

Rayner elsewhere describes an increase in group and grid as, respectively, increases in the "demands of incorporation and regulation" (1992, p. 88), while Grendstad and Selle (1995, p. 12) provide the following definition: "[g]rid connotes the social distinctions and delegations of authority that limit how people behave toward one another. Group connotes the social demarcations that people have erected between themselves and others." Figure 6.1 summarizes the two dimensions.

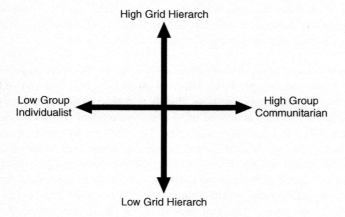

Figure 6.1 Grid and Group Dispositions and the Four Cultural Types.

112   *Cultural Legitimizing*

At the heart of the grid-group version of cultural theory is a mechanism of sociocultural viability in which cultural biases (shared values and beliefs) interact with social relations (patterns of interpersonal relations) to sustain a way of life (Thompson, Ellis, & Wildavsky, 1990, p. 2):

> The viability of a way of life ... depends upon a mutually supportive relationship between a particular pattern of social relations [and a bias]. These biases and relations cannot be mixed and matched. ... Shared values and beliefs are thus not free to come together in any which way; they are always closely tied to the social relations they help legitimate.

While empirical observation may not always be able to perfectly tease out these three components—biases or values, social relations, and way of life—in general an investigator would expect to see coherence among them, including in situations where an actor must interpret and choose among policy options. Thus, preferences and perceptions—an outward expression of values and beliefs— should cohere with the types of social relations in which one engages, and vice versa. And a way of life will, if it is socioculturally viable, cohere with both. In this study, the focus is on the coherence of governance preferences as an organization-level expression of individual social relations and measurable indicators of values and beliefs expressive of a way of life.

This process of coherence is closely bound to the process of risk appraisal. I use the word risk to describe "the possibility that an undesirable state of reality (adverse effects) may occur as a result of natural events or human activities" (Renn, 1992, p. 56). The subjective quality of risk is essential to my use of that term. Slovic (1992, pp. 119–120) states:

> Risk does not exist "out there," independent of our minds and cultures, waiting to be measured. Human beings have invented the concept "risk" to help them understand and cope with the dangers and uncertainties of life. There is no such thing as "real risk" or "objective risk." ... [We assume] risk is subjectively defined by individuals who may be influenced by a wide array of psychological, social, institutional, and cultural factors.

The link between culture and risk was developed early by Douglas and Wildavsky (1983). Concisely, people have selective attention spans and can only worry about so many risks at any one time. People will tend to give attention to the risks that threaten the cultural way of life—and the attendant social relations and values and beliefs—to which they subscribe. These values and relations are what individuals risk losing under different courses of action (see Figure 6.2). An individualist, then, would amplify risks to independence, autonomy, and self-sufficiency, trying to avoid or manage those courses of action he associates with such risks. And one could make similar statements for the other three cultural types. When risks enter into cognitive processes for evaluation, then, it is through cultural filters that amplify the risks most adverse to preferred values

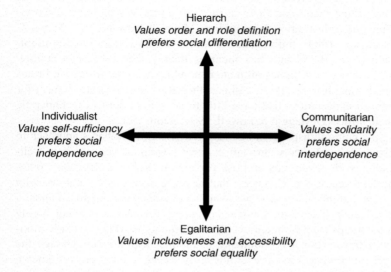

Figure 6.2 The Values and Preferred Social Relations of the Four Cultural Types.

and social relations. This is how legitimizing works with regard to culture, and it provides insight in general into how legitimizing works for any institutions, including regulative and normative ones. The more illegitimate an attitude or behavior is in any of the three dimensions, the more we would tend to amplify the risks it presents.

Thus, by way of summary, some of us are individualists who find little comfort in working together to solve a problem. Others among us are communitarians who possess internalized prescriptions to cooperate even if we know this will not maximize economic utility. The notion that "two heads are always better than one" would be a standard communitarian trope. This is the group dimension. On the grid dimension, some of us are hierarchs who place value in differentiation among people according to their social and economic indicators. For the hierarch, it makes sense for men to earn more than women. It makes sense to preserve the right to marry only for opposite-sex couples. It is natural and right that a child should be treated as subordinate to the parent. Others are egalitarians who would bristle at these sentiments. Our cultural dispositions accord a value to desirable social arrangements that exists apart from any economic cost and benefit. We receive a selective "warm glow" benefit from engaging in or preferring behavior that matches our social ideal, and we use our cultural worldview as a filter for the information we encounter in the world.

Rayner (1992, p. 90) notes, "[t]he fundamental purpose of grid/group analysis is to provide a framework within which a cultural analyst may consistently relate differences in organizational structures to the strength of arguments that sustain them." The behaviors of organizations—including the adoption of a formal

114 *Cultural Legitimizing*

interlocal cooperative agreement—derive from the attitudes and behaviors of the actors that constitute them, and these in turn are partially a product of worldviews that function as institutional constraints (Meyer & Rowan, 1977; Meyer & Scott, 1983; Zucker, 1983). Individuals are fully *embedded*, to use the terminology of Granovetter (1985), and this includes their embeddedness in culture. Classification, scripts, and frames all matter, in addition to the norms and rules that other institutionalists privilege. Culture, therefore, may operate to push for the fulfillment of expectations that have little to do with notions of technocratic or economistic utility (DiMaggio & Powell, 1991; Scott, 1987).

How might a cultural disposition be measured? I choose Kahan's approach to operationalizing cultural theory through *cultural cognition*, because it is well-suited to dealing with uncertainty and risk perception (Kahan & Braman, 2006). Recall from the discussion in Chapter 3 that land use decisions are imbued with uncertainty, and that this is true whether planning or zoning are organized under a cooperative structure (like a joint municipal planning agreement) or remain highly localized and perhaps even competitive. This uncertainty is what originally motivated the shift from rational economizing to rational legitimizing. Though the appearance of cultural cognition as a term is fairly recent, it draws on well-known sociological and psychometric perspectives on risk. Cultural cognition relies on variation in risk perception as its central mechanism. If a policy is inappropriate, we amplify the likelihood of incurring a cost, while diminishing the likelihood of receiving a benefit. If a policy is appropriate, we do the opposite: we amplify the probability of gains while diminishing the probability of losses. Psychometry provides a way to measure cultural disposition by using survey methods to ascertain how strongly someone values solidarity and equality (Slovic, 1992).

Reconciling Cultural Theory with Rational Choice Institutionalism

In the sociocultural collective action framework I develop, both the transaction cost economizing approach and cultural theory can coexist. Most pointedly, "it is important to note that unlike many other cultural theories, [the cultural theory of Douglas and Wildavsky] is highly complementary of rational choice and institutional theories" (Swedlow, 2011, p. 703). Culture and rules and norms are not warring claims on an actor's mental processes (Chai, 1997; Grendstad & Selle, 1995). They are not perfect substitutes, but are rather complementary. Both the transaction cost economizing approach of Williamson and the cultural theory account of the world can be used to explain how actors decide among different modes of organizing.[1] What cultural theory offers is an account in which individuals are not simply adopting ways of organizing—including cooperative ways—because of their short-term, economic interests. Rather, even in the absence of clarity about such interests, individuals will sort into different organizational structures because such structures promote appropriate social relations that cohere with personal worldviews, or because of coercion that has been sanctioned under the rule of law.

Cultural Legitimizing 115

Cultural cognition supplies a concise way of filtering through the messiness of values and ensuring they remain analytically distinct from attitudes and behaviors, which are the conscious, superficial manifestations of values.[2] It has some readily apparent benefits when applied in a regional governance context. Earlier I criticized rational choice institutionalist accounts of metropolitan governance for their inability to deliver functional policy recommendations. Culture lights a new path: if individuals are *not* rational economizers but are instead rational legitimizers, then we have a few more policy levers to pull. We can use framing, de-biasing, and other well-known "soft" interventions to promote the idea of interlocal cooperation. These are discussed in Chapter 7. I do not test them in this book, and they are not guaranteed to work, but they at least become possibilities well-supported by theory and open to evaluation.

The turn I am charting is not a dramatic one. Rational choice institutionalism and sociological institutionalism are both branches of the new institutionalist tree. They are both concerned with turning away from the behavioralist theories and pure rational choice models that dominated the post-World War II social scientific thought of the late 1940s, 1950s, and 1960s. Both perspectives can be reduced to the simple observation that institutions matter. Both are concerned with the threshold tasks of any institutional analysis: identifying problems that require new institutions for their solution (here, a formal cooperative agreement among local governments, and the norms that attach to it), and then figuring out why these institutions are discerned by relevant decision-makers to be the only possible outcome. Where the perspectives differ is their model of how individuals interact with institutions, and in their behavioral assumptions, in the ways I have outlined. It is only in sociological institutionalism, too, that one finds a role for cultural worldviews. Under some institutional circumstances, the logic of appropriateness and the logic of instrumentality may align. For some types of regional governance, such as the cooperative delivery of basic functions like wastewater treatment, garbage collection, or fire protection, the individual can be readily and fairly depicted as a boundedly rational utility satisficer. But for other types of regional governance, costs and benefits are potentially large and uncertain. This would be true of attempts at cooperation over land use planning and regulation, or tax base sharing agreements, or—most obviously—voluntary structural reforms. It is in these situations that individuals are most likely to rely on heuristic reasoning.

Connecting Dispositions to Governance

Because culture is at the heart of a person's identity, evaluating risks through a cultural filter is known as identity-protective risk appraisal. Kahan and Braman build on this idea when they define the cultural cognition of public policy as "the psychological disposition of persons to conform their factual beliefs about the instrumental efficacy (or perversity) of law to their cultural evaluations of the activities subject to regulation" (2006, p. 149). To elaborate, members of the public and their representatives disagree, often strongly, about what policies

116 *Cultural Legitimizing*

will achieve material well-being as an empirical matter, but this disagreement is neither randomly distributed nor correlated with education. The factual disagreement is not simply a product of lack of knowledge or information. Rather, conflict can exist even within various social groups that we would expect to have similar views and experiences of a policy, and even among experts in a policy area. The authors suggest that individuals' cultural ways of life act "as a kind of heuristic in the rational processing of information" (2006, p. 149).

Coyle (1993, p. 31) extends the idea of cultural theory to the practice of land use planning and zoning, noting that those who are high group (communitarian) desire "broad participation in decision making, as in regulatory procedure" and those who are low grid (egalitarian) want "greater substantive equality of resources."[3] By contrast, those who occupy a low group position promote individuated control of land use. And those who are high grid would be fine with a system of land use that allowed for inequality. Again, the themes of solidarity versus self-determination on one hand, and equality versus differentiation on the other, are clear. Coyle further remarks, "[w]e are likely to stress the problems with land use and be receptive to solutions that are compatible with our basic cultural orientation" (1993, p. 38). The question, then, is which of the cultural types will be wary of the risks of autonomy and receptive to the solution of *interlocal land use cooperation*, and which will be wary of the risks of cooperation and receptive to the continuation of the status quo?

If local elected officials, like everyone, are engaged in identity-protective cultural cognition (and there is no reason to suspect they are not) then some alignments become readily apparent. Consider an example. Suppose we send a thousand strangers to an island already developed into 1,000 parcels, and that each arrives with whatever wealth she has at the time. We assume that some outside force is present to maintain the rule of law and prevent a descent into anarchy. Two options are possible for how to govern land and deal with conflicts about it. In one, everyone is allowed to go about choosing a parcel on the first day, and then these parcels are divided into sets of 50, yielding 20 such collections. From that point on, those within each group must appoint leaders who plan the use of land and adjudicate conflicts. In the other option, the same process occurs but with 200 parcels in each set, resulting in five total. In the island example, as people are choosing which parcels to secure they are likely sorting based on who they want to live next to as neighbors.

The social science literature has well established the tendency of people to want to live with others who are like them or seem like them on the surface, a tendency that persists even among individuals who are not inherently racist or classist by other measures of attitude and preferences. Pursuant to this inherent clannishness, we would expect that each person on the island would try to settle down around as many similar individuals as possible. Because this must be judged superficially, the judgment would have to be made on the basis of appearance. Sorting might also arise simply because some places on the island are more desirable, and wealthy individuals could outbid for these. Some interaction of these mechanisms might occur: the most desirable locations could only be settled

Cultural Legitimizing   117

by the wealthiest, and so this provides a signal to other wealthy islanders who might want to live among those of a similar class. People would have multiple ways, in short, to settle among similar neighbors.

Now consider the two options and the likelihood of each being chosen by people according to their grid and group dimensions. The group dimension is about the relationship of the individual to government, where "government" is being used in the abstract sense. The basic balance is between freedom of action from government interference (individualism), and government intervention to address the problems of individual decisions (communitarianism, or solidarism). Which of the options outlined above is most likely to be chosen by someone who is a low group individualist? Arguably, it is the first option, which reflects the greatest degree of freedom from interference and self-determination, values that are cherished by the individualist. The high group communitarian would see the potential for more trouble under option one as the divided sets of parcels can get into more conflict, and with no definition of community at a scale able to address these issues.

This stylized example reflects a basic truth about the group dimension: all else being equal, as one moves lower in the scale of government, one is getting closer to a purely individualist arrangement, and as one moves higher in scale, one gets closer to pure communitarianism in which more and more people can participate, at least through the mechanism of representation. The process of sorting is integral to this truth. In a smaller arrangement of people, a person can know how homogeneous the other members are, and how likely it is that someone else shares his views about a number of issues and the best ways to address them. A low group individualist can be more secure in such a context that the public interest aligns well with his preferred mode of dealing with the world. The problems of moral hazard and adverse selection are much lower at a small scale. Increase the scale, and the situation becomes more and more uncertain—the individualist faces a much greater risk of having his individual autonomy fettered. For a communitarian, the heterogeneity and messiness of agreement in a larger community is acceptable because it reflects the awareness of interdependence—of being "in it together."

Sorting, of course, is a process of differentiation, and one can—with similar reasoning—conclude that option one described above would be more desirable to the high grid hierarchs. These individuals heartily approve of differentiation, as it accords with values favoring stability and order, and social relations that depend on roles and positions. One of the major positions that people occupy in society attaches to where they live. The well-known discussions of the geography of opportunity, for example, refer to the reality that individuals of a certain position (mostly in terms of class and race) occupy well-defined places often defined by municipal boundaries. In the island example, the smaller groups of 50 would have a much better ability to enforce this differentiation. As the groups get larger, it would be harder to maintain a common identity and prevent the mixing in of "others." In the island society, knowing that someone is from Group A has much more meaning when the group has only a few people, and

118 *Cultural Legitimizing*

this type of social meaning would be valuable to someone with a high grid disposition but anathema to an egalitarian. The alignments between grid and group and views toward interlocal land use cooperation are shown in Figure 6.3.

Returning to the real world, a summary of the links between the risks of cooperation (or autonomy) and cultural dispositions is useful. First, risks of loss include the familiar mechanisms of exit and voice (Hirschman, 1970). Residents and firms can leave the municipality or the region, or they can remain and express disapproval through voting and other political tools. These are not risks that have a knowable probability, but are rather the possibility of loss arising as a product of uncertainty. Second, risks can attach to both cooperation and autonomy. In terms of exit, neither option can guarantee specific action or inaction on the part of developers, residents, or firms necessary to improve municipal fiscal and economic well-being, or coerce beneficial and non-opportunistic behavior by other municipalities. Whatever behaviors have led to the pattern of municipal success and decline, or stability and instability, can continue to function under either form of governance. In terms of voice, neither governance option usually has the imprimatur of *ex ante* residential approval, or a clear partisan signal to assist the local elected official. Third, risks are present both for high-performing and low-performing municipalities, and neither form of governance is inherently capable of removing these risks for a specific type of municipality.

In short, the local elected official exists in a condition in which risks of loss—whether municipal or individual or both, since the two may be hard to separate—are pervasive. What cultural theory supplies is a heuristic with which local elected officials can appraise these risks and make a decision that coheres with her preferred way of life. If a high group communitarian, she will see only an

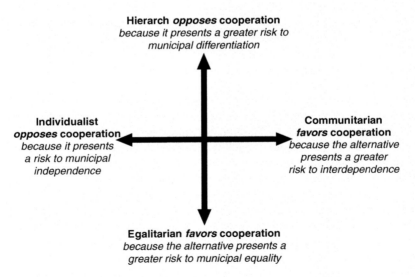

Figure 6.3 Cultural Dispositions and Preferences about Interlocal Cooperation.

Cultural Legitimizing   119

upside to cooperation because it promotes everyone working together and is an outward expression of interdependence and solidarity. Even if she recognizes the possibility for cooperation to be used in a negative way, this possibility will be diminished, and this diminution will persist whether she is in a high performing municipality or low performing municipality. The vice of parochialism, however, will be persistently amplified. A low grid egalitarian will have a similar preference but for a different reason. For him, the values of redistribution and fairness are most likely to be supported with a blurring of municipal boundaries that create artificial social divisions. In his preferred social relations, where a person is from should not be a defining social or economic feature. The egalitarian runs the risk that cooperative processes will simply reify existing race and class divisions, but the chance of this happening will seem small. The cultural heuristics will always be at work, but will function most aggressively in the process of preference formation where no countervailing political signals or other institutional signals are present. One could construct similar narratives for the high grid and low group individuals, but in the opposite direction.

What I have described is the process of cultural legitimizing as applied to questions of regional governance. Among two similarly situated local elected officials, even two occupying the same position in the same community, the one with a higher group, more communitarian disposition or a lower grid, more egalitarian disposition will be more likely to prefer a form of governance that is more cooperative, and that vests more authority in government at a larger scale. This choice of governance is most likely to promote an ordering of interlocal relations more reflective of the values these types of individuals have, and their preferred forms of social relation. By contrast, those with a higher grid, more hierarchical disposition or a lower group, more individualistic disposition will prefer a form of governance that preserves a relatively higher degree of local autonomy.

The Cultural Dispositions of Local Elected Officials

The short form cultural cognition items used in the work of Kahan are useful in this study for several reasons (Kahan, 2012).[4] First, they do not invoke cooperation directly—they do not use words like "cooperation" or "regional," which might lead to an inevitable positive correlation between dispositions and preferences. For example, a respondent who agrees "working as part of a team is valuable" should be more likely also to favor joint municipal land use planning. One would learn very little from this positive association except that people who prefer group work generally also prefer it specifically. Second, the questions—despite often addressing "hot button" political topics—are not ones for which a culturally sanctioned response is expected. Americans are far from uniform in their opinions about the role of government and issues of equality. Third, the questions measure different valences of cultural dispositions. Half the grid questions positively measure a hierarchical disposition if evaluated with "strongly agree" while the others positively measure an egalitarian disposition. A respondent giving the same answer repeatedly would have a neutral value on an additive

120 *Cultural Legitimizing*

index. A true "strong egalitarian" would have to strongly agree with three items and strongly disagree with the other three. The same would be true for a strong hierarch, strong communitarian, or strong individualist.

It is possible these questions are not the best items drawn from the original longer survey in the work of Kahan. The original factor analysis used data from a large-scale national survey of the general population, and the latent cultural dispositions of local elected officials may not load well on the 12 items in the short form survey. For this reason, I used exploratory factor analysis to test whether grid and group are indeed measuring different dimensions, and whether all the questions used for each dimension are worth including. To ensure parsimony in the multivariate models used to estimate the *ceteris paribus* associations between dispositions and preferences, I applied a factor analysis using polychoric correlations (which is appropriate when variables are ordinal) with varimax rotation to achieve orthogonal factors. A sample size of at least 300 with at least ten observations per variable is a rule of thumb for "good" factor analysis, and my dataset exceeds both thresholds easily (Comrey & Lee, 1992). The analysis, in plain terms, reveals that most of the variation across the 12 items—about 81 percent—loads onto a single factor, and that the six group items are the principal components in this factor. Another roughly 13 percent of the latent variation loads onto a second factor, and two of the grid items—the first and third items of the three with a hierarchical valence—are the principal components in that factor.[5]

The 12 survey items used to measure grid and group disposition included six questions for each dimension. Each question measured dispositions with a six-point, forced choice, Likert-type scale. Although prior research by others using these questions on the general population has demonstrated that the latent variation in a much longer questionnaire load most heavily onto these 12 items, factor analysis was used on the full set of 12 questions to narrow how the items would be used in analysis. All the group items loaded very strongly on one factor, while a second factor corresponding to two grid items[6] explained much of the remaining latent variation.

In this section I discuss each cultural item, and then the grid and group indices. Three items had a valence toward individualism (i.e., agreement would suggest the local elected official has a *low group* disposition). For the item *"The government interferes far too much in our everyday lives"* about 60 percent of respondents agreed while 40 percent disagreed ($n=535$). The split was almost exactly 50:50 for the item *"It's not the government's business to try to protect people from themselves"* ($n=531$). For the third item, *"The government should stop telling people how to live their lives,"* the ratio of agreement to disagreement was about 70:30 ($n=530$).

The other three group dimension items had a communitarian valence (a *high group* local elected official would find them easy to agree with). Nearly three-quarters of respondents agreed *"Sometimes government needs to make laws that keep people from hurting themselves"* ($n=536$). However, only a quarter felt "The government should do more to advance society's goals, even if that means

Cultural Legitimizing 121

limiting the freedom and choices of individuals" ($n=529$). And even fewer (22 percent) agreed that *"Government should put limits on the choices individuals can make so they don't get in the way of what's good for society"* ($n=525$).

For ascertaining grid disposition, the survey had three items with a hierarchical valence (those with which a high grid person should agree) and three with an egalitarian valence (those with which a high group person should agree). The first hierarchical item was *"We have gone too far in pushing equal rights in this country,"* and nearly two-thirds expressed some level of disagreement ($n=536$). The 528 local elected officials who responded to the statement *"It seems like blacks, women, homosexuals and other groups don't want equal rights, they want special rights just for them"* were almost exactly divided between agreement and disagreement. The third hierarchical item—*"Society as a whole has become too soft and feminine"*—received support from only about a third of respondents ($n=503$) and was the most skipped of all survey items. The three items with an egalitarian valence provoked fairly divided responses. About 58 percent of respondents ($n=536$) agreed that *"Our society would be better off if the distribution of wealth was more equal."* Slightly more than half ($n=533$) agreed that *"We need to dramatically reduce inequalities between the rich and the poor, whites and people of color, and men and women."* And slightly less than half ($n=533$) felt that *"Discrimination against minorities is still a very serious problem in our society."*

For the group and grid indices, I used two alternative approaches for the grid index and only one for the group index. The most basic index construction is additive: a simple sum of the six group items for the group index, and the six grid items to generate the grid index. Both indices range from negative to positive fifteen (−15 to +15). At the negative extreme for the group index, for example, a respondent would have answered *strongly agree* for all the individualist items and *strongly disagree* for all the communitarian items. At the zero value for the index, a respondent would have had responses that perfectly cancelled out.[7] A likely explanation would be that a respondent was responding the same for every item, such as all *strongly agree*, likely indicating repetitive answering without full item comprehension. Only 29 respondents had a zero response for the grid index, and only 34 had a zero response for the group index, a rate of about 5 percent for each index.

The group index values occupied the full range, with a mean of −2.57, mode of −3, and standard deviation of 6.62. The interquartile range is from an index value of −7 to 2. The histogram below shows the distribution of the grid index (see Figure 6.4). The grid index also ranges from −15 to +15. It has a mean of −0.85, mode of −1, and standard deviation of 7.19, with an interquartile range from −6 to 5. In research using the grid and group dimensions, a common approach is to intersect the two and divide respondents into four types based on this. Much of that research finds that the more common pairings are high group with low grid and low group with high grid. If someone is a communitarian, then she is more typically an egalitarian; if an individualist, then more typically a hierarch. This pattern somewhat persists among local elected officials in this study. The correlation

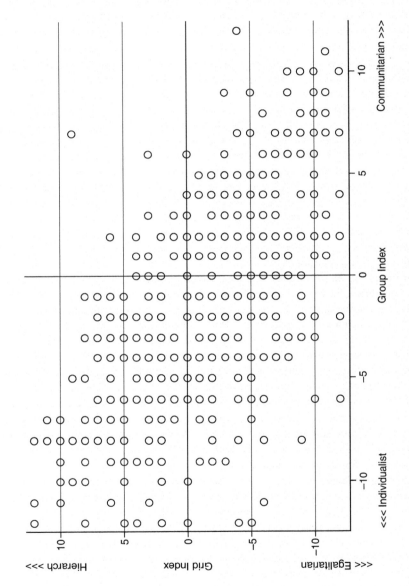

Figure 6.4 Cultural Dispositions of Respondent Local Elected Officials.

between grid and group is –0.64. Only 21 of 538 respondents (about 4 percent) are hierarchical communitarians (high grid and high group), making this the rarest combination by far. About one-fifth of respondents are *egalitarian individualists* who are low grid and low group). Another quarter are *egalitarian communitarians* who are low grid and high group. Lastly, about 40 percent are *hierarchical individualists* who are high grid and low group). Only two individuals were at the "center" with a value of zero on both group and grid indices.

The distribution reveals the importance of considering the dimensions separately. If we were to simply categorize a local elected official as a hierarchical individualist, for example, this would treat the person with a paired grid/group score of 15/–15 the same as one with a score of 7/–7, or 15/–1, or 1/–1. A large amount of valuable information would be lost in this approach. We would also have to consider how to treat the few individuals falling on the axis separating two categories, most of whom were still within the coordinate space for the other dimension. Besides the basic map, I include a political party cultural map (see Figure 6.5). We can see that Democrats tend to be egalitarian communitarians while Republicans are more often hierarchical individualists. However, many do not match this general typology, and the third party and independent candidates are all over the map.

Dispositions and Partisan Identity

Given the wording of the statements used to measure cultural dispositions, a logical question is whether the items are simply a reflection of political party affiliation. However, this is not problematic for the use of cultural cognition as a

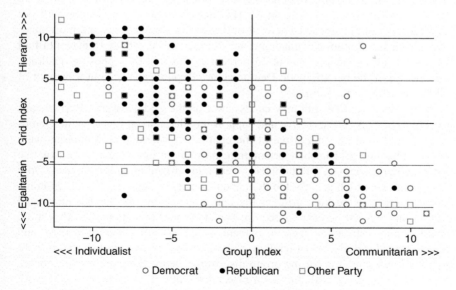

Figure 6.5 Cultural Dispositions by Partisan Self-Identification.

124   *Cultural Legitimizing*

mechanism, or for the use of the survey items. Swedlow (2011, p. 704) notes that cultural theory

> goes beyond the liberal-conservative continuum in American politics to specify the ideological and institutional sources of conflict and coalition in two dimensions of social and political relations, and consequently cultural theory provides a more accurate basis for characterizing ideological and institutional sources of partisanship.

Beyond enhanced accuracy, it is important to note the mutability of party affiliation, both over time and across space (Wildavsky, 1987). For example, a Republican currently might align well with the values that suggest a weak role for the government in individual behavior and clearly defined social roles based on easily recognized personal characteristics. A Libertarian might also fit squarely within the individualist affiliation, though the balance between hierarchy and egalitarianism might be trickier to predict. A Democrat would probably fit well with the communitarian's preference for a strong role for government and lack of defined social roles. Indeed, a lack of any alignment between party affiliation and cultural disposition should lead one to be suspicious of the items used to measure grid and group.

The relationship between party affiliation and cultural dispositions does not mean we should favor the former (because the information is more readily available) or the latter (because it allows for a richer variation than possible with the standard divisions of political party), and discard the other. Rather, the two are complementary: we can think of them as measures of identity. For example, if one is a hierarch and an individualist, then choosing to represent the Republican Party is protective of one's identity. This does not mean that friction will not exist. In my sample, about 10 percent of those who are hierarchs and individualists (the classic Republican quadrant) are Democrats, i.e., about 15 percent of all Democrats in the sample. About 15 percent of those in the opposing quadrant, the domain of the paradigmatic Democrat, are Republicans—about 9 percent of all Republicans in the sample.

While the party line split may be less clear on the grid questions, Republicans tend to be socially conservative and support the hierarchical items, while Democrats should be more supportive of the egalitarian statements. Democrats were consistently low grid in their orientation: only about one of every four or five gave high grid responses. Republicans were more mixed in their responses. Only 35 percent were high grid for the item about society being too soft and feminine, and 45 percent were high grid for the item about going too far pushing equal rights. But only 10 percent agreed our society would be better off with a more equal wealth distribution (i.e., 90 percent were high grid). The third party and independent local elected officials were quite mixed in their responses on these items. As was the case for the group disposition items, the pattern of responses suggests using party affiliation as a proxy for cultural disposition would work some of the time, but the linkage is not nearly as clean as we might expect.[8]

Cultural Legitimizing 125

The six group questions are suggestive of a "small government" or "big government" mindset, so it would be reasonable to expect some alignment, respectively, with Republican and Democrat party affiliation. To an extent, the findings support this. On the first individualist question, for example, of the 318 local elected officials expressing some level of agreement, only 37 were Democrats ($n=138$) while 178 were Republicans ($n=221$). But the divide was not as stark on other questions. Of the 270 local elected officials agreeing with the second individualist item, 130 were Republican ($n=217$), while 47 were Democrat ($n=137$). And for the second communitarian question, 149 of 221 Republican respondents agreed (about 67 percent), as did 109 of the 140 Democrats (about 78 percent).

The relationship between party affiliation and cultural dispositions does not mean one should favor the former (because the information is more readily available) or the latter (because it allows for a richer variation than possible with the standard divisions of political party), and discard the other. Rather, the two are complementary: both are measures of identity. For example, if one is a hierarch and an individualist, then choosing to represent the Republican Party is protective of one's identity. This does not mean that friction will not exist. In my sample, about 10 percent of those who are hierarchs and individualists (the classic Republican quadrant) are Democrats, i.e., about 15 percent of all Democrats in the sample. About 15 percent of those in the opposing quadrant, the domain of the paradigmatic Democrat, are Republicans—about 9 percent of all Republicans in the sample. I find it valuable in this study, an early consideration of cultural cognition, to focus on the grid and group dimensions and comment in later analysis, as necessary, on how party affiliation performs as an indicator in the place of cultural dispositions. Notably, all the findings presented later include political party affiliation as a control.

Evidence of Cultural Legitimizing

We can now consider the evidence about cultural legitimizing from multivariate, multilevel regression analysis (see tables in Appendix G). Group disposition is strongly significant and positive, as hypothesized. We can interpret the odds ratio as meaning that a one unit increase on the group dimension (moving toward being communitarian and away from being an individualist), corresponds to nearly a 7 percent increase in the odds of being in a higher dependent variable response category (for example, the odds of being neutral versus opposing, or favoring versus being neutral). A more useful change to consider is a six unit change, which would be the difference between a two respondents who were a full response category apart on all six group items. This type of shift—the difference, say, between a strong communitarian and a communitarian—would lead to a 47 percent increase in the odds of a more favorable response.

Grid disposition, which measures the disposition toward social equality or differentiation, was slightly below one as expected, but was not significant in this model. There were also no interactive effects between the grid and group

126　*Cultural Legitimizing*

measures. The only intersection that had a strong and positive effect (a value of roughly 1.96) was egalitarian (low grid) and communitarian (high group); a respondent having both dispositions was about twice as likely to favor cooperation as those in the other three cultural quadrants.

How are municipalities in the Detroit and Grand Rapids metropolitan areas different from each other? Cultural dispositions play a slightly stronger role in the latter region. The group index parameter has a larger magnitude, and the grid index parameter is significant and below one, as expected. Perception of residential support is strongly positive and highly significant in both regions. The variable measuring discretion is also positive and significant in the Grand Rapids area while it is not significant in the Detroit area.

Preferences about full coverage cooperation should be more divided. Rather than cooperating over land use in part of the municipality, under a full coverage agreement a common vision with one's partners must be reached regarding the planning of all the municipal land—not just commercial or industrial site assembly, or open space coordination, but multiple types of residential use and agricultural use. Such cooperation involves current residents and their properties much more directly, and the risk calculus is likely to be much different under a full coverage scenario.

The cultural political variables once again perform well and in line with expectations. A local elected official who is one unit higher on the grid disposition is 8 percent more likely to be in a more favorable response category; and the difference between dispositional categories (for example, between a communitarian and a strong communitarian) is about 57 percent. Conversely, a local elected official who is a strong individualist versus a weak individualist is about 56 percent more likely to be in a less favorable category. The two dispositions are mirrors of each other, and this makes sense with the reasoning behind the cultural cognition of governance mechanism.

Conclusion

Overall, the evidence from Michigan strongly suggests cultural legitimizing plays a significant role in shaping preferences about interlocal land use cooperation. The strength of the relationship across multiple model specifications and all outcome variables, and while controlling for a wide array of other institutional features, is quite remarkable. It is not inevitable, for example, that attitudes about women, Blacks, and gays, or about the need for government to play a protective role toward people, would correspond at all to notions about local versus regional governance of land use. But latent cultural dispositions reflected by these attitudes clearly do play a vital role in the legitimizing process. Individualists and hierarchs tend to oppose cooperation, and to favor more advisory forms of it. Communitarians and egalitarians tend to support it, and to favor more authoritative forms. And we can craft a logical narrative grounded in the tenets of cultural theory to support these alignments. In the final chapter, I consider how we might deal with the problem of cultural pluralism among actors facing the possibility of regionalizing reforms, including interlocal cooperation.

Notes

1 Hierarchy and market—the polar modes of organizing activity in Williamson's transactional economy—can be regarded as aligning with different ends of the grid and group dimensions (Thompson et al., 1990, pp. 13–14).
2 This is a view of values, attitudes, and behaviors consistent with social psychology, specifically the theory of planned behavior.
3 Coyle uses the traditional intersectional terminology of grid-group, such that those who are low grid and high group are egalitarians, those who are high grid and high group are hierarchs, and those who are low group and low grid are libertarians. The final quadrant (low group and high grid) is ignored, as is often the case.
4 See survey items 19 through 30, Appendix B.
5 In the final analyses I ran models including full cultural disposition indices (reflecting answers to all six questions for each disposition) and an alternative index for grid which summed only the two items that performed best in factor analysis.
6 The items were "We have gone too far in pushing equal rights in this country" and "Society as a whole has become too soft and feminine."
7 The component questions had no zero values due to being forced choice.
8 A discussion of the distribution in responses to the 12 items by individual and municipal attributes may reveal interesting patterns, but it is outside the scope of this book.

References

Chai, S. K. (1997). Rational choice and culture: Clashing perspectives or complementary modes of analysis? In A. B. Wildavsky, R. Ellis, & M. Thompson (Eds.), *Culture matters: Essays in honor of Aaron Wildavsky* (pp. 45–56). Westview Press.

Comrey, A. L., & Lee, H. B. (2013). *A first course in factor analysis*. Psychology Press.

Coyle, D. J. (1993). *Property rights and the constitution: Shaping society through land use regulation*. SUNY Press.

DiMaggio, P. J., & Powell, W. W. (Eds.). (1991). *The new institutionalism in organizational analysis*. University of Chicago Press.

Douglas, M. (2003). *Purity and danger: An analysis of concepts of pollution and taboo*. Routledge.

Douglas, M., & Wildavsky, A. (1983). *Risk and culture: An essay on the selection of technological and environmental dangers*. University of California Press.

Granovetter, M. (1985). Economic action and social structure: The problem of embeddedness. *American Journal of Sociology, 91*(3), 481–510.

Grendstad, G., & Selle, P. (1995). Cultural theory and the new institutionalism. *Journal of Theoretical Politics, 7*(1), 5–27.

Hirschman, A. O. (1970). *Exit, voice, and loyalty: Responses to decline in firms, organizations, and states*. Harvard University Press.

Kahan, D. M. (2012). Cultural cognition as a conception of the cultural theory of risk. In *Handbook of risk theory* (pp. 725–759). Springer Netherlands.

Kahan, D. M., & Braman, D. (2006). Cultural cognition and public policy. *Yale Law & Policy Review, 24*(1), 149–172.

Kahan, D. M., & Braman, D. (2003). More statistics, less persuasion: A cultural theory of gun-risk perceptions. *University of Pennsylvania Law Review, 151*(4), 1291–1327.

Kahan, D. M., Braman, D., Slovic, P., Gastil, J., & Cohen, G. (2009). Cultural cognition of the risks and benefits of nanotechnology. *Nature Nanotechnology, 4*(2), 87–90.

128 *Cultural Legitimizing*

Kahan, D. M., Peters, E., Wittlin, M., Slovic, P., Ouellette, L. L., Braman, D., & Mandel, G. (2012). The polarizing impact of science literacy and numeracy on perceived climate change risks. *Nature Climate Change, 2*(10), 732–735.

Meyer, J. W., & Rowan, B. (1977). Institutionalized organizations: Formal structure as myth and ceremony. *American Journal of Sociology, 83*(2), 340–363.

Meyer, J. W., & Scott, W. R. (1983). Centralization and the legitimacy problems of local government. *Organizational Environments: Ritual and Rationality, 199*, 215.

Rayner, S. (1992). Cultural theory and risk analysis. In S. Krimsky & D. Golding (Eds.), *Social theories of risk* (pp. 83–115). Praeger.

Renn, O. (1992). Concepts of risk: A classification. In S. Krimsky & D. Golding (Eds.), *Social theories of risk* (pp. 53–79). Praeger.

Scott, W. R. (1987). The adolescence of institutional theory. *Administrative Science Quarterly*, 493–511.

Slovic, P. (1992). Perception of risk: Reflections on the psychometric paradigm. In S. Krimsky & D. Golding (Eds.), *Social theories of risk* (pp. 117–152). Praeger.

Swedlow, B. (2011). A cultural theory of politics. *PS: Political Science & Politics, 44*(4), 703–710.

Thompson, M., Ellis, R., & Wildavsky, A. (1990). *Cultural theory*. Westview Press.

Wildavsky, A. (1987). Choosing preferences by constructing institutions: A cultural theory of preference formation. *American Political Science Review, 81*(1), 3–21.

Zucker, L. G. (1983). Organizations as institutions. *Research in the Sociology of Organizations, 2*(1), 1–47.

7   Conclusion

> *[I]t is the minds of the American public, and not the governmental framework in which it operates, that impose the major barrier to regionalism.*
> — Reynolds (2003, p. 111)

The previous two chapters discussed the evidence about the different sources of legitimizing.[1] Getting lost in the forest of all these numbers and verbiage is easy, and so it is useful to gain some altitude and consider what all this means to the practice of interlocal land use cooperation and regional governance more broadly. What can we say in general about how the different sources of legitimizing perform in the preference formation processes of the typical local elected official? In Table 7.1, I provide a summary of all the results at a glance across the dependent variables and all hypotheses. Rather than report coefficient estimates, I simply use positive (+) and negative (–) symbols for ease of clarity.[2]

The most consistent performer—across all model specifications and broken down by metropolitan area—is the measure of group disposition. Consider the power of that finding. Even when controlling for a wide array of variables reflect transaction cost and responsiveness norms—and various individual level controls—the measure of group was significant. More plainly, being more of a communitarian was associated with preferring not only the adoption of cooperation, but also a more authoritative structure. This is not simply a case of attitudes predicting attitudes, an obvious concern since I have just used terms like "communitarian" and "cooperation" which seem quite synonymous. The measure of the group disposition was based on six items, none of which used the word "cooperation" or "regional" or anything of the sort. While they did refer to individuals and government, there is no *inherent* link between a more individualistic society and one with more autonomous local land use, or a more communitarian society and one with more cooperative land use. Indeed, the use of government to proscribe individual behavior could be more fully realized with many more local governments, while an individual might feel free to do as he likes without government supervision in a much larger group. What the hypothesized relationship was based on was coherence between the values of the high group way of life, the ideal social relations that arise in it, and the tendency of cooperation to advance both.

Table 7.1 Support of the Hypotheses

Hypothesis	Partial Area JMPA Adoption			Full Coverage JMPA Adoption			JMPA Structure (Following Partial Area Adoption)			JMPA Structure (Following Full Coverage Adoption)		
	Full	Detroit	Grand Rapids	**Full**	Detroit	Grand Rapids	**Full**	Detroit	Grand Rapids	**Full**	Detroit	Grand Rapids
Cultural legitimizing												
Group (+)	+	+	+	+	+	+	+	+	+	+		+
Grid (−)			−	−	−	−	−	−		−	−	−
Political responsiveness (normative legitimizing)												
Alignment (−)				−	−		−		−	−	−	
Discretion (+)	+		+	+								
Residential support (+)	+	+	+	+	+	+	+	+		+	+	
Transaction cost economizing—municipal factors (normative legitimizing)												
Fiscal distress (+)												
Socioecon. distress (+)				+	+							
Growth (−)	−				[+]							
Homeowner lobby (−)		−						−		−		−

Transaction cost economizing and reciprocity—intermunicipal factors (normative legitimizing)

Interlocal ties (+)								+*		+*
Relative fiscal distress (+)				[−]					[−]	
Relative fiscal health (−)		−				−	[+]			
Relative socioecon. distress (+)				[−]				+		+
Relative socioecon.health (−)									−	
Relative high growth (−)					−					
Relative low growth (+)										
Racial heterog. (−)			[+]		[+]		−	[+]		[+]
Other										
JMPA awareness	+	+								
Republican	+									
Democrat										
Tenure				+	+		−			
Education				−	−					

Note

Sign indicates significance at $p<0.05$; sign by hypothesis indicates expectation; [brackets] around a sign indicate a significant result in the direction opposite expectations; multiple cell entries may occur because some hypotheses had several measures)

* This was for the variable *number of neighbors* only.

132 *Conclusion*

Grid disposition also worked quite well as a measure, attaining significance in all but one full model, one for Grand Rapids, and one for Detroit. The values were always below 1.0 when significant, suggesting a higher grid, more hierarchical individual will be more likely to oppose cooperation and an authoritative form of it. Interestingly, when the preferences had to do with *full coverage* adoption and structure, the grid measure was *always* significant, suggesting that such preferences cohered more closely with concerns of differentiation and equality.

The one other variable that performed well across nearly every model specification was the perception of residential support. Earlier I cautioned about the limitations of this variable. While not highly correlated or well explained by the various preferences, there may still be enough of an effect from survey respondents intentionally aligning this response with their own (since it came closely after the JMPA preference scenarios) that the magnitude—if not the significance—may be overstated.

The findings for the rest of the variables are a true mixed bag. One notable feature perhaps not readily apparent in this visual review is that many of the variables for municipal and intermunicipal attributes had two or three different measures that could have been significant. For example, the eight intermunicipal vectors had 20 variables included in them. These variables were tested with multiple transformations in myriad model specifications, all in attempts to make them perform in line with expectations. They only rarely did, and sometimes they performed against expectations.

These findings were only based on cross-sectional evidence from one state, and they only considered preferences rather than behaviors. These are, of course, limitations. But the use of a large sample, hierarchical linear modeling that accounted for individuals nested within municipalities, and a quite exhaustive selection of variables included in model specifications makes the findings very hard to disregard. Because preferences *do* tend to predict behaviors so well, knowing that public officials have strong cultural heuristics that seem to play a persistent role in how they think about a key form of voluntary regionalizing reforms matters a great deal for our shared metropolitan futures.

The viability of a sociocultural collective action framework also matters for two other reasons, and it is these that I explore in the final chapter. First, it matters for how we reform the policy space within which metropolitan governance occurs. Second, it matters for shaping the future study of metropolitan governance.

Avenues for Policy Reform under Legitimizing

Sociological institutionalism has tended over the course of its scholarly life toward explanations for why organizations become similar (DiMaggio & Powell, 1983). But in the arena of metropolitan governance, this kind of pursuit would not be satisfying because the status quo is very much the problem. The local government, through a combination of coercive and normative forces, is very much pushed toward competition rather than cooperation. I detailed this in

Conclusion 133

Chapter 2. Moreover, cultural opposition to meaningful cooperation—which clearly exists among many local public officials—could be very difficult to overcome, because of just how deeply cultural worldviews sit in our cognitive processes. To realize an increase in the frequency and endurance of cooperation over land use planning and regulation, and other lifestyle services, we would need to make it more legitimate.

An advantage of sociocultural collective action is that it has so many points from which policy recommendations can generate. If we found regulative barriers were a lingering problem, we would want to advocate for appropriate changes to state enabling legislation to create a local policy space within which cooperation is less discouraged (Barron, 2003; Frug & Barron, 2013; Cashin, 1999; Gillette, 1991). If normative economizing is the impediment, then the state or a third-party broker might also play a role in providing incentives. If a lack of reciprocity creates cognitive de-legitimization that thwarts cooperation, then councils of government or smaller regional bodies may need to play a more active role, or longer tenures in local government may need to be enabled and rewarded. If local officials are concerned about making decisions that are not legitimate in the eyes of constituents, then soft policy interventions such as education campaigns and participatory processes may need to be used to create a dialog between representatives and residents. And, lastly, cultural biases can be addressed through the means discussed in the next section.

Thus, depending on what empirical evidence reveals over time, we would need either to make a desired reform more legitimate in the institutional sphere in which it encounters the greatest deficit, or constrain an actor to consult only those internalized prescriptions that will *ex ante* legitimate cooperation or other regionalizing reforms. Given the focus of this book on cultural legitimizing, I pay the most attention in this final chapter to dealing with cultural pluralism. I assume negative biases—those attached to hierarchy and individualism—will be distributed into most organizational settings. Just as the minds of the American are a potential hurdle to regionalism, as Reynolds notes in the opening quote of this chapter, so too can the minds of local elected officials be a problem.

Dealing with Cultural Pluralism through De-Biasing

Scholars developing grid-group cultural theory over the last 30 years have spent very little time considering the policy implications of their findings, devoting most of their attention instead to generating empirical evidence that will support their theoretical perspective as accurately descriptive of the real world. Much of the difficulty is in the necessary conceptualization of cultural dispositions as foundational and nearly immutable. Dispositions are at the core of one's self, as developed and reinforced through the power of socialization. Absent this deep anchorage, cultural theory would have minimal explanatory power across diverse settings and would be a poor alternative to rational choice. If cultural dispositions exist, then the logical conclusion is that we will continue to deal with polarization and tension, and that our efforts at negotiation and compromise will

134   *Conclusion*

address only superficial issues. Not only does culture frame many problems as deeply ideological, but it seems to force a begrudging acceptance of the intransigence of these problems because of their underlying cultural affiliation.

Kahan and his colleagues in the cultural cognition project, whose work was described at length in Chapter 6, have made two contributions beyond the theoretically important drawing together of cultural theory and the psychometric theories of risk. First, they provided a more rigorous and conceptually sound approach to measuring grid and group cultural dispositions. Second, they had a willingness to directly consider policy recommendations. While the cultural cognition project was directed at understanding ideological polarization among members of the lay public regarding technological and environmental risks, the implications Kahan and others consider can be adapted to policymakers engaged in policy processes.

These implications are grounded in the psychological and social mechanisms by which cultural cues translate new information, lead to preference formation, and, ultimately, generate behavior. The mechanisms Kahan has proposed include identity-protective cognition, identity affirmation, biased assimilation, credibility, and availability (2012, p. 739). The notion of *identity-protective cognition* depends on an almost tribal image of people with similar cultural dispositions sorting into groups that can provide material and non-material benefits. Those with the strongest stake in this group membership—those who enjoy the most benefits from such association—will resist risks to their identity. Kahan gives the example of hierarchs who oppose gun control but do so most strongly when they are also white and male, because gun ownership is disproportionately beneficial to those hierarchs with such racial and gender characteristics. In other words, gun control is perceived as risky by *any* hierarch, but it is *especially* risky to the hierarchical identity of those who culturally attach gun ownership and freedom of use to that identity (Kahan, 2012, pp. 741–742). Cultural *identity affirmation* suggests a policy can be framed to neutralize information that would otherwise be threatening to cultural worldview, making it valuable to "communicate information about risk in a way that affirms rather than threatens their cultural worldview" (2012, p. 753). Affirmation can also occur in the design of policy. For example, registering guns by providing a tax rebate would be a path to registration that affirms ownership with a positive stimulus. Identity affirmation is the positive side of identity protection, allowing acceptance of a risk that would otherwise be unacceptable.

Culturally biased *assimilation* occurs when an individual "selectively attend[s] to evidence and arguments, crediting those that reinforce their beliefs and dismissing as non-credible those that contravene them" (2012, p. 742). This occurs both when individuals have prior, culturally grounded beliefs (creating a reinforcing, filtering effect toward future information) and when they are starting from a blank slate. In the latter case, even an initial presentation with balanced information does not prevent biased assimilation. Cultural *availability* is not about information uptake but rather about information recall: those risks most at odds with one's cultural disposition will be remembered as having greater

Conclusion 135

significance, and therefore remembered more readily (2012, p. 747). Last, cultural credibility is the functioning of cultural cues but with regard to individuals: we favor and recall information from those who signal they share our cultural worldviews (2012, pp. 749–750).

All these mechanisms create or reinforce cultural bias. Providing simply *more* information is not enough, and is likely to lead to polarization in attitudes and behaviors. Rather, the information about a policy must be packaged and presented in a way that will make it affirming of *any* cultural worldview, or at least of the cultural worldviews held by participants in a decision process. A few examples illustrate how issues can be packaged to be broadly acceptable across multiple cultural worldviews.

First, to address the credibility mechanism, one can attempt to create what Kahan calls a purposely pluralistic advocacy condition (2012, p. 752). Kahan and colleagues (2010) studied public risk perceptions about the human papillomavirus (HPV) vaccine, and found that subjects receiving an argument they were culturally predisposed to reject from an expert whose values they shared significantly decreased polarization in risk perception. The opposite was true as well. By having information about the vaccine delivered by sources who seem culturally credible to people of multiple worldviews—a condition of culturally pluralistic advocacy—a broader base of public support for a particular viewpoint might be built.

Experiments are useful for developing theory, but what about putting this logic into practice? Consider two similar examples drawn from the real world. One is from France, where conflict about abortion decreased after a policy was enacted in which the procedure required an unreviewable certification of personal distress. Kahan and Braman (2006, pp. 168–169) suggest this policy was popular and quelled polarization because requiring certification was appealing to hierarchs and communitarians (the typical profile of religious traditionalists) while making it unreviewable was appealing to egalitarians and individualists (the typical profile of those supporting a woman's bodily autonomy). The second is about the consensus surrounding tradable emissions permits as an acceptable form of pollution regulation in the late 1980s and early 1990s. The authors argue this occurred because improving air quality (a goal appealing to communitarians) would be achieved using a market mechanism (a means appealing to individualists) and the symbolic empowerment of large firms (a message appealing to hierarchs).

A more contemporaneous account comes from southeast Florida (Kahan, 2014, pp. 36–39). There, four county commissioners—both Republicans and Democrats—took the lead in ratifying a detailed, five-year joint climate action plan as members of the Southeast Florida Regional Climate Change Compact. The action was necessary in the wake of a mandate that all municipal subdivisions update their comprehensive plans to address the threat of rising sea levels and coastal flooding. The plan and the public processes used to create it were able to succeed despite a population that is politically diverse and which has similarly diverse views about the causes and dangers of climate change. Kahan

136 *Conclusion*

argues success has been possible because the question before participants was about *what they knew* about dealing with a decades-old regional problem, rather than about "who they are, whose side they are on" (2014, p. 35). By focusing on the concrete symptoms of a well-known problem rather than the cause of the problem, the polarization that existed about anthropogenic climate change was diminished and the need for local government effectiveness—an agreeable, culturally neutral position—was emphasized.

The process at work in all these examples is cultural "de-biasing": the management of potentially threatening information so that it enters cognitive processes through a positive cultural filter, allowing a more open-minded appraisal of competing facts and opinions. Kahan and Braman (2006, p. 151) note, "[t]he key to debiasing … is to frame empirical information in terms that make assent to it compatible with, rather than antagonistic to, the commitments of individuals of diverse cultural persuasions." De-biasing has not yet been well-tested. No evidence exists yet that we should credit to de-biasing the success of French abortion reform, or tradable emission permits, or southeast Florida climate change action planning. However, it does at least suggest ways to deal with cultural pluralism beyond a mere shrug of the shoulders in the face of deep conflicts. How might we translate the logic of de-biasing to the context of governance choice among local officials confronting regional dilemmas? And is de-biasing the only method through which we might address cultural pluralism in policy processes?

Let us presume for the sake of generating prescriptions that interlocal cooperation is normatively good by some external measures—e.g., that it would yield more efficiency, equity, effectiveness—and that we are policymakers with an interest in spurring its adoption and endurance. Cultural cognition of governance suggests merely explaining the inherent goodness of cooperation is not enough. In many of my conversations with planning academics and practitioners, this logic would be readily accepted. But among many others, including many of the local elected officials I interviewed and surveyed, it would not be. The mechanisms through which cultural bias operates would simply lead to retrenchment.

De-biasing as described above requires culturally affirmative framing. Based on the findings in this study, we already have evidence that those with high group (communitarian) and low grid (egalitarian) cultural dispositions tend to favor joint land use planning, even when that mode of land use governance is not attached to any substantive end (whether social justice, economic development, or something else). The trick, then, is to make it appealing to individualists and hierarchs who value, respectively, autonomy and differentiation.

One way might be to appeal to hierarchs specifically by characterizing joint land use as a differentiating mechanism. The possibility of using a joint agreement as a guard against exclusionary zoning challenges—as a way to preserve the unique character of the cooperating communities—would be affirming to the *hierarch*'s view of local government. If this characteristic were included explicitly in the authorizing statute rather than discussed as a legal possibility, hierarchs might view cooperation more favorably. Cooperation can also give the region a competitive advantage over other regions in attracting firms and

Conclusion 137

residents, and this possibility would be affirming to hierarchs. Organizations interested in promoting land use cooperation could emphasize this in their messaging about the benefits of a joint agreement. For *individualists*, the flexibility in the governance structure with regard to local autonomy (that it can be purely advisory in nature and need not lead to dissolution of the local planning bodies and regulations) should be appealing. Cooperation that is merely advisory in form is more protective of an identity that values autonomy. However, finding a culturally affirming way to sell a stronger form of voluntary cooperation to an individualist—who values self-sufficiency and prefers social independence—may be much more difficult.

The creation of a pluralistic advocacy condition may be one option. The correlation between political party affiliation and cultural identity, discussed in Chapter 6, suggests advocacy for interlocal cooperation should come from politically diverse individuals and organizations—Republicans, Democrats, Libertarians, and others. An organization such as the Land Information Access Association (LIAA), which, in Michigan, acted as a third party supporting the processes leading to joint land use planning implementation, could help create such a condition. If hierarchs and individualists hear about the benefits of joint land use planning from culturally credible people, they may be receptive not only to advisory cooperation but even to that which reduces land use autonomy.

Because the present study addresses cultural cognition among local *elected* officials expressing preferences about governance, we must think about how cultural pluralism interfaces with politics. Recall that respondents who perceived residential support for joint land use planning were much more likely to prefer adopting both partial and full coverage versions and were more likely to favor an authoritative structure. Local elected officials were not strictly partisan political creatures (i.e., a respondent's Democrat or Republican identity had only a weak relationship to preferences); rather, they were quite responsive to their appraisal of the sentiment among residents in their community. Recall, too, that most respondents felt serving resident interests was important but still felt the ability to contravene these interests to serve their own idea of the public interest (in the terminology I adopted, they simultaneously perceived a condition of both high alignment and high discretion). By making the adoption and repeal of a joint land use planning agreement an activity for local elected officials, the JMPA by design adds another potential layer of cultural pluralism: that existing among constituents. To the extent hierarchs and individualists have electoral power in a community—whether from speaking as the majority voice or having other influence—de-biasing must also target them.

Kahan's account of climate change action planning in Florida may provide a clue to how this could be done. There, the success of the policy process was credited to its consistent framing as a response to concerns about flooding, rather than as a debate on participants' views toward anthropogenic climate change. For joint land use planning to garner culturally widespread public support, it may need to be framed as an effective local government response to a well-known and long-standing concern—such as sprawl, fiscal crisis, or natural

138 *Conclusion*

resource degradation—rather than as a verdict about the benefits of localism versus regionalism. Indeed, the municipalities where joint land use planning was adopted tended to be those where it was an essential tool for dealing with a fairly well-defined problem. The near complete absence of joint land use planning in metropolitan areas may be due to how potent the local versus regional dynamic can be there, as often seen in the conflicts between suburbs and central city or between an affluent community and its distressed neighbors.

It is here that we see a point of intersection with transaction cost economizing under the institutional collective action framework. Scholarship on interlocal cooperation has long emphasized the necessity of joint gains or collective benefits, as I discussed in Chapter 3. While this seems intuitive from a rational economic perspective, the success of projects with joint gains may also be due to their ability to appeal across cultural divisions and neutralize bias. The hypotheses about fiscal and demographic characteristics may have had little supportive evidence in the Michigan research presented in this book because survey scenarios were purposefully generic. Local public officials—and their constituents—may require a narrative link between unique municipal problems and cooperation as a specific solution. In other words, simply knowing one's community is in distress—which is what would show through in socioeconomic and fiscal data—may not lead one to see cooperation as a path toward a better future, particularly given the uncertainty and risk attached to cooperation in land use that I outlined in earlier chapters.

Even if de-biasing among local officials and the public can secure support for and adoption of joint land use planning, this does not guarantee continued support. In the story of the Manchester Community, the turnover in elected leadership in Bridgewater Township seemed to play some role in the eventual repeal of membership. The views of residents can change too, particularly in quickly growing communities. To avoid these possibilities, it may be necessary to consider depoliticizing joint land use planning. Why introduce political difficulties by requiring a vote of local elected officials? While dissolution of local planning and zoning would still require a vote of representatives or a public referendum, advisory forms might be successfully made the subject of administrative oversight. If land use cooperation could somehow be made purely a part of the work of planning staff and appointed commissioners, or made more durable against electoral turnover by requiring supermajority repeal votes or setting up other roadblocks, the political calculus about cooperation might be successfully bypassed.

Staff planners can be especially well-positioned to encourage lifestyle function cooperation among culturally pluralistic groups, whether members of the public or local elected officials. The two major conceptualizations of the planner in the last 70 years are, first, as a technocratic participant in administrative processes and, second, as a participant in and manager of discursive, highly public political processes. We can view each of these roles as a different way of dealing with the problem, if it is one, of cultural pluralism.

The technocratic, comprehensive planner was not only a reflection of the dominance of classical rationality but was complementary of the broader

Conclusion 139

movement toward progressive reform that brought with it council-manager forms of local government and the professionalization of government activity. If we take political ideology as one expression of a deeper cultural identity, then the planner who is used for the rational, scientific management of social problems, removed from and even superior to the messiness of politics, represents a depoliticizing reaction to cultural pluralism. When I earlier mentioned the possible need to remove cooperation from the domain of city councils and township boards and place it in the planning department, the recommendation very much embraced this view of the planner as wise bureaucrat.

When the planner or analyst is described as part of communicative, discursive, and consensual processes, it is a nod to the processes of de-biasing (Innes and Booher, 2010; Healey, 2003; Forester, 1999). However, for as much attention as this perspective gives to framing, dialog, and rhetorical persuasion, and as frequently as it talks about the values underlying these mechanisms, few attempts have been hade to quantify and empirically study the substance of these values. We know processes should be open to diverse stakeholders, but that diversity is usually expressed in terms of race, class, political identity, or role within the process (such as developer versus community organization). We do not think of the cultural diversity that cuts across and may even unite people who are superficially different, nor do we consider how our language within these processes might be threatening or affirming to those of different cultural values.

The practice of planning in either form, then, can be seen as simply as a justifiable response to cultural pluralism, rather than as an attempt to run away from politics (an oft-made critique of rational planning in both its comprehensive and incremental forms) or to become an inherently political creature who risks capture by capitalist elites while never fully engaging in equitable advocacy (a common critique of communicative action and related paradigms). By bringing cultural cognition into planning, we can begin to develop empirically testable narratives about what planners have done and should do in response to the pluralistic world with which they engage in their practice.

The Prospects for Regional Governance through Voluntary Interlocal Cooperation

The findings in this study suggest de-biasing may be an important step to engendering supportive preferences across cultural groups. While communitarians and egalitarians were quite consistent in their support for cooperation, support that exists among hierarchs and individualists was much more common under partial area coverage or an advisory structure. Weaker forms of interlocal cooperation—those that preserve more local autonomy either territorially or structurally—are more culturally affirming and, therefore, acceptable to hierarchs and individualists. However, this does once again put us into the same corner identified by Donald Norris (2016) and many others: regionalizing reforms are possible, but when they are voluntary they will never be able to tackle the really difficult

140 *Conclusion*

problems caused by fragmented, parochial land use planning and regulation, and other lifestyle functions. Partial area cooperation and advisory cooperation are not valueless, but we should harbor no illusions that they vindicate the polycentrist and localist vision of public choice adherents.

Cultural de-biasing deserves vetting as a pathway to realizing voluntary regionalizing reforms in areas where they have traditionally underperformed. But I propose the greater value of this book lies in the sociocultural collective action framework. By providing an account of local government in which decisions are made by legitimacy-seeking actors embedded in multiple types of institutions—rules, norms, and culture—the book encourages an attentiveness to empirical work targeted at individuals and the multiple sources of rationality they might employ. Rather than model all local public officials as boundedly rational opportunists, or some variant on that, we can acknowledge that decisions about regionalizing reforms are likely reflective of multiple, competing legitimizing calculi.

This book animates the formal debate about polycentrism and localism versus and centralizing reforms—the government versus governance approaches of, respectively, the reform and public choice advocates—with evidence about how interlocal cooperation is perceived by local elected officials. When interlocal cooperation or other voluntary regionalizing reforms are not adopted or do not endure over time, we now have some more clues about the possible hurdles that might need to be crossed. The significance of group and grid cultural dispositions in this study should be interpreted as simply a first step. To truly speak to the limitations of interlocal cooperation in the policy domains it has not traditionally reached, we need to now embark on research that tests the full sociocultural collective action framework and evaluates the policy recommendations suggested by it. Future research will need to more directly study local elected and administrative officials and treat them as rational legitimizers embedded in rich institutional settings that include cultures. It will need to marshal evidence across multiple states to incorporate institutional variation not only in cultural and normative prescriptions, but also in regulative ones.

What must be acknowledged, finally, is that using a framework built on a sociological institutionalist perspective may lead us to a familiar end despite taking a different path: the need for centralizing reforms, or at least adjustments to the sphere of local autonomy enjoyed by municipal governments. The expansion of research to multiple states with heterogeneous laws will be essential to discerning the marginal impact of polycentrist and localist regulations, while controlling for multiple normative and cultural influences. The insights provided by the sociocultural collective action framework will be just as essential for understanding the viability and endurance of regional government as they are for regional governance.

Notes

1 This is also summarized in the tables in Appendix F.
2 A positive sign means "an odds ratio greater than 1.0" and a negative sign means "an odds ratio less than 1.0."

References

Barron, D. J. (2003). Reclaiming home rule. *Harvard Law Review*, 2255–2386.

Cashin, S. D. (1999). Localism, self-interest, and the tyranny of the favored quarter: Addressing the barriers to new regionalism. *Geo. LJ*, *88*, 1985.

DiMaggio, P., & Powell, W. W. (1983). The iron cage revisited: Collective rationality and institutional isomorphism in organizational fields. *American Sociological Review*, *48*(2), 147–160.

Forester, J. (1999). *The deliberative practitioner: Encouraging participatory planning processes*. MIT Press.

Frug, G. E., & Barron, D. J. (2013). *City bound: How states stifle urban innovation*. Cornell University Press.

Gillette, C. P. (1991). In partial praise of Dillon's Rule, or, can public choice theory justify local government law. *Chi.-Kent L. Rev.*, *67*, 959.

Healey, P. (2003). Collaborative planning in perspective. *Planning Theory*, *2*(2), 101–123.

Innes, J. E., & Booher, D. E. (2010). *Planning with complexity: An introduction to collaborative rationality for public policy*. Routledge.

Kahan, D. M. (2015). Climate-science communication and the measurement problem. *Political Psychology*, *36*(S1), 1–43.

Kahan, D. M. (2012). Cultural cognition as a conception of the cultural theory of risk. In *Handbook of risk theory* (pp. 725–759). Springer Netherlands.

Kahan, D. M., & Braman, D. (2006). Cultural cognition and public policy. *Yale Law & Policy Review*, *24*(1), 149–172.

Kahan, D. M., Braman, D., Cohen, G. L., Gastil, J., & Slovic, P. (2010). Who fears the HPV vaccine, who doesn't, and why? An experimental study of the mechanisms of cultural cognition. *Law and Human Behavior*, *34*(6), 501–516.

Norris, D. F. (2016). *Metropolitan governance in America*. Routledge.

Reynolds, L. (2003). Intergovernmental cooperation, metropolitan equity, and the new regionalism. *Washington Law Review*, *78*, 93.

Appendices

Appendix A Local Governments and Local Elected Officials in Michigan

Michigan—like most states—has strong local governments that have access to many avenues for cooperation. If asked to express a preference about interlocal land use cooperation, local elected officials are likely to have appreciation of the tensions between regional and local governance. In the following paragraphs, I describe the framework of local government form, interlocal cooperation, and local land use in the state, and also briefly summarize the nature of regional government in the Detroit and Grand Rapids areas. I then conclude with a more detailed discussion of the Joint Municipal Planning Act.

Six types of local government exist in Michigan: mayor-council (sometimes known as "strong mayor") cities, council-manager ("weak mayor") cities, general law villages, home rule villages, general law townships, and charter townships. Unlike the townships in many states, Michigan townships are corporate entities and have all the powers expressly granted or fairly implied by the law. Every square mile of the state is covered by some form of sub-county local government. Therefore, no city, township, or village is without a jurisdictional neighbor of some kind. The liberal constitutional construction of township powers means that they function very similarly to cities and villages. Village residents have a sort of dual citizenship: they participate in township elections and can hold township office, and the townships in which they are nested assess property, collect taxes, run most elections, and provide most other services. Villages usually handle police protection and sanitary water and sewer service. Michigan governments do not need to meet a high bar for population or density before they can incorporate, and this encourages a strong link between fragmentation and urbanization. Although the state ranks 12th in the number of local governments as of 2012, per capita measures place it closer to average. Michigan has 1,773 sub-county general-purpose governments, including 533 cities and villages and 1,240 townships.

The key difference between home rule and general law units is that the latter have limited ability to generate own source revenue from taxes. With regard to land use, all local government types have the same statutory grant of land use

Appendices 143

planning and zoning power under the state enabling acts.[1] The major statutory limitation on local land use regulations and decisions is a prohibition on exclusionary zoning.[2] Neighboring jurisdictions can comment on each other's comprehensive land use plans, but the commentary has no binding effect on policy decisions. The legal framework for planning and zoning in Michigan is similar to that found in many other states.

While the state has been described as having a strong home rule tradition, most local jurisdictions in the state—like those across the country—engage in interlocal collective action to provide at least one service, and often to provide many. Municipalities in Michigan have endured a long-term, state-wide recession, declines in state revenue-sharing programs, limits on increases in property tax rates, and increases in the cost of providing local goods and services. If a local government does not want to reduce services or try to generate more revenue through an expanded or increased fee schedule, both of which may place it at a competitive disadvantage for attracting new firms and households, then interlocal arrangements become a critical way to address resource scarcity

Above this panoply of local governments, Michigan has several regional structures. I focus on those present in the Grand Rapids and Detroit metropolitan areas. The state is divided into 14 federal- and state-designated regional councils. Four overlap with the Detroit and Grand Rapids metropolitan areas.[3] In 2013, Governor Snyder also established ten "prosperity regions" across Michigan, though it remains to be seen what impact they will have over time.[4] Contrasting the top-down councils of government, metropolitan planning commissions, and regional planning and development commissions (and now prosperity regions), a few voluntary associations of local governments also exist in Michigan. The Grand Valley Metropolitan Council (GVMC) was formed under Michigan's Metropolitan Councils Act.[5] Thirty-four municipalities are members; only Kent County and Ottawa County are formal members of the GVMC, although a few municipalities in the other metropolitan counties are members. Community conferences have also formed in a few areas in Wayne County, like the Downriver Community Conference and the Conference of Western Wayne. And smaller councils of government, like the Southwest Washtenaw Council of Governments described in Chapter 3, can work more closely with local governments than their larger counterparts. Functionally, however, all these regional bodies have had no real impact on land use regulation. As is evident in Chapter 4, their theoretical relevance to interlocal cooperation is through their ability to inculcate trust by facilitating the development of bridging ties.

The substantial autonomy Michigan municipalities enjoy over land use decision-making through state planning and enabling acts is matched by a similar degree of autonomy over voluntary cooperation. These acts were described at length in Chapter 2.

The local elected officials in the final sample ranged in age from 24 to 88 years old, with an average of about 56 years old. Age did not correspond directly to tenure, but the two shared a positive, linear relationship, as one would expect:

144 *Appendices*

every additional year in age added about three months to tenure for the typical respondent. The vast majority identified as non-Hispanic White (about 83 percent, $n=502$), demonstrating that suburban representation is still predominantly non-minority, even in communities in which roughly three of every four residents are non-White. The gender split was about even in the sample. About two-fifths of the local elected officials identified as Republicans, and another quarter identified as Democrats. Most of the remaining third indicated they were Libertarians or independents. Republicans tended to serve about three years longer in office, but on every other individual attribute—gender, race, educational attainment, and age—were highly similar to Democrats and all other elected officials.

Appendix B Survey of Local Elected Officials

To gather data on local elected officials' preferences, perceptions, cultural dispositions, and other personal characteristics, I developed and administered a survey in 2013 and 2014 targeting all elected officials who serve on legislative bodies in Michigan cities, townships, and villages located within the 17 metropolitan counties around Detroit and Grand Rapids. I populated my own contact list by scanning the municipal websites of the 508 municipalities in the two metropolitan areas—288 in the Detroit area and 220 in the Grand Rapids area. The contact list included mayors, city council members, township board members, and village board members, as well as staff planners. Where municipal websites were outdated, non-existent, or lacked contact information, I expanded my search to county-level sources. In the early development of the contact list for the Detroit region I attempted further supplementation through telephone calls to local clerks and other officials, but in many of the municipalities in which emails were not originally available telephone calls were not successful due to non-response or privacy concerns. The titles of officials can vary slightly depending on the community. The findings regarding staff planners are outside the scope of this book.

In total, the contact list included 3,036 local elected officials—1,799 in Detroit and 1,237 in Grand Rapids. The final contact list had only 92 staff planners, reflecting the common use of outside consulting firms. Only about 60 percent of the officials on the contact list had email addresses available: 1,219 in Detroit and 621 in Grand Rapids. This disparity reflects the presence of more semi-rural and rural areas within the eight Grand Rapids counties. These counties had a lower email availability rate and most had lower response rates. One can also see that the municipalities represented in the study are higher in population and taxable value (the two tend to travel together) and slightly higher in median home value. I discuss in the analysis whether the slight underrepresentation of rural, smaller, and less wealthy municipalities introduced meaningful bias into the findings. Overall, the response rate was about 27 percent.

The survey had 31 items, and is included at the end of this appendix. The order of the items was intentional. Earlier items were non-personal and not controversial; the more controversial cultural cognition items were all reserved for

Appendices 145

the end of the survey once buy-in was more likely. Three of the items were about prior awareness of the JMPA and use of it or another land use cooperation instrument by the municipality in which an official served. The next four were the items measuring the dependent variable: preferences toward interlocal land use cooperation scenarios under the JMPA. These were followed by an open-ended text box in which respondents could comment about the idea of interlocal land use cooperation. Next, respondents offered perceptions on three items about their relationship with residents specifically with regard to land use planning and zoning and interlocal land use cooperation. The seven individual-level demographic measures followed; these were included mainly to use as controls in later analysis. Lastly, respondents were asked to evaluate 12 statements reflective of cultural dispositions. These responses would be used to construct the key explanatory variables.

I administered the survey via Qualtrics (using the University of Michigan's license) through an emailed link to an online version of the instrument. On average, the survey took about 12 minutes to complete. Respondents were not allowed to go back and change answers. I used a pop-up caution box to verify whether they wanted to leave a question blank. Tables B.1 and B.2 provide the response rates by government type and by county.

Table B.1 Detroit Region, Institutional Representativeness of Sample of Local Elected Officials by Government Type and County

	All Elected Officials Percent (Frequency)	*Sample Percent (Frequency)*
Government form (response rate, %)	100% (1,785*)	100% (349)
Township (29.7)	49.7 (888)	51.6 (180)
General law (29.5)	*32.6 (582)*	*45.8 (160)*
Charter (31.7)	*17.1 (306)*	*5.7 (20)*
City (28.4)	39.9 (712)	41.3 (144)
Council-mgr (29.4)	*32.0 (571)*	*33.8 (118)*
Mayor-council (24.5)	*7.9 (141)*	*7.4 (26)*
Village (25.0)	11.0 (196)	7.2 (25)
*Counties (response rate, %**)*		
Wayne (25.3)	17.2 (307)	16.0 (56)
Oakland (28.4)	22.2 (396)	27.8 (97)
Macomb (29.9)	9.2 (165)	12.3 (43)
Livingston (35.6)	7.2 (128)	10.3 (36)
Lapeer (17.8)	8.2 (147)	2.3 (8)
St. Clair (35.5)	9.1 (162)	6.3 (22)
Genesee (30.4)	9.7 (173)	8.9 (31)
Monroe (21.3)	7.5 (133)	4.6 (16)
Washtenaw (36.1)	10.4 (185)	11.5 (40)

Notes
* The total population is a list of all officials available from public websites, such as those maintained by municipalities, counties, and other organizations.
** Sample/sampling frame. The sampling frame was limited to those local elected officials with available email addresses, regardless of whether those addresses were functional.

146 *Appendices*

Table B.2 Grand Rapids Region, Institutional Representativeness of Sample of Local Elected Officials by Government Type and County

	All Elected Officials Percent (Frequency)	Sample Percent (Frequency)
Government form (response rate, %)	100% (1,237*)	100% (189)
Township (31.9)	64.8 (802)	65.6 (124)
General law (30.7)	*56.3 (697)*	*53.4 (101)*
Charter (38.3)	*8.5 (105)*	*12.2 (23)*
City (31.5)	21.7 (269)	32.8 (62)
Council-mgr (30.1)	*19.2 (238)*	*26.5 (50)*
Mayor-counc (38.7)	*2.5 (31)*	*6.3 (12)*
Village (8.9)	13.4 (166)	1.2 (3)
*Counties (response rate, %**)*		
Kent (32.3)	17.5 (217)	25.9 (49)
Ottawa (40.9)	11.7 (145)	24.9 (47)
Barry (17.6)	9.0 (111)	4.8 (9)
Montcalm (22.7)	13.3 (165)	5.3 (10)
Ionia (33.3)	7.5 (93)	3.7 (7)
Newaygo (30.8)	12.5 (155)	8.5 (16)
Muskegon (30.8)	12.9 (159)	10.6 (20)
Allegan (25.6)	15.5 (192)	16.4 (31)

Notes
* The total population is a list of all officials available from public websites, such as those maintained by municipalities, counties, and other organizations.
** Sample/sampling frame. The sampling frame was limited to those local elected officials with available email addresses, regardless of whether those addresses were functional.

Table B.3 Detroit Area, Demographic and Fiscal Representativeness of Municipalities Represented by Elected Officials in Sample

Demographic/Fiscal Characteristic	*Mean*	
	All Munis (288)	*Sample (166)*
Average population (2009–2012)	**16,619**	**28,239**
Average % of pop. identifying as White (2009–2012)	90.2	87.7
Average % of properties vacant (2009–2012)	9.2	8.6
Average % of housing units owner-occupied (2009–2012)	80.8	78.7
Average % of housing units that are single-family detached (2009–2012)	77.6	72.8
% of built structures built since 2000 (2012)	12.6	13.0
% of households moved in since 2000 (2012)	51.7	55.3
Average median household income (2009–2012) ($)	61,595	66,522
Average med. owner-occ. house value (2009–2012) ($)	**178,700**	**200,883**
Average level of operations funding* (2008–2012)	1.9	2.7
Average expenditures burden** (2008–2012)	1.3	1.4
Average taxable value (2008–2012) ($)	**566 million**	**$1.1 billion**

Notes
* operations funding = (general fund revenues – general fund expenditures)/general fund revenues. Above zero is a surplus; below zero is a deficit.
** expenditures burden = general fund expenditures/taxable value.

Appendices   147

Table B.4 Grand Rapids Area, Demographic and Fiscal Representativeness of Municipalities Represented by Elected Officials in Sample

Demographic/Fiscal Characteristic	Mean	
	All Munis (220)	Sample (96)
Average population (2009–2012)	**6,408**	**12,677**
Average % of pop. identifying as White (2009–2012)	93.4	91.7
Average % of properties vacant (2009–2012)	13.4	12.0
Average % of housing units owner-occupied (2009–2012)	82.2	80.8
Average % of housing units that are single-family detached (2009–2012)	76.5	74.1
% of built structures built since 2000 (2012)	13.2	15.4
% of households moved in since 2000 (2012)	52.1	56.1
Average median household income (2009–2012) ($)	49,371	54,750
Average med. owner-occ. house value (2009–2012) ($)	**133,800**	**156,106**
Average level of operations funding[*] (2008–2012)	−0.05	2.5
Average expenditures burden[**] (2008–2012)	0.90	0.97
Average taxable value (2008–2012) ($)	**214 million**	**441 billion**

Notes
[*]   operations funding = (general fund revenues − general fund expenditures)/general fund revenues. Above zero is a surplus; below zero is a deficit.
[**]   expenditures burden = general fund expenditures/taxable value.

Survey Instrument

Consent.
This is a survey of local elected officials and staff planners in Michigan, including members of city and village councils and township boards. It is part of a study being conducted at the University of Michigan Department of Urban and Regional Planning. Your participation is voluntary. Your identity will remain confidential at all times, including in any written or oral publication of the findings of this research. The survey takes on average about 10 minutes to complete, and we thank you in advance for your time. Please click "Yes" if you would like to continue to the survey. ___ Yes ___No

Questions about the Joint Municipal Planning Act
Throughout this survey, the general term "municipality" is used to refer to cities, villages, charter townships, and townships. In questions and graphics, words such as "city," "township," and "village" can be read interchangeably.

1   In 2003, Michigan passed the Joint Municipal Planning Act (JMPA). Under the JMPA, cities, villages, and townships can use an intermunicipal agreement to plan and zone jointly with other municipalities. Before taking this survey, had you ever heard of the JMPA?

___Yes ___No5

148 *Appendices*

2 Does your municipality currently have a JMPA agreement with one or more other municipalities?

___Yes ___No ___I don't know

3 Does your municipality currently have any other agreements with one or more other municipalities that affect decisions about land use planning and zoning?

___Yes ___No ___I don't know

Municipalities can structure a JMPA agreement in a variety of ways. In the next section we'll present you with four scenarios about how a municipality might use a JMPA agreement. The scenarios may or may not seem applicable to the municipality in which you currently live, but we ask that you simply react to the general scenario to the best of your ability.

4 Local officials are considering using the JMPA to govern land use policy in an area shared among neighboring municipalities. The agreement would *not* affect land use decisions outside that area (respondent shown graphic). How do you feel about such an agreement?

___Strongly oppose ___Oppose ___Indifferent ___Favor ___Strongly favor

5 Local officials enter the agreement and are trying to decide how to structure it. They have two options for how to govern *only the land within the JMPA area*. Option 1: Advisory Joint Planning Commission for the JMPA area with a non-binding land use plan; Option 2: Joint Planning Commission and Joint Zoning Board of Appeals for the JMPA area with dissolution of municipal planning and zoning for the JMPA area. Which option do you prefer? (respondent shown graphic from item 4 again)

___Strongly prefer option 1 ___Prefer option 1 ___Indifferent
___Prefer option 2 ___Strongly prefer option 2

6 Local officials are considering using the JMPA to govern land use policy for *all* the land in two or more participating municipalities (respondent shown graphic). How do you feel about such an agreement?

___Strongly oppose ___Oppose ___Indifferent ___Favor ___Strongly favor

7 Local officials enter the agreement and are trying to decide how to structure it. They have two options for how to govern *all* the land within their municipal boundaries. Option 1: Advisory Joint Planning Commission for the JMPA area with a non-binding land use plan; Option 2: Joint Planning Commission and Joint Zoning Board of Appeals for the JMPA area with dissolution of municipal planning and zoning for the JMPA area. Which option do you prefer? (respondent shown graphic from item 6 again)

___Strongly prefer option 1 ___Prefer option 1 ___Indifferent
___Prefer option 2 ___Strongly prefer option 2

8 Do you have any questions or comments about the Joint Municipal Planning Act or the scenarios presented above? Please share them in the space below:_____

Questions about the perceived relationship to residents
The next two statements are about the planning and zoning process. Please give your reaction.

9 "It is important that decisions about planning and zoning reflect what the residents in my municipality want."

___Strongly disagree ___Disagree ___Neither agree nor disagree

___Agree ___Strongly agree

10 "I am free to make decisions about planning and zoning that I think are in the best interest of the municipality, even if those decisions are not popular among residents."

___Strongly disagree ___Disagree ___Neither agree nor disagree

___Agree ___Strongly agree

11 Earlier you answered questions about the Joint Municipal Planning Act. Complete the following statement: "In general, residents in my municipality would _____ a JMPA agreement with another municipality."

___Strongly oppose ___Oppose ___Be neutral about ___Support

___Strongly support

Individual level controls

12 About how many years have you served in local government in your current municipality (including both elected and appointed positions)? Please round to the nearest number of years. If six months or less, enter 0. ____.
13 What year were you born? ____.
14 What is your gender? (optional) ___Male ___Female
15 What is your race? (optional) (eight-choice drop-down menu)
16 Are you of Hispanic, Latino/a, or Spanish origin? (optional) ___Yes ___No
17 With which political party do you identify? (six-choice drop-down menu)
18 What is the highest level of education you've attained? (diploma or GED; some college; associate degree; bachelor degree; some graduate school; professional or graduate degree)

150 *Appendices*

Cultural disposition questions

In this final section we will ask for your personal reaction to twelve statements about government and society. These statements have been used extensively in other social research. We appreciate your time and honesty in completing this part of the survey. As with all your responses, your answers will remain confidential and are analyzed with hundreds of other responses. First, here are six statements about the relationship between individuals and government.

19 "The government interferes far too much in our everyday lives." (Individualist valence item 1, reverse coded)

___Strongly disagree ___Disagree ___Neither agree nor disagree
___Agree ___Strongly agree

20 "Sometimes government needs to make laws that keep people from hurting themselves." (Communitarian valence item 1, straight coded)

___Strongly disagree ___Disagree ___Neither agree nor disagree
___Agree ___Strongly agree

21 "It's not the government's business to try to protect people from themselves." (Individualist valence item 2, reverse coded)

___Strongly disagree ___Disagree ___Neither agree nor disagree
___Agree ___Strongly agree

22 "The government should stop telling people how to live their lives." (Individualist valence item 3, reverse coded)

___Strongly disagree ___Disagree ___Neither agree nor disagree
___Agree ___Strongly agree

23 "The government should do more to advance society's goals, even if that means limiting the freedom and choices of individuals." (Communitarian valence item 2, straight coded)

___Strongly disagree ___Disagree ___Neither agree nor disagree
___Agree ___Strongly agree

24 "Government should put limits on the choices individuals can make so they don't get in the way of what's good for society." (Communitarian valence item 3, straight coded)

___Strongly disagree ___Disagree ___Neither agree nor disagree
___Agree ___Strongly agree

Appendices 151

Next, here are six statements about issues relating to society.

25 "We have gone too far in pushing equal rights in this country." (Hierarchical valence item 1, straight coded)

___Strongly disagree ___Disagree ___Neither agree nor disagree

___Agree ___Strongly agree

26 "Our society would be better off if the distribution of wealth was more equal." (Egalitarian valence item 1, reverse coded)

___Strongly disagree ___Disagree ___Neither agree nor disagree

___Agree ___Strongly agree

27 "We need to dramatically reduce inequalities between the rich and the poor, whites and people of color, and men and women." (Egalitarian valence item 2, reverse coded)

___Strongly disagree ___Disagree ___Neither agree nor disagree

___Agree ___Strongly agree

28 "Discrimination against minorities is still a very serious problem in our society." (Egalitarian valence item 3, reverse coded)

___Strongly disagree ___Disagree ___Neither agree nor disagree

___Agree ___Strongly agree

29 "It seems like blacks, women, homosexuals and other groups don't want equal rights, they want special rights just for them." (Hierarchical valence item 2, straight coded)

___Strongly disagree ___Disagree ___Neither agree nor disagree

___Agree ___Strongly agree

30 "Society as a whole has become too soft and feminine." (Hierarchical valence item 3, straight coded)

___Strongly disagree ___Disagree ___Neither agree nor disagree

___Agree ___Strongly agree

Appendix C Data Sources and Variable Specification

Data Sources

To connect the survey data to characteristics of the municipality, I first made a database of all the municipalities in the Detroit and Grand Rapids counties in my study, coded by metropolitan area. I also included several dozen municipalities that touched the borders of these counties to allow later construction of inter-municipal characteristics that were not artificially limited by county boundaries.

152   *Appendices*

This database included municipal name, government type, county location, metropolitan area, and—most importantly—a Federal Information Processing Standards code (FIPS). The FIPS code is used by the U.S. Census of Housing and Population, including the American Community Survey five-year estimates for 2009, 2010, 2011, and 2012 used in this study. The variables pulled from these estimates are described later in this appendix, along with their manipulation into intermunicipal variables. An advantage of this approach was the ability to have averages and change-in measures for a period that is very contemporaneous for the local elected officials I surveyed in 2013 and 2014. On average, it would be unlikely that the trends or conditions observed in this period would change dramatically enough for a large enough subset of well over 500 municipalities for a one- to two-year time gap to be meaningful in a large scale quantitative study. For fiscal data, I used the data available from the Munetrix Corporation public listings online, which allow a user to look up several key measures of fiscal health for each municipality every year beginning mostly in 2008 and, at the time of data collection, running through mostly 2012. Only the largest municipalities had 2013 data. I entered 20 different fiscal measures in my own database and joined these through municipality name to the census data. This same municipal name was then used to link all the municipal data—from both ACS estimates and Munetrix data—to each survey respondent (who was listed with municipal name in the original contact list). Thus, for Ann Arbor City, as an example, eight respondents completed the survey, and for all eight the municipal level variables would be the same while the individual level responses would, on most survey items, vary.

Cultural Indicators

The short form cultural cognition items used in the work of Kahan are useful in this study for several reasons.[6] First, they do not invoke cooperation directly—they do not use words like "cooperation" or "regional" that might lead to an inevitable positive correlation between dispositions and preferences. For example, a respondent who agrees "working as part of a team is valuable" should be more likely also to favor joint municipal land use planning. We would learn very little from this positive association except that people who prefer group work in general also prefer it in a specific case. Second, the questions—despite often addressing "hot button" political topics—are not ones for which we would expect a culturally sanctioned response. Americans are far from uniform in their opinions about the role of government and issues of equality. Third, the questions measure different valences of cultural dispositions. Half the grid questions positively measure a hierarchical disposition if evaluated with "strongly agree" while the others positively measure an egalitarian disposition. A respondent giving the same answer repeatedly would have a neutral value on the final index. A true "strong egalitarian" would have to strongly agree with three items and strongly disagree with the other three. The same would be true for a strong hierarch, strong communitarian, or strong individualist.

Appendices   153

It is possible these questions are not the best items drawn from the original longer survey in the work of Dan Kahan and colleagues (see Chapter 6). The original factor analysis used data from a large-scale national survey of the general population, and the latent cultural dispositions of local elected officials may not load well on the 12 items in the short form survey. For this reason, I used exploratory factor analysis to test whether grid and group are indeed measuring different dimensions, and whether all the questions used for each dimension are worth including. To ensure parsimony in the multivariate models used to estimate the *ceteris paribus* associations between dispositions and preferences, I applied a factor analysis using polychoric correlations because the variables are ordinal, with varimax rotation to achieve orthogonal factors. A sample size of at least 300 with at least ten observations per variable is a rule of thumb for "good" factor analysis, and my dataset exceeds both thresholds easily. The analysis, in plain terms, reveals that most of the variation across the 12 items— about 81 percent—loads onto a single factor, and that the six group items are the principal components in this factor. Another roughly 13 percent of the latent variation loads onto a second factor, and two of the grid items—the first and third items of the three with a hierarchical valence—are the principal components in that factor. In the final analyses, I ran models including both full indices (reflecting answers to all six questions for each disposition) and an alternative index for grid that summed only the two items that performed best in factor analysis.

The Relationship between Residents and Local Elected Officials

The relationship between residents and local elected officials is reflected in three variables, which I term alignment, discretion, and support. These can be seen in survey items 9, 10, and 11, respectively, in Appendix B. All are with regard to land use planning and zoning and cooperation specifically. It would be less informative to ask how an elected official *generally* perceives these dynamics, since they are likely to be quite different across policy areas.

These survey items are meant to capture how respondents interpret their role as representatives of residents and/or the public interest (the two may not be identically defined). I shorthand these as *support, alignment*, and *discretion*. The literature reviewed in Chapter 5 suggests this interpretation matters. While we have theoretical arguments and empirical evidence suggesting alignment between city policies and resident political views (or between legislators and constituents in general), it remains unclear how persistent the connection is for local elected officials. This is particularly true when we consider those from communities with populations under 25,000, a feature characteristic of most municipalities in the U.S. and in my study. The three items measure the extent to which responsiveness is to residents or to the municipality, and this distinction matters when we think later about policy interventions that might spur cooperation. Framing cooperation as having electoral benefits because of its appeal to residents is a much different task than framing it as being instrumentally

154   *Appendices*

beneficial to the municipal corporation, where projections about fiscal health and growth might have more play.

For the *support* measure, a concern is that respondents would simply align their perceptions of resident preferences with their own preferences, such that any significance of residential support as an explanatory variable would be suspect. We would expect some alignment between local elected officials' preferences about interlocal land use cooperation and their perceptions of residential support. However, the measure of support does not simply parrot the preference measures. Correlations between these items are about 0.40 and 0.36 for the preferences about partial area and full coverage adoption, and are about 0.19 and 0.15 for preferences about advisory versus authoritative forms of cooperation after adoption. This difference makes sense: from the viewpoint of an elected official, residents are likely to be more engaged with the adoption decision and have less input on implementation. Of course, the ideal measure of residential support would be a survey of residents about cooperation or some external measure of support such as a public referendum. But for purposes of the present study, I am comfortable enough with the perceptual measure of residential support to include it.

Interlocal Ties

Several studies on network effects in interlocal cooperation suggest that ties in one policy or membership in regional bodies can lead to cooperation in other areas. Although the research is often associational rather than over time, the reasoning is that the links among the municipalities create relationships of trust and a positive norm of reciprocity among the elected and administrative officials working in those municipalities. When scholars discuss metropolitan governance as a manifestation of administrative conjunction, it is this type of relational effect to which they are referring.

I am not confident in the notion that cooperation in other areas begets land use cooperation. Cooperation in public works or public safety and other systems maintenance functions is generally not part of how a community differentiates itself from others, or maintains a specific community character. In general across the state of Michigan one finds thousands of interlocal agreements targeting systems maintenance, but few about land use or other lifestyle services. Elected officials are typically not a part of the networks that create or maintain interlocal cooperation in systems maintenance. Most interlocal agreements do not require legislative oversight or participation in implementation after adoption.

In general, municipal membership in an agreement or a regional body does not mean that a respondent elected official was involved in adopting an agreement or approving membership, or is part of ongoing maintenance or attending meetings. These would be the mechanisms through which trust among the elected officials of neighboring municipalities might generate, paving the way for more supportive preferences toward joint land use planning. From a data collection and analysis perspective, having a binary variable reflecting the presence of any interlocal agreements would not yield enough variation (nearly all municipalities have at least one). A count variable would not perform much better, since from the perspective of the local elected official the difference between having two local agreements and having five might simply reflect the areas in which a community has needed outside help. The only linkage that should really matter is the cooperation that happens in areas affecting land use decisions. Regional bodies have more regular meetings and one could view them as creating a regional consciousness beyond that arising from linkages through mutual aid agreements and memoranda of understanding, or service contracts. Elected officials might have a general awareness of being part of a broader "community" because of this, and I would expect this to be truer if the association was voluntary.

Based on the above reasoning, in the final database I included dichotomous perceptual measures of whether a community already had a JMPA agreement, whether it had another cooperative interlocal agreement that affected land use planning and zoning decisions, and whether it was a member of a voluntary regional association, including the Grand Valley Metropolitan Council, Downriver Community Conference, and Conference of Western Wayne. I also included a dichotomous measure of SEMCOG and other COG membership, though I did not expect it to be significant and it was, indeed, not.

Measures of Municipal and Intermunicipal Conditions

The perception of the local elected official about the municipal fiscal and demographic context requires some consideration. In earlier studies of interlocal cooperation, variable specification suffered from two conceptual flaws. First, most variables are about the municipality only, even though theory suggests comparative performance is critical to how an official might appraise potential costs and benefits. Looking at the municipality only has its limits, because cooperation is relational. A measure of median home value likely means little beyond serving as one indicator, perhaps, of fiscal distress if the figure is quite low or falling. We would also want to know, however, how a municipality's median home value compares to those of its neighbors.

This is the idea of homophily discussed in the transaction cost framework detailed in Chapter 4: cooperation is easier among similarly situated municipalities, for several reasons. A few studies include a comparison of the municipality to the average for the county or metropolitan statistical area on a dimension, but this is not a pertinent comparison. A municipality might be on par with the average county or MSA municipality, but performing much better (or much worse) than its immediate neighbors. It is these neighbors who matter most in every interlocal cooperation policy area. While cooperation might extend beyond these immediate neighbors, it is hard to imagine a community looking for mutual aid or service provision two municipalities away. For land use, contiguity is quite important—one cannot effectively plan to protect a watershed or connect recreational uses or assemble a site without sharing common borders. Thus,

156   *Appendices*

when local actors think about how their municipality compares to others, the "others" which matter most are adjacent, not some imagined average other.

Having all the data linked through federal information processing standards (FIPS) codes within a geographic information system allowed me to overcome this first problem. Using the Python interface in Quantum GIS (QGIS), I created a code that would sum a given dimension for all the municipalities touching a target municipality, or neighbor. I would then divide by the number of neighbors to get the average. The technique, clearly, is imperfect because it weights all communities the same. However, knowing how a local elected official might privilege one community over another in considering interlocal land use cooperation was simply unknowable. Using weights reflecting population or area, for example, might have yielded a result that made one neighboring municipality seem much more important than it would be in the local official's thought process.

Let us use median home value as an example, and work specifically with Livonia, a suburban city in northeastern Wayne County. The average median home value in Livonia for the years 2009 through 2012 was $107,900 (eighth lowest of the 41 municipalities in Wayne County; Detroit ranks third). In the three-county urban area (Wayne, Oakland, and Macomb counties), the average value for the same time period was $200,362, and in Wayne County alone it was $159,426. But using the GIS analysis technique described above, we learn that the average median home value in the ten municipalities bordering Livonia is $173,015, and this has the advantage of allowing us to compare Livonia both to the municipalities in Wayne County and in Oakland County that it borders. For those communities on the border of the study area, I included all municipalities bordering my study area in making these calculations to ensure accuracy. For the purposes of ascertaining heterogeneity, a municipality versus metro area comparison would measure Livonia as 46 percent below average, overstating its relative weakness on this dimension. A municipality to county comparison would yield a negative 32 percent measure. The comparison to those neighboring municipalities with which it actually shares contiguous land—the most likely candidates for land use cooperation—gives a figure near negative 38 percent.

Measuring heterogeneity against nearest neighbors solves, as practically as possible, the problem of using conceptually sound comparative measures. A second problem is that measures are usually taken without reference to the timing of the adoption of cooperation. For example, if considering a measure of fiscal distress as a signal, in theory, of greater interest in cooperation, the measure should correspond to the timing of adoption. Having a decade-old interlocal agreement made in a time of fiscal distress and then still having the agreement at the time of the study when the condition of distress has passed would cause us to miss the relationship. The opposite could also happen, which would lead to an association between the measure of distress and the presence of cooperation, when the two had no relationship at the time of adoption. Circumstances change in local governments, sometimes quite rapidly from year to year, and having relatively contemporaneous measures reflecting municipal and intermunicipal conditions of which a local actor could be aware for making a calculus of cost and benefit. The second problem was addressed by using fiscal and census data for 2008 to 2012 and 2009 to 2012, respectively, with the survey conducted mostly in late 2013 and early 2014.

For fiscal measures, I use four variables to reflect municipal conditions. Average operations funding for 2008 to 2012 measures how well a municipality is covering its general fund expenditures with general fund revenue. If the variable is negative, then this means the municipality has a deficit. If positive, the municipality is running a surplus. The shift from positive to negative values is likely more important than any other in the range of values for this variable, and I reason a local elected official is likely to know if a deficit or surplus is being run. I use a dummy variable as an alternative measure of operations funding. The other fiscal measure is average annual change in taxable value from 2008 to 2012. This should be a stronger indicator of fiscal health than median home value, since taxable value includes non-residential property which may be substantial in some municipalities. Relative or intermunicipal fiscal measures should also be significant. I included a measure of heterogeneity for both operating deficit and change in taxable value.

For municipal housing and population variables, I used average annual change in population, average annual change in median home value, the average share of housing units occupied by owners, and the share of structures built since the year 2000. All measures used data from 2009 through 2012. Intermunicipal or relative measures included average annual change in population, average annual change in median home value, average median home value, and the share of structures built since the year 2000, plus the average share of population that identifies as White. These numbers were all calculated in the same way as the relative fiscal dimensions—by comparing the target municipality to the average figure for immediate neighbors.

Because a local elected official is likely to simply have a rough sense of how her municipality is performing compared to others, I also broke the heterogeneity measures for fiscal, population, and housing variables into quartiles. Using median home value as an example, those municipalities in the top 25 percent of all municipalities on the measure of median home value heterogeneity—those strongly outperforming their neighbors—are deemed high relative median home value communities. A dummy variable codes which municipalities are in this group.

Examples in Wayne County include Canton Charter Township and Grosse Pointe Park City. The same is done for the bottom quartile, producing a dummy variable for low relative median home value. Livonia and Detroit are both in this low group, with values of about negative 37 percent and negative 54 percent, respectively. About three quarters of the municipalities in both the high and low quartiles are from the Detroit region, reflecting the well-known narrative of extreme class segregation in that metropolitan area. If continuous measures are not significant as a reflection of heterogeneity, a municipality's position as an extreme "winner" or "loser" on a dimension may have a stronger explanatory role.

158 *Appendices*

Even though municipal and intermunicipal fiscal and demographic variables are not behind the key explanatory mechanisms in my model, truly controlling for context requires thoughtful specification of these variables. If preferences regarding interlocal land use can be explained by municipal and intermunicipal cues, then supportive evidence should be found in these measures.

Appendix D Summary of Hypotheses

The measures in this study reflect: (1) cultural dispositions (group and grid indices); (2) the perceived relationship of elected officials with residents (perceptions of alignment and discretion, and perception of residential support); (3) interlocal relationships (membership in voluntary regional associations, prior cooperative agreements affecting land use, prior JMPA agreement, number of neighbors, whether a municipality is an "island" municipality, and having a council-manager form of government); (4) several measures of municipal and intermunicipal socioeconomic and fiscal conditions (population change and population density; share of population identifying as White; median home value and median home value change; share of units owner occupied; share of structures built since 2000; share of households moved in since 2000; taxable value per capita and taxable value change; and operations funding); (5) individual-level and other controls, such as years in office and level of educational attainment.

The variables reflect normative legitimizing—through transactional economizing, reciprocity, and political responsiveness—as described in Chapter 5, and cultural legitimizing as described in Chapter 6. In Table D.1, I provide plain English articulations of the hypothesized relationships.

In Table D.2, I use these measures to translate the general hypotheses to terms that resonate with the estimation technique (see Appendix E). In the right column, I present hypothesized odds ratios because I later use ordinal logistic regression. To the extent the value of these odds ratios are significant and match the relationship to 1.0 listed below, the reader can interpret the finding as evidence supporting the relevant hypothesis.

Table D.1 General Hypotheses Based on Different Types of Rational Legitimizing

Type of Cognition	Mechanism at Work	General Hypothesis about Local Elected Officials' Perceptions toward Interlocal Land Use Cooperation (Versus Autonomy)
Cultural (cultural legitimizing)	Group	Support for cooperation will be higher among those with a higher group, more communitarian disposition. Support for autonomy will be higher among those with a lower group, more individualist disposition.
	Grid	Support for cooperation will be higher among those with a lower grid, more egalitarian disposition. Support for autonomy will be higher among those with a higher grid, more hierarchical disposition.

Type of Cognition	Mechanism at Work	General Hypothesis about Local Elected Officials' Perceptions toward Interlocal Land Use Cooperation (Versus Autonomy)
Political (normative legitimizing)	Alignment	*Support for cooperation will in general be lower, and for autonomy be higher, among those who attach more importance to doing what residents want with regard to land use policies.*
	Discretion	*Support for cooperation will in general be higher, and for autonomy be lower, among those who perceive greater ability to make decisions about land use policies that contravene what residents want if it serves the best interests of the municipality.*
	Support	*Support for cooperation will in general be higher, and for autonomy be lower, among those who perceive more support for land use cooperation among residents.*
Municipal (transaction cost legitimizing)	Fiscal distress	*Support for cooperation will in general be higher, and for autonomy be lower, among those who perceive greater fiscal distress in the community.*
	Socioeconomic distress	*Support for cooperation will in general be higher, and for autonomy be lower, among those who perceive greater socioeconomic distress in the community.*
	Homeowner lobby	*Support for cooperation will in general be higher, and for autonomy be lower, among those who from communities with a higher share of homeowners.*
Intermunicipal (transaction cost and reciprocity legitimizing)	Interlocal ties	*Support for cooperation will be higher, and for autonomy be lower, among those from municipalities connected through membership in voluntary regional associations, prior cooperative agreements affecting land use, and an existing JMPA agreement, as well as those from municipalities with a lower number of neighbors, those from "island" municipalities, and those from council-manager cities.*
	Fiscal homophily	*Support for cooperation will in general be higher, and for autonomy be lower, among those from communities that are much worse off than neighboring communities in terms of fiscal performance (and vice versa)*
	Socioeconomic homophily	*Support for cooperation will in general be higher, and for autonomy be lower, among those from communities that are much better or much worse off than neighboring communities in terms of socioeconomic performance (and vice versa)*

160 *Appendices*

Table D.2 Hypotheses Based on Measures and Estimation Techniques Used in the Current Study

Mechanism	Hypotheses about Perceptions toward Interlocal Land Use Cooperation as Indicated by Preferences toward JMPA Adoption (Favor/Oppose) and Structure (Advisory/Authoritative)	Odds Ratio*
Group	A more favorable response toward adoption and an authoritative structure will be more likely for respondents with a higher group index score.	>1.0
Grid	A more favorable response toward adoption and an authoritative structure will be more likely for respondents with a lower grid index score.	<1.0
Alignment	A more favorable response toward adoption and an authoritative structure will be more likely for respondents who perceive a lower importance of aligning land use actions with what residents want.	<1.0
Discretion	A more favorable response toward adoption and an authoritative structure will be more likely for respondents who who perceive a greater ability to contravene in land use policies what residents want in favor of the best interests of the municipality.	>1.0
Residential support	A more favorable response toward adoption and an authoritative structure will be more likely for respondents with a higher perception of residential support for joint land use.	>1.0
Fiscal distress	A more favorable response toward adoption and an authoritative structure will be more likely for respondents from municipalities experiencing greater fiscal distress as measured by the extent of average operating fund deficit and a decline in taxable value.	<1.0
Socioecon. distress	A more favorable response toward adoption and an authoritative structure will be more likely for respondents from municipalities experiencing greater socioeconomic distress as measured by the extent of population decline and decline in median home value.	<1.0
Growth	A more favorable response toward adoption and an authoritative structure will be more likely for respondents from municipalities experiencing lower recent growth as measured by the extent of population increase, share of structures built since the year 2000, and share of population moved in since 2000.	<1.0
Homeowner lobby	A more favorable response toward adoption and an authoritative structure will be more likely for respondents from municipalities with a lower share of households that are owners as opposed to renters.	<1.0

Mechanism	Hypotheses about Perceptions toward Interlocal Land Use Cooperation as Indicated by Preferences toward JMPA Adoption (Favor/Oppose) and Structure (Advisory/Authoritative)	Odds Ratio*
Interlocal ties	*A more favorable response toward adoption and an authoritative structure will be more likely for respondents from municipalities connected through membership in voluntary regional associations, municipalities with prior cooperative agreements affecting land use, and municipalities with an existing JMPA agreement, as well as respondents from municipalities with a lower number of neighbors, those from "island" municipalities, and those from council-manager cities.*	>1.0
Fiscal homophily	*A more favorable response toward adoption and an authoritative structure will be more likely for respondents from municipalities experiencing **relatively** greater fiscal distress, as measured by the percent difference in average operating fund deficit and a decline in taxable value between the home municipality and the average value in adjacent municipalities.*	<1.0
Socioecon. homophily	*A more favorable response toward adoption and an authoritative structure will be more likely for respondents from municipalities experiencing **relatively** greater socioeconomic distress, as measured by the percent difference in population decline, median home value, and share of population identifying as White between the home municipality and the average value in adjacent municipalities.*	<1.0
Growth homophily	*A more favorable response toward adoption and an authoritative structure will be more likely for respondents from municipalities experiencing **relatively** lower recent growth, as measured by the percent difference in extent of population increase, share of structures built since the year 2000, and share of population moved in since 2000.*	<1.0

Appendix E Estimation Technique

In the study, data exist at multiple levels: survey data about individuals, measuring their preferences, perceptions, dispositions, and various control attributes; demographic and fiscal data about municipalities; and transformations of this demographic and fiscal data to reflect how a municipality compares to its immediate neighbors. The municipalities are also nested within counties, about which we do not have data beyond identity. Still, the county identity may be relevant, particularly if it matters to how local elected officials think about land use cooperation in a way that was not captured by municipal variables. The municipalities are also within metropolitan areas. These latter two attributes—county and MSA location—can be easily accommodated through the inclusion of dummy variables, or the inclusion of pertinent attributes.

162 *Appendices*

Still, we are left with a situation in which we have individuals within each municipality. The data, in statistical terms, are *nested* or *multi-level*. This feature violates the assumption of independence necessary for standard ordinary least squares regression models. The clustering of individuals within municipalities would lead to correlated error terms (and a higher incidence of Type 1 errors, i.e. false positives), biased estimates of parameter standard errors, and errors in interpreting the importance of independent variables. Multi-level modeling allows for the possibility that higher levels (in the case of this study, municipalities) have an effect on the intercepts and coefficients at the lower level (individual local actors). Given the established instrumental and structural approach in the literature on cooperation, we would expect this possibility to be high.

One of the useful features of multi-level modeling is the ability to calculate the components of variance: for each observation, the variance from the grand mean (the mean of all the observations) can be partitioned into that share arising from the municipal level and the individual level. An unconditional or null model contains no covariates, and allows us to partition the variance in the dependent variable. In Table E.1, the first column gives the municipal level variance for each of the dependent variables under an unconditional model. For three of the dependent variables, the variance ranges from 20 to 30 percent. For the preference regarding how to govern a partial area agreement, the figure is near zero, reflecting at least in this data a lack of influence from municipal level attributes—whatever those might be—on that preference. These variance numbers make intuitive sense. When we run models including a set of demographic and fiscal variables that we would expect to have some effect on preferences, we see that the amount of variance explained at the municipal level drops (see Table E.1, column 2).

A difficulty with my data is that many of the municipalities—99 of 262—have only one individual. While this is not detrimental to the estimation of models using a multi-level approach, it does make the interpretation of variance more difficult. Whatever variance exists is being read only in those municipalities with at least two individuals. To get a better idea of the functioning of the structuralist approach, it would be helpful to see how the variance numbers change when one is dealing only with municipalities in the sample that have a larger number of individuals. Since most local governments only have five to seven elected officials, having three respondents is actually quite a healthy response. If we restrict our unconditional model to only those municipalities with at least three respondents, we should get a stronger sense of the true variance attributable to the municipal level. The variance under this restriction is reported in column three of Table E.1. We see little effect on the variance attributable to the municipal level.

Appendices 163

Table E.1 Share of Variance Attributable to Municipal Level in Multi-Level Ordinal Logistic Models

Preference for:	Unconditional Model (n = 538)	Municipal Model (Fiscal, Demographic Variables) (n = 538)	Unconditional Model for High Sample Munis (at Least Three Respondents) (n = 292)
Partial area joint planning	29.05	9.03	32.09
Full coverage joint planning	27.06	9.08	34.11
Governance-partial area	~0.00	~0.00	~0.00
Governance-full coverage	20.47	10.07	20.55

Appendix F Preferences about Interlocal Land Use Cooperation

The dependent variables are in survey items 4 through 7. The first two items deal with scenarios in which partial JMPA coverage is used to cooperatively plan in a specific area that is smaller than the entire municipality. Corridor development, highway interchanges, rivers, waterfronts, and other man-made and natural features that disregard municipal boundaries can be targeted through this use of an agreement. The second two survey items deal with full coverage, which is self-explanatory. Measurement was with a five-point, non-forced choice, Likert-type scale ranging from strongly oppose to strongly favor.

Preferences about Partial Area Cooperation

Overall, local elected officials were supportive of using a joint agreement for advisory planning of a part of their jurisdiction (see Figure F.1). Of the 538 respondents who answered this survey item, 285 (more than half) favored cooperation and another 63 (nearly 12 percent) strongly favored it. A total of 113 respondents (about one-fifth) neither favored nor opposed the agreement. Only 77 respondents expressed opposition (less than 15 percent), and only 19 of these were strongly opposed.

In total, then, about five of every six respondents had a supportive or neutral preference, suggesting elected officials are fairly receptive to this type of cooperation. Since partial area cooperation is the weakest use of the JMPA, one might wonder about the characteristics and contexts of those who expressed strong *opposition*. These individuals are about as diverse as those holding other opinions about partial area cooperation. They come from all municipal types (both in terms of form—township, mayor-council city, council-manager city, and the like—and fiscal and demographic characteristics), places with few

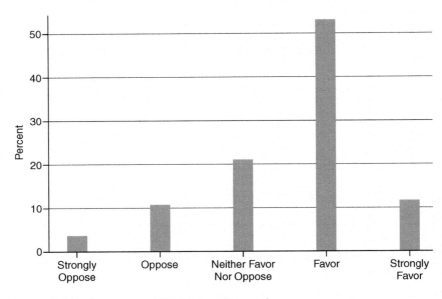

Figure F.1 Preferences about Partial Area Cooperation.

neighbors and many neighbors, in both the Detroit and Grand Rapids metropolitan areas, and in most counties within the two metropolitan areas. Their perceptions of political dynamics, discussed more in Chapter 5, are not exceptional, and they are similar to the full sample of respondents in time in office, age, and other individual characteristics. As one might expect, nearly all were also opposed to full coverage cooperation and, if given the choice, would prefer an advisory JMP agreement if one had to be adopted. As Chapter 6 shows, the one distinguishing characteristic is that they had a very distinct cultural worldview.

In the group of respondents holding favorable or highly favorable views toward cooperation, about 13 percent more city and village elected officials were supportive than were those from townships. Within the city-village/township dichotomy, council-manager cities and charter townships had more respondents express strong support. Most of the respondents from mayor-council and council-manager cities were council members (respectively, 34 of 38 and 135 of 168), meaning the comparison is not skewed by responses from mayors who have very different roles in each type of community. Township officials, overall, had a higher frequency of neutral responses, with about a quarter of respondents choosing this option (versus 10–16 percent in the cities)

Mayors were very supportive of partial area cooperation. Of the 37 mayors in the sample, 33 favored or strongly favored it; the other four were neutral. This may be due to increased electoral pressure. However, only four of the 37 were from mayor-council cities, where the mayor is independently elected. Still, the position of mayor may still be highly visible in council-manager cities, with a

Appendices 165

stronger link to constituents than other council members. For the other positions, preferences lined up fairly well with those for the overall population. This is logical, since differences in responsibilities between, say, a township supervisor and treasurer or trustee should not matter in land use cooperation decisions.

Support for partial area cooperation was much higher in more densely populated municipalities, perhaps because of the higher demand for services. In the bottom quartile of municipalities, those with a population density roughly less than four persons per acre, half the respondents favored cooperation, and about one-fifth opposed it. In municipalities with a population density exceeding about 40 persons per acre, the top quartile, more than 70 percent of the respondents were supportive, and less than 10 percent were not. Breaking down municipalities into quartiles by their four-year average expenditures and expenditures burden (expenditures relative to taxable value) showed a similar shift in preferences as one moved from low to high general fund outlays.

Among Democrat respondents ($n=140$), about 71 percent were supportive and 7 percent opposed; among Republicans ($n=221$), about 65 percent to 11 percent. Third-party and independent respondents ($n=168$) were the least supportive: about 58 percent favored, and about 23 percent opposed. Respondents who held a graduate or professional degree showed scant opposition to partial area cooperation (about 80 percent were supportive, and another 14 percent were neutral). Also, neutral responses were more common for those with lower educational attainment (for example, more than a third of those with a high school diploma or GED, versus less than 15 percent in categories at or above a bachelor degree). The other individual level attributes such as tenure, age, and gender did not exhibit any interesting preference patterns.

Preferences about Full Coverage Cooperation

I expected that when the *scope* of a joint planning agreement increased (from partial area to full coverage), support for cooperation would likely decrease because of the declining amount of land over which municipal leaders would have complete autonomy. Also, respondents may have found it easier to imagine partial area scenarios that made sense: the coordinated development of a shared corridor, natural resource, or industrial site, for example. The distribution of preferences supports this reasoning. Of the 538 elected officials who responded to this question, 147 favored an agreement (only 12 of these strongly favored it), while 276 opposed it (76 expressing strong opposition). The numbers of respondents who neither favored nor opposed a joint planning agreement were nearly identical between full coverage and partial area cooperation. Figure F.2 shows the preferences for full coverage adoption by each metropolitan area (left) and compared to the partial area preferences (right).

Local elected officials from municipalities with more heterogeneous land uses might be less receptive toward full coverage cooperation because it would require agreement across a broader range of use categories. Agreeing on a common vision about a natural resource or a commercial development, for example, might

166 *Appendices*

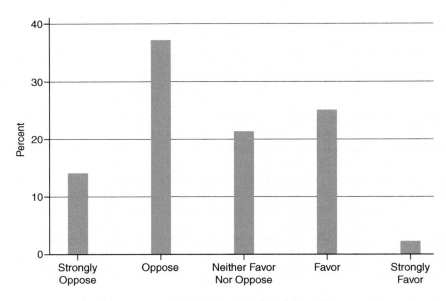

Figure F.2 Preferences about Full Coverage Cooperation.

be easier than negotiating how to coordinate the planning of commercial, residential, and agricultural land. I do not have a measure of land use heterogeneity for municipalities because of data collection challenges. However, the share of residential units that are single-family detached dwellings may provide a rough indicator of heterogeneity; generally, municipalities with more multi-family and attached dwellings also have more commercial development. However, the breakdown of preferences among municipalities along this dimension showed little variation. The same was true for population density, which might be another rough indicator of heterogeneity of land uses. Respondents from the densest municipalities were fairly similar to those from the least dense ones.

Still, preferences did track to a few individual and municipal attributes. Respondents from municipalities in the bottom quartile for general fund expenditures and expenditures relative to taxable value had a rate of opposition more than 10 percent above their counterparts in the top quartile. This was a similar result to what happened with preferences for partial area cooperation. Support was lowest from elected officials in townships. In charter townships only 18 percent of respondents were supportive while more than 58 percent were not. The numbers were similar in general law townships. Respondents in mayor-council cities expressed favorable views at a rate of almost 45 percent, but a nearly equal number expressed opposition; neutrality was uncommon in this form of government.

Republicans differed from Democrats. The rate of support was lower for Republicans by about 10 percent (about 21 percent versus 31 percent), and the rate of opposition was more than 10 percent higher (about 55 percent versus 44 percent). Third-party and independent respondents expressed neutrality less often; a little more than half opposed full coverage cooperation and roughly a third favored it. Looking at the swing away from support (either a "favor" or "strongly favor" response becoming a "neutral," "oppose," or "strongly oppose" response) with a change in geographic coverage, Democrat respondents were supportive at a rate 40 percent lower; Republican respondents, about 44 percent lower; third-party and independent respondents, about 27 percent lower.

Favorable responses decreased as respondents moved from having some college to having a graduate or professional degree. Those in the latter category were actually most similar to those with only a high school diploma or GED in the breakdown of preferences. Comparing results across geographic coverage, the shift among respondents in the highest education category was the most extreme. While only about 6 percent opposed the partial area agreement, 46 percent opposed the full coverage agreement; the number of those expressing a "neutral" response more than doubled, and the rate of support, overall, dropped by 60 points.

The breakdown in preferences for full coverage cooperation by tenure suggests that being in office longer may make local elected officials more receptive to cooperation. Those in the top quartile with at least 14 years in office favored cooperation at a rate of about 44 percent; about 41 percent opposed it. For those with three years or fewer in office (the bottom quartile), the corresponding figures were about 21 percent and 55 percent. The other individual level attributes showed no clear patterns.

Considering the two coverage scenarios together, I expected those who opposed partial area cooperation would not switch their preference and favor full coverage cooperation. While favoring a partial area agreement but opposing a full coverage agreement seems quite plausible (and logical under a risk-based calculation), and favoring both or opposing both would also make sense, it would seem counterintuitive for a local elected official to oppose partial area cooperation but then support full coverage cooperation. The results bear this out. Respondents who favor or strongly favor partial area cooperation ($n=348$) are split in their preferences about full coverage cooperation: 128 (37 percent) favor it while 143 (41 percent) oppose it. Thus, a large number are uniformly pro-cooperation, but for a similarly large number expanding the geographic coverage of land use cooperation makes a difference in their support. Of the 77 local elected officials who oppose or strongly oppose partial area cooperation, 57 also oppose full coverage cooperation while only five support it. Less than 1 percent of all elected officials, then, had a pair of preferences that on the surface seem incompatible. I considered the possibility that the five officials may have all had experience with a JMPA or other joint land use agreement and recognized a practical problem with cooperation in a defined area, leading to the unusual result of opposing partial area cooperation and favoring full coverage cooperation. However, this was not the case.

Preferences for Advisory Versus Authoritative Structures

The two other dependent variable items in the survey measured local elected officials' preferences toward a more advisory or more authoritative structure. The advisory structure was described as having two features: an advisory joint planning commission, and a non-binding land use plan. The authoritative structure, by contrast, had a joint planning commission and joint zoning board of appeals, and the dissolution of municipal (local) level planning and zoning. I expected that local elected officials would prefer an advisory structure, and that this would persist regardless of individual or municipal attributes simply because of the higher political risk of ceding all local autonomy to a joint body. I also expected strong preferences for the advisory form across partial area and full coverage interlocal cooperation scope, but I anticipated wariness about an authoritative structure would be slightly higher for the full coverage option.

In Figures F.3 and F.4, I show the preferences for advisory versus authoritative structure under partial coverage and full coverage by metropolitan area, and then compare the two coverage types for the full sample in Figure F.5.

The findings somewhat supported my expectations. Among the 538 officials, 205 (38 percent) preferred the advisory option, and another 81 (15 percent) strongly preferred it, when considering the governance of a partial area. Only 166 preferred the authoritative structure (31 percent) and another 25 (5 percent) strongly preferred it.

While more than half of respondents preferred the advisory structure, what is surprising is that more than a third preferred the authoritative alternative. Those 191 local elected officials tended to be Democrats. Support for the authoritative

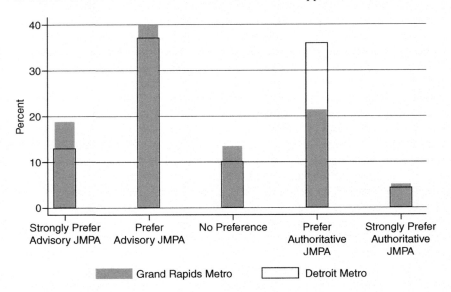

Figure F.3 Preferences about Governance under Partial Area Cooperation, by Metropolitan Area.

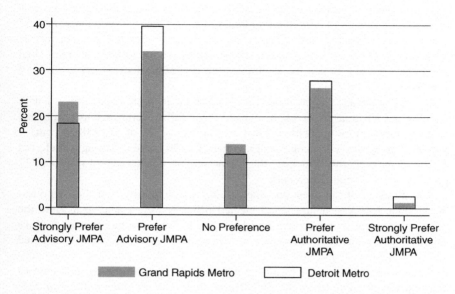

Figure F.4 Preferences about Governance under Full Coverage Cooperation, by Metropolitan Area.

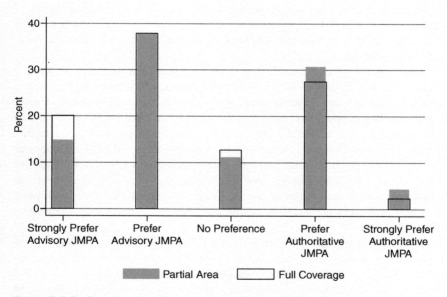

Figure F.5 Preferences about Governance, by Extent of JMPA Coverage.

170 *Appendices*

structure versus the advisory structure was more common among Democrats (48 percent versus 42 percent) than among Republicans (29 percent versus 57 percent) or third-party and independent elected officials (33 percent versus 57 percent). Otherwise, the descriptive statistics on individual and municipal attributes were highly similar for those preferring authoritative versus advisory structures.

For full coverage cooperation, the distribution in preferences aligned with that for partial area cooperation, even though full coverage cooperation had received much more opposition. Most respondents—203 of 538 (38 percent)—preferred an advisory structure, and another 108 (20 percent) strongly preferred it. For an authoritative structure, the corresponding figures were 147 (about 27 percent) and 12 (about 2 percent).

The phrasing of the questions may explain the similarity. For the two questions about JMPA structure, local elected officials were asked to assume the decision to adopt an agreement had been made. With the question of *will we cooperate?* off the table, the question of *how will we cooperate?* is likely tied less to geographic scope. Of course, in the real world the negotiation about adoption and structure selection would be intertwined. The correlation in responses between the two questions is 0.563. Nearly half the respondents (240 of 538, about 45 percent) have a preference for the advisory structure across both survey items, and another fifth (118 of 538, about 22 percent) have a uniform preference for the authoritative structure. However, there are still 92 respondents (about 17 percent) with unmatched preferences—choosing an advisory structure under partial area cooperation and an authoritative structure under full coverage cooperation, or vice versa.

Local elected officials mostly favor interlocal land use cooperation when it covers only a select area of their municipality, perhaps corresponding to a shared corridor, business development area, or natural resource. Opposition is more common when cooperation implicates the entire municipality, but close to half the respondents still had a favorable or neutral response even with this scenario. In practice, the difference is important because the ability of land use cooperation to address some regional problems may depend on it being comprehensive in its scope. Preferences about how to structure the interlocal agreement—as authoritative or advisory—were consistent across geographic scope, with more than half preferring the advisory option and about a third favoring the authoritative option.

Some logical alignment was present among the four interlocal land use cooperation items. Specifically, local elected officials who opposed partial area cooperation but favored full coverage cooperation were exceptional: less than 1 percent (five of 538) had this pattern of responses. And those who preferred an advisory structure under partial area cooperation but supported an authoritative structure under full coverage cooperation were also rare: less than 6 percent of all respondents (30 of 538). These findings support the survey items used to measure preferences, suggesting that respondents were able to make internally coherent distinctions. The fairly low rates of neutral responses, such as "neither favor nor oppose" or "indifferent," is also an encouraging sign. While nearly half the respondents ($n=248$) gave at least one neutral response, only 12 respondents (about 2 percent) gave neutral responses on all four cooperation preference items. Neutral responses were about twice as frequent for the coverage items (the partial area and full coverage scenarios) than for the structure items (advisory versus authoritative). The coverage questions came first, suggesting that survey fatigue or disinterest was not an explanation. Local elected officials may have simply been more undecided about *whether* to cooperate than about the form it should take.

Appendix G Results Tables for Quantitative Analyses

Table G.1 Preferences[†] for Partial Area Land Use Cooperation, For All Respondents across Both Metro Areas

Variables	Final Model[a] (n = 495)
	Odds Ratios
Cultural and political (2013–2014)	
Group disposition	1.066***
Grid disposition	0.982
Perception of discretion	1.233*
Perception of residential support	2.120***
Municipal and intermunicipal (2008/2009–2012)	
Very low share of recently built structures relative to neighbors	0.650*
Individual (2013–2014)	
Aware of Joint Municipal Planning Act	1.608**
Republican party (self identification)	1.711*
Fit statistics/criteria[b]	
Akaike's information criterion (AIC) (unconditional model: 1378.233)	*1,124.479*
Bayesian information criterion (BIC) (unconditional model: 1399.672)	*1,191.622*
Cox-Snell R^2	*0.231*
McKelvey and Zavoina's R^2	*0.265*
Craig-Uhler R^2	*0.251*

Notes
† Five Item, Non-Forced Choice, Likert-Type; Strongly Oppose to Strongly Favor
*** $p<0.001$; ** $p<0.01$; * $p<0.05$.
a Besides grid and group disposition, which as the key explanatory variables are always included for comparison across models, the figures reported here are only those that are significant. All of the final models had between nine and 12 covariates.
b Note: Pseudo-R^2 tests conducted on ordinal logistic regression estimation (removal of multi-level structure did not change parameter estimates or level of significance). AIC and BIC figures are based on corresponding multi-level modeling, with municipalities as level-2 clusters.

Table G.2 Preferences[†] for Partial Area Land Use Cooperation, Comparing Respondents by Metropolitan Area

Variables	Detroit Metro[a] (n = 315)	Grand Rapids Metro[a] (n = 196)
	Odds Ratios	Odds Ratios
Cultural and political (2013–2014)		
Group disposition	1.062**	1.133***
Grid disposition	1.024	0.886*
Perception of discretion		1.691**
Perception of residential support	2.301***	2.150***
Municipal and intermunicipal (2008/2009–2012)		
Very high share of owner occupied housing units	0.573*	
Operations funding relative to neighbors		0.956***
Very high decline in taxable value relative to neighbors		0.286**
Very low share of population identifying as White relative to neighbors		3.287**
Individual (2013–2014)		
Aware of Joint Municipal Planning Act	1.985**	
Fit statistics/criteria[b]		
Akaike's information criterion (AIC) (unconditional model)	708.6922 (868.137)	403.309 (508.371)
Bayesian information criterion (BIC) (unconditional model)	772.4859 (883.558)	454.037 (524.580)
Cox-Snell R^2	0.244	0.398
McKelvey and Zavoina's R^2	0.280	0.438
Craig-Uhler R^2	0.268	0.430

Notes

† Five Item, Non-Forced Choice, Likert-Type; Strongly Oppose to Strongly Favor

*** $p<0.001$; ** $p<0.01$; * $p<0.05$.

a Besides grid and group disposition, which as the key explanatory variables are always included for comparison across models, the figures reported here are only those that are significant. All of the final models had between nine and 12 covariates.

b Note: Pseudo-R^2 tests conducted on ordinal logistic regression estimation (removal of multi-level structure did not change parameter estimates or level of significance). AIC and BIC figures are based on corresponding multi-level modeling, with municipalities as level-2 clusters.

Appendices 173

Table G.3 Preferences[†] for Full Coverage Land Use Cooperation, For All Respondents across Both Metro Areas

Variables	*Final Model*[a] *(n = 495)*
	Odds Ratios
Cultural and political (2013–2014)	
Group disposition	1.078***
Grid disposition	0.929*
Perception of alignment	0.817**
Perception of discretion	1.198*
Perception of residential support	1.871***
Municipal and intermunicipal (2008/2009–2012)	
Very high average annual population decline	1.615*
Very high population decline relative to neighbors	0.590*
Individual (2013–2014)	
Number of years in office	1.025*
Level of educational attainment	0.906*
Fit statistics/criteria[b]	
Akaike's information criterion (AIC) (unconditional model: 1520.264)	*1,272.702*
Bayesian information criterion (BIC) (unconditional model: 1541.703)	*1,331.538*
Cox-Snell R^2	*0.242*
McKelvey and Zavoina's R^2	*0.251*
Craig-Uhler R^2	*0.258*

Notes

† Five Item, Non-Forced Choice, Likert-Type; Strongly Oppose to Strongly Favor

*** $p<0.001$; ** $p<0.01$; * $p<0.05$.

a Besides grid and group disposition, which as the key explanatory variables are always included for comparison across models, the figures reported here are only those that are significant. All of the final models had between nine and 12 covariates.

b Note: Pseudo-R^2 tests conducted on ordinal logistic regression estimation (removal of multi-level structure did not change parameter estimates or level of significance). AIC and BIC figures are based on corresponding multi-level modeling, with municipalities as level-2 clusters.

Table G.4 Preferences[†] for Full Coverage Land Use Cooperation, Comparing Respondents by Metropolitan Area[a]

Variables	Detroit Metro (n = 315)	Grand Rapids Metro (n = 176)
	Odds Ratios	Odds Ratios
Cultural and political (2013–2014)		
Group disposition	1.060**	1.123***
Grid disposition	0.905*	0.882*
Perception of alignment	0.826*	
Perception of residential support	2.010***	2.149***
Municipal and intermunicipal (2008/2009–2012)		
Very high median home value	1.623*	
Very high share of structures built since the year 2000	1.970*	
Very high share of structures built since the year 2000 relative to neighbors	0.484*	0.472*
Very high operations funding (i.e., surplus) relative to neighbors		
Very low share of population identifying as White relative to neighbors	1.776*	
Individual (2013–2014)		
Years in office	1.035**	
Level of educational attainment	0.837**	
Fit statistics/criteria[b]		
Akaike's information criterion (AIC) (unconditional model)	803.302 (972.783)	450.751 (554.743)
Bayesian information criterion (BIC) (unconditional model)	867.096 (992.059)	491.967 (570.951)
Cox-Snell R^2	0.259	0.300
McKelvey and Zavoina's R^2	0.272	0.340
Craig-Uhler R^2	0.276	0.324

Notes

† Five Item, Non-Forced Choice, Likert-Type; Strongly Oppose to Strongly Favor

*** $p<0.001$; ** $p<0.01$; * $p<0.05$.

a Besides grid and group disposition, which as the key explanatory variables are always included for comparison across models, the figures reported here are only those that are significant. All of the final models had between nine and 12 covariates.

b Note: Pseudo-R^2 tests conducted on ordinal logistic regression estimation (removal of multi-level structure did not change parameter estimates or level of significance. AIC and BIC figures are based on corresponding multi-level modeling, with municipalities as level-2 clusters.

Table G.5 Preferences[†] for Authoritative Versus Advisory Structure, For All Respondents across Both Metro Areas

Variables	Grand Rapids Metro[a] (n = 176)	Variables	Detroit Metro[a] (n = 315)
	Odds Ratios		Odds Ratios
Cultural and political (2013–2014)		*Cultural and political (2013–2014)*	
Group disposition	1.063***	Group disposition	1.044**
Grid disposition	0.887***	Grid disposition	0.865***
Perception of alignment	0.840*	Perception of alignment	0.859*
Perception of residential support	1.446***	Perception of residential support	1.328**
Municipal and intermunicipal (2008/2009–2012)		*Municipal and intermunicipal (2008/2009–2012)*	
Very high operations funding (i.e., surplus) relative to neighbors	1.496*	Very high share of housing units occupied by owners	0.614*
Location in Detroit CMSA	1.417*		
Individual (2013–2014)			
Number of years in office	0.979*		
Fit statistics/criteria[b]		*Fit statistics/criteria*[b]	
Akaike's information criterion (AIC) (unconditional model: 1519.751)	*1,327.755*	*Akaike's information criterion (AIC) (unconditional model: 1505.603)*	*1,312.900*
Bayesian information criterion (BIC) (unconditional model: 1536.902)	*1,390.793*	*Bayesian information criterion (BIC) (unconditional model: 1526.063)*	*1,375.847*
Cox-Snell R²	*0.154*	*Cox-Snell R²*	*0.136*
McKelvey and Zavoina's R²	*0.163*	*McKelvey and Zavoina's R²*	*0.141*
Craig-Uhler R²	*0.164*	*Craig-Uhler R²*	*0.145*

Notes

† Five Item, Non-Forced Choice, Likert-Type; Strongly Prefer Advisory to Strongly Prefer Authoritative

*** $p<0.001$; ** $p<0.01$; * $p<0.05$.

a Besides grid and group disposition, which as the key explanatory variables are always included for comparison across models, the figures reported here are only those that are significant. All of the final models had between nine and 12 covariates.

b Note: Pseudo-R² tests conducted on ordinal logistic regression estimation (removal of multi-level structure did not change parameter estimates or level of significance). AIC and BIC figures are based on corresponding multi-level modeling, with municipalities as level-2 clusters.

Table G.6 Preferences[†] for Authoritative Versus Advisory Structure, by Metropolitan Area

Variables	*Grand Rapids Metro*[a] *(n = 176)*		Variables	*Detroit Metro*[a] *(n = 315)*	
	Partial Area	*Full Coverage*		*Partial Area*	*Full Coverage*
	Odds Ratios	*Odds Ratios*		*Odds Ratios*	*Odds Ratios*
Cultural and political (2013–2014)			*Cultural and political (2013–2014)*		
Group disposition	1.094***	1.060*	Group disposition	1.040*	1.030
Grid disposition	0.950	0.889*	Grid disposition	0.842***	0.854***
Perception of alignment	0.691*	–	Perception of alignment	–	0.806*
Perception of resid. support	–	–	Perception of resid. support	1.541***	1.326*
Municipal and intermunicipal (2008/2009–2012)			*Municipal and intermunicipal (2008/2009–2012)*		
Difference in the avg. share of population identifying as White	1.065**	1.071**	Very low share of housing units occupied by owners	1.867*	
Very low share of housing units occupied by owners		3.502**	Very high share of pop. White relative to neighbors	0.572*	
Very low median home value relative to neighbors	4.683**	3.255**	Very high incr. in pop. relative to neighbors		0.561*
			Very high decline in tax. value relative to neighbors		0.578*

Interlocal ties

Number of neighbors (adjacency)		
	805.463	831.887

Fit statistics/criteria[b]

Akaike's information criterion (AIC) (unconditional model)	805.463 (961.215)	831.887 (972.791)
Bayesian information criterion (BIC) (unconditional model)	857.999 (976.635)	888.176 (992.066)
Cox-Snell R²	0.195	0.169
McKelvey & Zavoina's R²	0.215	0.180
Craig-Uhler R²	0.210	0.180

Interlocal ties

Number of neighbors (adjacency)		
	1.231**	1.328***

Fit statistics/criteria[b]

Akaike's information criterion (AIC) (unconditional model)	495.149 (553.120)	484.569 (558.243)
Bayesian information criterion (BIC) (unconditional model)	539.535 (566.077)	522.614 (554.452)
Cox-Snell R²	0.212	0.167
McKelvey & Zavoina's R²	0.222	0.167
Craig-Uhler R²	0.224	0.178

Notes

† Five Item, Non-Forced Choice, Likert-Type; Strongly Prefer Advisory to Strongly Prefer Authoritative

*** $p < .001$; ** $p < .01$; * $p < .05$.

a Besides grid and group disposition, which as the key explanatory variables are always included for comparison across models, the figures reported here are only those that are significant. All of the final models had between nine and 12 covariates.

b Note: Pseudo-R^2 tests conducted on ordinal logistic regression estimation (removal of multi-level structure did not change parameter estimates or level of significance). AIC and BIC figures are based on corresponding multi-level modeling, with municipalities as level-2 clusters.

Notes

1 Michigan Compiled Laws 125.3203(1) (2006).
2 Michigan Compiled Laws 125.3207 (2006).
3 The West Michigan Shoreline Regional Development Council (WMSRDC) is a federal and state designated regional planning and development agency, and the planning agency for the MPO program for Muskegon and northern Ottawa counties. The West Michigan Regional Planning Commission (WMRPC) serves seven counties including five in the Grand Rapids metro area. The Southeast Michigan Council of Governments (SEMCOG) serves Livingston, Macomb, Monroe, Oakland, St. Clair, Wayne, and Washtenaw counties. Genesee and Lapeer counties, with Shiawassee County, are in the Region 5 Planning and Development Commission.
4 Region 6, the East Michigan Prosperity Region, includes Genesee, Lapeer, St. Clair, and four other counties. The Detroit Region, number 10, includes Detroit, Oakland, and Wayne counties. Washtenaw, Livingston, and Monroe counties, with three others, are part of the Southeast Michigan Prosperity Region. Seven of the eight metro counties around Grand Rapids are in the West Michigan Prosperity Region (Region 4b) while Newaygo County and five others are in the West Central Prosperity Region (Region 4a).
5 Act 292 of 1989.
6 See Chapter 6 for a discussion of the work by Dan Kahan and colleagues. See survey items 19 through 30, Appendix B, for the cultural cognition items.

Index

Page numbers in *italics* denote tables, those in **bold** denote figures.

Act 425; Michigan 44
administrative actor 9, 42, 46; *see also* city
   manager; planner
affordable housing 6, 43, 47, 71
agreement: interlocal 11–13, 18–19, 20,
   21–2, 42–3, 48n6, 83, 94, 115;
   intergovernmental 19, 44, 48n6; joint land
   use planning 24, 28n14, 34–6, 45–6,
   67–8, 84–7, 136–7
agriculture 34, 87
Ambrose, Jerry 3
annexation 6–8, 27n3, 37–40, 43, 46, 70;
   extraterritorial jurisdiction 27n3, 37, 39;
   unincorporated land 6, 37
asset specificity *see* transaction cost
   economizing

balkanization 6; *see also* decentralization;
   fragmentation; polycentrism
bargaining cost *see* transaction cost
   economizing
behavior: economizing 19, 52, 58–9;
   instrumental 11, 51, 78; internalized
   prescriptions about 10, 25, 42, 79, 82–7,
   91–2, 110, 113–15; planned behavior 25,
   76, 127n2; preferences and 9, 15, 21, 24,
   75–6, 132
beliefs *see* cultural theory
biases *see* cultural theory
Bloomington School *see* public choice
bureaucracy 12; *see also* administrative
   actor

California 17, 39, 40, 48n4, 100
capacity: cognitive 77; municipal 54, 60; *see*
   also fiscal: capacity
central city 4, 6, 21, 24, 27n2, 37, 39, 70,
   138; Atlanta 39; Boston 37; Detroit 37,
39, 47n2; Philadelphia 37; St. Louis 37;
   San Antonio 6, 27n3, 39; *see also*
   metropolitan area
centralization 4, 27n5, 40, 99; *see also*
   structural reform
charter township *see* general-purpose local
   government
Chicago school, economics 76
city *see* general-purpose local government
city council *see* elected official, local
city council member *see* elected official,
   local
city manager 12, 55–6, 58, 96
city–county consolidation *see* structural
   reform
city–suburb interdependence 4, 19
Clinton, Hillary 3
Coaseian costs *see* transaction cost
   economizing
cognition *see* cultural cognition; rationality
collective action 9, 13, 19, 42, 59–60;
   collective incentives 13, 138; joint gains
   13, 54, 92, 138; selective incentives 13;
   see also institutional collective action;
   sociocultural collective action
communitarian *see* cultural theory
comprehensive plan 35, 41, 135, 138; *see*
   also regional plan
conditional transfer agreement *see* Act 425
consolidation *see* structural reform
cooperation *see* interlocal cooperation
council of governments (COG) 41, 58;
   SEMCOG 178n3; SWWCOG 36, 86,
   143; *see also* metropolitan planning
   organization (MPO)
council-manager city 46, 58, 139, 142,
   158–64
county *see* general-purpose local government

180 *Index*

creatures of the state, local governments as 7, 40
cultural cognition 114–16, 119, 123, 125–6, 134–7, 139
cultural theory 10, 109–12, 114, 116, 118, 124, 126, 133–4; beliefs 9–10, 25, 60, 112, 115, 134; biases 9, 21, 112, 115, 133–40, 144, 162; communitarian **111**, **113**, 116–18, **118**, 119–21, 122–6, 129, 135–6, 139, 150, 152, 158; cultural differentiation 9, 18, 83, 110, 113, 116–18, 125, 132, 136; cultural legitimizing 109, 113–14, 125–6; cultural map **122**; cultural types **111**, **113**, **123**; disposition **111**, **118**, **122**, **123**; divergence, of orientations 22, 60–1, 69, 71; egalitarian **111**, **113**, 116, **118**, 119–21, 123–6, 127n3, 135–6, 139, 150–2; equality 9, 106, 109, 114, 118–19, 125, 132, 152; grid 110–13, 116–21, **122**, 123–6, 152–3, 158, 160; group 110–13, 116–21, **122**, 123–6, 152–3, 158, 160; hierarch **111**, **113**, 127n1, 132–7, 139, 152–3, 158; individualist **111**, **113**, 116–18, **118**, 119–21, 122–6, 129, 135–6, 139, 150, 152, 158; pluralism 126, 133, 135–9; prescriptions, internalized 10, 25, 110, 113–15; orientations 60–1, 80, 116, 124; solidarity 9, 106, 111, 113, 114, 116, 119; values 9–10, 41, 66, 70, 77, 79, 109, 111–12, **113**, 113–15, 117, 119, 121, 123–4, 127n2, 129, 135–7, 139–40; worldviews 9–10, 21–3, 25–6, 46, 68–9, 81–3, 88, 113–15, 133–5, 164

de-biasing 115, 133, 136–40
decentralization 5, 27n5; *see also* fragmentation; polycentrism
density: of governments 27n2, 57; of population 13, 34, 142, 158, 165–6
Detroit 1–3, 37, 39, 47n2
Detroit Water and Sewerage Department (DWSD) 3–4
Dillon's rule 38, 43
discriminating alignment hypothesis *see* transaction cost economizing
disparities 19
dispositions *see* cultural theory
district bill 38

ecological inference 12
economic development 4, 13–14, 47, 54–5, 64, 97–8, 136

economizing *see* behavior: economizing; *see also* legitimizing; transaction cost economizing
egalitarian *see* cultural theory
elastic cities 6, 40
elected official, local 3, 13, 15, 20–3, 26, 45–6, 58–9, 62–4, 66–9, 71, 82, 84, 86–8, 91–106, 118–20, 136–8, 142–7, 153–9
embeddedness 9, 51, 60, 75, 78, 80, 81–2, 84, 114, 140
emergency manager, financial 3–4
enabling legislation 24, 43, 47n3, 66, 81, 133, 143
enclave 6, 19, 27n2; *see also* ghetto
epistemic network 58
equality *see* cultural theory
exit: from cooperation 27n5, 36, 42–3; as political action by households and firms 17, 20, 62, 118
extraterritorial jurisdiction *see* annexation
exurb 21

fiscal: capacity 38, 63; determinants of collective action 68, *85*, 86–7, 93–4, 101, *130*, *131*, 138; distress 13, 54, 55, 64, 93–4, 137, 156, 159–60; federalism 18; health 13, 20, 64, 118, 154; homophily 58, 159, 161; indicators 64, *146*, *147*, 152, 155, 157; zoning 118
Flint 3–5, 70–1; *see also* New Flint
Flint Water Crisis 3–5
Florida 22, 100, 135–7
foreclosure crisis 6, 64
formal agreement *see* agreement
fragmentation 2, 6–7, 11, 16, 19, 27n2, 36, 40, 44, 46–7, 140, 142; *see also* decentralization; polycentrism

General Motors 2–5
general-purpose local government 2, 6, 16–17, 19, 23, 40, 41, 42, 47, 58, 142; charter township 7, 23, 28n14, 92–4, 100, 142; county 37, 39–41, 43–4, 48n3, 58, 62, 70–1, 99–100, 135; municipality 4, 6–8, 13, 17, 20, **23**, 27n2, 35, 37–8, 42–7, 64–6, 86–8, 92–6, 100–6, 118–19, 138; township, general-law 1, 9, 23–4, 42–4, 46, 84–7, 96, 100, 142; village 9, 23–4, 42, 44, 46–7, 102, 142; *see also* special-purpose government
general-purpose regional government 40
Genesee County, Michigan 3–5, 70–1
ghetto 18–19; *see also* enclave
governance 11, 17, 26n1; *see also*

Index 181

metropolitan governance; regional governance
Grand Rapids 23, 93–5, 100, 126
Grand Valley Metropolitan Council 93, 143, 155
Granholm, Jennifer 44
Greater Manchester Area Council 36
grid *see* cultural theory
group *see* cultural theory

heuristic 9–10, 71, 77–9, 81, 83, 115–16, 118–19, 132
hierarch *see* cultural theory
hierarchical linear modeling (HLM) *see* multi-level modeling
hierarchy, as governance *see* transaction cost economizing
home rule 4, 7–8, 17, 37–9, 41, 43–4, 46, 142–3
homophily *see* transaction cost economizing
housing *see* affordable housing

immunity: from state interference 37–8, 47
incentive 13, 15, 20, 24, 41–2, 65, 67–8, 86, 96, 98; *see also* collective action
incorporation, of local government 4, 6–8, 10, 37–40, 42, 46, 48n6, 111, 142
Indianapolis 7, 39
individual–organizational linkages 12, 20–1, 60
inequality 18–19, 116
initiative 8, 37–8, 47
individualist *see* cultural theory
institution 25, 60–1, 63, 65, 75, 77–84, 88, 110, 113–15, 140: cultural *see* cultural theory; mediation 12, 47, 80; normative *see* norms; regulative *see* rules; signal strength 9–11, 16, 25, 27n1, 65, 68; *see also* embeddedness; institutionalism; prescriptions, internalized
institutional collective action 11–12, 15, 54, 59–60, 75, 80, 83, 98, 138
institutionalism, new 9, 12, 75, 115; actor-centered 80; Institutional Analysis and Development (IAD) 80, 88n3; New Institutional Economics (NIE) 51, 79; rational choice 11–13, 14–15, 25–6, 51, 63, 65, 80, 84, 87, 114–15; sociological 9–11, 79, 81, 90, 115, 132, 140–1
intergovernmental: agreement 19, 44, 48n6; state-local grant 2, 41–2, 55; versus interlocal 42

Intergovernmental Contracts Between Municipalities Act, Michigan 44
interlocal agreement *see* agreement
interlocal cooperation 8, 12, 15, 20–2, 24–5, 27n5, 42–3, 46–7, 48n8, 53–4, 56, 58–60, 62–3, 64–6, 75, 79–80, 99, 106, 110, 115, 138–40; geographic scope of 24, 69, 92–6, 105–6, 137, 139–40, *163*, 163–7; governance of 24, 35, 68–9, 86, 96, 106, 126, 137–40; 148, 168–71, **168, 169**; in land use planning and regulation 24, 71, 87–8, 91–2, 95–6, 99, 105, 116, 118, 144–5, *163*; as transaction *see* transaction cost economizing; voluntariness of 8, 42–3; *see also* Joint Municipal Planning Act (JMPA); lifestyle services; systems maintenance
intermunicipal cooperation *see* interlocal cooperation
internalized prescriptions *see* prescriptions, internalized
Iowa 22, 66
irrationality *see* rationality
island municipality 6–7, 40, 158, 159, 161; *see also* general-purpose local government

jobs–housing imbalance 6
joint agreement *see* agreement
joint gains *see* collective action
joint land use planning agreement *see* agreement
Joint Municipal Planning Act (JMPA) 24, 44, 48n8, 66, 142, 155

Karegnondi Water Authority (KWA) 3
Kurtz, Ed 3

LaGuardia, Fiorello 62–3
land use: planning 13, 64–5, 67, 105, 116, 119, 133, 137–8, 140, 152, 154–5; regulation 13, 64, 67, 105, 116, 133, 140, 152, 155
legitimacy *see* legitimizing
legitimizing 9–12, 20, 22, 24–6, 46–7, 59, 68, 75, 81, 83, 129–33, 140; cultural *see* cultural theory; internalized, normative *see* norms; internalized prescriptions *see* prescriptions; political *see* norms; regulative *see* rules; subjective versus objective 45, 60; versus economizing 9–10, 12, 84

182 *Index*

Lifestyle Model of Urban Politics 27n5; *see also* lifestyle services; systems maintenance

lifestyle services 8, 13–15, 19, 20, 22, 25–6, 27n5, 46–7, 62, 84, 92, 133, 138, 140; *see also* systems maintenance

local autonomy 7, 13, 18, 47, 64, 81, 83, 86, 101, 119, 137–40

local elected official *see* elected official, local

local government *see* general-purpose local government; *see also* special-purpose government

localism 4, 7, 14, 15, 36, 40, 46–7, 65, 71, 138, 140; *see also* parochialism

logic of appropriateness 8–9, 26, 69–70, 79, 82, 91, 115; *see also* legitimizing

logic of instrumentality 11, 26, 70, 82, 91, 115; *see also* transaction cost economizing

market failure *see* transaction cost economizing

mayor *see* elected official, local

mayor-council city 46, 98, 100, 142, 145, 163–6

measurability *see* meterability

median voter 20, 57, 99, 104

merger *see* structural reform

meterability 55–6

methodological collectivism 12

methodological individualism 12

metropolitan area 2, 6–8, 11, 15–18, 27n2, 40–1, 47, 61, 64–6, 100, 138, 143; Detroit 23, 93–5, 126; Grand Rapids 23, 94–5, 126; *see also* central city

metropolitan governance 8, 12, 16; *see also* regional governance

metropolitan planning organization (MPO) *see* council of governments (COG)

metropolitan services district 7

metropolitan transit system 1–2

Michigan Land Use Leadership Council 44

Moore, Michael 3

multi-level modeling 125, 132

multi-purpose government *see* general-purpose local government

municipality *see* general-purpose local government

network 11–12, 26n1, 36, 46, 53–4, 56–8, 66, 78, 154

New Flint 4–5, 70–1

New Institutional Economics *see* institutionalism, new

new institutionalism *see* institutionalism, new

new regionalism 18–19

New York City 6

norms 8–12, 15–16, 21–2, 47, 60, 65, 78–80; economizing 10–12, 15, 63, 79, 82; legitimizing 49, 59, 79, 81–3, 86–8, 91–3, 96, 99, 101, 106, 158, 159; political responsiveness 13–14, **103**, 105; professionalization 21, 58, 82, 139; reciprocity 58, 82–3, 86, 91–3, 96, 106, *131*, 133, 154, 158; trust 13, 40, 58, 78, 82, 86, 93, 154

optimizing *see* rationality

opportunism *see* transaction cost economizing

opting out 1, 5, 7–8

organizational–individual linkages *see* individual–organizational linkages

orientations *see* cultural theory

parochialism 14, 119; *see also* localism

partisanship 62–3, 84, 86, 97, 118, **123**, 124, 137

path dependency 20

picket fence regionalism 9

plan *see* comprehensive plan

planner 70, 81–2, 138–9, 144

planning commission 24, 34–5, 43–4, 68, 84, 106

pluralism *see* cultural theory

politician *see* elected official, local

polycentrism 14, 26, 36; *see also* decentralization; fragmentation

preferences *see* behavior: preferences and

prescriptions, internalized *see* cultural theory

principal-agent 57

private sector 26n1, 42, 61–4

property tax 44, 70, 143

property values 64, 87, 96

public choice 16–19, 27n8, 65, 140; Bloomington School 16

public interest 20–1, 27n8, 57, 68, 82, 91, 96–8, 101, 117, 137, 153

public welfare *see* public interest

quiet revolution 41–2

Index 183

rational choice institutionalism *see* institutionalism, new

rationality 9, 51, 61–2, 70, 75–6, 78, 81, 138, 140; bounded 12–13, 47, 51–2, 77–9, 81, 110, 115, 140; cultural *see* cultural theory; material 9–13, 60, 70, 75, 76, 79, 110, 116, 134 (*see also* logic of instrumentality); opportunism *see* transaction cost economizing; optimization 11–12, 76–7, 88n1; satisficing 12–13, 77–8, 115; second-generation 11; self-interest 19, 51, 61, 76, 78–9, 110; thin 11; through legitimizing *see* legitimizing

Reagan administration 41

reasoning *see* rationality; behavior

redistribution 15, 17

referendum 5, 8, 39, 42, 47n3, 154

regional governance 8

regional plan 35–6, 43, 57, 84, 87, 99, 143

Regional Planning Act, Michigan 43

regional reform 7–8, 11, 14–16, 22, 40, 47, 82, 92; *see also* centralization; structural reform

Regional Transit Authority (RTA), Michigan 1–2

regionalism 7, 11, 18–19, 41–2, 46–7, 65, 71, 129, 133, 138; *see also* centralization; localism; new regionalism; regional reform

representation *see* norms: political responsiveness

resilience 6

responsiveness *see* norms: political repsonsiveness

revenue-sharing 13, 143

risk 10, 27n7, 138; cultural 111–19, 134–5; political 94, 98, 99; transactional 52–7, 60, 63–4, 76, 78, 126; *see also* uncertainty

Robertson, James 1–2

rules 10–11, 13, 15, 25, 26n1, 45, 52, 59–60, 65, 77, 79–82, 88n2, 114; regulative legitimizing 82–4, 86–8, 114, 140

satisfying *see* rationality

segregation, by race and class 1, 6, 15, 19, 157

single-purpose district *see* special-purpose government

single-purpose government *see* special-purpose government

site assembly 65, 126

small town 7, 21, 34, 100

sociocultural collective action 9, 11

sociological institutionalism *see* institutionalism, new

solidarity *see* cultural theory

Southeast Florida Regional Climate Change Compact 135

Southeast Michigan Council of Governments (SEMCOG) *see* council of governments (COG)

Southwest Washtenaw Council of Governments (SWWCOG) *see* council of governments (COG)

special-purpose district *see* special-purpose government

special-purpose government 18, 40

sprawl, suburban 7, 34, 137

state court *see* state judiciary

state judiciary 17–18, 27n4

state legislature 24, 38, 40

statutory interpretation 27n4, 38

structural reform 8, 14, 20, 37, 40–1, 70, 115; consolidation 5–8, 14, 37–40, 42–3, 46, 47n3, 70, 86, 99; dissolution 16, 24, 40, 42; merger 43; *see also* annexation; incorporation

suburb 3, 16

suburban dependence *see* city-suburb interdependence

systems maintenance 8, 14, 16, 20, 22, 24–5, 27n5, 40, 46, 54, 62, 64–5, 71, 82–4, 154; *see also* lifestyle services

technocrat 20, 21, 42, 114, 138

territorial restructuring *see* structural reform

theory of the firm 51

Tiebout model 17, 18, 65

township *see* general-purpose local government

township board member *see* elected official, local

transaction cost economizing 10–13, 19, 51, 53, 61–2, 65–6, 80, 82, 84, 98, 114, *130*, *131*, 138; asset specificity 51–3, 55–6; bargaining cost 52, 53, 57–8; Coaseian costs 13, 56; discriminating alignment hypothesis 52; division of gain 13, 56, 58; frequency 51, 54; hierarchy governance 51–3, 61–2, 127n1; homophily 15, 57, 155, 159, 161; hybrid governance 51–3, 61–2; joint gains *see* collective action; market governance 17, 51–3, 56, 61–3,

184 *Index*

transaction cost economizing *continued*
127n1; meterability 55–6; negotiation
cost 52, 53, 63, 98; as a norm 82, 84,
87, 92, 129; uncertainty in 10, 14,
51–3, 56, 92
Transfers of Functions and Responsibilities
Act, Michigan 44

uncertainty 10, 14, 60, 63, 65, 76, 78, 96,
97, 114, 118, 138; *see also* transaction
cost economizing
unincorporated land *see* annexation
Urban Cooperation Act, Michigan 44
urban growth boundary 7
values *see* cultural theory

veto player 13
village *see* general-purpose local
government
voice 20, 62, 70, 118, 137

West Michigan Regional Planning
Commission (WMRPC) 178n3
West Michigan Shoreline Regional
Development Council (WMSRDC)
178n3
worldviews *see* cultural theory

zoning 24, 34–5, 44–5, 64, 67–9, 86, 92,
105–6, 114, 116, 136, 138, 143; board
of appeal 24, 106